The Life of

WILLIAM PINKNEY

The Life of

WILLIAM PINKNEY

By The Rev. William Pinkney

DA CAPO PRESS • NEW YORK • 1969

A Da Capo Press Reprint Edition

This Da Capo Press edition of *The Life of William Pinkney*
is an unabridged republication of the first edition
published in New York in 1853.

Library of Congress Catalog Card Number 75-75276

Published by Da Capo Press
A Division of Plenum Publishing Corporation
227 West 17th Street
New York, N. Y. 10011
All rights reserved

Printed in the United States of America

The Life of

WILLIAM PINKNEY

ENGRAVED BY T. B. WELCH.

THE LIFE

OF

WILLIAM PINKNEY,

BY HIS NEPHEW,

THE REV. WILLIAM PINKNEY, D.D.

"Tanta vis animi, tantus impetus, tantus dolor, oculis, vultu, gestu, digito denique isto tuo, significari solet: tantum est flumen gravissimorum optimorumque verborum, tam intigræ sententiæ, tam veræ, tam novæ, tam sine pigmentis fucoque puerili, ut mihi non solum tu incendere judicem, sed ipse ardere, videaris.—CICERO DE ORATORE.

"His opinions had almost acquired the authority of judicial decisions."
ROB. GOODLOE HARPER.

NEW-YORK:
D. APPLETON AND COMPANY,
200 BROADWAY.
MDCCCLIII.

TO

THE BAR OF MARYLAND,

EVER RENOWNED FOR THE ELOQUENCE AND LEARNING OF ITS
ADVOCATES,

THIS WORK

IS RESPECTFULLY DEDICATED

BY

THE AUTHOR.

PREFACE.

MARYLAND has been far more favored by Divine Providence in her list of illustrious sons, and exciting historic incidents, than by the pen of skilful and enlightened historians or faithful and competent biographers. This is just matter of surprise, and good ground of impeachment. Next to the production of great men, who inscribe their names upon the monuments of their country's glory, is the energetic endeavor to hand down to after ages a true and faithful record of their deeds ; and, what is of greater importance still (for deeds lose something of their power to fascinate and charm by the changing scenes of the present moment), of their intellectual qualities and moral virtues, which are the true picture of the man, and make up his claim to an immortality on the earth.

It is no less the duty than the interest of the State to be jealous of the glory of the past. It is her treasury of wealth, from which she may draw largely not only for present exigencies but for future advancement. The most illustrious of the historians of Rome thus wrote :—" Nam sæpe audivi, O. Maxumum, P. Scipionem, præterea civitatis nostræ præclaros viros solitos ita dicere, cum majorum imagines intuerentur, vehementissume sibi animum ad virtutem accendi. Scilicet, non ceram illam, neque figuram, tantam vim in sese habere ; sed memoria rerum gestarum eam flammam egregiis viris in pectore crescere neque prius sedari, quam virtus eorum famam atque gloriam adæqua-verit."

The very sight of the statues of our ancestors is inspirit-ing, for though in themselves but cold marble, they have a voice that speaks at once to the heart and hopes of the young who are grouped around them. But if mere statues be thus eloquent and instructive, what must be said of the life-like and life-revealing biography? If the chisel of the sculptor, or the pencil of the artist, can accomplish so won-derful a work as the retaining here on the earth the image of departed worth, what may not the pen of the historian do?

In history we have accomplished much, though not so much as the rich variety of our material demands; but in biography we have scarce made more than our first essay. Bozman, of old and fragrant memory, has earned just praise for the facts he has rescued from oblivion; which, while they diminish naught from the stirring glories of Plymouth Rock, show conclusively that a higher Rock, of firmer basis and more broad protecting shade, was laid in this western world by our forefathers in the colonizing of Maryland— where liberty in higher form pervaded our charter, and a more enlightened toleration was secured to the pioneers of freedom. The gifted historian of Frederick City has added another flower to our garden of history that will never fade. McMahon, our most illustrious living orator, who wears the robe of our old renown in great names so gracefully, has given to the country and the world a good pledge of what her sons can accomplish in this most difficult field of literary pursuit. It is deeply to be regretted that his vigorous pen has ceased to record the glowing deeds of the past, and sketch with those master-strokes the moral beauty and intellectual grandeur of her sons, whose names and deeds are inseparably blended with her history. It is to our shame and disgrace, that the historian is yet alive, patient in study, and skilled in all that can give force and beauty to narrative; and yet that narrative be not completed. It is a burning reproach that one of the original thirteen stars (whose very first scintillations of liberty were the solace and consolation of the oppressed, and whose peculiar brilliancy was always meekly blended with that of the blazing galaxy) is not yet fixed in the firmament of history. We sincerely hope that the day is not far distant, when the pen of McMahon shall once more recall to mind the fact that Rome had her Livy; and enable us, with the modesty of truth, to say that Maryland may exultingly point to hers.

But in biography what have we done ? With the exception of Wirt's Life, by Kennedy, the hand of strangers has had to write the only lives of our lamented dead; and we all know that a stranger cannot so well gather up the lights and shades of character as those who, familiarized with the hearth-stones whence are reflected the daily habits of the daily life, tread the very soil they trod and illuminated with their glory.

We are not ignorant of the difficulties that compass the path of those who would fain write biography; nor are we insensible to the rashness of the undertaking. We have not the vanity to suppose that we can execute it with such skill as to disarm criticism and win her approval.

Ours is a work of peculiar hazard. We follow in the steps of one who adorned the republic of letters, and illustrated the virtues that belong to the enlightened and accomplished American citizen while he lived; and, in death, received the most touching tributes of the admiration of a sorrowing country—and that too at a time when many of the most interesting incidents are lost, and some of the most copious and important written documents that survived him were mingled in the wreck. We have studiously collected together all that has been preserved; and where we have drawn from oral tradition, we have been careful to test the accuracy of each statement by direct and unimpeachable testimony.

Mr. Pinkney's real character is but little known and appreciated in the present day. That character we have endeavored to draw; and the facts collated more than sustain the justice and accuracy of the portrait. It is not possible to write such a life as would be most edifying and pleasing. There is not enough of the requisite material. We had either to adopt the plan selected, or give up the idea altogether. The alternative was promptly chosen, for we thought that the faintest sketch would be better than nothing.

In the execution of our work we have had occasion now and then to review the opinions and statements of others; and, while we have been careful to deal as tenderly as possible with their motives, we have unflinchingly exposed what we deemed to be injustice to the memory of the subject of our memoir. Passages in his life, which were obviously misunderstood or seemingly misrepresented, have been cleared up, and his title to the admiration and confidence of the present and future established, based upon what he was, and the part he enacted proved him to be. Less than this would have been gross injustice to his memory—a connivance at the wrong perpetrated. We know that critics have labored hard to cry down this habit of defending the character; and we are free to admit that there may be vicious extremes to which it may be pushed ; but, while we vindicate the propriety of the one, we have been careful to guard against the other. Against but three classes of assailants have we raised our voice ; and we have met those, not with the weapons of argument or declamation, so much as with stubborn and incontrovertible facts.

Some may be tempted to charge us with extravagant eulogy. We only ask to be judged by our facts. If they condemn us, we are prepared to plead guilty to the charge and sue for pardon. If they condemn us not, we may well challenge the approval of mankind.

It has been said, that he who causes a spire of grass to grow where none grew before, is a public benefactor. If so, what shall be said of him who succeeds in setting forth an illustrious character in its true light. Criticism may sneer at the style, and denounce the over-estimate of ability, which pursues an aim above its reach. But surely the endeavor to accomplish so good a purpose under so many discouragements, and amid such a dearth of materials, may well confound the critic, and shield us from his poisoned shafts.

If those "who discommend will mend" the work, they will find me the first to offer them the sincerest tribute of gratitude ; and may rest assured that none will rejoice more in a failure, which shall secure for William Pinkney a biographer worthy of his fame, than myself.

A number of public and private letters never before incorporated in a biography, some of them never before published elsewhere, are now given to the world.

He wrote some most admirable articles, under the signature of " Decius," in favor of Madison's re-election, and against the pretensions of De Witt Clinton, which I have endeavored in vain to secure for publication in this work. They were known to be his by his more intimate friends.

LIFE OF WILLIAM PINKNEY.

WILLIAM PINKNEY was born at Annapolis in the State of
Maryland on the 17th of March, 1764. The place of his
birth was every way worthy of her illustrious son. Situated
on the banks of the Severn, girded in by a belt of waters, almost an island, in full view of the noble old Chesapeake,
the paragon of bays ; and surrounded by a scenery richly
variegated, of mingled beauty and sublimity,—it is not possible to look out upon this ancient city, even amid the
touching monuments of her decline, without admiration.
She was, at the period of which I speak, the seat of refinement, elegance, and taste—the Athens of the New World.
Genius and wealth lend their combined attractions to grace
the legend of her glory. She was also the theatre of stirring revolutionary scenes. It was within her precincts
that the offensive and unjust legislation of the mother country met with a rebuke, full as significant and emphatic as
that which has since given to Boston an immortality of
renown and made her, as it were, the consecrated cradle of
liberty. Young Pinkney loved and honored this the place
of his birth. Possessed of a soul which was peculiarly
attuned to those nobler feelings of our nature which delight
in the thrilling reminiscences and ennobling associations of
the past ; and more than ordinarily susceptible to the power
of local attachments, he always prided himself upon Annapolis, the place of his birth. His heart clung to it with
peculiar tenacity even amid the beauties of London. Stand-

ing on the shores of classic Italy, and drinking in, with every sense, the potent spell that lingers by the spot where the past so gloriously mingles with the present, he was often known to look over the wide waste of waters, and sigh that his eye rested not upon the city washed by Chesapeake's broad waves.   To wander by the banks of her rivers, and survey her exquisite natural scenery, was ever his delight.   It was there he fed his strong natural taste for the beautiful and sublime, and kindled the flame of his boundless ambition.   If those banks had a voice, or those grottoes were now vocal, they would, doubtless, echo back the stirring notes of his youthful eloquence.   How he loved Annapolis and treasured through all after years the touching memory of her beauty, may be ascertained from the following passage of one of his published letters.

"In itself the most beautiful, to me the most interesting spot on earth, I would fain believe that it is destined to enjoy the honors of old age, without its decrepitude.

"There is not a spot of ground in its neighborhood, which my memory has not consecrated, and which does not produce as fancy traces it a thousand retrospections that go directly to the heart."

Demosthenes was not more proud of Athens nor Cicero of Rome.   Webster was not more proud of Boston than was William Pinkney of Annapolis.   And she was pre-eminently worthy of his ardent attachment and exulting pride ; for in all that can give dignity and honor, the charm of patriotism and the fascination of genius to the character of man, she was at that time most richly endowed.

Mr. Pinkney's ancestors came over from Normandy to England with William the Conqueror.   His father sprung from one of the most respectable and ancient families of Britain; the same that gave to Carolina some of her most brilliant and illustrious names.   It has been sometimes affirmed that his origin was obscure ; but nothing could be

farther removed from the truth. The elder Pinkney emigrated to the United States, and located himself at Annapolis,
where he lived in quiet seclusion and illustrated the virtues
that adorned his character. He was a hero in spirit, a man
of indomitable moral courage and the highest moral integrity, who never sacrificed conscience to expediency, and never
yielded up its dictates but to clear convictions of duty. He
adhered with a mistaken but honest firmness to the cause
of the mother country, and suffered severely the consequences of his conscientiousness. Even those who may be
disposed to censure his adherence to the oath he had taken
as a subject of the British crown, must admire the sterling
and heroic spirit he displayed, in sacrificing his ease and comfort and fortune to what he believed to be his duty, and con-
fronting, unawed and unappalled, the violent outbreaks of
the popular feeling, that branded his conduct as unpatriotic
and disgraceful. He died as he lived, without a stain upon
his honor, the victim of a mistaken sense of duty. The
mother of young Pinkney was a lady of most vigorous understanding and tender sensibilities. Her image was the
guiding star of his destiny. He always spoke of her as the instrument, under Providence, of all that gave him any title to
public confidence and esteem. She watched over his infant
years with the fondest solicitude, and aided by her pious
counsel and beautiful example in the development of his
mind and heart. It was his misfortune to lose her fostering
care when but a boy ; and he retained, through all after-life,
the freshest recollection of her many virtues and superior intellect, and never mentioned her name but with deepest veneration and truest and most heartfelt affection. Poverty was the
portion of his early childhood. His father's property con-
fiscated by the government, whose infant struggles at once enlisted his warmest sympathies, he was thrown penniless on the
world. Without money or the patronage money brings with
it, through exertions all his own, the giant resolve to be

something and do something to reflect some new lustre on the city and State of his birth—he pushed on in his enterprising career with a steadiness and industry, that were the surest pledge of success.

Concerning the early education of Mr. Pinkney, there has been much misapprehension. During the lifetime of his father, and before his troubles began, no expense was spared in securing for him the best and most skilful instruction. He was sent to King William school, a first class academy, founded in 1696. "It stood on the south side of the State House, and is said to have been a plain building, containing school-rooms and apartments for the teacher and his family." At the time he entered its walls, it was under the government of a gentleman by the name of Bref-hard, who was a first-rate scholar and pre-eminently fitted to have charge of youth. Perceiving the extraordinary abilities of his young pupil, Mr. Bref-hard took uncommon pains in imparting to him the rudiments of a first-rate education. He left school about the age of thirteen—but his teacher, conscious of the uncommon promise of his interesting charge, continued to give him private lessons at his own house ; and watched with unbounded interest the development of his mind, as long as he remained in the country. This gentleman formed for his pupil a warm personal friendship, which was never afterwards withdrawn. That he received a first-rate English education and was well grounded in the classics is indisputable ; but it is more than probable, that his reading in the classics at that early period was not extensive, as he did not long continue to enjoy those invaluable privileges.

This school has been sometimes confounded with St. John's College, and therefore that institution has been not unfrequently regarded as his alma mater. The misapprehension no doubt originated in the fact, that the funds of King William school were by an act of assembly consigned in 1785 to St. John's College. The college was founded in 1784 and opened and dedicated in 1789; so that the school may be said truly to have been merged in the college.

For St. John's Mr. Pinkney felt a strong attachment. It was with not less pride than pleasure that he saw her become the boast and pride of Maryland ; and witnessed her distinguished success in rewarding the State's liberal patronage by returning to her bosom, sons who were qualified, by profound and elegant scholarship and high toned manly principles, to guide and control her future destinies. This venerable edifice still stands, and fulfils her important mission. The strong hand of power struck her down in her bright career, but Mr. Pinkney left his indignant and decisive protest against the mad policy of her foes, by pronouncing the day, that witnessed her degradation, the darkest Maryland had known. Old St. John's once more enjoys the fostering care of the State, and prosecutes with quiet and unobtrusive dignity her allotted work.

Academic instruction was all, then, that the subject of this memoir enjoyed. And even in academic groves he was permitted to rove but for a few fleeting years. While a resident in London it is well known that he employed his leisure moments in the study of the Latin language and the critical study of his own. Finding himself far behind the classical attainments of the prominent men of England, he devoted time and attention, under the superintendence of a private tutor, to the renewal of those studies ; and never rested satisfied until he had made up all deficiencies. He became an admirable Latin scholar, and acquired a knowledge of his own tongue, singularly accurate and discriminating, rarely if ever equalled, never excelled. Unwilling to appear in the learned and polite circles of English scholars ignorant ; and unwilling to affect a knowledge he did not possess, he at that late period put himself to school, and thought it no degradation to assume the attitude of a learner, although the representative of one of the proudest nations of the world, and placed in almost constant contact with the most experienced statesmen and profound jurists of another.

There are many floating traditions, which conspired to give to his early years the pledge of his future vast renown. But still for the most part, his youth was passed in the struggles of pride and a lofty aspiration with the rough and appalling realities of life, when poverty settles down, like night upon the sea, on the youthful aspirant.

His first thoughts were directed to medicine. He entered the office of Dr. Dorsey and pursued his studies for a short time.

Discovering that it was an uncongenial pursuit, he very soon abandoned it for that, which owned him pre-eminent. Judge Chase, of distinguished memory, was his patron and his friend. He studied in his office, and received many facilities in the accomplishment of his desires in this new and untried field, from that able jurist ; which he lived to repay in after years to Chase's descendants. In the bright catalogue of the illustrious men (whose names are still the boast and ornament of the Maryland bar) Pinkney felt the exciting stimulus for exertion. The field of fame was preoccupied. Laurels were strewed all around him in wild profusion, worn by other brows and kept in unfading lustre by their energetic efforts. In the splendors of Dulany, her setting luminary (one of the most remarkable men of his age), and in the meridian blaze of her Chase and Martin, who were just then culminating to their zenith, he felt as the sons of genius ever feel, whose steppings are in an illuminated pathway, that those, who would follow in their steps, must give their days and nights to study and emulate their greatness by emulating their love of labor. He studied for the mastery. His aim was high from the start, and he never withdrew his eye from the goal. In the struggles of the debating club, with his young associates around him (each one doing his utmost to eclipse his fellows and win the palm of ascendency against all competitors), Pinkney easily acquired an enviable pre-eminence ; and yet he did not dare *even then* to enjoy it in ease. He was indefatigable as a student. He studied the grand principles of the law in the writings of its profoundest and deepest expounders ; and in those earliest struggles, where he acquired his training for the more earnest conflicts of the forum, he poured forth all his powers, and often extorted praise from the admiring crowd, who were the delighted spectators of those youthful contests.

He was admitted to the bar in 1786. Harford county was chosen as the arena of his first professional efforts. She received and rewarded the young adventurer. She saw his worth and appreciated it. In April, 1788 (but two years after his settlement in the county), he was elected a delegate to the convention of the State of Maryland, which ratified the constitution of the United States. This was the beginning of his illustrious public career. Unhappily there is no record preserved of the debates of that body, and consequently we are not able to determine what part young Pinkney took in its deliberations, or in what way he signalized himself. But the bare privilege of sitting in such a body, and mingling in the councils of the fathers of the Republic, and recording an affirmative vote in the adoption of such an instrument as the constitution of the United States—the being considered by so intelligent a constituency (among whom he had been but two years a resident) worthy of so high and responsible a post, was honor enough and distinction enough for so young a man. There seems to be, to my mind at least, a beautiful and appropriate coincidence in the beginning and the close of Pinkney's career. It opened amid the splendors of the new formed constitution (that wise substitute for the impotent and inadequate confederation) ; and it closed in the very act of giving a last and finishing exhibition of the truest, safest, profoundest principles of its interpretation.

In October, 1788, he was elected a member of the House

of Delegates. In those days Maryland had cause to be proud of that body. They were men chosen for their intelligence, purity, patriotism, learning and eloquonce. He there met with competition to test the strength of the strongest, and fire the enthusiasm of the most aspiring. His style of speaking is represented by those who were competent to judge, to have been singularly rich and attractive. With a voice of uncommon melody and power, an elocution beautifully accurate, and action graceful and impressive, he held the listening crowds upon his tongue in rapt astonishment and wonder. The tradition is still alive in Maryland, which echoes the wide-spread rumor of his fame ; and those are still living, known to this writer, who heard from competent lips the confident prediction of his future pre-eminence.

It was there he raised his voice, in bold and manly tone, against the law that would deny to the holder of slaves the right of manumission. Twice on the floor of the House, in speeches of considerable power and fervid eloquence, he deprecated the insertion of such an odious and despicable principle in the State's legislation. The sentiments delivered on that occasion were such as did infinite credit to his heart. They indicated a spirit that shunned not the responsibility of speaking out its honest opinions and convictions of public policy, without reserve or equivocation. But those opinions and convictions were not in disloyalty to the Union or in contravention of the constitution. In advocating the right of the power to manumit, and holding up to universal scorn and rebrobation the law that would have laid low that right, Mr. Pinkney was speaking to Marylanders on a subject exclusively their own. He was addressing himself to the representatives of a Southern State in relation to an institution purely local, and enforcing the wisdom and propriety of clemency and moderation in the legislation about to be adopted. I dwell upon this, because the views of Mr. Pinkney have been singularly misconceived and misrepresented on the floor of the American Senate. His name has been identified with modern abolitionism. The speeches of his youth have been arrayed against the grand effort in the Missouri compromise in the maturity of his years ; with what show of justice will be seen, when we compare the positions in which he stood in the one case and the other. In the Legislature of Maryland, he raised his voice against what appeared to him to be cruel and oppressive legislation, touching an institution all her own, within the express terms and spirit of the constitution. He implored Marylanders to do, what it was perfectly competent for them to do with their own, in the spirit of an enlightened and elevated humanity. There was not one word uttered against the clear constitutional rights of a sovereign State of this Union—not one principle advanced that was in violation of that great constitutional compromise. He was pleading on Maryland soil with Marylanders, for the exercise of a clemency and justice in her legislation, that was perfectly in consonance with her constitutional rights and privileges. He who can discover any sort of affinity between this earnest remonstrance, addressed to the constitutional authorities of a sovereign State, and the revolutionary and inflammatory appeals of abolitionism, which assail constitutional prerogatives and war upon State sovereignty, possesses a power of tracing resemblances between things that are intrinsically unlike ; and confounds all the existing and well established distinctions that divide contrarieties from each other.

In the Missouri compromise, on the floor of the American Senate, Mr. Pinkney maintained the right of the State under the constitution to regulate and control this institution for itself, and denied the power of Congress to place any restriction upon a State applying for admission. There is no antagonism between the views of Mr. Pinkney during any period of his public career upon this delicate and important subject. He was too zealous and consistent a supporter of the constitution to have ever sanctioned aggression, either of the States upon the general government or the general government upon the States.   Those who have invoked his name to the support of principles, that are destructive of the peace, harmony, and perpetuity of the Union, have done great injustice to his memory ; and for lack of knowledge or want of reflection have failed to distinguish between things essentially diverse.   The perpetration of the injustice is not so wonderful as the failure to rectify it when pointed out.

At this early period of his professional and legislative career, he was noted for the careless simplicity of his dress and manners; the very opposite of the punctilious and studious elegance and attention to dress, which he acquired in foreign courts, to avoid singularity, and which he retained to the close of life.

In 1789 Mr. Pinkney was united to Miss Ann Maria, daughter of John Rodgers, Esq., of Havre de Grace, and sister of Commodore John Rodgers ; a man of bold, chivalrous spirit, who never tarnished the flag under which he sailed, and lost no opportunity of seeking to plant it in triumph, whenever he navigated the seas.

Ten children were the fruit of this marriage, all of whom, with the beautiful and accomplished lady who united her happiness and destiny to his, survived him.   Mrs. Pinkney lived to an honorable old age ; and her declining years, though saddened by severe bodily infirmity, were soothed by those who best knew her worth, until death gently closed the scene.   She was in early life the picture of health and feminine beauty.   Her easy manner, affability of disposition, and strong vigorous intellect, eminently qualified her to adorn the social position she was called to fill, and fitted her to cheer the anxious careworn pilgrimage of her illustrious consort.   She paid his memory the most precious tribute of affection and respect, and sought and found, in the bosom of her family and a few select and tried friends, the solace of her widowhood.

In 1790 he was elected a member of Congress by the citizens of his adopted county. His election was contested, but, after a most powerful and conclusive argument in his own behalf, ratified and confirmed. He however subsequently declined the honor for reasons of a prudential and private nature.

In 1792 he was elected a member of the Executive Council of Maryland, of which he was for a time the president. This position of great responsibility, under the old Constitution, he filled with increasing reputation and ability.

In 1796 he was appointed commissioner to England under the seventh article of Jay's treaty in connection with Mr. Gore. This was a truly honorable appointment, the more honorable because conferred without solicitation by the discrimination of a Washington, who in his own State was surrounded by the very stars of the Republic, and in the bestowment of office looked to the qualifications, and refused to be swayed in his choice by narrow, contracted or local prejudices ; which alas ! in our day too much influence executive patronage. Official position adds nothing to the intrinsic intellectual power and moral greatness of a man. It only affords a sphere for the display of the talent, and exhibition of the high qualities for rule that are possessed. It does not enrich or endow. It only developes. But still in those early days it was a sure and unerring indication of talent ; for office was then conferred, not sought, the reward of distinction, not the price of servile partisanship. The manner in which he discharged the duties of his high functions during this embassage is matter of history; and his recorded opinions are splendid specimens of profound and eloquent argumentation, worthy of the country he represented and the distinguished legal ability that characterized the discussion he was called upon in part to adjudicate. He also rendered most valuable service to the State of Maryland in recovering 800,000 dollars, which was acknowledged in a public vote of thanks by the Legislature.

Mr. Pinkney's private correspondence during the period of his absence on this mission is very beautiful and interesting. Although much of it has been unhappily lost, it is in my power to add a few letters, that have never before graced the pages of any preceding biography. Dr. Johnson in his life of Pope admonishes us that "epistolary intercourse affords the strongest temptation to fallacy and sophistication," and scouts the idea that "the true character of men may be found in their letters." There is doubtless much force and truth in the views of the venerable Doctor; but still we incline to the opinion of another of England's noble writers "that the comparison of letters, from whatever hand, will assist materially in estimating the disposition as well as the talents of a writer." A criterion it is;—but one which must be narrowly watched, entertained with caution, and carefully weighed. In interweaving portions of Mr. Pinkney's letters into this memoir, I do not so much design to illustrate character as to give currency to his views and reflections on men and things. A rich variety was put into the hands of Mr. Wheaton, consisting of letters from England, Naples, Russia, and Italy, written to individuals in different parts of the country and never designed for the perusal of any but the warm, tried friends of his heart. Of those that were not published (among which were some of the most beautiful) none, that I know of, were returned to his friends. A few have been received from unexpected quarters; these will be read with satisfaction, and leave an increased regret that the lost cannot be now recovered. There is one noble quality in those letters, viz., their freedom from haughty egotism and bitter acrimony. There is no effort at what may be called fine writing; no gush of heart-revealing in them. They are the natural, unaffected, artless interchange of thought.

To entertain, please and instruct, was his end and aim—to describe what he saw and felt, was his simple, single-minded desire. We read without effort, and rise from the perusal, charmed with their natural eloquence, simplicity and beauty. We listen to his first impressions of England and her great and distinguished sons, and find them delivered with freedom, but in a spirit of friendly criticism. He held the mind of Pitt in august admiration. He admired Wilberforce ; revered his character, and secured his warmest friendship and most unbounded admiration. He duly appreciated the power and skill of the Bench and Bar of that great country; and showed his high respect for parliamentary eloquence by a patient and unflagging attendance upon its debates.

MR. PINKNEY TO HIS BROTHER JONATHAN.

" LONDON, 26th August, 1796.

" DEAR J. :—We are now London housekeepers. I found it would not answer to take lodgings unless we meant to do penance instead of being comfortable. Our present residence is merely temporary. I have taken a short lease of a new house in Upper Guilford-street, No. 5, to which we shall remove in about six weeks. The situation is airy, genteel, and convenient enough to the commissioner's office. We are compelled to live handsomely, to avoid singularity; but our view is still to be as economical as the requisite style of living will admit. We do not, and shall not want for the most respectable and agreeable society. The American families here are on the most friendly and intimate footing with us, and we have as many English acquaintances as we desire. In short, we may pass our time here (for a few years to come) with considerable satisfaction—not so happily, indeed, as at Annapolis, but still with much comfort and many gratifications. My health is apparently bettered, and Mrs. P. is evidently mending,—but we have not yet had

sufficient experience of the climate to be able to conjecture
its future effects on us.   The child continues well.

"Our namesake (the late American Minister) is an amiable man.   We have been much with him, and have received
from him every possible attention.   He unites with an excellent understanding the most pleasing manners, and is at
once the man of sense and the polished gentleman.   Every
body speaks well of him, and deservedly.   There is no doubt
of our relationship.   His family came from the North—I
think from Durham, where he tells me he still has relations.
The loss of his wife appears to have affected him deeply, and
has doubtless occasioned his anxiety to return to America.
He leaves us soon, and I am sorry that he does so.

"Yesterday we appointed the fifth commissioner *by lot*.
He is an *American* (Colonel John Trumbull), and was secretary to Mr. Jay, when envoy at this court.   I made the
draft.   We all qualified this morning before the Lord Mayor,
and shall commence business very soon.   Every thing in relation to the commission wears *at present* a favorable aspect,
and I have now expectations of being able to return to my
friends within a period much shorter than I had ventured to
hope for.

"2d Sept. 1796, P. S.—Your letter of the 26th June has
just reached me.   Be assured that nothing can diminish my
attachment to Annapolis.   I have nothing to complain of
from the inhabitants ; on the contrary, they have done me
honor beyond my merit.   I feel the worth of their attentions, and shall never lose the grateful recollection of them.
They have treated me with flattering and friendly distinctions, and I will never give them cause to regret it.   In a
word, the hope of once more becoming an inhabitant of my
native city forms one of my greatest pleasures.   If I cannot
be happy there, I cannot be happy any where.   If I were to
settle in any other place, interest, not inclination, must give
rise to it.   I know not where the wish of procuring a com-

petence may hereafter fix me ; but if that competence can be obtained at Annapolis, there will I labor for it.

"I intended to have written to Mr. James Williams, but have been so much interrupted and engaged as not to be able to do so. Indeed I have no subject for a letter but what is exhausted in this. His friendly offices on the eve of my departure, proved the goodness of his heart, and made a deep impression on mine. Let me be remembered to him in the warmest terms. I will write to all my friends in due time, and in the interim tell them to write to me—a letter is now of real value to me.

"Sept. 18th, P. S.—I missed the opportunity of sending my letter, and do not now know when I shall have another.

" The shooting season began here the 15th inst., but I have not yet had a gun in hand. I envy Dr. Sheaff the sport he will have in the neighborhood of Annapolis. There can be none in this country to equal it.

" Adieu : if I keep my letter by me much longer, it will become a volume of postscripts.

" October 14th.—I have just got yours of the 14th Aug. It is kind in you to write thus often. Persevere in a practice so well begun, and you will oblige me highly. The commissioners commenced business the 10th inst. I was presented to the King on Wednesday last at St. James's. It was necessary, and I am glad it was, for while I am here I wish to see as much as possible. I was in the House of Lords at the opening of Parliament, and heard his majesty deliver his speech ; but I was not able to hear the debate upon it in the House of Commons, as I wished to do. I have attended the theatre pretty often, and have seen all their great performers. Be assured that we are accustomed in America to rate their excellence too high. There is hardly an exhibition in London which report does not exaggerate to us. I was led to expect more than I have been able to find. There are subjects, however, upon which I have not been disappointed ; the beauty and flourishing appearance of the country—the excellence of the roads—the extent and perfection of their various manufactures—the enormous stock of individual wealth which town and country exhibits, &c., &c., cannot be too strongly anticipated."

MR. PINKNEY TO THE HON. VANZ MURRY.

LONDON, *February 9th,* 1797.

"MY DEAR SIR :—I thank you for requesting to hear from me, but did not intend to wait for such a request. I wished to feel a little at home before I troubled you with a letter—and a stranger in London continues a stranger for some time. I find it difficult, even now, to accommodate myself to a world in all respects new to me. My habits were at variance with a London life, and habits contracted at an early period, and long cherished, are stubborn things. I have, however, made a virtue of necessity, and struggled with considerable industry to like what I must submit to whether I like it or not. Still I cannot look back upon my own country without strong regrets. Absence has consecrated and swelled into importance the veriest trifles I have left behind me. You have doubtless experienced this enthusiastic retrospect, and know with what soft and mellow colorings imagination paints the past in a situation like mine, and how the visionary picture indisposes one to the scenes of the moment. Upon the whole, however (when I can keep down this picture drawing propensity), I manage better than I expected. I have found here those whom it would be want of liberality not to esteem. I have found much to amuse and more to instruct me.

" Our circle of acquaintance is a pleasant one, and as extensive as we wish it ; and if I did not find some *friends,* too, in such a place as London, I should be afraid that I did not deserve any. In short, my time passes *agreeably*, though not so *happily* as in Maryland : my fancy is more amused and my understanding more widely occupied, but the heart is not so much interested.

" It is the misfortune of almost all travellers, that they set out with expectations so extravagant that their gratification is absolutely impossible. This was in great measure my case, and the consequence has been frequent disappointment. I presume it is to be attributed to my too sanguine anticipation, that I have seen Mrs. Siddons in her most favorite character without emotion or approbation—that I have heard Mr. Fox on the most interesting and weighty subjects, without discovering that he is an orator—that I have heard Mr. Grey on the same occasions, without thinking him above mediocrity—in short, that I have seen and heard much that I was told I should admire, without admiring it at all. Mr. Pitt indeed has not disappointed me. He is truly a wonderful man. I never heard so clear and masterly a reasoner, or a more effectual declaimer. They have all one fault, however. They do not understand the power which may be given to the human voice by *tones* and *modulations*. In consequence of our public character, Gore and myself are allowed to sit under the gallery of the House of Commons—a privilege of which you will suppose I do not omit to avail myself—I could sit there for ever to listen to Mr. Pitt. In argument he is beyond example correct and perspicuous—and in declamation energetic and commanding. His style might serve as a model of classical elegance, and has no defect, unless it be that it is sometimes overloaded with parentheses. You have seen and heard him, and therefore need not be told that his manner is against him—that his voice is full and impressive and his articulation unusually distinct. I thought at first that his pronunciation was too precise and analytic. It is, in fact, a sort of spelling pronunciation, that gives unnecessary body and importance to

every syllable ; but I am now familiarized to this scholastic
particularity, and hardly feel its impropriety.   I observe that
he, as well as Mr. Fox, closes his periods with a cadence
unknown in America.   I think it unmusical and harsh.   It
is, however, so completely fashionable, that you meet with it
even in Westminster Hall.   Of Mr. Fox, I think that he
has a vigorous mind—but that he is a speaker *in spite of
nature and his stars*.   He is, notwithstanding, generally powerful in debate.   I have heard Mr. Erskine once—in the
House of Commons.   I thought nothing of him, but I am
assured by good judges that at *the Bar* he is formidable, and
indeed eloquent, although he makes no figure in parliament.
I do not understand this—but I know one half of the fact to
be true in Mr. Erskine's case.

"Mr. Secretary Dundas is *mediocre*.   I incline to think
that in America the *art of speaking* is more advanced than
any other country.   We have, it is true, swarms of *praters*,
but we have also more (I mean a greater number of) able
speakers than are to be found here or elsewhere.   The *Bar*,
in this country, are sound lawyers, but nothing more.   In
America they are something more.   Perhaps in all this I
make my estimate a little too petulantly, and with too much
pride of country about me ; but I am writing to you who
have the same prejudices, and can make allowance for me.

"You will have heard, before my letter reaches you, of
the wonderful victory obtained by Bonaparte over the fifth
army of the Emperor in Italy—23,000 prisoners and 6,000
slain !   It is almost beyond belief—and we have yet nothing
upon which to ground belief but the French accounts.   They
state, however, the official dispatches of Bonaparte to the
Directory—and there seems to be no reason to doubt them.
If they be true, the fate of Italy is decided.   Wurmser,
however, still holds out in Mantua—but it is uncertain
whether Alvinzi succeeded in throwing provisions into the
garrison or not.   That Wurmser was in great want of pro-

visions is certain, and to relieve him in this respect was the great object of the attack of the Austrians on Bonaparte.

" You will also have heard of the attempt by the French to make a descent on Ireland. The weather defeated it ; but the greatest part of the vessels sent on this wild expedition have returned safe to France. We do not know precisely how Mr. Pinkney stands at Paris. He has not been received, and the papers here state that he is about to leave Paris for Amsterdam, to wait the orders of his government ; but this wants confirmation.

" The Emperor of Russia seems to embarrass all the belligerents. An universal pacification is supposed to be his object. He has much in his power ; and it is fervently to be wished that he may make a proper use of his situation.

" Our commission has experienced some unexpected embarrassments, but the government has removed them in a way highly honorable and satisfactory. The king's agent objected to our jurisdiction in a case—a leading feature of which was *that the Lords Commissioners of appeal had affirmed the original condemnation.* When the fifth commissioner, Gore, and myself were ready to overrule this objection, our right *to decide upon our own jurisdiction* was brought into question ! The government has said that both points were against those who started them, and we are now prosperously under way again. I have no fears of a fair execution of the 7th article by this country.

" This letter is becoming so unreasonably long, that I will only add that I am in every sense of the word your sincere friend.

" P. S.—When you go to Baltimore, if you should have any curiosity to know the precise nature of the embarrassments above alluded to, Mr. Chase will show you an explanation of them which I send him by the same vessel which carries this ; be good enough to write to me as often as your leisure will allow. Mr. McDonald (one of the commissioners on the part of this government under the 6th article of the Treaty), who is just on the point of sailing for America, I am acquainted with. If you should meet him, I need not ask you to attend to him when I inform you that he is an amiable, well-informed gentleman, and carries with him the best disposition towards our country."

MR. PINKNEY TO HIS BROTHER JONATHAN.

"LONDON, 26th April, 1799.

"DEAR J. :—I have received your letter of the 4th of March, inclosing one for Mr. Trumbull; but that of the 17th of April, covering a duplicate of Mr. Trumbull's letter, I have not received. Mr. T. has charged me with his thanks for your attention, and will, I presume, write to you himself.

"I am grieved by the style of your letter. If I have neglected you, it has not been from want of affection or forgetfulness of what I owe to your worth. I did not know that it would be acceptable to you to hear very often or very fully from me; and if on that account I have sometimes made you trust to others for tidings of me, and at other times have written rather scantily on subjects that might have been interesting to you, I ask to be forgiven.

"To say the truth, a long letter of a mere friendly complexion is not easily made. It would be idle to give you in such a letter the news of the moment, for the news would cease to be so before the letter could reach you; and I should fatigue you to death if I were to doom you to read accounts of London amusements, or of the manner in which I pass my time. Such details would soon have no novelty to recommend them, and would lose all attraction.

"I have seen in this country, and continue to see much that deserves the attention of him that would be wise or happy; but I would prefer making all this the subject of *conversation*, when Providence shall permit us to meet again, to putting it imperfectly on paper for your perusal when we are separated. There is not perhaps a more dangerous thing for him who aims at consistency, or at least the appearance of it, than to hasten to record impressions as they are made upon his mind by a state of things to which he has not been accustomed, and to give that record out of his own possession. I have made conclusions here, from time to time, which I have afterwards discarded as absurd; and I could wish that some of these conclusions did not show themselves in more than one of the letters I have occasionally written to my friends. I have made false estimates of men and things, and have corrected them as I have been able; in this there was nothing to blush for, for who is there that can say he has not done the same? But I confess that I do feel some little regret, when I remember that I have sent a few (though to say the truth, *very few*) of those estimates across the Atlantic, as indisputably accurate, and have either deceived those to whom they were sent, or afforded them grounds for thinking me a precipitate or superficial observer. The consciousness of this has indisposed me to a repetition of similar conduct; and I have desired so to write in future as to be able to change ill-founded opinions without the hazard of being convicted of capriciousness or folly. You will observe that I am all this time endeavoring to make my peace with you on the score of your complaint of negligence; but after all, I must in great measure rely upon your disposition to bear with my faults, and to overlook those you cannot fully acquit. I must not, however, omit to state my belief that you do not receive all the letters I send you, and of course that I appear to you more culpable than I really am.

"I wish I could tell you when I shall be likely to see you; although my time passes in a way highly gratifying, I am anxious to return. Our acquaintance has lately very

much enlarged itself, and our situation is altogether peculiarly pleasant for foreigners ; but I sigh now and then for home.
I am told I am considerably altered since I came here, and I
incline to think there is some foundation for it ; but I shall
not grow much wiser or better by a longer stay.   I am becoming familiar with almost every thing around me, and do
not look out upon life with as much intentness of observation as heretofore, and of course I am now rather confirming
former acquisitions of knowledge than laying in new stores
for the future—I begin to languish for my profession—I want
active employment.   The business of the commission does
not occupy me sufficiently, and visiting, &c., with the aid of
much reading, cannot supply the deficiency.   My time is always filled in some way or other ; but I think I should be
the better for a speech now and then.   Perhaps another
twelvemonth may give me the opportunity of making *speeches*
till I get tired of them—and tire others too.

"There are some respects in which it may be better that
I should remain here a little longer ; my health, though
greatly mended, is still delicate—I *look* better than I *am ;*
and perhaps a summer at *Brighton* or *Cheltenham* may make
me stronger.   The last winter has been unfavorable to me,
by affecting my stomach severely, and I have at this moment the same affection in a less degree accompanied with a
considerable headache.   I ought to have good health, for I
take pains to acquire it ; and have even gone so far as to
abandon the use of tobacco, to which I was once a slave.   It
is now about eighteen months since I have tasted this pernicious weed ; but I did not forbear the use of it solely on
account of my health ; I found that it was considered here
as a vulgar habit, which he who desired society must discard."

MR. PINKNEY TO THE SAME.

"LONDON, 14th February, 1800.

"DEAR J. :—It is now so long since I have had a line from you that I must conclude I have been unlucky enough to give you offence, for which it is necessary I should atone. What it can be I have no means of conjecturing ; but let it be what it may, you ought to believe that it has been wholly accidental. You complained to me some time ago that I was a negligent correspondent ; I explained the cause, and asked to be forgiven. If that explanation did not satisfy you, at least my prayer of pardon had some claim to be well received. I think I know you so well that I may venture to be certain you are not angry with me for the *old* reason. There must be some *new* ground of exception. Let me know it, I entreat you, and I will make amends as far as I am able. I had indeed hoped that it would not be for ordinary matters that you would forget my claims to your *friendship*, if not your *affection*. I had supposed that you would not lightly have been induced to treat me as a stranger ; and to substitute the cold intercourse of ceremony for that of the heart. Why will you allow me to be disappointed in expectations so reasonable, and so justly founded on the natural goodness of your disposition, and the soundness of your understanding ? Can you imagine that I do not recollect how much I am indebted to your kindness on various occasions, and how strong is your title to my attachment and respect ? If I have appeared to slight your letters by sometimes giving them short answers, and sometimes delaying to give them any, can you think so meanly of me as to suppose that therefore I have not placed a proper value on them and you ? I declare to God that if you have made this supposition, you have been unjust both to yourself and me. There is not a person on earth for whom I have a more warm and sincere regard, nor is there one whose correspondence, while you permitted it to last, was more truly grateful to me. I beg you, therefore, to resume it, and to resume it cordially. But if, after all, you are so different from yourself as to persist in regarding me as one who has no better ties upon you than the rest of the world, at least tell me why it is that this must be so.

"Of the late revolution in France and of Bonaparte's advances to negotiation, with the rejection of these advances, you will have heard before this can reach you. I was present very lately in the House of Commons at the debate on the rejection of these overtures. So able and eloquent a speech as Mr. Pitt's on that occasion I never witnessed. Experience only can decide how far the conduct he vindicated was wise. Administration have undoubtedly sanguine hopes of restoring the House of Bourbon ; and prodigious efforts will be made during the next campaign with that object. I do not think that this will succeed. The co-operation of Russia still remains equivocal; but even if Russia should give all her strength to the confederacy, it will not have power to force upon France the ancient dynasty of that country with all the consequences inseparable from it. The present government of that ill-fated nation is a mockery—a rank usurpation by which political freedom is annihilated ; but it is a government of energy, and will be made yet more so by an avowed attempt to overturn it by a foreign army in favor of the exiled family. This is my opinion ; but the war in Europe has so often changed its aspect against all calculation that prophecies about its future results, are hardly worth the making. The death of General Washington has ascertained how greatly he was every where admired. The panegyrics that all parties here have combined to bestow upon his character have equalled those in America.

"P. S.—As our commission is at a stand on account of the disagreements under the American commission, I can form no guess as to the probable time of my return. There is little prospect, however, of its being very soon. I must be patient, and am determined *to see it out ;* but I wish most ardently to revisit my country and my friends. I think it likely that my brother commissioner, Gore, will take a trip to America next summer, and come back in the course of the autumn. I am afraid we shall both have *leisure enough* for a voyage to the East Indies. I have nothing to do here but to visit, read, write, and so forth. In this idle course I certainly grow older and perhaps a little wiser; but I am doing nothing to expedite my return.

"Pray can you make out to send me a box of Spanish cigars ? If you can, I will thank you; for I find it beneficial to smoke a cigar or two before I go to bed. This I do by stealth, and in a room devoted to that purpose ; for smoking here is considered a most ungentlemanlike practice. Having left off chewing tobacco, which was prejudicial to me, I have taken up the habit of smoking to a very limited extent in lieu of it ; and as I find it serviceable to me, and *nobody knows it,* I think I shall continue it. Remember me affectionately to Ninian, and tell him I mean to write to him soon. Mrs. Pinkney hears that William is able to write something like a letter. If this be so, she begs you will request Ninian to make him write to her."

MR. PINKNEY TO THE SAME.

"LONDON, *August 27th,* 1800.

"DEAR J.: I received your letter of the 27th May, while in the country, and delayed answering it till my return to town. For your good intentions relative to the cigars, I am much obliged to you, and I heartily wish it was in my power to thank you for the *cigars themselves,* of which I have heard nothing otherwise than in your letter. Perhaps I may still get them—but I have not much hopes. Make my acknowledgments to Mr. Williams for the box you speak of as being a present from him. As there is no person for whom I feel a more warm and sincere regard, and upon whose friendship I more value myself, you may be assured that this little proof of his recollection gives me the greatest pleasure. I shall not easily forget the many kind attentions I have received from him ; nor can I ever be more happy than when an opportunity shall occur of showing the sense I entertain of them.

"Whether the justification you offer for ceasing to write to me is a sound one or not, it is not worth while to inquire. You *have* written at last, and this puts out of the question all past omissions. Perhaps we have been both to blame— or perhaps the fault has been wholly mine. I will not dispute with you on this point, but I entreat that in future it may be understood between us that trifles are not to be allowed to bring into doubt our regard for each other, and that our intercourse is not to be regulated by the rules of a rigorous ceremony. While I admit what you urge in regard to my neglect of *you*, I take leave to enter my protest in the strongest terms against the general charge made in your letter that I have neglected several others in the same way. I have had no correspondent in America (I have excepted you) who has not generally been in my debt. The truth is, my friends have overlooked me in a strange way, and I have been compelled to jog their memories more than perhaps I ought to have done. As to Ninian, you know very well that in writing to you I considered myself as writing to him ; for I did not imagine it was desirable that I should make two letters, which should be little more than duplicates, when one would serve just as well. But since I have discovered that Ninian wished me to write to him, I have taken pleasure in doing so ; and for some time past, I think he has no cause to complain of me on this score.

"It is my earnest wish to return home without loss of

time, and to apply in earnest to my profession for the purpose of securing, while my faculties are unimpaired, a competence for my helpless family. For several months past I have thought of desiring from my government to be recalled, and if the prospect of our resuming our functions does not greatly change for the better before next spring, I shall undoubtedly have recourse to this step. At present, it is not practicable to form even a conjecture upon this subject. We have been stopped by the difficulties that have occurred under the 6th article of the treaty, and not by any thing depending on ourselves, or connected with our own duties. If we had not been thus arrested in our progress, we should have finished ere now, or at farthest by Christmas, to the satisfaction of all parties. The arrangement under the 6th article will be accomplished, I am afraid, very slowly, if at all; and even when that arrangement shall be made, the execution of it will demand several years ; and we are not, it seems, to outstrip the advances it shall make. Thus it is probable that I shall grow old in this country, unless I resign. In short, I see very little room to doubt that I shall be driven to this expedient. So much for the mismanagement and folly of other people !

" The commission in America has been wretchedly bungled. I am entirely convinced that with discretion and moderation a better result might have been obtained ; be this as it may, it is time for me to think seriously of revisiting my country, and of employing myself in a profitable pursuit. I shall soon begin to require ease and retirement ; my constitution is weak and my health precarious. A few years of professional labor will bring me into the *sear and yellow leaf of life;* and if I do not begin speedily, I shall begin too late. To commence the world *at forty* is indeed dreadful; but I am used to adverse fortune, and know how to struggle with it ; my consolations cannot easily desert me—the consciousness of honorable views, and the cheering hope that Providence will yet enable me to pass my age in peace. It is not of small importance to me that I shall go back to the bar cured of every propensity that could divert me from business—stronger than when I left it—and, I trust, somewhat wiser. In regard to legal knowledge, I shall not be worse than if I had continued ; I have been a regular and industrious student for the last two years, and I believe myself to be a much better lawyer than when I arrived in England. There are other respects, too, in which I hope I have gained something—how much, my friends must judge. But I am wearying you with prattle about myself, for which I ask you to excuse me.

"I received Ninian's letter by Mr. Gore, but have not now time to answer it. I wrote him very lately. Request him to get from Mr. Vanhorne the note-book, or note-books I lent him, and to take care of them for me. In one of my note-books I made some few reports of General Court and Chancery decisions. Let it be taken care of. When I write again, I hope to be able to state when it is probable I shall have a chance of seeing you. When I do return, it is my present intention to settle at Annapolis, unless I go to the federal city. No certainty yet of peace—but I continue to prophesy (notwithstanding the Emperor of Russia's troops) that a *continental* peace will soon take place. The affair between this country and Denmark will probable be settled by Denmark's yielding the point. I have no opinion of the armed neutrality so much talked of. It could do nothing *now*, if it were formed——but I doubt the fact of its formation."

MR. PINKNEY TO HIS BROTHER NINIAN.

"LONDON, *July* 21*st*, 1801.

"DEAR N. :—Report has certainly taken great liberties with my letter to Mr. Thompson. Undoubtedly I have never written to any person sentiments that go the length you state. When the contest for President was reduced to Mr. Jefferson and Mr. Burr, my judgment was fixed that the former ought to be preferred—and I went so far as to think that his superiority in every particular that gives a title to respect and confidence, was so plain and decided as to leave no room for an impartial and unprejudiced man to hesitate in giving him his voice. Of course, it is probable that in reference to the result of this competition, when it was known, I have expressed myself in some of my letters to my friends as highly pleased, and that before it was known, I expressed my wishes that the event might be such as it has been. It is highly probable too that, even before the contest was brought to this alternative, I have said that, whatever may have been my wishes, I felt no alarms at the idea of Mr. Jefferson's success. I do not remember that I *have* said thus much, but I believe it to be likely, because it would have been true.

"I have at all times thought highly of Mr. Jefferson, and have never been backward to say so. I have never seen, or fancied I saw, in the perspective of his administration the calamities and disasters, the anticipation of which has filled so many with terror and dismay.

"I thought it certain that a change of *men* would follow his elevation to power—but I did not forbode from it any *such* change of *measures* as would put in hazard the public happiness. I believed, and do still believe him to be too wise not to comprehend, and too honest not to pursue, the substantial interests of the United States, which it is in fact almost impossible to mistake, and which he has every possible motive to secure and promote. I did not credit the suggestions that unworthy prejudices against one nation, or childish predilection for another, would cause him to commit the growing prosperity of his country to the chances of a war, by which much might be lost, but nothing could be gained, except the fruits of petty hostility and base pillage on the ocean. I did not credit, and often did not understand, the vague assertions that he was a disorganizer—an enemy to all efficient government—a democrat—an infidel, &c. &c.

" In the past conduct of Mr. Jefferson, so far as it had come to my knowledge, I discovered no just foundation for these assertions—and I am not to be influenced by mere clamor, from whatsoever quarter it may come. In short, I never could persuade myself to tremble lest the United States should find in the presidency of Mr. Jefferson the evils which might be expected to flow from a weak or a wicked government. I am, on the contrary, satisfied that he has talents, knowledge, integrity, and stake in the country suffi- cient to give us well-founded confidence, that our affairs will be well administered so far as shall depend on him ; although he may not always perhaps make use of exactly the same means and agents that our partialities or peculiar opinions might induce us to wish.

" I hope you are deceived as to the possible consequences of the ensuing State elections. What has Mr. Jefferson's being President of the United States to do with your Gen- eral Court, Chancery, &c.? Without tracing the peril in which these establishments manifestly are, to the ascendency of this or that political party in the nation at large, it may be found in the local interests of the different counties at any distance from the seat of justice—in the interests of the attorneys who swarm in every part of the State, and in the House of Delegates—in the plausible and popular nature of the theory that justice should be brought home to men's doors, and that it should be cheap, easy, and expeditious—in the love of change which half the world believe to be synon- ymous with improvement—in the disgust of parties who have lost their cause and their money at Annapolis or Easton, and who imagine they would have done better in the county court—and in a thousand other causes that a long speech only could enumerate. Five years ago your House of Delegates voted the abolition of the General Court, and yet Maryland was at that time in high reputation as a *federal State*. The Senate, it is true, rejected the bill; not, however, because they were more federal than the House of Delegates, but simply because they had good sense enough to perceive that the bill was a very foolish affair; and I have confidence that your next Senate, whether Mr. Jefferson's partisans or opposers, will manifest the same soundness of mind and firmness of conduct. I profess I am a good deal surprised that you at Annapolis, who are interested locally, as well as generally, in preserving the General Court, &c., should be so imprudent as to cause it to be understood that you consider the whole of a great and triumphant party in the State as hostile upon principle to these establishments. For my part I would hold the opposite language, and would industriously circulate my unalterable conviction that *this* was no party question, but such a one as every honest man, a friend to the prosperity of Maryland, and to the purity of justice, cannot fail to oppose. By making a party question of it, you are in greater danger of a defeat than you otherwise would be, because you may give *party men* inducements to vote for it who in a different and more correct view of the subject might vote the other way. You are on the spot, however, and must have better means of judging on this head than I have. No man would lament more sincerely than I should do, the destruction of what I consider the fairest ornaments of our judicial system. If I was among you, I would spare no honest effort to stem the torrent of innovation, which has long been threatening the superior courts, and will finally overthrow them. But I should not believe that I was promoting my object by putting in array against me, and insisting on considering and treating as adversaries, a numerous and zealous body of men with whom I happened

to differ on some other topic, and who perhaps, if I would allow them to take their own stations, would be found on my
side."

MR. PINKNEY TO THE SAME.

"LONDON, *July* 21*st*, 1803.

"DEAR N. :—I received your kind letter of the 31st of
May on yesterday. You had omitted to write to me for so
great a length of time, that I had despaired of again hearing
from you during my stay in England. Your letter has, of
course, given me more than usual pleasure.

"I offer you my congratulations on your marriage, which
you have now for the first time announced to me. Mrs. P.
desires me also to offer you hers. We both wish you all the
happiness you can yourself desire.

"It is now certain that I am not to see you this year.
Our commission will, however, close next winter, and in April
or May, if I live and do well, I shall undoubtedly be with
you. In the mean time, such insinuations as you mention,
let them come from what quarter they will (and I can form
no conjecture whence they come), can give me no uneasiness.
I am not so inordinately fond of praise as to be disappointed
or provoked, when I am told that there are some who either
do or affect to think less of my capacity than I would have
them. What *station* you allude to I am wholly unable to
judge, but I know that I have never solicited any. I am no
office-hunter. Without professing to shun public employment when it seeks me, I can truly say that I disdain to
seek it. My reliance, both for character and fortune, is, under Providence, on my profession, to which I shall immediately return, and in the practice of which I do not fear to
silence those insinuators. What I am must soon be seen
and known. The bar is not a place to acquire or preserve a
false or fraudulent reputation for talents ; and I feel what is

I hope, no more than a just and honorable confidence, in which I may indulge without vanity, that on that theatre I shall be able to make my depreciators acknowledge that they have undervalued me.

" I shall mingle too in the politics of my country on my return (I mean as a private citizen only) ; and then I shall not fail to give the world an opportunity of judging both of my head and my heart. Enough of this.

" I have constantly believed that America has nothing to fear from the men now at the head of our affairs—and in this I think you will soon agree with me, notwithstanding the interested clamor of their adversaries. Time will show in what hands the public power in America can be most safety deposited. To that test you will do well to refer yourself. In the mean time it appears to be a rational confidence that no party can *long* abuse that power with impunity."

MR. PINKNEY TO MR. COOKE.

"LONDON, *August 8th*, 1803.

" My Dear Sir :—The kindness of your last letter, which I received about a week ago, and which I shall long bear in mind, will not allow me to forego the pleasure of writing you once more (though but a few lines) during my stay in England. I say *once* more, because I trust that early in the spring I shall commence my voyage for America, and of course shall have no inducement to write again. I was entirely convinced before the receipt of your last, that your letter of December, on the subject of the Maryland business, was dictated, as you say, by friendship ; and I not only felt all the value of the motive, but thanked you sincerely for the communication itself.

" I had not heard of your rejection of the appointment to

the Court of Appeals, and I am truly sorry that you have rejected it. Of the circumstances attending the offer, or the views by which it was either influenced or resisted, I know nothing; but I know that the appointment would have been the best that could have been made; and I believe that the public have a right to your services, now that it is no longer necessary that you should labor for yourself. I have, however, so much reliance on the correctness of your judgment, that I must presume you have done right, and that I see only half the subject.

"I am prepared on my return to find the spirit of party as high and frenzied as the most turbulent would have it. I am even prepared to find a brutality in that spirit which in this country either does not exist, or is kept down by the predominance of a better feeling. I lament with you that this is so; and I *wonder* that it is so—for the American people are generous, and liberal, and enlightened. We are not, I hope, to have this inordinate zeal, this extravagant fanaticism, entailed upon us—although really one might almost suppose it to be a part of our political creed that internal tranquillity, or rather the absence of domestic discord, and a rancorous contention for power, was incompatible with the health of the state, and the liberty of the citizen. I profess to be temperate in my opinions, and shall put in my claim to freedom of conscience; but when both sides are intolerant, what hope can I have that this claim will be respected? At the bar I must contrive as well as I can, for I *must* return to it. I have no alternative; and if I had, choice would carry me back to the profession. I do not desire *office*, although I have no such objections to the present administration, as, on what are called party principles, would induce me to decline public employment. It is my wish to be a mere professional laborer—to cultivate my friends and my family, and to secure an honorable independence before I am overtaken by age and infirmity. My present intention is to fix in Baltimore, where I will flatter myself I shall find some who will not regret my choice of residence. I had understood with unfeigned concern the severe loss you alude to, and knew the pain it would occasion. You have, however, the best of consolations in those whom she has left behind ; and it is my earnest wish that they may be long spared to you, and you to them. In a family like yours every loss must be deeply felt ; for none can be taken away without diminishing the stock of worth and happiness to which each is so well calculated to contribute. But you have still about you enough to preserve to life all that belongs to it of interest and value, to which, my dear sir, you can add that which many cannot, the perfect consciousness of having deserved it. I beg you to remember me in the most friendly terms to your sons, and to present our affectionate compliments to Mrs. Cooke."

MR. PINKNEY TO THE SAME.

"LONDON, *February 15th*, 1804.

"MY DEAR SIR :—Your letter of the 2d of December, which I received on the 23d of last month, is among the most pleasing of the many proofs which my long absence from America has procured me of your valuable friendship. It is not in my power to manifest by words the sensibility which such kindness excites in my heart. I must leave it to time therefore to offer me other means.

"The application to the government of the United States, for an outfit, was the joint application of Mr. Gore and myself ; and as it was addressed wholly to the *justice* of the government, and asked no favor, I did not suppose that it would be proper to endeavor to interest my friends generally in its success. It seemed to me that this would have argued a distrust either of the claim itself, or of those to whom it was preferred ; and as I really had the most perfect confidence in both, I was not disposed to act as if I had none. Accordingly, I mentioned the subject only to General Smith, as a Senator of the United States, requesting of him, in case the President should lay it before Congress, such explanations and support as it might seem to him to require, and his view of it (*as a demand of right*) would justify.   More than this, I could not prevail upon myself to do, although I began several letters to diff erent persons whose good offices I thought I might venture to ask.   General Smith has answered my letter, and otherwise acted on this occasion in a way to deserve my particular thanks.   I have no doubt, however, that the claim has been rejected ; and I understand that I am not likely to derive much consolation for this rejection, from the manner in which our application has been received and treated.   It would not be proper to say more upon a transaction of which I have at present such scanty knowledge, and the result of which may not be such as I conjecture it to be.

" General Smith mentions another matter, of which you also take notice—I mean the desire expressed by some gentlemen of Baltimore, who have been benefited by my services in England, to make me some pecuniary acknowledgment. My answer, written in a hurry, and therefore, perhaps, not exactly what it ought to be, declines this proposal, for which, however, I cannot but be sincerely thankful to those from whom it proceeds.   General Smith will probably show you my letter, and I should be glad that you would even ask him to do so.

"As to the arrangement of a loan, it is liable, in substance, to all the objections applicable to the other, and consequently inadmissible.   I must, therefore, do as well as I can with my own resources—and I have the satisfaction to know that I shall leave England with my credit untouched, and in no *tradesman's* debt.   If it will distress me to return to Maryland, with my large family (as I am not ashamed to confess it will), I shall at least have to sustain me under it, the consciousness that no vice has contributed to produce it—that my honor has no stain upon it—and that although it may be a misfortune to become poor in the public service, it is no crime. For the rest, I rely upon Providence and my own efforts in my profession.

"I am not ashamed, my dear sir, that almost every word of this letter has myself for its subject; and I should be yet more so, if I did not recollect that it is to you, who have encouraged me thus to play the egotist. I am not likely, however, to sin in this respect, at least for some time, as I hope to leave this country in March, for the United States, and shall of course be under no temptation to write again, even to you.

"The affair of the Maryland stock is in train, and I have now a fair prospect of settling it (as I hope satisfactorily) after much anxiety, vexation and difficulty. A week or two more will, I trust, conclude it. I shall not make any communication on this subject to the government of the United States, or of Maryland, until I am enabled to say that the stock has been transferred. Some sacrifice on our part has been found indispensable—but if with that sacrifice the residue can be immediately secured, we ought, in my opinion, to rejoice. That business closed, I shall only wait for a vessel sufficient to accommodate my family, bound to Baltimore. None has yet offered—and I begin to have some fears on that score. I must have patience."

Mr. Pinkney was absent from the United States until August, 1804, when he returned once more to the spot he most loved on earth, to begin again at the age of forty the struggles of the forum. He returned however with a mind enriched with foreign travel, panting to gain fresh laurels, and stimulated by the master minds of the Law, in the mother country, in contact with whom he had been brought by the business of his mission. He led a very active life while abroad. He observed every thing worthy of note, and studied every thing he saw. His society was much sought by distinguished noblemen and commoners, and it was his happiness to form some warm friendships, which relieved the period of his temporary exile. He continued to pursue with unabated ardor and energy his professional studies, and kept up his habit of extempore speaking in private. Nothing was permitted to entice him from this severe mental discipline and labor. With the eye of an intelligent and discriminating critic he instituted a comparison between the bar of England and that of the United States ;—and the comparison was far from being prejudicial to the rising character of his countrymen. Privileged to sit within the bar of the English parliament, he was a constant frequenter of the debates of that body; and was therefore qualified to form and express his opinion. He made the most of his circumstances, and appropriated with consummate skill all the benefits of this close and critical analysis of the legal and parliamentary mind of England.

By this course of patient application, and constant practice in private of the habit of speaking (kept up and persevered in, amid the brilliant displays of a Parliament preeminently distinguished for oratorical ability), he retained all his freshness as an advocate, and entered on the renewal of professional conflict, as though he had not abandoned for a moment the courts of justice. Baltimore was the field selected for the re-commencement of his labors. He no sooner entered upon it than business flowed in, and he found himself occupied with a practice extremely lucrative. He took his stand at the head of the Maryland Bar, and won honors in every contest. His arguments enlightened the tribunals he addressed, and the courts acknowledged his supremacy.

In 1805 he was appointed Attorney-General of the State. This office he consented to hold for the benefit of one of his early and most revered friends, between whom and himself there existed a warm personal attachment. I allude to Mr. Johnson, who was afterwards the Chancellor of Maryland, a gentleman of uncommon force of intellect and purity of character—the father of the Hon. Reverdy Johnson and John Johnson, the former one of the very first lawyers of the Union, who as Senator and Attorney-General of the United States displayed a statesmanlike ability and profound legal learning which have won for him a most enviable distinction ; and the latter, the present accomplished and able Chancellor of the State.

In 1806 he was again sent to England to assist Mr. Monroe in the adjustment of our difficult and delicate negotiations with that august and mighty nation. This appointment he received from President Jefferson. The mode in which it was conferred was alike honorable to each. He was chosen for his peculiar fitness for the work, and solicited to accept the trust for the good of the country. In a letter from Mr. Jefferson (now given to the public for the first time), in his own beautiful autograph, from which I copy, dated August 5th, 1809, I find the following explicit language :

"I am happy in an occasion of expressing to you my great esteem for you personally, and the satisfaction with which I noted the correctness, both as to matter and manner, with which you discharged the public duties you *were so kind as to undertake* at my request.

"I witnessed too, with pleasure, the esteem with which you inspired my successor, then more immediately engaged in correspondence with you. Accept the just tribute of mine also, and of my great respect and consideration."

It is refreshing at this day to look back to the time when a public trust so delicate and important was assumed, as a kind compliance with the earnest request of the President, with whom was lodged the appointing power. Mr. Pinkney had been abroad. He was at this time in the full flush of professional success, amassing a fortune for his large and helpless family, with nothing to desire but health and strength to reap the field that was literally groaning beneath the burden of the harvest. He was exactly in the sphere he most coveted to fill, when the eye of the President was turned towards him—a President, too, whom he could be scarcely said to know except by name and a large reputation. He was called to turn aside once more from the forum, and the scenes he most loved to contemplate, and the circle of friends in which he most delighted; and embark on a mission that promised nothing but toil and self-sacrifice. It was the call of the country, however, and his patriot heart beat responsive to it. A kind compliance with the President's request was the thing asked of him, and the boon was no sooner asked than granted.

The manner in which he executed this trust, or afterwards filled the sole responsibilities of Minister Plenipotentiary to the court of St. James, will be discussed in another portion of this memoir.

It may be refreshing to pause a moment in our narrative, and turn to the correspondence of Mr. Pinkney, and see what was the state of his mind, his views and feelings, during this his second embassage to England.

MR. PINKNEY TO HIS BROTHER NINIAN.

"LONDON, *April 28th,* 1808.

" DEAR N. :—I received a few days ago your very short letter on a very large sheet of paper. I expected a volume, and was obliged to put up with half a dozen lines. This is not well. After all, it is so much clear gain to hear from you; and, giving you credit for good intentions and a good stock of affection, I thank you for your letter, which furnishes much evidence of both. I should have been gratified undoubtedly by a little intelligence about Annapolis, the health of friends, and so forth; but you will give me all these in your next letter; and so we will settle the account.

"I congratulate you on the growth of your daughter. She is, I doubt not, worthy of all your care, and will, I sincerely hope and trust, give you many a delightful hour, employed in watching her improvement, and cultivating and forming her mind and manners: the purest, the most completely unmixed of all our enjoyments; for even its anxieties are happiness!

"How does it happen that Jonathan has not written to me? It is odd enough that I, who seem to have a host of friends, as kind as heart could wish, when I am in Maryland, appear to have none the moment I leave it. This is poor encouragement to travel. I think, if ever I live to get back to the *fontes et flumina natæ*, this consideration will induce me to make a vow to quit them no more on any errand whatever. Even *you* recollect me only when some striking event forces me, as it were, upon you; and Jonathan of course forgets me, because I keep no cash at the Farmers' Bank. Notwithstanding all this, remember me to him in the most affectionate manner. Tell him I think of him often. *How* I think of him he need not be told.

"I have been more frequently indisposed within the last six months, than has been usual with me. I am, indeed, just recovered from an attack. Too much employment and some inquietude may have laid me open to these indispositions. The climate does not suit me as well as it did. I hope to do better in future; but these warnings are not to be slighted.

"You have not mentioned the Governor in any of your letters. You must like him, I am sure; for he is of a liberal, generous temper. I do not meet with your newspapers as often as I could wish ; but, from those I have seen, the Governor's conduct appears to have been active, spirited, and judicious on every occasion that has occurred since his first appointment. It was to have been confidently expected that it should be so. His principles have always been those of ardent patriotism ; and his mind, naturally strong and vigorous, has been enlightened by great experience. In my letter to him by Mr. Rose (which, as Mr. Rose did not go to Annapolis as he expected, was not perhaps delivered), I asked to have the pleasure of hearing from him when he should have a leisure hour which he could not otherwise employ. Will you take an opportunity of intimating this to him ? Remind Mr. H. and Mr. D. of me. Tell them that they neglect me ; but that I remember them with as much cordial esteem as ever. Where is my friend, Mr. E. ? If you should see him, say to him for me a thousand kind things. Inform Mr. M. that I wrote to him last autumn ; but fear my letter miscarried. As to Mr. C., he has given me up entirely. There are many other friends of whom I could speak ; but I have not time. There is one, however, of whom I will find time to speak ; and to her I beg you to say that she shares in all the regard I feel for you."

MR. PINKNEY TO THE SAME.

"LONDON, *August 29th*, 1808.

" DEAR N. :—I have had the pleasure to receive your letter of the 16th of July, and am happy to see that you do not forget me.

" I should reluctantly quarrel with your domestic felicity ; but I might perhaps be in danger of doing so, if it appeared to engross you so entirely as to leave no leisure for a recollection now and then of us who are absent.

"The letter of which you speak (inclosing one from Mrs. P.) came safe to hand; and if it had not, I should have invented half a dozen apologies for you. I know you so well, that, when you appear to neglect me, I am ready to throw the blame upon fortune, upon accident (who are, I suspect, the same personages), upon every thing, and every body, rather than upon you.

"My health *has been* rather worse than I wished it; but I am now convalescent. A short absence from town (my family are still out of town), sea-air and sea-bathing, have put me up again.

"Such a result of my labors for the public as you would flatter me with, would make me, I doubt not, the healthiest man in England. There is a sort of moral health, however, which crosses, and difficulties, and disappointments, tend very much to promote. I must endeavor to console myself with the opinion that I have laid in a good stock of that while I was losing some of the other.

"After all this philosophizing, I am half inclined to envy you the smooth, even tenor of your life. You are every way happy—at home—abroad. Nothing disturbs your tranquillity farther than to show you the value of it.

"Beloved by your family—respected and esteemed every where—your official capacity acknowledged—your official exertions successful—what have you to desire? But I have been so tossed about in the world, that, although I am as happy at home as my neighbors, I can hardly be said to have had a fair and decent share of real quiet. The time may come, however, when I too shall be tranquil, and when, freed from a host of importunate cares, that now keep me company whether I will or not, I may look back upon the way I have travelled with a heart at ease, and forward with a Christian's hope. I suspect I am growing serious when I meant to be directly the reverse. Thus, indeed, it is with the great mass of our purposes.

"I am rejoiced that Annapolis holds up its head. In itself the most beautiful, to me the most interesting spot on earth, I would fain believe that it is doomed to enjoy the honors of old age without its decrepitude. There is not a foot of ground in its neighborhood which my memory has not consecrated, and which does not produce, as fancy traces it, a thousand retrospections that go directly to the heart. It was the scene of our youthful days. What more can be said? I would have it to be also the scene of my declining years.

"Tell Jonathan that I would write to him if I could—but that I have scarcely leisure for this scrawl. He knows my affections, and will take the 'will for the deed.' I offer him, through you, my felicitations upon the stability and wholesome effects of the Farmers' Bank. Ask him why it is that I do not hear from him? All days are not discount days, and a man may be cashier of the Bank of England, and yet have a moment to spare to those who love him. I beg you to remember me to the Governor, and to Dr. J., and to other friends."

MR. PINKNEY TO MRS. NINIAN PINKNEY.

"LONDON, *June 24th*, 1809.

"MY DEAR MADAM :—If I had not found it impossible to answer your letter by the return of the Pacific, it would have been answered. Business occupied my time, and anxiety my heart, to the last moment. I would have cheated the last of these tyrants of an hour or two by conversing with you; but the first forbade it, and I had no choice but to submit. From this double despotism I am now comparatively free, and the use which I make of my liberty is to trespass on you with a few lines.

I shall not condole with you on your loss, though I am able to conjecture how keenly it has been felt; you have yourself suggested one of the consolations which best support the good under the heaviest of all human calamities : *We shall meet again in purity and joy the friends who are every day falling around us.* There is nothing which more effectually cheers the soul in its dark mortal pilgrimage than this noble confidence ; life would, indeed, be a sad journey without it ; the power of death is, in this view, nothing ; it separates us for a season merely to fit us for a more exalted and holy communion. I have clung to this thought ever since I was capable of thinking, and I would not part with it for worlds ; it has assisted me in many a trial to bear up against the evil of the hour, and to shake off in some degree (for who can boast of having entirely escaped from) the influence of those passions that betray and degrade us. If I may dare to say so, it gives a new value to immortality, while it furnishes powerful incentives to virtue. You cannot, I think, have yet met with " Morehead's Discourses." One of his sermons turns upon the loss of children ; and he sets forth, with that eloquence which comes warm from the heart, the softenings which this bitter affliction derives from religion. When you can get the sermon, read it ; in the mean time, the following short extract will please you. It is exquisitely beautiful ; and the best of our modern Reviews has quoted it as a soothing and original suggestion :

" ' We are all well aware of the influence of the world. We know how strongly it engages our thoughts, and debases the springs of our actions : we all know how important it is to have the springs of our minds renewed, and the rust which gathers over them cleared away. One of the principal advantages, perhaps, which arises from the possession of children, is, that in their society the simplicity of our nature is constantly recalled to our view ; and that, when we return from the cares and thoughts of the world into our domestic circle, we behold beings whose happiness springs from no false estimates of worldly good, but from the benevolent instincts of nature. *The same moral advantage is often derived in a greater degree from the memory of those children who have left us.* Their simple characters dwell upon our minds with a deeper impression ; their least actions return to our thoughts with more force than if we had it still in our power to witness them ; and they return to us clothed in that saintly garb which belongs to the possessors of a higher existence. We feel that there is now a link connecting us with a purer and a better scene of beings ; that a part of ourselves has gone before us in the bosom of God ; and that the same happy creatures which here on earth showed us the simple sources from which happiness springs, now hover over us, and scatter from their wings the graces and beatitudes of eternity.'

" Who can read this passage without feeling his heart in unison with it ? It cannot be read without inspiring a pleasing melancholy, and lifting the mind beyond the low contamination of this probationary state, ' to scenes where love and bliss immortal reign.' "

MR. PINKNEY TO HIS BROTHER NINIAN.

"LONDON, *September 23d*, 1809.

" DEAR N. :—I received, a few days ago, your letter of the 26th of June. I am obliged to you for the intelligence given in a part of it, and still more for the kindness and affection which pervade the whole. A better choice of *Governor* could not, I should think, have been made. It must have been very agreeable to you, and I congratulate you upon it accordingly. I have not yet received the letter which you tell me I am to expect from the Governor and Council. I shall be happy to do all in my power to fulfil their wishes, whatever they may be. William is most fortunately fixed, and I have the utmost confidence that he will do well. If he does otherwise his condemnation will be great indeed. The children who are with me have shot up at a prodigious rate, and require much care and expense. Charles, who is a remarkably promising boy, has finished his preparatory course, and is now at Eton. Edward will be placed, after Christmas, at the school which Charles has left. The rest will continue to have masters at home.

" My anxiety to return does not diminish. On the contrary, it grows upon me, and I find it necessary to wrestle with it. You know that I have as many and as strong inducements to be contented here as any American could have ; but England is not Maryland ; and foreign friends, however great, or numerous, or kind, cannot interest us like those of our native land,—the companions of our early days, the witnesses and competitors of our first struggles in life, and the indulgent partakers of our sorrows and our joys ! I trust that I have as little disposition as any man to repine at my lot, and I know that I endeavored to form my mind to a devout and reverential submission to the will of God. Yet I cannot conceal from myself that every day adds something to my cares and nothing to my happiness ; that I am growing old among strangers ; and that my heart, naturally warm and open, becomes cold by discipline, contracted by duty, and sluggish from want of exercise. These may be called imaginary ills ; but there is another, which all the world will admit to be substantial—I speak to you in confidence—my salary is found by experience to be far short of the actual necessities of my situation. It was fixed at its present rate many years ago, when the style of living and the prices of articles would not bear a comparison with those of the present time. I have no right to complain, however ; and, therefore, I write this for your own perusal merely."

THOMAS JEFFERSON TO WILLIAM PINKNEY.

"MONTICELLO, *August 5th*, 1809.

" DEAR SIR.—The bearer hereof, Mr. Alexander McRae, and Major John Clarke, proposing to go to Great Britain on their private concerns, I take the liberty of presenting them to your notice and patronage. Mr. McRae, a lawyer of distinction, has been a member of the council of state of Virginia and Lieutenant-Governor, highly esteemed for his talents and correctness of principle, moral and political. Major Clarke was long also in public employ as director of the armory of this State, recommended as such by his great mechanical ingenuity and personal worth. Any good offices you may be so kind as to render them will be deservedly bestowed ; and their knowledge of the present state of our affairs may enable them to add acceptably to your information.

" I am happy in an occasion of expressing to you my great esteem for you personally, and the satisfaction with which I noted the correctness, both as to matter and manner, with which you discharged the public duties you were so kind as to undertake at my request.

" I witnessed too with pleasure the esteem with which you inspired my successor, then more immediately engaged in correspondence with you. Accept the just tribute of mine also, and of my great respect and consideration."

MR. PINKNEY TO THOMAS JEFFERSON.

"LONDON, *April 30th*, 1810.

" DEAR SIR :—It was only a few days ago that I had the honor to receive your letter of the 5th of August last, by Mr. McRae. I need not say that I shall be happy to show that gentleman every attention, and to do him every service in my power.

" I cannot express to you how sensibly I feel the kindness of the last paragraph of your letter. If any thing could give new strength to the affectionate sentiments which bind me to you, it would be the assurance it contains, that in your retirement you look back with approbation on my humble endeavors to be useful to our country, and that you honor me with your esteem. I lay claim to no other merit than that of disinterested zeal in seconding your views for the public honor and prosperity ; views which I heartily approved, and which every day demonstrates the wisdom.

" I sincerely hope that my conduct during the remainder of my mission (which, without utter ruin to my private affairs, can scarcely be very long) will not deprive me of your good opinion. I am quite sure that it will not shake your confidence in the rectitude of my intentions.

" When I return to the private situation in which you were so good as to distinguish me, it will be in my power to show as I wish the veneration in which I hold your character, and the impression which your friendly conduct towards me has made upon my heart."

Amid the exciting and agitating discussions that were going on in England, and the often clouded sky of our political horizon, it is delightful to trace the workings of private friendship, and recall the sentiments of respect with which our Minister inspired those with whom he was brought in contact. The alienation of countries, so closely allied to each other in all that can cement and bind them together, is exceedingly painful. The aggravating perseverance in an odious and oppressive policy (sanctioned by no principle of the great international law, on the part of successive administrations of public affairs in England), which ultimately terminated in a disastrous war, is a subject of reflection not less painful in the retrospect. But there are evidences of a kindliness of feeling, a generosity and magnanimity, which set forth the personal character of those most intimately connected with such grave discussions in beautiful and striking contrast, and prove that while each was true to their national claims, they knew how to admire and appreciate what was personally winning and attractive in the other. The following letters from Wilberforce, the pure-hearted and eloquent champion of humanity, and Lord Holland, the consummate statesman and refined gentleman, though in themselves but mere expressions of personal regard, will be read with interest.

FROM LORD HOLLAND TO MR. PINKNEY.

LONDON, *June 1st*, 1808.

"DEAR SIR :—From fear that you might have thought what I said to you about your boy a mere matter of form, I write again to you after I have talked it over with Lady Holland, to say that if we are to encounter the misfortune of a war with America, and upon leaving this country you should wish your son to pursue his education *here*, Lady Holland and myself beg to assure you, that without the least inconvenience to us, we can take care of him during the holidays ; and between them ascertain, that he is going on properly, and give you all the information you would require upon the progress of his studies, state of his health, &c. I only entreat you to adopt this plan, if otherwise agreeable and convenient, without scruple, as I assure you we should not offer it if we did not feel pleasure in the prospect of its being accepted.

"I see in the Morning Chronicle of yesterday the statement you gave me in a letter signed *Veritas*. Where it comes from I know not. I was preparing to send the statement to the papers, and it has saved me the trouble."

FROM WILBEREORCE TO MR. PINKNEY.

"*March* 13*th*, 1811.

" MY DEAR SIR :—It has been, for above a week past, my intention to do myself the honor of calling on you, to take my chance of obtaining a conference with you ; but having always been, and still being prevented, may I take the liberty of begging the favor of you to appoint a day, when between 11 and 1 (if you can spare me a few moments between those hours), I may have the honor of a little conversation* with you. Indeed, if you should stay in England longer than I fear you design, I would hope that you might indulge me with your company at dinner ; but I am anxious to *secure* a little intercourse with you. I cannot lay down my pen without expressing (and with no unmeaning words) my deep concern on the event of your quitting this country; fearing that it has at least a face of declining friendship between our two countries, which it is one of the fondest desires of my heart, as it is recommended by the clearest judgment of my understanding, that they should be united in the bonds of close and indissoluble attachment."

Mr. Pinkney returned to the United States in the month of June, 1811. He was not suffered to continue long in retirement ; for in the September following he was elected a member of the Senate of Maryland. This position he occupied but a few months, for in December he was appointed, by President Madison, Attorney-General of the United States. This was an office eminently congenial to his tastes and feelings. It gave a splendid scope to the peculiar powers of his mind, and opened up a field of usefulness and of fame most tempting to behold, and profitable to cultivate and till. There was something too in the manner in which it was conferred, that was exceedingly gratifying. He had just returned from England. His whole public career, while at the court of St. James, had passed under the immediate review of Mr. Madison ; and it was a noble tribute to his worth, to be selected almost immediately on his return to fill so important and dignified a position, in a relationship so near to that wise and great statesman. The manner in which his new duties were discharged is best illustrated by the might and majesty of his arguments before the Supreme Court, and the cogency and convincing power of his written legal opinions. The passage of a law, which made it necessary for the Attorney-General to reside at the seat of government, compelled him to resign the post within the short period of two years. His practice was too lucrative to admit of so great a sacrifice, and Madison was left to mourn his loss to the public councils of the nation. This necessity was just cause for regret. Mr. Pinkney's great industry, methodical mode of doing business, and high professional ambition, would have been productive of most admirable results to the public service ; while his profound acquaintance with the constitution and deep legal learning and skill in diplomacy, would have made him an invaluable aid the administration, and an astute defender of the rights of the government.

During the war he was as ready to serve the country in the field, as he had been to uphold her dignity and maintain her honor in discussion with English diplomatists. He assumed the command of a company, and in the disastrous engagement at Bladensburg (where in the judgment of impartial history our arms will be found to have deserved a better fate), he was severely wounded. The effects of that wound he carried with him to the grave.

He wielded his pen with signal success in the defence of the war, and in a pamphlet over the signature of Publius, addressed to the people of Maryland, he thus expressed himself.

EXTRACTS FROM A PAMPHLET WRITTEN BY MR. PINKNEY, UN-
DER THE SIGNATURE OF " PUBLIUS."

" But it is impossible that, in weighing the merits of a
candidate for a seat in the General Assembly, you should be
occupied by considerations which are merely local. You are
bound to give to your inquiries a wider range. You neither
can, nor ought, to shut your eyes to the urgent concerns of
the whole empire, embarked as it is in a conflict with the
determined foe of every nation upon earth sufficiently prosperous to be envied. Maryland is at all times an interesting
and conspicuous member of the Union ; but her relative position is infinitely more important now than in ordinary
seasons. The war is in her waters, and it is waged there
with a wantonness of brutality, which will not suffer the
energies of her gallant population to slumber, or the watch-
fulness of her appointed guardians to be intermitted. The
rights for which the nation is in arms are of high import to
her as a commercial section of the continent. They cannot
be surrendered or compromised without affecting every vein
and artery of her system ; and if the towering honor of universal America should be made to bow before the sword, or
should be betrayed by an inglorious peace, where will the
blow be felt with a sensibility more exquisite than here in
Maryland !

" It is perfectly true that our State government has not
the prerogative of peace and war ; but it is just as true, that
it can do much to invigorate or enfeeble the national arm for
attack or for defence ; that it may conspire with the legislatures of other States to blast the best hopes of peace, by embarrassing or resisting the efforts by which alone a durable
peace can be achieved ; as it may forward pacific negotiation
by contributing to teach the enemy that we who, when our

means were small, and our numbers few, rose as one man, and maintained ourselves victorious against the mere theories of England, with all the terrors of English power before us, are not *now* prepared to crouch to less than the same power, however insolently displayed, and to receive from it in perpetuity an infamous yoke of pernicious principles, which had already galled us until we could bear it no longer.

" That the war with England is irreproachably just, no man can doubt who exercises his understanding upon the question. It is known to the whole world, that when it was declared, the British Government had not retracted or qualified any one of those maritime claims which threatened the ruin of American commerce, and disparaged American sovereignty. Every constructive blockade, by which our ordinary communication with European or other marts had been intercepted, was either perversely maintained, or made to give place only to a wider and more comprehensive impediment. The right of impressment, in its most odious form, continued to be vindicated in argument and enforced in practice. The rule of the war of 1756, against which the voice of all America was lifted up in 1805, was still preserved, and had only become inactive because the colonies of France and her allies had fallen before the naval power of England. The Orders in Council of 1807 and 1809, which in their motive, principle, and operation, were utterly incompatible with our existence as a commercial people, which retaliated with tremendous effect upon a friend the impotent irregularities of an enemy; which established upon the seas a despotic dominion, by which power and right were confounded, and a system of monopoly and plunder raised, with a daring contempt of decency, upon the wreck of neutral prosperity, and public law ; which even attempted to exact a tribute, under the name of an impost, from the merchants of this independent land, for permission to become the slaves and instruments of that abominable system ; had been adhered to (notwithstanding the acknowledged repeal of the Berlin and Milan decrees in regard to the United States) with an alarming appearance of a fixed and permanent attachment to those very qualities which fitted them for the work of oppression, and filled us with dismay. Satisfaction, and even explanation, had been either steadily denied, or contemptuously evaded. Our complaints had been reiterated till we ourselves blushed to hear them, and till the insolence with which they were received recalled us to some sense of dignity. History does not furnish an example of such patience under such an accumulation of injuries and insults.

"The Orders in Council were indeed provisionally revoked a few days after the declaration of war; in such a manner, however, as to assert their lawfulness, and to make provision for their revival, whenever the British Government should think fit to say that they ought to be revived. The distresses of the manufacturing and other classes of British subjects had, at last, extorted from a bigoted and reluctant cabinet what had been obstinately refused to the demands of justice. But the lingering repeal, inadequate and ungracious as it was, came too late. *The Rubicon had been passed.*

"'Nothing is more to be esteemed than peace' (I quote the wisdom of Polybius), 'when it leaves us in possession of our honor and rights; but when it is joined with loss of freedom, or with infamy, nothing can be more detestable and fatal.' I speak with just confidence, when I say, that no federalist can be found who desires with more sincerity the return of peace than the republican government by which the war was declared. But it desires such a peace as the companion and instructor of Scipio has praised—a peace consistent with our rights and honor, and not the deadly tranquillity which may be purchased by disgrace, or taken in barter for the dearest and most essential claims of our trade and sovereignty. I appeal to you boldly: Are you prepared to purchase a mere cessation of arms by unqualified submis-

sion to the pretensions of England ? Are you prepared to
sanction them by treaty and entail them upon your posterity, with the inglorious and timid hope of escaping the wrath
of those whom your fathers discomfited and vanquished ?
Are you prepared, for the sake of a present profit, which the
circumstances of Europe must render paltry and precarious,
to cripple the strong wing of American commerce for years to
come, to take from our flag its national effect and character,
and to subject our vessels on the high seas, and the brave men
who navigate them, to the municipal jurisdiction of Great
Britain ? I know very well that there are some amongst us (I
hope they are few) who are prepared for all this, and more ; who
pule over every scratch occasioned by the war as if it were an
overwhelming calamity, and are only sorry that it is not
worse ; who would skulk out of a contest for the best interests
of their country to save a shilling or gain a cent ; who, having
inherited the wealth of their ancestors without their spirit,
would receive laws from London with as much facility as
woollens from Yorkshire, or hardware from Sheffield. But I
write to the great body of the people, who are sound and
virtuous, and worthy of the legacy which the heroes of the
Revolution have bequeathed them. For *them*, I undertake to
answer, that the only peace which they can be made to endure, is that which may twine itself round the honor of the
people, and with its healthy and abundant foliage give shade
and shelter to the prosperity of the empire.

" I passed rapidly in a former number over the justifying
causes of the war. But you must permit me in this place,
and for a single instant, to recur to one of them, as introductory to a consideration which you will do well to lay to your
hearts when you are assembled at the polls. The foundation upon which the claim of Great Britain reposes, to send
a pressgang on board of our ships upon the ocean, as if
they were the docks or the alehouses of Liverpool, is simply
the right of the crown, as it is recognized by her laws, to the

services of every subject in time of war. The doctrine amounts to this, that a man born within the British dominions is, in a qualified sense, the property of the government, in virtue of an artificial and slavish notion of perpetual allegiance ; that, though he may have been forced by poverty or persecution to emigrate, and has become the citizen or subject of another state, his allegiance cleaves to him for life ; that no time, or distance, or sanctuary, or new obligations can save him from its mysterious and inextinguishable power ; and that, of course, he may be seized wherever and whenever he can be found.

" But the abominable doctrine is associated with another which says, that although no state can be suffered to hold British seamen in its service by naturalization or otherwise, Great Britain may encourage the seamen of other states to enter into *her* service, and may keep them there till she wants them no longer ! And, that nothing may be wanting to the *consistency* of the British doctrine on this head, it goes on to maintain that if a foreign seaman should happen to marry and settle (as it is phrased) in an English port, he may be impressed as an English sailor, and may be retained as such against his own remonstrance, seconded by that of his country.

" In the execution of the first of those rules, which the associated rules so pointedly discountenance, our vessels were stopped on their lawful voyages, and their mariners taken away by violence upon the bare allegation, whether true or false, that they were British subjects. Many of these persons were native Americans, many of them were neutral Europeans over whom Great Britain had no lawful control, and many more were fairly entitled to be considered as American seamen, according to the law which Great Britain had (as I have already stated) laid down and enforced against us and the rest of the world. It was impossible that, with the best disposition, such a rule should be made to act only on the professed objects of it. But it was often exercised with wanton tyranny by proud and upstart surrogates in naval uniform; and the abuses grew to be enormous and intolerable. The approach of a British cruiser, in the bosom of peace, struck a terror in our seamen which it cannot *now* inspire, and almost every vessel returning from a foreign voyage, brought affliction to an American family, by reporting the impressment of a husband, a brother, or a son. The government of the United States, by whomsoever administered, has invariably protested against this monstrous practice, as cruel to the gallant men whom it oppressed, as it was injurious to the navigation, the commerce, and the sovereignty of the Union. Under the administration of Washington, of Adams, of Jefferson, of Madison, it was reprobated and resisted as a grievance which could not be borne; and Mr. King, who was instructed upon it, supposed at one time that the British Government were ready to abandon it, by a convention which he had arranged with Lord St. Vincent, but which finally miscarried. You have witnessed the generous anxiety of the late and present chief magistrates to put an end to a usage so pestilent and debasing. You have seen them propose to a succession of English ministers, as inducements to its relinquishment, expedients and equivalents of infinitely greater value to England than the usage, whilst they were innocent in themselves and respectful to us. You have seen these temperate overtures haughtily repelled, until the other noxious pretensions of Great Britain, grown in the interim to a gigantic size, ranged themselves by the side of this, and left no alternative but war or infamy. We are at war accordingly, and the single question is, whether you will fly like cowards from the sacred ground which the government has been compelled to take, or whether you will prove by your actions that you are descended from the loins of men who reared the edifice of American liberty, in the midst of such a storm as you have never felt.

" As the war was forced upon us by a long series of unexmpled aggressions, it would be absolute madness to doubt that peace will receive a cordial welcome, if she returns without ignominy in her train, and with security in her hand. The destinies of America are commercial, and her true policy is peace ; but the *substance* of peace had, long before we were roused to a tardy resistance, been denied to us by the ministry of England ; and the *shadow* which had been left to mock our hopes and to delude our imaginations, resembled too much the frowning spectre of war to deceive any body. Every sea had witnessed, and continued to witness, the systematic persecution of our trade and the unrelenting oppression of our people. The ocean had ceased to be the safe highway of the neutral world ; and our citizens traversed it with all the fears of a benighted traveller, who trembles along a road beset with banditti, or infested by the beasts of the forest. The government, thus urged and goaded, drew the sword with a visible reluctance ; and, true to the pacific policy which kept it so long in the scabbard, it will sheathe it again when Great Britain shall consult her own interest, by consenting to forbear in future the wrongs of the past.

" The disposition of the government upon that point has been decidedly pronounced by facts which need no commentary. From the moment when war was declared, peace has been sought by it with a steady and unwearied assiduity, at the same time that every practicable preparation has been made, and every nerve exerted to prosecute the war with vigor, if the enemy should persist in his injustice. The law respecting seamen, the Russian mission, the instructions sent to our Chargé d'affaires in London, the prompt and explicit disavowal of every unreasonable pretension falsely ascribed to us, and the solemn declaration of the government in the face of the world, that it wishes for nothing more than a fair and honorable accommodation, would be conclusive proofs of this, if any proofs were necessary. But it does not require to be proved, because it is self-evident. What interest, in the name of common sense, can the government have (distinctly from that of the whole nation) in a war with Great Britain ? It is obvious to the meanest capacity that such a war must be accompanied by privations, of which no government would hazard the consequences, but upon the suggestions of an heroic patriotism. The President and his supporters have never been ignorant that those who suffer by a war, however unavoidable, are apt rather to murmur against the government than against the enemy, and that while it presses upon us we sometimes forget the compulsion under which it was commenced, and regret that it was not avoided with a provident foresight of its evils.

" It will, therefore, be no easy matter to persuade you that this war was *courted* by an administration who depend upon the people for their power, and are proud of that dependence ; or that it will be carried on with a childish obstinacy when it can be terminated with honor and with safety. You have, on the contrary, a thousand pledges that the government was averse to war, and will give you peace the instant peace is in its power. You know, moreover, that the enemy will not grant it as a boon, and that it must be wrung from his necessities. It comes to this, then : whom will you select as your champions to extort it from him? upon whom will you cast the charge of achieving it against him in the lists ? "

In 1815 he was elected a Representative in Congress from the city of Baltimore.

In 1816 he was appointed by President Monroe, Minister Plenipotentiary to the court of Russia and special minister to that of Naples. This was another gratifying tribute of respect and confidence from one who best knew his qualifications as a statesman. Of his conduct in those missions I shall have occasion to speak hereafter. I have it in my power to lay before the public a letter written to Robert

Goodloe Harper. It is a gem of its kind, a living, breathing picture, full of beauty and exquisite taste. It exhibits a power of graphic composition not easily paralleled. I am sure it will be read with interest. His sketch of the reigning empress is inimitable ; and his fine appreciation of all that is truly beautiful and fascinating in the charm of woman shines out in each and every paragraph—and what is most remarkable, the hues of the portraiture are so shaded and blended, that while they seem to catch their coloring from the skies, they are not unreal. It goes as near extravagance as it could, to be just and faithful ; and never oversteps the bounds of probability and of fact, as the pen of history has since testified. There is nothing that I remember so beautiful in the English language, except it be Wordsworth's touching and exquisite picture of his wife. Mr. Pinkney was held in peculiar estimation by the reigning Emperor Alexander, who opened a new page in the history of Russia, and redeemed his court from the intrigues and excesses that had well-nigh disgraced it in the eye of the world, during some of the preceding reigns.

MR. PINKNEY TO ROB. GOODLOE HARPER.

"St. Petersburg, *August 10th*, 1817.

" Dear Sir :—Major General the Baron de Tevyll, who is about to proceed to the United States as the successor of Mr. Daschkoft, wishes me to make him acquainted with some of my friends in Baltimore ; and you will, I hope, take it in good part that I introduce to you the worthy minister of such a monarch as Alexander.

" The Baron has seen a good deal of service as a soldier, and has won an honorable reputation. By birth a Dutchman, he was originally in some corps in the pay of England, and thence passed into the staff and line of Russia. He has, however, been more employed as a *diplomatist*, and has recently returned from a mission to Rome in which he conducted himself satisfactorily and ably. In this department he is said to be very skilful. But what I think of yet greater consequence is, that he is an excellent man and an accomplished gentleman. I speak in part from my own observation (for I have seen him often here), and partly from what I learn from others who have long known him. He carries with him a great regard for our country, in unison with the sentiments of the Emperor; and this feeling, combined with his characteristic good sense and discretion, will, I am sure, make him an acceptable minister, not only to our government but to our people.

"As I know the interest which you take in whatever concerns this government, you will not, I think, be displeased if, now that I have begun to write, I give you a very brief sketch (not of its policy—for with that you are well acquainted—but) of the great personages who are at the head of it, I mean the principal members of the Imperial family, of whom little is known in America.

"*The Emperor* is a remarkably handsome man, and of an admirable address. Every body justly ascribes to him the merit of *good intentions*, and, with equal justice, the additional merit of knowing how to use the best means for the fulfilment of those intentions. He is one of the few men in the world who, having been seen at a distance in great enterprises and achievements, gain by being approached and closely examined. I am mistaken in him if he is not a man of great abilities. He appears to me to have a clear, vigorous and cultivated mind—to be steady and sagacious in the pursuit of his purposes—to be well read in men as well as books—to be prompt and dexterous in the management of affairs—to have the wholesome habit of thinking for himself—to be of a generous, though perhaps somewhat hasty temper—and, in a word, to be signally fitted for his high vocation.

"*The Empress Mother* is still a most charming woman,

and when young must have been extremely handsome ; she may be said to do the honors of this splendid court, and it is right that she should. Her manners are infinitely pleasing at the same time that they are lofty ; and she is a perfect mistress of the arts of conversation. She is, moreover, exemplary in all the relations of life, and is beloved for her goodness by all classes.

"Of *the reigning Empress* it is impossible to speak in adequate terms of praise. It is necessary to see her, to be able to comprehend how wonderfully interesting she is. It is no exaggeration to say that, with a slight abatement for the effects of time and severe affliction (produced by the loss of her children), she combines every charm that contributes to female loveliness, with all the qualities that peculiarly become her exalted station. Her figure, although thin, is exquisitely fine. Her countenance is a subduing picture of feeling and intelligence. Her voice is of that soft and happy tone that goes directly to the heart and awakens every sentiment which a virtuous woman can be ambitious to excite. Her manner cannot be described or imagined. It is so graceful, so unaffectedly gentle, so winning and yet so dignified, that (I had almost said) an angel might copy it and improve his own. Her conversation is suited to this noble exterior. Adapted with a nice discrimination to those to whom it is addressed, unostentatious and easy, sensible and kind, it captivates invariably the wise and good, and (what is yet more difficult) satisfies the frivolous without the slightest approaches to frivolity. If universal report is to be credited, there is no virtue for which this incomparable woman is not distinguished ; and I have reason to be confident, from all that I have observed and heard, that her understanding (naturally of the highest order) has been embellished and improved to an uncommon degree by judicious and regular and various study. It is not surprising, therefore, that she is alike adored by the inhabitant of the palace and the cottage, and that every Russian looks up to her as to a superior being. She is indeed a superior being; and would be adored although she were not surrounded by Imperial pomp and power. It is time, however, to have done with these sketches, and to return to the subject of this letter, into which I did not intend, when I sat down to write, to introduce any other subject.

"The Baron sets out from St. Petersburgh in a few days; but probably will not arrive in the United States until next winter, as he goes by the route of Vienna, Munich, Holland, and England."

Mr. Pinkney returned to the United States in 1818 at his own request, and it is remarkable, that while he never solicited directly or indirectly a foreign appointment, he was never recalled but upon his own expressed wish long resisted and reluctantly entertained.

He lost no time in indolent inactivity, but immediately resumed the practice of the law ; and soon proved that he had lost nothing during his absence from the forum. Maryland was too proud of his fame to allow him to continue in private practice at the bar. She had honored him with almost every post of distinction in her gift, and she now gave him the finishing proof of her attachment and confidence by electing him to the Senate of the United States. On the 4th January, 1820, he took his seat. The country was in the deepest state of anxiety. A question of momentous interest was then under deliberation. The first men of the land were participators in the discussion. On the 15th February he delivered his immortal speech on the Missouri Compromise. A member of the committee of conference on the part of the Senate, he proposed the report which was subsequently adopted by that committee. Little more than one month a member of that body, he delivered a speech that electrified the country, was placed upon the committee that settled the difficulty and proposed the report that was made. Such pre-eminence in so short a time is not often paralleled in the history of legislation.

During the brief period of his Senatorial career he was incessantly occupied in the conflicts of the forum ; discussing questions of the greatest magnitude with competitors from all quarters of the country, who were rarely if ever equalled, and never excelled in any other period of the history of the American Bar. He was preparing a great speech on the constitution at the time he died ; and from the zest with which he entered on its preparation and the interest he felt, it may be affirmed, that, had he lived, he would have doubled his claim to the lasting gratitude of his countrymen and recalled the early days of the Republic when constitutional discussions were rich in wisdom and pre-eminently patriotic in purpose. But it pleased Divine Providence to forbid that the topmost stone should be placed by his own hands upon the vast pyramid of his fame. Death palsied the tongue, ere its trumpet tones were heard in that discussion ; and none were privileged to share in the noble thoughts that were flitting through his brain and panting for utterance.

I now draw near the close of his life. It will be seen that from the early age of 24 to the day of his death, he was constantly occupied in the public service at home or abroad, a service he neither sought nor shunned ; that he contrived all the while to pursue with unabated zeal his professional studies, and retained a practice at the bar without a parallel in the history of the past or the present. The few last years of his life were marked with exertions well-nigh incredible, and rewarded with an income that it would be deemed exaggeration to name. His intellectual labors exceeded his physical strength. In the very pride of his power, in the fifty-eighth year of his age, with a robust constitution, upon which time seemed scarcely to have left its impress, " his eye not dimmed nor his natural force abated," he fell before the stroke of the destroyer. He had exerted himself in the discussion of a great cause before the court only a few days before. On the night of the 17th February, 1822, he sat up very late, amusing himself with the perusal of the Pirates; and poured forth into the ear of private friendship his beautiful strictures upon the characters introduced. His mind was powerfully excited. I remember to have heard a gentleman, who sat with him for a short time during that eventful evening, say that he playfully exhibited the most astonishing feat of a powerful and retentive memory he had ever witnessed. That night he was struck down by disease. He lingered on until the night of the 25th, in severe bodily suffering, wandering at times and then again in the full possession of his powers, when he breathed his last. His physician, Dr. Theophilus Parsons, thought him at first quite out of danger, and so wrote to his afflicted lady. But he was mistaken in his opinion, as the event sadly proved. His illness, so sudden and unexpected, produced a profound sensation in the country. His fellow-citizens, who had so recently witnessed his wondrous eloquence and still more wonderful legal logic, and were high in expectancy, as he was just beginning his preparation for his argument with Tazewell of Virginia, were illy prepared to follow in the funeral train that bore him to his resting-place, near the banks of the beautiful Potomac. He disappeared with startling suddenness from the sphere of glory he had so long filled; and grave Senators and learned judges paid a befitting tribute to his memory.

There was no gradual breaking down of his giant intellect, no progressive, slowly developed decay in his splendid faculties. He fell in his might before the tribunal he delighted to address and on the arena he most loved to tread. He fell where the patriot and the hero would ever desire to fall, with his eyes on the floating stars and his armor on. Conscious that he would not survive the shock, he prepared to meet the summons and gently fell asleep. There was a grandeur in the close of his brilliant career. He could never brook the idea of rusting out. He preferred the higher destiny of the candle that consumes itself in burning. He toiled to the last and spurned the idea of intermitted exertion. His body now rests in the same grave-yard where lie so many of his illustrious compeers. A simple stone monument indicates the spot. Resting my hand upon it, with my eye on the few letters inscribed thereon, I then and there realized the emptiness of earth, and asked myself the question, what is life with all of earthly renown it has to give, but a vapor that soon passeth away? There is a sweet and touching simplicity in this the chosen sepulchre of our distinguished countrymen. There is a calm, quiet beauty about it, that speaks directly to the heart. The green grass has grown up around it, and the birds sing in the leafy boughs that overshade it.

Crowds throng the capitol and gaze with delight upon the lofty dome and ornamented grounds. They hang with pride and pleasure on the tongue of eloquence which still finds within its walls an echo. But its burial-ground is to me a still more attractive object. I love to go and stand amid the monuments of our past greatness; and in the sad and pensive solitudes that are scarce broken by a sound, I love to muse and meditate on the memories of men long since dead, as fresh and fragrant as the day they died. *There* is the school of patriotism—*there*, the nursery of thoughts, great and pure and noble.

I come now to discuss the intellectual and moral character of Mr. Pinkney; and I am free to confess that I have chosen a task most difficult to execute. I am impelled to the undertaking by natural affection, and the conviction that the exhibition of such a character, in all the hues of its blended beauty and strength, would be an acceptable offering to the young men of the profession, and serve to stim-

ulate and cheer them on in their earnest endeavor to emulate
and if possible excel him of whom I write.

Mr. Pinkney's character (those peculiar and striking
moral and intellectual elements, which were its very warp
and woof) has been pronounced, by Story, a study worthy of
the young men of the land; one of the grandest themes the
tongue of eloquence can touch or the mind of genius analyze. And while I feel, and, feeling, deplore my inability to
do any thing like justice to the theme, I hope that the end
will more than justify the effort. The portrait, which I
shall endeavor to draw, is for the most part intellectual, a
daguerreotype of the soul. His life, as has been already
proved, was not without incident. A large portion of it was
spent in the most stirring events of the most eventful period
of modern history. But alas! many of those incidents, which
constitute so important a portion of the attractiveness and
usefulness of biography, have been unhappily lost in the ever
shifting tide of time, or else only survive in a dim oral tradition. His habits and mode of private life are to be seen,
when seen at all, in mere floating report, good as far as it
goes, but necessarily defective in minute and copious detail.
For many of the incidents which ordinarily make up history
and biography I possess no very high regard, because they
do not serve to illustrate the subject. There are a thousand
facts, the recital of which may amuse the superficial and
unreflecting; but which, as they do not set forth in stronger
light the philosophy and moral of the subject, overload the
memory and are nothing worth. There are other incidents,
however, of the very last importance. Every thing, for example, connected with the personal history of a man on
whom the eyes of an admiring world are fixed, is of interest.
All are eager to know his inner life—how he inured his soul
to the stern discipline of study, and sacrificed ease and
pleasure to patient, secluded labor—what were his habits of
reflection and the pastimes to which he resorted for amuse-

ment—who were the favorite authors that cheered his hours of solitude, and what the peculiar tastes that adorned his private walk among men. There is a sort of mystery in the inner life of the great, which all are eager to explore. The biographer, who can, out of his abundant materials, gratify this natural and yearning desire, possesses a powerful hold upon the sympathies of his readers and exercises a most potent influence for good. It is to be regretted, that so many of the touching and beautiful incidents, which characterized the life and illustrated the individuality of William Pinkney, are lost beyond the hope of recovery. It is to be deeply regretted, that his observations on men and things, made in the exciting scenes of his foreign service, were not registered to be preserved and handed down to the ages following; for he was a close and discriminating observer of both men and things. Often was his intercourse with his more confidential and intimate friends seasoned with minute and graphic criticisms of what passed under his notice. Some of the most brilliant specimens of his rare eloquence and profound thought were poured forth in those unreserved critiques. He wrote much, and published a good deal while in England, which is now lost. A number of documents were left in charge of my father, containing powerful discussions on a vast variety of the leading topics of the day, which were returned to him; all of which have perished.

It has been often the topic of remark and a matter of surprise, that a mind so active and prolific, exercised in constant contact with so much to thrill and excite it, should have left so little written behind. But the wonder is solved by the fact, that there was no effort made to preserve and hand it down. Could the observations that fell from his lips in torrents of the richest eloquence extending to an almost infinite variety of topics be now recalled, they would supply a sad chasm in his eventful life and constitute one of the most attractive pages of biography. For it is in the unreserved communion of heart with heart, that the character shines out and the man is most fully developed. But alas ! there was no Boswell equally competent and eager to retain those splendid passages of a life that nowhere shone so resplendently as in the endearments of a friendship he fully trusted. It was this constant contact and faithful transcript, which enabled the writer of the life of Johnson to give to the world the most beautiful and accurate idea of what a biography should be, and which lent the most bewitching attraction to its pages.

I possess no such advantages. The time was when like diligence would have been rewarded by like results. But that time has passed. And in the dearth of this pleasing and instructive material, I must do the best I can, and let the moral and intellectual devlopment make up as best it may for the sad deficiency.

It is as an orator, lawyer, statesman and man, that I propose to consider him. In the analysis, while I am free to confess I write under the influence of long cherished and ardent admiration, and lay no claim to exemption from the ordinary infirmities of our nature, I hope I shall not be found to sacrifice the great principles of truth and justice to my inordinate attachment to the memory of the dead.

WILLIAM PINKNEY AN ORATOR.

WILLIAM PINKNEY was an orator. But what is oratory, and who is worthy of this august title ? This is a most interesting inquiry, interesting in itself and more so still in the light it casts upon the illustrious subject of this memoir. If we take Cicero's definition, who most admirably illustrated the thing he defined, " composite, ornate, copiose eloqui "—or the still more comprehensive " quam ob rem, si quis universam et propriam oratoris vim definire complectique vult, is orator erit, mea sententia, hoc tam gravi dignus nomine, qui, quæcumque res inciderit, quæ sit dictione, explicanda, prudenter, et composite, et ornate et memoriter dicat, cum quadam etiam actionis dignitate." I repeat, if we take Cicero's definition, there are few among the living or the dead, who can be found equally entitled to the term. Not to dwell upon his physical advantages, his fine commanding person, his voice of singular sweetness, variety, compass and flexibility of tone, and his impressive and emphatic action ; he possessed a most vigorous and brilliant imagination, and a depth of keen, discriminating analysis in union with the most lively and acute sensibilities. His command of language was marvellous in the extreme. For beauty, force and splendor of diction, he was unrivalled. It flowed forth in a continuous stream of surprising accuracy and richness ; no word misapplied, no word misapprehended. True it is, he had some few natural defects of manner and some few artificial. But still with all, and despite of all, he was an orator of the very first class and among the very foremost of that class. If by oratory we mean the power to mould and

melt the heart at pleasure, captivate and thrill the understanding and sway the judgment—if by oratory we mean
not only the magic tone, and emphatic look, and commanding
gesture, but the capacity to express in words best suited to
the theme the vivid and grand conceptions of the brain, and
the imagination to combine and weave them together, and
then the power to breathe into them life and energy—if all
this be meant by oratory, then William Pinkney was an
orator.

There are different kinds of oratory as there are different
degrees in its perfection.   There is the soft and persuasive,
which falls on the heart like dew and lingers on the enchanted
ear like dulcet notes of music ; and there is the impetuous
and overpowering, which bears down all before it, like the
onward rush of the foaming cataract. Mr. Pinkney's oratory
was impetuous and overpowering.   He could touch the tender chords with the hand of a master, and call forth, when
he willed, the softest tones to melt and subdue the listener ;
but most commonly he spoke to command and bear down,
and such was the might and majesty of his eloquence that it
took captive every hearer at its will.   It was masterful and
victorious.   The elements of power were blended in it so exquisitely, that you could scarce discover where the one began
or the other ended.   Matter and manner alike conspired to
make him an orator.   He was as deep as he was brilliant.
His rhetoric was thus convincing and his oratory thus masterful, because they were the lustre and the solidity of the
diamond combined.   Full of the most magnificent illustrations, the birth of an imagination naturally strong, and
cultivated with the most studious care and exquisite taste,
and enriched with the latest stores of an ever accumulating
learning ; he threw all over the dry discussions of the law
a bewitching fascination, and set forth its august principles
with a fulness and a power seldom evoked.

The testimony which is borne to the marvellous impressiveness of Mr. Pinkney's speaking upon any subject on any forum, at the bar or in the Senate chamber, or before the populace, cannot be mistaken. It comes up from too many sources to falsify itself. Report speaks of verdicts forced from juries by his eloquent tongue ; and learned judges, who were compelled to bring around them, and summon to their aid, all the sterner attributes of their office in their endeavor to dissipate the spell of the charmer ; not once, but again and again. The writer of this memoir has often heard the late John Stephen (one of the judges of the old court of Appeals, one of the purest and most upright of judges, an ornament of the bench where he dispensed law and justice, not more respected for his ripe learning than his rare modesty, nice sense of judicial propriety and love of genuine forensic eloquence) say, that he had heard Mr. Pinkney indulge in such strains of lofty eloquence in so many pleadings before the court, that he wholly despaired of ever hearing any thing like it again ; and that too, when returning from the capitol of the country and the presence of the American Senate chamber in the day of its proudest fame. Judge Story, another of the bright lights of American jurisprudence (I might say one of the brightest), tells us in his exquisite sketch, that "no one could listen to him for many minutes without forgetting all the defects of art or taste in the overpowering sensations of delight !" And in Story's life just issued from the press, there are many additional proofs of the power wielded by Pinkney over that consummate judge. In letter after letter, Story pours forth expressions of wonder and astonishment at the surpassing splendor of his mind, and the depth of his ratiocination, and copiousness and compass of his legal learning. Amid the living forms of Dexter and Emmet, orators of whom any land might be proud, Pinkney stood forth the confessed favorite of Story. That I may not be supposed to overestimate his opinion of Mr. Pinkney, I will insert one or two extracts from letters recently published.

" Every time I hear Pinkney he rises higher and higher in my estimation. His clear and forcible manner of putting his case before the court, his powerful and commanding eloquence, occasionally illuminated with sparkling lights, but always logical and appropriate, and above all, his accurate and discriminating law knowledge, which he pours out with wonderful precision—give him in my opinion a great superiority over every man whom I have known. I have seen in a single man each of those qualities separate, but never before combined in so extraordinary a degree." Again: "His genius and eloquence were so lofty, I might almost say, so unrivalled, his learning so extensive, his ambition so elevated, his political and constitutional principles so truly just and pure, his weight in the public councils so decisive, his character at the bar so peerless and commanding, that there seems now left a dismal and perplexing vacancy. I write to you while sitting in court, and as the argument is now taking an interesting turn, I must now stop and listen ; but never do I expect to hear a man like Pinkney. He was a man who appears scarcely once a century." Speaking of Dexter he adds: "I always considered him second only to our inimitable friend Pinkney. In the phrase of a painter, I would say Pinkney's character and mind would be a great study."—*Story's Life.* Vol. I.

And who was Story ? Himself one of the first men the country has produced, in whom the very soul of eloquence glowed ; a stern judge called upon to weigh arguments and resist eloquence, save where they were the faithful echoes of law and justice, with no spirit of rivalry to bias his judgment, and all his enthusiastic love of the North to excite his sectional pride—is spell-bound, thrilled, transported by the wonderful powers of Pinkney's oratory. A mixed audience might have been deceived, and juries hurried on beyond discretion, by the melodious tone, the look, or gesture ; but Story could only have been so moved and excited by the true genius of oratory. I know nothing which affords a more demonstrative evidence of the power of an orator, than the ability to move and sway so consummate a judge, himself pre-eminently skilled in all the mysteries of the moving art. Marshall, a more severe judge of oratory, because not himself of the imaginative cast, paid a no less marked and splendid tribute in the memorable opinion in the Nereide.

"With a pencil dipped in the most vivid colors, and guided by the hand of a master, a splendid portrait has been drawn, exhibiting this vessel and her freighter as forming a single figure, composed of the most discordant materials of peace and war. So exquisite was the skill of the artist, so dazzling the garb in which the figure was painted, that it required the exercise of that cold investigating faculty which ought always to belong to those who sit on this bench, to discover its only imperfection—its want of resemblance."
—*Marshall's Opinion in the Nereide.*

I dwell upon these frank and ingenuous attestations, because it has been sometimes denied that Mr. Pinkney was an orator.

The distinguished biographer of Mr. Wirt, whose transcendent talents I am neither slow to acknowledge nor reluctant to praise, has done injustice—I will do him the justice to believe, unintentional—to the memory of Mr. Pinkney. That accomplished scholar says (page 400, Vol. I.) that "impartial and judicious estimate of Mr. Pinkney's powers and acquirements seems rarely to have been accorded to him" —and then again he speaks "of exaggerated praise." Now the learned and Hon. Ex-Secretary of the Navy will, I think, find it difficult to sustain his judgment, when he remembers, that a Story professes himself the delighted captive of an eloquence as rare as it was brilliant, "embellished, when the occasion called for it, with all the gorgeous amplitude and magnificence of a Bolingbroke and Burke;" and listens to the warnings of a Marshall, declaring that it required all the

sterner quailities of the judge to resist the power of the advocate. If this be exaggerated praise—if impartial and judicious estimate of power and acquirement be not here accorded, we must adopt the opinion that Marshall and Story
were not competent to judge, or else given to sycophantic
and servile praise. The trophies of Mr. Pinkney's powers
are too numerous and exalted to admit of depreciation with
impunity, now that the winding-sheet and shroud are the
only covering of the mighty dead ; and surely on no soil less
appropriate, and by no pen less befitting, could the wrong be
perpetrated, which would dim in the least the fame of Pinkney, than on the soil of his birth, and by the pen of one,
whom his fellow-citizens have delighted to honor as another
of her distinguished sons.

The title of Mr. Pinkney to the character of an orator depends not then on the breath of mere popular applause. It
is based on a rock impervious to the assaults of envy—the
possession of the highest intellectual endowments and the
achievement of the rarest intellectual victories, not obtained
over ignorance and folly, but over the noblest and most commanding intellect ; not once, but again and again, amid competitors with whom it would be a signal honor to dispute the
palm for ascendency.

That Mr. Pinkney was the butt of much illiberal and
envious depreciation, I am ready to admit. But the names
of his depreciators will perish, while his own endures. Who
need be reminded that a member of Congress held up his
speech on the Missouri compromise to public scorn and ridi-
cule ; and is ignorant that the anonymous calumny has outlived every other deed of the author. Defamation is easy.
Fault-finding is the work of little minds. If the fact that
Mr. Pinkney was "hawked at by such mousing owls, birds
of the night," who could not endure the bright shining of
the sun, be proof that judicious and impartial estimate has
been rarely accorded to him ;—why then, indeed, the biogra-

pher of Mr. Wirt has proved his point. But if the facts above enumerated—the power wielded by Mr. Pinkney over such minds as Story's and Marshall's ; his holding, time and again, large promiscuous audiences spell-bound through the long discussions of dry questions of law—be not proof of oratorical power and profound acquirement, why, then, there can be no proof adduced which is conclusive of the point.

There will be always envious detractions, jealous out-breakings. Some minds are proof against proof. I do not mean to intimate that so distinguished a scholar as Mr. Kennedy, can be classified with such. I only regret that he should have permitted himself to lend even a seeming sanction to their crude criticisms, and recorded, as his deliberate judgment, the opinion "that judicious and impartial estimate of Mr. Pinkney's power and acquirements was rarely accorded to him." I regret it, because the severity of his censure must fall upon the best judges of forensic ability in the land, and place him among the critics of one, whom, to use the language of Johnson, if we are correct in our facts, "it is vain to blame and useless to praise."

Had I undertaken to indulge in a mere indiscriminate praise and immoderate eulogy, Mr. Kennedy would be safe from impeachment ; for his competency to judge would be deemed greater than my own. But facts are stubborn things, and no man can overturn them. It is to facts I appeal. The *claim* to oratory is one thing ; the *achievements* of oratory are another. The claim I predicate on the achievements, and I feel a strong confidence, that the judgment of Mr. Kennedy cannot stand so long as those achievements exist. My appeal is from Mr. Kennedy to the Storys and Marshalls of the land.

John Randolph knew and felt the power of Mr. Pinkney ; and on the floor of Congress, after full opportunities of judging, he pronounced the following eulogy :

" We have been talking of General Jackson, and a greater

man than he is not here, but gone for ever ! I allude, sir, to
the boast of Maryland and the pride of the United States,—
the pride of us all, and particularly the pride and ornament
of that profession of which you, Mr. Speaker (Stephenson),
are a member, and an eminent one. He was a man with
whom I lived when a member of this house, and a new one
too ; and ever since he left it for the other—I speak it with
pride—in habits not merely negatively friendly, but of kindness and cordiality. The last time I saw him was on Saturday, the last Saturday but one, in the pride of life, and
full possession and vigor of all his faculties, in that lobby.
He is now gone to his account (for as the tree falls so must
it lie) where we must all go—where I must soon go, and by
the same road too—the course of nature ; and where all of
us, put off the evil day as we may, must also go. For what
is the past but a span ; and which of us can look forward
to as many years as we have lived ? The last act of intercourse between us was an act, the recollection of which I
would not be without for all the offices that all the men of
the United States have filled, or ever shall fill. He had, indeed, his faults, his foibles; I should rather say his sins.
Who is without them ? Let such, such only, cast the first
stone. And these foibles, if you will, which every body
could see, because every body is clear-sighted with regard to
the faults and foibles of others, he, I have no doubt, would
have been the first to acknowledge on a proper representation
of them. Every thing now is hidden from us,—not, God
forbid, that utter darkness rests upon the grave, which, hid-
eous as it is, is lighted, cheered, and warmed with light from
heaven ; not the impious fire fabled to be stolen from heaven
by the heathen, but by the Spirit of the living God, whom
we profess to worship, and whom I hope we shall spend the
remainder of the day in worshipping ; not with mouth honor,
but in our hearts, in spirit and in truth ; that it may not be
said of us also, ' this people draweth nigh to me with their

lips, but their heart is far from me.' Yes, it is just so; he is gone. I will not say that our loss is irreparable, because such a man as has existed, may exist again. There has been a Homer, there has been a Shakspeare, there has been a Milton, there has been a Newton. There may be another Pinkney, but there is none now. And it was to announce this event that I have risen. I am almost inclined to believe in presentiments. I have been, all along, as well assured of the fatal termination of that disease with which he was afflicted, as I am now; and I have dragged my weary limbs before sunrise to the door of his sick chamber (for I would not intrude on the sacred grief of the family), almost every morning since. From the first, I had almost no hope."

"In those early and pious visitations to the sick chamber of virtue and genius (says Mr. Garland, the accomplished biographer of Randolph), he was frequently accompanied by the Chief Justice. What a beautiful and touching tribute to the memory of Pinkney, that the greatest orator and statesman, and the greatest jurist of his age, should watch with so much interest and tenderness the last expiring breath of him, who in life had rivalled the one in eloquence and the other in profound learning."--*Randolph's Life*, vol. ii. 169, 170.

No man was more sparing of his praise,—and yet he bowed in willing homage before the oratory of Pinkney, because it was genuine and pure; thought and feeling combined, dressed in the most exquisite garb; words of beauty and images of fire.

I make on this head no comparisons. I desire to make none. In a country that has given birth to a Patrick Henry, an Ames, a Dexter, a Wirt, a Clay, a Calhoun, and a Webster, orators who may well vie with those of Greece, and Rome; it is not my purpose to institute invidious comparisons. But still among them, in the foremost rank, stood William Pinkney; and that as I have shown, not in my too partial estimate, but upon the authority of those who were farthest removed from the bias of prejudice, and otherwise most competent to decide.

A contributor to the North American, vol. xxiv. page 68, thus writes :

" To the time of his last appearance in public in Washington, the court room was always thronged with the wise, the learned and the fashionable, when it was known that he was to speak ; and he uniformly riveted the attention of his auditors through the technical detail of his longest and dryest arguments." And the same might be said, with equal truth, of his repeated efforts in other tribunals in other portions of the Union. This one fact is worth a thousand assertions, in proof of his power as an orator.

The discussions of the Senate chamber are of deep and absorbing interest to the crowds that are accustomed to attend upon them. The orator has in his subject a strong and powerful chord of sympathy between himself and his audience. Not so, except in a few particular cases, in the discussions before the court. And yet Mr. Pinkney kept his fascinating spell upon the large and promiscuous crowd, at the same time he poured into the ear of judicial wisdom the wonderful stream of his concise and profound legal logic. The wise and the learned would sit for hours delighted and thrilled, while such masters of the law, as the judges of the supreme court, were time and again greeted with a chain of legal argument as massive and solid in its structure, as though each link was of diamond solidity and the whole a cable of impregnable strength.

I give to the malicious and envious the full weight of the defects they are able to discover,—I listen unmoved to their fastidious criticisms, so long as this one fact (excelled in none of the features of mental and moral grandeur by the present or the past) remains undisputed and indisputable. The eloquence of Pericles is known chiefly by its effects, and it has been said of him by one competent to judge, " that he was strong in the weakness of his audience." Not so, the subject of this memoir. Mr. Gilmer of Virginia furnishes me, in his masterly sketches, with a happy conclusion to this portion of my portraiture ! " The powers of Mr. Pinkney's mind seemed to strengthen with his years and expand with his subject. Of all the exhibitions of his eloquence, his reply to Mr. King in the Senate on the Missouri restriction " (of which I shall have occasion to speak hereafter), "was, perhaps, that in which the force of his genius was the most conspicuous and overwhelming, and enough of itself to entitle him to the *first place among living orators.* He not only sustained his reputation, but surpassed the most exaggerated ideas which had been entertained of his abilities. Seldom in either hemisphere has the English language been the medium of sublimer eloquence. He shed lustre upon letters, renown upon Congress, glory on the country! The United States owe lasting obligations to Mr. Pinkney for having scattered the forces of political crusaders before they began their devastations."—*Gilmer's Sketches*, p. 53.

Eloquentiâ aut æquavit præstantissimorum gloriam aut excessit. Quis sententiis aut acutior aut crebrior ? Quis verbis aut ornatior aut elegantior ? Audax orator, cumulatus omni laude.

PINKNEY A LAWYER.

MR. PINKNEY was more than an orator. He was a consummate lawyer. The bar was his own chosen and favorite arena. If he left it for a season, it was only to serve his country and recruit his exhausted strength, after labors that would have crushed a less vigorous constitution; and to return to it with increased ardor and intensity, and with additional stores of vast and varied learning. He studied law, as before stated, intently amid the blandishments and glitter of foreign courts, and never for a moment lost sight of this, the calling in life most suited to his tastes and congenial to his habits. Not more remarkable for depth and accuracy than extent and variety of legal learning, he stood by universal suffrage in the very foremost rank of advocates. Every inch of his fame in this department was won by giant struggles and herculean labors. He relied not on the singular quickness of his perceptions. He depended not on force of genius. Not satisfied with having mastered all the great principles of the legal science, he sought in each case he argued, to enlarge his own professional attainments. His hard-earned fame he kept constantly before him; and each succeeding effort was but a struggle to surpass himself.

It was his great ambition to toil night and day in the investigation and elucidation of the merits of a cause, so that he might hope to enlighten each tribunal he addressed. By turning to the law reports of the day, meagre and insufficient as most of them are, we shall find not a few acknowledgments from sources whose names are praise, that he did not labor in vain. Those records teem with the matured fruits of his large experience and profound learning. The philosophy of the Law was his study and delight ; and ever animated by the most exalted sense of the dignity and grandeur of his profession, he always addressed himself to the higher feelings and principles of our nature.

Mr. Pinkney possessed two very rare qualities, rare at least in their combination, viz., the power of concentration, and the power of amplification. And each he possessed in marvellous perfection. He could go down to the very kernel, and contract the lines of his argument, until at the very heart of his subject you could see it through and through ; or he could sow his arguments broadcast, and expand and amplify them, until you were completely overpowered by the surpassing luxuriance of thought and fertility of intellectual resources.

He particularly excelled in the statement of a cause. Judge Story says of him, that his very statement was an argument. And I know not that a more striking proof could be afforded of the power of condensation. There was one thing that marked the character of Mr. Pinkney's mind, as I have already intimated, and strikingly distinguished it from that of most other men, ancient and modern. I allude to the union of depth and brilliancy. He was the most argumentative of speakers ; and when he chose, he could be dazzlingly gorgeous. Judge Marshall bore honorable witness to his argumentative powers, of which he possessed a rare opportunity of judging, when he pronounced him, as Story tells us, the closest reasoner he had ever heard. Of the scope and vigor of his imagination it would be idle to speak.

The opinion has been entertained, and not unfrequently advanced, that brilliancy and depth are, as it were, antagonistic to each other ; *dissociabiles res,* which are incapable of combination in a single mind. Profundity has been associated with dryness. Tropes and figures of rhetoric, similes and metaphors, have been deemed beneath the use of a logical reasoner. That they are, in point of fact, oftentimes *dissociabiles res,* no one will or can dispute, who has witnessed the mental developments of the age, and seen how one will excel in splendid declamation who is totally disqualified to unravel the intricate thread of an argument, and pursue a close logical discussion; and another exhibit great powers of reasoning, who is incapable of soaring, on strong wing, among things grand and beautiful. But that there is any antagonism between the two I totally deny. The imagination is not opposed to the reasoning faculty, or inconsistent with it. On the contrary it is, when possessed in perfection, one of its most valuable and powerful auxiliaries. It groups and combines, and then all over the dry field of argumentation it diffuses the energy of an ever active life. Johnson maintained "that metaphorical expression is of great excellence in style, where it is used with propriety, because it gives us two ideas for one, and conveys the meaning more luxuriously, and generally with a perception of delight." It is a gross and unwarrantable disparagement of the imagination, to consider its chief office to be embellishment. The imagination is eminently practical. It sees things in their strongest light and sets them forth with uncommon vigor. When combined with a faculty mighty to reason, it is eminently argumentative. By making the discussion more grand, and imparting something of its own magnificence to the mere deductions of reason, it does not diminish the strength or abate the vigor. It throws light and heat all around it. It illustrates, enforces, deepens the impression. It is the soul of argument, and in its sublimest and mightiest soarings, it is vehement argumentation. Of course, I am speaking of imagination when in combination with logical precision and mental force —imagination in its highest form and noblest development; the imagination of a well-balanced and thoroughly disciplined mind. Where the reasoning faculty is weak, the imagination cannot supply the deficiency. It may dazzle and corruscate, but it cannot enlighten. It may inflame and excite the feelings, but it will not assist or inform the judgment.

But where the reasoning power exists and exerts itself, the imagination, seizing hold of the deductions of reason, and following it *pari passu* in its most elaborate processes; or else anticipating it in its somewhat prophetic spirit, gives them life, and clothes them with increased might and power. I am not combating a shadow—endeavoring to refute a mere figment of my own fancy. For what is more common than the expression, that a speech or argument is beautiful and splendid, but that it wants depth and force—or that a speech is solid and convincing, but dry and argumentative. The expression has its foundation in the popular misapprehension of the subject. What is dry, is oftentimes deemed profound, because it is dry; and what is splendid is deemed unsubstantial, because it is splendid. Men forget that there is a diamond in the mind, a diamond brilliancy and a diamond solidity,—that the imagination is the handmaid of reason, —that where the power to explore the depths of a subject exists, the imagination is an efficient helper in the exploration. The union of the imaginative with the reasoning faculty, is as rare as the possession of first-rate intellect. But it is not a thing impossible. It has existed,—it does exist; and where it exists, there can be no reasonable doubt that the one strengthens and enriches the other,—that the two are more powerful in union. " It was not a chain of reasoning, though close and cogent as if delivered in the Areopagus; it was not only a display of imagination, however chastened from Asiatic luxuriance; nor an appeal to the passions, however moving and vehement; it was a combination of all that in the language of a distinguished Greek scholar gave to the eloquence of Pericles its power and charm, and secured for him the title of the Prince of eloquence in his generation." It was a like combination that gave to Mr. Pinkney his vast celebrity as an orator and lawyer, during a life spent in the constant struggles of the forum. His imagination never degenerated into mere vapid declamation. It burned and glowed all along the path of his argument, and enriched it occasionally with what Judge Story calls "sparkling lights," never alien to the strict line of the argument or held up in the wrong place. His imagination was but the poetic form of his ratiocination—the dazzling garb now and then thrown over the cooler deductions of his reasoning. Indeed, the imagination and the reasoning faculty were the workshop, in which his massive argument was woven, and it would have been impossible to separate the golden and silver threads of the woof, without wholly marring the texture. Burke was the profoundest of philosophers, and yet he possessed a huge imagination, which poured a flood of light over the pathway of his argumentation; and he must be pitied, who cannot see that the profound was rendered more profound by the vast compass and gorgeous magnificence of the imagination, which enlightened while it delighted. Barrow was a profound theological reasoner, and yet he was a man of marvellous scope of imagination. Hooker was the most masterful of them all, and who doubts that his immortal work was made the more immortal by the gorgeousness of the imagination that glows and burns through all its pages.

Mr. Pinkney was accustomed to sound all the depths of the subjects he investigated and discussed. Superficiality he detested,—a false and spurious pretence to learning he abhorred,—and yet he could indulge at times in passages of such inimitable beauty and power, so natural and artistically woven into the thread of his argument, that you could scarce discover where they began or ended. They seemed, as indeed they did, to grow out of the subject, to be an essential element in it, the outbursting flower from the parent stem, the living germ on the thrifty and vigorous plant. No one held in greater abhorrence or more severely reprobated, as will be seen in his own rich criticism on political sketches, what might be called a sickly sentimentalism of style, or an extravagant and irregular indulgence of fancy. Perspicuity was the thing of primary importance in his estimation. He allowed nothing to darken or obscure his meaning. His figures were never crowded together, or jumbled up in motley confusion. They were never far-fetched or unnatural. Exquisite taste guided the helm, and the imagination in its richest glow was ever obedient to the pilot. He never used it for mere ornament. He used it as the handmaid of reason. Force and appropriateness of diction and simplicity of illustration were the chosen vehicles of his thoughts. Strength made beautiful, when the occasion called for it, gave a peculiar fascination and nerve to his style. Thought, however, always predominated over expression. Imagination in its highest and purest form occupied in all his discussions the place of an uncurbed, unrestrained, artificial fancy. To convince, not dazzle, was his high object ; and yet from the native splendor of his mind, he insensibly dazzled in the very act of convincing.

His style of argument on legal questions was peculiar to himself, founded on no particular model. It was original and striking. In many discussions before the Supreme Court, those peculiar powers were conspicuously displayed. I will mention but two, the Bank case and the Nereide ; and I cite these two, because while in themselves of deepest magnitude, I am enabled to review a criticism of Mr. Legaré of South Carolina on the former, and an animadversion of Mr. Phillips, the Irish barrister, in his life of Curran, on an incident connected with the latter. The array of counsel in the Bank case was truly splendid. By the side of Pinkney stood Webster and Wirt, "the Gothic and Corinthian" pillar ; opposed to them were Martin, Hopkinson and Walter Jones —the last named, the connecting link that binds the past to us, a man of the rarest powers of eloquence, and the profoundest powers of reasoning. It was not possible for six such minds to be brought into such stirring proximity, without the keenest intellectual rivalry. The theme was worthy of the men, and the scene of the conflict worthy of both. It was in this bright array of talent, that Mr. Pinkney rose to conclude the argument; and although he was three days in the discussion, Judge Story tells us that it was "worth a journey from Salem to hear it."

Mr. Legaré pronounces a rather dogmatic opinion on the merits of the argument. He jeers Mr. Pinkney for not going beyond the English text-books, and taunts him for not going more deeply into the subject than Dr. Blackstone. It almost excites a smile to hear such a charge brought against one who stood, in his day, the very embodiment of legal learning and patient research. Our surprise is increased, because of this very speech Justice Story thus writes (vol. I. page 325): "I never in my whole life heard a greater speech. He spoke like a great statesman and patriot, and sound constitutional lawyer—all the cobwebs of sophistry and metaphysics about State rights and State sovereignty he brushed away with a mighty besom."

Mr. Legaré does not do Mr. Pinkney's argument in that cause full and ample justice. He says that Mr. Pinkney "began his argument by declaring that he did not consider the constitutionality of the Bank as an open question, because it had been *assumed* by Congress and acquiesced in for thirty years." Let us now look into the report in Mr. Wheaton, and see how the case really stands. After a most admirable and masterly discussiou of the powers of the State and General Governments, Mr. Pinkney contended, that the question of the constitutionality of the Bank was to be settled on authority and principle. "The constitution acts on the people by means of powers communicated directly from the people. No State in its corporate capacity ratified it, but it was proposed for adoption to popular conventions. It springs from the people precisely as the State constitutions spring from the people, and acts on them in a similar manner. The federal powers are just as sovereign as those of the States.

The constitutionality of the establishment of the Bank, as one of the necessary means to carry into effect the authority vested in the General Government, is no longer an open question. It has been long since settled by *decisions of the most revered authority, legislative, executive, and judicial.* A legislative construction in a doubtful case, persevered in for a course of years, ought to be binding on the court. This however is not a question of construction merely, but of political necessity, on which Congress must decide. The members of the convention, who framed the constitution, passed into the first Congress by which the new government was organized. They must have understood their own work. They declared that the constitution gave to Congress the power of incorporating a bank. It is an historical fact of great importance in this discussion, that amendments to the constitution were actually proposed, in order to guard against the establishment of commercial monopolies. The legislative precedent established in 1791 has been followed up by a series of acts of Congress, all conferring the authority."

It was not the mere assumption by Congress of the power, but the settlement of the question by the most revered authorities, legislative, executive, and judicial, upon which Mr. Pinkney relied in the discussion of that great cause ; and that, too, in a doubtful case of construction. The report of the cause may be found in Wheaton's reports, vol. 4, February term, 1819. And whoever desires to test the value of Mr. Legaré's strictures need only turn to Mr. Pinkney's argument, where he will find, even in the skeleton gleanings of the accomplished reporter, one of the ablest and most unanswerable expositions of the great constitutional question, which has since been exhumed by the refined metaphysicians of South Carolina to agitate and disturb the peace of the Union, but with no other result than their own chagrin and disappointment. It is sufficient to remind the reader of Mr. Legaré's critique, that the reasonings of this speech upon the principles of constitutional law involved, were endorsed by the Storys and Marshalls of this land; and ingrafted on the statute books of the court, though not deeper than Dr. Blackstone. Judge Marshall's opinion gives a judicial clothing to many points of Pinkney's argument.

I regret the necessity of being compelled to notice the review in question, because Mr. Legaré is not now alive; but at the time he wrote it the voice of Pinkney had been hushed in death, and his name was inscribed on the cold marble.

The speech on the Nereide, though not so successful with the court, was a splendid specimen of forensic power. It has been long before the public, though in mutilated form and garbled extracts, and they can judge of it for themselves.

I will be excused for pausing a moment, while I examine a statement made by Mr. Phillips in his life of Curran, of a collision between Mr. Emmet and Mr. Pinkney in the cause of the Mary and that of the Nereide, which is wide of the truth. Speaking of Mr. Pinkney's assault he says, "Emmet's demeanor was such in noticing it, that shame extorted next day from his defeated adversary a eulogium which he doubtless estimated at what it was worth," and then he puts into Mr. Emmet's mouth the following language: "I know not by what name arrogance and presumption may be called on this side of the water, but I am sure he never could have acquired those manners in the polite circles of Europe which he had long frequented as a public minister." He refers for authority to Madden's lives of United Irishmen. By particular examination, I find the affair thus stated by him: "The latter (Mr. Pinkney) closed his argument in a very important cause, and with his characteristic arrogance alluded to the fact of Mr. Emmet's emigration to the United States. When he had concluded his argument, Mr. Emmet rose and took up the mode and manner in which his opponent had

treated him. He said he was Mr. Pinkney's equal in birth,
rank, and connections, and he was not his enemy. He knew
not by what name arrogance and presumption might be called
on this side of the ocean, but sure he was that Mr. Pinkney
never acquired those manners in the polite circles of Europe,
which he had frequented as a public minister. Mr. Pinkney was not ready at retort, and made no reply. But a
few days afterwards, it so happened that Mr. Emmet and
Mr. Pinkney were again opposed to each other in a cause of
magnitude, and it fell to Mr. Emmet's part to close the
argument, who was determined that his antagonist should be
put in mind of his former deportment and expressions. Pinkney was aware of the thunderbolt in store, and took the opportunity of paying to Mr. Emmet's genius, fame, and private worth, the highest tribute of respect. This respect was
never again violated."—*Madden's Life of Thomas A. Emmet.*
He added further—" When Mr. Emmet rose out of his place
as before stated, Chief Justice Marshall indicated great uneasiness, thinking that something unpleasant might be the result. Mr. Justice Livingston remarked in a whisper, ' Let him
go on ; I will answer that he says nothing rude or improper.'
With this, as well as the result, the Chief Justice was satisfied." Mr. Phillips gives Madden as his authority, and Madden makes his statement, supported by not so much as a
shadow of authority. Mr. Phillips improves upon his authority, and speaks of Mr. Pinkney as a defeated adversary.
Justice Story witnessed the first competition of those two
illustrious men in the highest court of the Union : and so
did Mr. Wheaton. We have their evidence in the case. In
the first cause, that of the Mary, in which Mr. Pinkney indulged in some warmth of expression, justified as he at the
time thought by the too free strictures of Mr. Emmet on one
of his clients, so far from being the routed champion Mr.
Phillips would represent, Justice Story, who sat in the cause,
tells us in his published sketch of Mr. Emmet, that Mr.

Pinkney " won an easy victory, and pressed his advantages
with vast dexterity, and, *as Mr. Emmet thought,* with somewhat the display of triumph." So much for one of the assertions of Mr. Phillips made professedly on authority, and
yet unsustained by his own authority, and disproved by another. In the case of the Nereide, in which Mr. Emmet
delivered a most masterly speech, Justice Story informs us
that Mr. Emmet began by paying a generous tribute to the
talents and acquirements of his opponent, whom fame and
fortune had followed both in Europe and America. It is
impossible, at this late day, to state what Mr. Emmet in
reality said. But one thing is certain, the representations
of excited partisans must be received with great distrust ;
especially where the recorded statement of so distinguished
a witness as Justice Story or Mr. Wheaton gives it no manner of countenance. Mr. Pinkney made the amende honorable, and avowed his regret that he should have indulged in
a seemingly unkind criticism upon his illustrious opponent,
which was " deepened by the *forbearance* and *urbanity* of his
reply." Is it credible that Mr. Pinkney would publicly, in
the presence of the court, where language so grossly insulting
as that put into Mr. Emmet's lips must have been used, if
used at all, have spoken of the forbearance and urbanity of
a reply which had just branded him with insolence and presumption and ill-breeding ? Will any one (who was at all
acquainted with Mr. Pinkney, or the court of which Judge
Marshall was the honored head) believe that such common
billingsgate abuse was either endured by him or the court.
I have far too much respect for Mr. Emmet to believe that
his lips were so employed. I think the statement sufficiently
disproved by Mr. Emmet's high praise of Mr. Pinkney as recorded by Story ; and the terms of Pinkney's own apology,
an apology which does him infinite credit, whose eloquence
is only equalled by its magnanimity; as well as the inherent
probabilities of the case. As to the insinuations of Mr. Mad-

den, that Mr. Pinkney was induced by fear to disarm Mr. Emmet of the thunderbolt of vengeance by an unfelt and hypocritical profession of admiration, or that he was not ready at retort, it may pass current among foreigners, though a mere unproved assertion ; but where Mr. Pinkney was known, it will be read with a smile; for he was afraid, physically or intellectually, of no man. To use his own expression to Lord Wellesley, which an Englishman should be the last to forget, he neither sought nor shunned discussions, of which the tendency is merely to irritate. In the discussion on the Mary he had met with nothing to excite his fears, for Story represents him as a victor; and in the Nereide, although he failed to carry conviction to the court, he carried one of the brightest lights of that court with him, and based his argument upon principles, that were almost simultaneously sanctioned by the highest judicial wisdom of England, and delivered a speech which, even in its present mutilated form, will ever rank among the finest specimens of forensic eloquence and power.

Since writing the above, my attention was drawn to a passage in the life of the late Jeremiah Smith, a distinguished judge of New Hampshire. It is in these words : " Judge Spencer related to me the anecdote of Mr. Pinkney's attack on Emmet in the Supreme Court of the United States. They were on opposite sides in an important cause, and one which Mr. Pinkney had much at heart, and was desirous of winning by fair or unfair means. In the course of the argument, he travelled out of the cause to make observations personal and extremely offensive on Mr. Emmet, with a view probably of irritating and weakening his reply. When the argument was through, Mr. Emmet said perhaps he ought not to notice the remarks of the opposite counsel. Then follows pretty much the above version, save these words: " He would only say that he had been informed that the learned gentleman had filled the highest office his country could be-

stow at the court of St. James.   He was sure he had never
learned his *breeding* in that school.   The court, the bar, and
audience were delighted."

This, it will be remembered, was not published until after
Mr. Pinkney's death.   In the first place, there is a gratuitous
and unproved charge, that Mr. Pinkney was bent upon gain-
ing the cause of the Mary by fair or unfair means—a charge
made by a warm personal friend of Mr. Emmet without one
tittle of evidence, and as I shall presently show, in the face
of evidence to the contrary, and in violation of the facts in
the case.   In the second place, there is the imputation of a
low and vulgar motive, at which every right-minded man re-
coils, upon *bare probability*, " with a view *probably* of irritating and weakening the reply."   The animus of this anecdote
is its own best and surest condemnation.   The charge of
unfairness, and the imputation of such a motive upon mere
probability, when brought against one whom Justice Story
represents as of the most peerless character at the bar, are
strange deeds in one, whose office it was to judge righteous
judgment and base assertions, touching the illustrious dead,
upon solid and substantial facts.   The motive attributed to
Mr. Pinkney is not only untrue, but impossible to be true.
Mr. Emmet's argument was concluded, and could not therefore be weakened by irritation.   Mr. Wheaton, who was present, gives us the true motive ; and Justice Story conclusively
proves, that there was no necessity for a resort to any thing
like trick, if indeed Mr. Pinkney were capable of it, as he
won by argument an easy victory.   It is strange that Judge
Story tells us nothing of the pleasure with which he listened
to language far too coarse to have ever greeted the ear of such
a tribunal as the Supreme Court of the Union.

I am not to defend Mr. Pinkney in what he, upon reflection, thought proper to acknowledge was not wholly de-
fensible ; and for which he offered a full and gratuitous public
atonement.   But when reports, extremely prejudicial to the

character of another, are circulated after his death, and accompanied by gross abuse ; it is surely within the province of a biographer to sift the assertion, and, as far as the evidence will admit, disabuse the public mind, and set the matter right.   A breath may tarnish the mirror of a peerless character, if suffered to remain upon it—and no one has a right to complain, if others are wounded in the mere sheer justice of rubbing it off.

The name of Thomas A. Emmet recalls many thrilling reminiscences.   The misfortunes of his early life, which was overhung with clouds, imparted a melancholy interest to his subsequent illustrious career.   A man of rare eloquence and most commanding abilities, he lived to shed an additional lustre upon old Ireland ; for although his soft and persuasive oratory, and the breathings of his pure and enlightened patriotism were hushed on the banks of Killarney, and he was compelled to fly the Ireland he loved, and seek and find a shelter beneath the outspread wings of the American eagle ; he enjoyed the enviable pleasure of knowing that the echoes of his fame became familiar sounds in every Irish homestead.   Casting his eye over the names of her illustrious sons, her Goldsmiths, Burkes, Sheridans, Grattans, Currans, and his own most gifted brother (the man whose epitaph will yet be written); he could, with something of the exultation of patriotic pride, console himself with the belief that he was not unmindful of their glory. If in the excitement of debate, there was a momentary jar between Ireland's favored son and Maryland's most admired, it was a jar in which neither was wholly blameless, and each triumphed by sacrificing obstinate self-pride in a cordial and mutual recognition and acknowledgment of all that was truly great in the other.   I leave to malevolence on either side the waters, the gratification of parading forth infirmities that are common to us all, and overlooking virtues that but few possess ; while the more pleasing and grateful task is

left me, of showing how the incidental misunderstanding between them was adjusted without dishonor to either.

Mr. Pinkney possessed an eminently legal mind ; quick,
keen, discriminating, incredibly patient in investigation, and
endowed with extraordinary powers of analysis.   He studied
Law as a science, and mastered it in all its departments.
The whole domain of the common law was as familiar to his
mind and thought, as the soil of his birth ; while the great
principles of international law, and the not less imposing
principles of our own august constitution, were thoroughly
explored and comprehended by him.   He was accustomed to
refresh himself at the well springs, and drew his legal knowledge from the great original sources, the masters whose expositions are decisions.   Nothing of importance escaped his
notice.   Thoroughness and comprehensiveness combined to
make him singularly learned in the Law.   He never engaged
in a cause without looking carefully and calmly into its
merits, and sifting them through all their intricacies, and
adjusting with the utmost precision the law to the facts.
Once in the cause, he was perfect master of the ground.   No
error committed by those with whom he was called to grapple, escaped his eager and eagle-eyed observation.   Cool and
cautious, he surveyed the whole field, and discovered at a
glance where were the weak and where were the strong points
of the assault and the defence.   His own line of argument was
most skilfully laid, and his authorities marshalled with consummate judgment.   Story says he never pressed weak points
upon the court, and therein he showed his good sterling common sense and high regard for professional propriety.   He ex-
pended his whole strength upon the really strong points in the
case. and warred with the weapons of a giant.   Investigation,
deep, searching, laborious investigation, preceded and accompanied all his discussions before the court.   His habit of careful
and diligent preparation (from which he never departed, and
which in reality constituted one of the marvels of his life),

gave rise to the idea that his mind was slow in its operation, and that his speeches were written out before they were delivered, and that he was deficient in what are called the powers of extemporaneous debate—an idea the farthest possible removed from the fact. Those who were accustomed to listen to his legal arguments, most elaborately prepared, were not unfrequently astonished at his prompt responses, when consulted as an *amicus curiæ*, upon points suddenly sprung upon the court, which resembled the gushings forth from an overflowing fountain, and were not more characterized by lofty eloquence, than wonderful precision and exactness. He who never presumed to present himself before a court, but after the most patient and profound examination of the case, in all its bearings, could, when the occasion called for it, pour forth his accurate and methodized legal learning with a force and precision truly wonderful. Those who were privileged to listen to his arguments continued hour after hour, have testified to the fact, that the scintillations of his genius, emitted in the heat and excitement of debate, whether before the court or the Senate, possessed a beauty and a brilliancy that were never afterwards gathered up. So far from being carefully written out beforehand, they could not have been written at all. They were, to use the poetic language of another, like dew-drops that hang on the petals of flowers, which cannot be gathered. Mr. Pinkney possessed all the peculiar qualities of a powerful extemporaneous debater, viz., unlimited command of language, inexhaustible fund of knowledge, a powerful and retentive memory, and admirable self-possession. But he valued his reputation too highly; he too much respected the court and the audience, to go forth to the discussion without the last finish of the most exact and minute investigation. The writer of this memoir has heard several anecdotes of an authentic character, illustrative of his wonderful quickness of comprehension;—one of which he begs permission to mention, as it came to him

direct. It does honor to another of the distinguished sons of
Maryland, who was himself a most eloquent and powerful
advocate. Mr. * * * had a case to argue, and Mr. Pinkney
was employed as associate counsel in the upper court. During the consultation, in giving a history of the cause, one
point was mentioned as of secondary importance. As soon
as Mr. * * * concluded, Mr. Pinkney said, " Do you take
the points you prefer, and I will see what I can do with the
one you reject." This excited curiosity, and when the argument of Mr. Pinkney opened, his professional colleague remained to see what could be made of it ; and very soon discovered that it was the very gist of the cause.

And yet, as I have shown, his quickness of comprehension never betrayed him into indolence. His perfect command of the most appropriate, beautiful, and forcible diction,
never surprised him into carelessness of preparation. His
intimate familiarity with the legal lore of the past, and the
enlightened decisions of the present, never tempted him
into a confident presumption of authorities. His quickness
of perception, compass of information, and brilliancy of
genius, all disciplined by the severest and most constantly
sustained study, gave him the pre-eminence he maintained
at the bar, and made him the wonderful legal logician the
North American Review pronounced him to be.

Mr. Pinkney entertained the most exalted idea of professional honor. There is a trifling circumstance mentioned
in a letter, addressed by him to Mr. Ridgely of Maryland,
now in my possession, which, as it sets forth this trait of
character in a very striking light, I beg leave to copy :

" October 22, 1821.

" Sir :—Since the writing of my letter of the 20th, in
answer to yours of the 16th, Mr. Purviance and Mr. Williams have, in your name and behalf, offered me a compensation (a check of one thousand dollars), in consequence of

my known determination to be neutral on your demand in the case of the Union Bank against you. But I could not, consistently with my notions of what I owe to my own character and the honor of the Bar, accept your fee, and therefore I refused it (as doubtless they have informed you), the moment it was tendered to me.

" I am the general counsel of the Union Bank, and had, moreover, undertaken for it this cause in particular, having no idea that after the return of your retainer, with your own previous assent, there was, or could be any objection to my doing so ; or that I was expected, without any recompense, to decline the duties of my profession altogether in your cause, and in every other that should involve the same questions ; and if, from considerations of delicacy, I retire from the fulfilment of my engagement with the Union Bank, I will not consent to be paid for it in any shape or manner by their opponent, or by any body else. My conduct on this occasion would cease to be worthy of the approbation of my brethren and the public if I suffered my neutrality to be purchased, or to appear to be purchased, or in any way to be compensated to the prejudice of those who have honored me with their confidence, and who, with their accustomed liberality, will, I am sure, excuse me for abandoning their cause upon disinterested motives under the circumstances in which I am unexpectedly placed.

" Your obedient servant,
" WILLIAM PINKNEY."

This letter speaks volumes. It exhibits a refinement of delicacy, and a nice sense of honor and propriety, that must receive universal commendation. It is the more beautiful, because it was a deed done in secret, and now only meets the public eye through the kind consideration of those who survive him, thirty years and more after he has passed from the sight of men.

Four years after Mr. Pinkney's death, William Wirt thus wrote of him : " If he shall have a biographer of genius, he will, by preserving the real echoes of his fame, do more for his immortality than Pinkney could have done for himself."—Vol. II, page 197.   Those echoes of his fame (the oracular decisions of a Marshall, a Story, and a Wheaton), can never die away ; and, as long as they live, Pinkney's name will live with them.   But still we must ever regret (Mr. Wirt's judgment to the contrary notwithstanding), that his speeches could not have been preserved as they were delivered ; since Wheaton and Story, both accomplished scholars and fastidious judges of style and matter, have told us that they lost in every effort to report them.

May we not justly say of him,—" Qui consulta patrum, qui leges juraque servat ? "

WIRT AND PINKNEY.

JUSTICE to the character and memory of Mr. Pinkney makes it my duty to devote a few pages to the consideration of a portion of the memoir of Mr. Wirt, written by the Hon. J. P. Kennedy, a gentleman of literary distinction, well known to the American people. Holding Mr. Wirt's reputation, as a profound lawyer and brilliant orator, in very high esteem, and recognizing in him a gentleman of varied accomplishments, an ornament of the State of his birth and the country at large, I cannot but regret that his biographer has forced upon me this necessity. Fault-finding is always irksome and distasteful, but especially so where there is much to commend, as both well and wisely written ; and, if it were not for the fact that another distinguished name in Maryland might suffer, I should pass it by in silence.

I do not animadvert upon this work merely because of the free expression of Mr. Kennedy's own opinion respecting the talents and acquirements of Mr. Pinkney ; or the insertion of the still freer criticisms of the illustrious subject of his biography. They both had a right to form their estimate of Mr. Pinkney, and then publish it to the world. True it is, as I think I shall be able to show conclusively, the exercise of that right was singularly unfortunate ; as the tone and temper of the criticisms will be found, upon examination, to reflect but little credit upon either the judgment or liberality of their authors. They mar the work, and are a spot on the disk of one of Maryland's bright orbs. The insertion of those criticisms was exceedingly indiscreet. But indiscretion is no breach of the biographer's privilege; nor is it all of which I feel myself entitled to complain on the part of Mr. Kennedy in this portion of his biography. He has thought proper to publish to the world letters, in which allusion is made to conversations that purport to have passed between Mr. Pinkney and Mr. Wirt alone (detrimental to the reputation of the former), upon Mr. Wirt's sole authority, long after the death of Mr. Pinkney, and at a time when it is impossible to offer either explanation or a denial of their correctness. He has done more. He has woven a portion of those letters (the most offensive) into the very typography of the text, and thus given them his most solemn and deliberate endorsement.

What man would be willing to have his occasional remarks (they might have been playfully made) thirty years after his decease, when he is totally incapable of defending himself, chronicled to the world by his own personal rival? Who would be willing to be thus personally judged? Without intentional misrepresentation (which I would be the last to impute to Mr. Wirt), we all know how easily a thing may be changed by a change in the tone and look, and how easily our own peculiar temperament at the time may give a coloring and bias to things in themselves perfectly trivial and unimportant. Trifles are not unfrequently magnified into some grave offence against the rules of good taste and high-toned bearing by a morbid and diseased sensitiveness, in moments of temporary excitement, when the power of a rival is felt. Impressions made at such a time, especially where we ourselves are the party directly concerned, are not to be trusted. If there be any principle of justice or propriety clearly established, it is this: that all repetition of conversations which occur in the privacy of personal intercourse, reflecting in the slightest degree on another, be published in his lifetime, or else be consigned to the tomb of oblivion. In the publication of those letters of Mr. Wirt which contain a mere intellectual critique on Mr. Pinkney, Mr. Kennedy has been singularly unfortunate ; while in the publication of those which are morally condemnatory, he has been unjust. The one is a fair subject of friendly criticism in return ; the other, a clear ground of impeachment.

I have said, that a careful inspection of Mr. Wirt's criticisms of Pinkney, will not enhance his discrimination as a judge, nor his magnanimity as a rival. Let me test the soundness of this assertion. And be it remembered that the biographer has opened this page of Mr. Wirt's life, and must therefore bear the consequences of its analysis. On page 402 of Vol. I. in a letter to Mr. Francis W. Gilmer, dated April 1st., 1816, we have a scathing dissection of Mr. Pinkney's mental calibre.

"Teach these boys,—as Pinkney said he would do,—' a new style of speaking.' But let it be a better one than his ; I mean his solemn style, to which, in Irish phrase, I give the back of my hand. If that be a good style, then all the models, both ancient and modern, which we have been accustomed to contemplate as truly great,—such as Crassus, Anthony, Cicero, the prolocutors of the Dialogue ' De causis corruptæ eloquentiæ,' Chatham, Henry, and others,—not forgetting ' Paul Jones and old Charon,'—are all pretenders. I know that this is not your opinion. But I was near him five or six weeks, and watched him narrowly. He has nothing of the rapid and unerring analysis of Marshall,—but he has in lieu of it, a dogmatizing absoluteness of manner which passes with the million,—which, by-the-by, includes many more than we should at first suspect,—for an evidence of power ; and he has acquired with those around him a sort of papal infallibility. That manner is a piece of acting; it is artificial, as you may see by the wandering of his eye, and is as far removed from the composed confidence of enlightened certainty, as it is from natural modesty. Socrates confessed that all the knowledge he had been able to acquire seemed only to convince him that he knew nothing. This frankness is one of the most characteristic traits of a great mind. Pinkney would make you believe that he knows every thing.

" —At the bar he is despotic, and cares as little for his colleagues or adversaries as if they were men of wood. He has certainly much the advantage of any of them in forensic show. Give him time—and he requires not much—and he will deliver a speech which any man might be proud to claim. You will have good materials, very well put together, and clothed in a costume as magnificent as that of Louis XIV. ; but you will have a vast quantity of false fire, besides a vehemence of intonation, for which you see nothing to account in the character of the thought. His arguments, when I heard him, were such as would have occurred to any good mind of the profession. It was his mode of introducing, dressing and incorporating them, which constituted their chief value—'materiem superabit opus.'"

This was not a hastily formed opinion. It was the result of mature reflection and close personal observation. Consistency may be said to be the very jewel of criticism. Not that I would intimate that our views may not be altered or modified by time and circumstances, without a forfeiture of our title to respect and confidence. But the criticism of to-day must be perfectly consistent with itself, to make it in any degree valuable. Where is the consistency of this criticism ? " Dogmatizing absoluteness of manner" not power ; "forensic show" is all that in the first part of this letter he is willing to concede to Mr. Pinkney, after five or six weeks' close and narrow watching. And yet, upon short notice he will deliver a speech which any man would be proud to claim ; and still after all, the arguments he used, when Mr. Wirt heard him, were only such as would have occurred to any good mind of the profession, with a vast deal of false fire. Such is the character of the first criticism that Wirt passed upon Pinkney ; and Mr. Kennedy has deemed it wise to hand it down to the generation following. How any man, who has in lieu of unerring and rapid analysis, a dogmatizing absoluteness of manner, which is not power, but passes with the weak-minded million for an evidence of power, should be able, upon short preparation, to deliver a speech which any man would be proud to claim;—and yet only stumble upon such arguments as would occur to any good mind of the profession, characterized with a vast deal of false fire, is a refinement of distinction, that I candidly avow I cannot penetrate. This criticism destroys itself. It was, as I have shown, not hastily formed, and cannot therefore plead negligence or haste in its extenuation; and although essentially modified in after years, the feeling that dictated it will serve as a key to help me to discover the true source of Mr. Wirt's strictures upon his rival. In a letter to Judge Carr, dated April 7th, 1816, he thus writes (Vol. I. p. 405):

"In this hopeless situation I went to court, to try the tug of war with the renowned Pinkney. When I thought of my situation,—of the theatre on which I was now to appear for the first time,—the expectation which I was told was excited, and saw the assembled multitude of ladies and gentlemen from every quarter of the Union, you may guess my feelings. Had I been prepared, how should I have gloried in that theatre, that concourse, and that adversary! As it was, my dear wife and children, and your features, look, and sympathetic voice and friendly inquietude, came over me like evil spirits. To be sure, these considerations gave me a sort of desperate, ferocious, bandit-like resolution; but what is mere *brute* resolution with a totally denuded intellect? I gave, indeed, some hits which produced a visible and animating effect; but my courage sank, and I suppose my manner fell under the conscious imbecility of my argument. I was comforted, however, by finding that Pinkney mended the matter very little, if at all.

"Had the cause been to argue over again on the next

day, I could have shivered him ; for his discussion revived all my forgotten topics, and, as I lay in my bed on the following morning, arguments poured themselves out before me as from a cornucopia. I should have wept at the consideration of what I had lost, if I had not prevented it by leaping out of bed, and beginning to sing and dance like a maniac."

It is a curious fact, that this letter was penned but six days after the one just commented on. It is not a little surprising that dogmatizing absoluteness of manner and forensic show should have produced such a state of feeling at the prospect of actual collision. Unfortunately for Mr. Wirt, but most fortunately for his antagonist, the bed, not the forum, was the scene of this hopeless rout ; and Wirt himself, the graphic narrator of the shivering effects that would have followed the renewal of the contest. It was a wonderful transition from the imbecile argument to the teeming cornucopia; and most fortunate for Pinkney was it, that the bed, being a non-conductor, saved him from the shivering bolt of legal eloquence and logic, before it laid him low in the dust of the dishonored forum. In a letter to Mrs. Wirt, dated April 7th, 1821 (Vol. II. p. 119), Mr. Wirt thus wrote :

"This is the fourteenth day since this argument was opened. Pinkney, before he began, promised to speak only two hours and a half. He has now spoken two days, and is, at this moment, at it again for the third day. You will be gratified to hear, that although there are four counsel on the same side with me, and the veteran General Harper,— hitherto the only Maryland rival of Pinkney,—among them, yet here the Attorney-General is regarded as his chief antagonist, and the comparison made by the court, the bar and the bystanders, far from being to my prejudice."

All this may have been so in point of fact (but there are those alive who have heard other testimony from the court, to say nothing of the bar); but did it not occur to Mr.

Kennedy, that other less interested witnesses would more gracefully and properly have attested the fact, and that the wise words of Solomon are still, as they ever have been, the safest and best to follow? Wirt may have eclipsed the veteran Harper, a man as great as he was learned, and as lofty in spirit as he was ambitious to excel. He may have eclipsed Pinkney in this cause. But the learned biographer will pity, if he does not excuse our incredulity, until he has explained to us how the opinion of the court, the bar and the bystanders, was gauged. Wirt doubtless thought as he wrote, and his friends may have told him so ; but friends are not always impartial, neither are they infallible. Our own opinions under such circumstances are surely as little to be trusted. Mr. Kennedy seems to have had a sort of presentiment, that the insertion of such a letter might be open to criticism ; and bespeaks for it exemption, on the score of the peculiar circumstances under which it was written. He adds, " Trifles such as these, which on other occasions might be liable to disparaging comment, acquire value in a biographical sketch, as exponents of characters. They are to be regarded as illustrative anecdotes, which often serve to cast a better light upon personal qualities or the features of the mind, than more earnest and acute dissertation. They are chiefly valuable in the present case, for the evidence they furnish us of that eager, sensitive, and stimulating desire in the breast of Wirt, to contend with and excel, if possible, the most renowned and skilful competitors in the theatre of his own art."—Vol. II. p. 119.

These trifles consist, it will be borne in mind, of three letters (one of which alone I have commented on), April 2d, 5th, and 7th ; in two of which Mr. Pinkney is held up to posterity in any thing but an amiable light, and in the 3d exhibited as comparing unfavorably with Wirt in the estimation of the court, bar, and bystanders. If they be, as Mr Kennedy affirms, exponents of character, I am greatly in error if the friends of Mr. Wirt do not join me in the expression of opinion, that they have been most unfortunately inserted into his biography. Would any one, who takes time for reflection, wish to wound the feelings of the friends of Mr. Pinkney, who survive him, (at a time too, when it is impossible for them to open the secrets of the past for his justification,) for the sake of inserting mere *trifles* and retaining the echo of a trumpet blast of victory sounded by Mr. Wirt's own lips? As private letters, restricted to the private circles, I should have never ventured to criticise them. But Mr. Kennedy has made them public and endeavored to defend them as "exponents of character," although two of them bear unkindly upon the memory of one not living at the time of their publication ; and the other is a self-appropriated claim to victory. In another letter to Judge Carr, May 14th, 1821 (Vol. II. p. 121), I read :

" Why, Sir, have not I been to Bel Air, in the midst of it all, and bearded that ' * * * * * * magician Glendower,' without suffering the thousandth part that the earth did, at the birth of the Welshman ; nay, without suffering by the struggle or in the comparison ?"

This reference to Glendower, the Welshman, seems to have been particularly pleasing to Mr. Wirt, as he introduces it on more than one occasion, when speaking of Mr. Pinkney. Judging from the tone and spirit of his letters, one might fancy that Wirt like Lancaster could "illy brook the mention of Glendower." I will not insinuate that the words of the Welshman could have been adopted by Mr. Pinkney.

> "Three times hath Henry Bolingbroke made head
> Against my power—thrice from the banks of Wye,
> *And sandy-bottomed Severn*, have I sent him
> Bootless home, and weather-beaten back."

But surely this much I may do. I may well express my regret, that Wirt had not with Mortimer's magnanimity have divided the disputed realm.

"England, from Trent and Severn hitherto,
By South and East is to my part assigned:
All westward, Wales, beyond the *Severn shore*,
And all the fertile land within that bound,
To Owen Glendower."—

It may not be that Wirt's Glendower, like Shakspeare's,
"gave the tongue a helpful ornament that was never seen
before"—but still comparisons are sometimes stronger and
more striking than we at first imagined.

Again in a letter to Francis W. Gilmer, May 9th, 1822,
p. 138, Vol. II.

"Poor Pinkney! he died opportunely for his fame.   It
could not have risen higher * * * *.

"He was a great man.   On a set occasion, the greatest,
I think, at our bar.   I never heard Emmet nor Wells, and,
therefore, I do not say the American bar.   He was an excellent lawyer; had very great force of mind, great compass,
nice discrimination, strong and accurate judgment: and for
copiousness and beauty of diction was unrivalled.   He is a
real loss to the bar.   No man dared to grapple with him
without the most perfect preparation and the full possession
of all his strength.   Thus he kept the bar on the alert and
every horse with his traces tight.   It will be useful to remember him, and in every case to imagine him the adversary
with whom we have to cope.   But, I assure you, I do not
enjoy more rest because that comet has set.   There was a
pleasurable excitement in wrestling with him on full preparation.   In my two last encounters with him I was well
satisfied, and should never have been otherwise when entirely ready.   To draw his supremacy into question, any
where, was honor enough for ambition as moderate as mine."

These words were penned in an hour of solemn interest,
over the closed coffin and grave of his contemporary—and
yet even here we have the rising of the same restless influence, that the name and fame of Pinkney always produced

on Wirt. Pinkney did die, in one sense, opportunely for his fame. He died in the full flush of honor, with his face fronting duty; not ingloriously reposing upon his laurels, but in the act of making a desperate struggle for still higher fame and vaster renown. But he had not reached the acme of either his aspirations or his hopes. Had he lived, and his powers continued unimpaired by disease, his countrymen would have heard of him yet again on the floor of the Senate, and the forum.

Mr. Wirt in this letter concedes, it is true, "that he was a great man; on a set occasion the greatest at the Maryland bar. He had not heard Emmet or Wells, and therefore he did not say the American bar. " He had heard Webster and Tazewell. This is high praise, and although not uttered until the orb that seemed to culminate so painfully on Mr. Wirt's vision had set, still I was disposed to say that it was praise gracefully spoken, when my eye rested upon the following passage: " In my two last encounters with him I was well satisfied, and should never have been otherwise, when entirely ready." No mention is made of him but in self-comparison. The fame of Pinkney (if these letters be a true index of the feelings of their author) was Wirt's disturbing ghost. Even when the great Lawyer and orator lay in the shroud, and criticism herself stood disarmed by his bier, that ghost could not be laid. Long after death had claimed its victim, it continued to haunt the memory and awaken unpleasant associations. In a letter to Judge Carr, February 9th, 1824 (Vol. II. p. 179), he thus wrote:

" There was Pinkney, who was certainly a great advocate. He was never heard to complain of a failure. He has made some speeches which would have half killed me. On a great occasion in Annapolis I heard him speak for three days. Of the first day, two or three hours were in his best manner; the rest of that day, and the whole of the following two,

were filled up with interminable prolixity of petty commentary upon one or two hundred cases. The court, bar and
every one were tired to death. He went home and told—
that he had made the greatest speech he had ever made in
his life."

From this judgment thus sweepingly made, with a sort
of oracular infallibility, if the occasion had been mentioned,
I apprehend an appeal might be safely made to those who
listened for three days to Mr. Pinkney. For, strange to say,
he never spoke in Annapolis without admiring audiences,
and the judges were always prompt to record their highest
appreciation of his power. In a letter to Francis W. Gilmer, April 2d, 1825, he writes further :

" His fame had a magnitude by refraction, which would
have been impaired by the publication of his speeches."

The letters, to which I take exception on the score of
propriety, because they are calculated to leave on the mind
of the reader the idea that Pinkney was disgustingly over-
bearing and jealous, while Wirt, his contemporary, was the
very impersonation of modesty and retirement, are to be
found on pages 80 Vol. II ; 119, do. ; 176, do. I again repeat, that I would most gladly have omitted this whole criticism on the work of Mr. Kennedy, if justice to the memory
of William Pinkney would have allowed. But that was not
possible. Thirty years had passed, since Mr. Pinkney was
laid in the grave, when, needlessly and without benefit to the
character of Wirt, his biographer gives publicity, not merely
to Wirt's depreciation of his rival, but to grave reflections
on his character. It will not do to say that these criticisms
(both severe in their tone and unkind) were subsequently
modified and changed. They were never so modified, as not
to be tinctured by the most transparent self-exaltation ; and
in their more objectionable features they were not modified
at all. The very name of Wirt gives importance to his opinions and statements ; and the superadded name of Kennedy

clothes them with additional authority. And surely, as the biographer has not hesitated to give all the perpetuity he can to the strictures on Mr. Pinkney and mere ex parte repetitions of conversations—no friend of Mr. Pinkney, in an attempt to write his life and vindicate his character, can be blamed for subjecting the criticism to the touchstone of a calm and impartial review, and entering a protest against those ex parte statements.

We must not be misunderstood. Mr. Kennedy and Mr. Wirt had a right to speak of Mr. Pinkney as they thought fit. I concede that right to the fullest extent. They were at liberty to dissect his mental calibre at pleasure. I complain not of the exercise of that right. But, having exercised it, and thereby submitted their own criticism to the world, they become in turn fair subjects of critical investigation, and no one has a right to complain if the result prove unsatisfactory or painful.

But I deny that Mr. Kennedy had a right to publish one-sided statements, that were never published in the lifetime of the person assailed.

Nil de mortuis nisi bonum, is a most admirable sentiment. The world may deny our claim to greatness or severely dissect our intellectual powers, if it please. But no man has a right to touch the character, unless upon charges made in the lifetime, and confronted with the accused, or on statements that have been submitted to the touchstone of full and fair investigation. A deeper wrong could not well have been inflicted on the memory of the lamented Wirt, than this indiscreet and improper publication. I can only once more regret, that it did not occur to the discriminating judgment of the biographer, that the supremacy of either of those illustrious men could never be satisfactorily settled by the assertions of either; and that he did not leave those letters in the privacy they were permitted to enjoy while Pinkney lived. They exhibit Mr. Wirt's character, which was in many respects worthy of the highest admiration, in a most unenviable light; and evince a weakness of jealousy upon which it is truly painful to animadvert.

N. B.—Some of the points in this portion of my memoir were introduced into an article I forwarded to the Literary World, which was published some time ago.

PINKNEY, A STATESMAN.

MR. PINKNEY's character in this aspect of it is not generally understood, and is not therefore properly appreciated. Before I enter upon a review of his conduct in the different embassages he filled, I propose to inquire what it was, which entitled him to the appellation of a statesman; in what school he was trained; and what were the mental and moral elements which combined to qualify him for the difficult and delicate functions that are always involved in the management and control of public affairs. He was a true-hearted American patriot, a sincere and ardent lover of his country, deeply versed in the grand principles of our glorious constitution, and a thorough master of every portion of its intricate and beautiful mechanism. He had studied the system in the writings of its august founders. Accustomed from infancy to the war-cry of the Revolution, his youthful imagination was fired with the thrilling associations of that giant struggle for freedom. He grew up in the meridian blaze of the period of '76. His profound knowledge of constitutional law enabled him, at a glance, to see how far any given measure comported with the dignity and true glory of the country, or put in jeopardy its substantial prosperity and success. He had the nicest conception of the powers of the General Government, and the separate jurisdiction and sovereignty of the States, and never for a moment lost sight of the boundary that divided the one from the other. No man was a truer, firmer, faster friend of the rights of the States, or viewed with a more jealous eye the least infringement of their clear constitutional prerogatives; and yet no man possessed a more admirable nationality of soul. He was out and out an American in all his views and principles. His spirit was as large as his country, and wherever the stars and stripes floated, through the whole extent of the national domain, he could exultingly say, with a full consciousness of the glory of the sentiment, "This is my country all." He was above the influence and dominion of sectional prejudices. Though a Southerner by birth, his noble heart beat high with the broadest nationality. The Union he prized as the proud palladium of our liberties, the fruitful source of all our past mercies, and the only hope of the still more glorious future. He saw in it the "seminal principle" of an unprecedented national exaltation, the more than germ of the most stupendous system of government the sun ever before shone upon. The union of independent and separate States—united in all that could give efficiency to the whole, while separate and sovereign in all that was essential to the largest desirable freedom of each—this union of equals for the purposes of mutual defence and glory, enlisted the purest sympathies of his soul, and called forth the mightiest strains of his eloquence. In his whole political career, he aspired to be the friend of the States in union; and nothing less than this broad nationality satisfied his ideas of what a true devotion to State rights required at his hands. He saw nothing but advancement, unparalleled success and far-reaching, illimitable prosperity, for the States, so long as they continued in a whole-souled fealty and devotion to the Union; while in the severance of that Union he saw nothing but the darkness and blackness of despotism, the most dismal and frightful chaos of anarchy and confusion. The following letter, written by Mr. Clay but a short time before his death, corroborates all that I have here stated, and beautifully expresses the confidence and admiration of one, who remembered to applaud the day that witnessed Mr. Pinkney's triumphant

vindication of the constitution in the discussion of the Missouri question.

"HAVANA, *March 29th*, 1851.

"MY DEAR SIR :—I request your acceptance of my
thanks for the Chart and History of Hayti, which you have
done me the favor to present to me. They relate to an
island, distinguished by great vicissitudes of prosperity and
adversity, and I shall take much pleasure in tracing them.
It is greatly to be regretted that an island so full of rich
resources could not be made more conducive to the supply
of the commerce and the consumption of our species.

" I beg your acceptance also of my acknowledgments
for your friendly consideration of me, and for your kind estimate (quite too high and flattering) of my public services.
On the recent perilous occasions in our councils, it was a
matter of great gratification and encouragement to have
been perfectly assured that the navy, as well as the army,
and the great mass of the people of the United States, were
true and faithful to that Union, which is at once the bond,
the security, and the glory of all.

" Had William Pinkney been alive, your illustrious relation, his eloquent voice would have been conspicuously and
effectively heard in the defence and support of that Union.

" With my best respects for your health, happiness, and
prosperity,

" I am, respectfully,
" Your obedient servant,
" Dr. Ninian Pinkney,   H. CLAY."
" U. S. Navy."

It was Mr. Pinkney's constant aim to be eminently just.
He scorned the questionable expedients so often resorted to
by petty politicians. Deeming honesty the crowning ornament of a diplomatist, and his country's honor the only safe
guiding star of public policy, he pursued his object with

bold independence and manly directness. Extraordinary quickness in comprehending the merits of a subject—extraordinary labor and patience of research in threading all its perplexing labyrinths, and extricating it from every thing extraneous or irrelevant—commanding and ready eloquence in enforcing his own deliberate and well-weighed conclusions —superiority to low and contemptible artifice—remarkable prudence and self-control in brushing away the " cobweb conceits " of shallow politicians—moral courage, the bravery of the heart, which is unappalled by difficulties and unawed in danger, and which always dares to assume responsibility and meet it—these all combined to make him a consummate statesman.

I speak now of his powers in the abstract—powers which a Washington was the first to discover, and a Jefferson, Madison, and Monroe were as prompt to appreciate and reward. If Mr. Pinkney had never been tried in the active duties of statesmanship, we might have confidently argued his pre-eminent fitness for the work from those well-known attributes of his character. Having been tried, let us now inquire how they were developed and exhibited. Was the fruit worthy of the tree ?

It will be remembered that his first appearance abroad was under the appointment of Washington, as commissioner on the part of the United States, under the 7th article of Jay's Treaty. The duties rendered under that appointment are recorded in history ; and it is not necessary to say more of them now, than that the result of his labors was the making award by the Board on the principles contended for by the American commissioners.

President Jefferson invited him to assist Mr. Monroe in the pending negotiations with Great Britain. His acceptance of this appointment subjected him to severe censure ; his motives were impugned, and his fidelity to his old political principles was called in question. I have shown, upon the authority of Mr. Jefferson's own letter, that the appointment came to him without solicitation, direct or indirect. The interests of the country seemed to call loudly for an extraordinary embassage, and the high character of Mr. Pinkney in England (which was the result of his former sojourn in that country) seemed to concur, with his known ability and prudence, in pointing him out as the very man for the position. Mr. Pinkney did not waver in devotion to his country's cause. In a spirit of noble self-sacrifice he stepped forth and laid on the altar of his country his large experience and the reputation he had already won. He was not the man to skulk from duty in such a crisis for a mere personal and selfish consideration, where principle and honor were to be neither compromised nor offered up in sacrifice. In his letter to Mr. Cooke, of Baltimore, of the 5th October, 1806, he thus eloquently and feelingly vindicates himself from those ungenerous imputations :

MR. PINKNEY TO MR. COOKE.

"LONDON, 5th October, 1806.

" My Dear Sir :—I am very much indebted to you for your truly kind letter of the 4th of August, which has just reached me. It contains the best proof in the world of your good opinion and regard. It speaks to me with candor, and, at the same time that it betrays the partiality of a long-tried friendship, guards me against the disappointment to which a sanguine and credulous temper might expose me, and enables me to anticipate in season the misconceptions and calumnies which are preparing for me. This anticipation is certainly wholesome ; but it is unpleasant notwithstanding. The language of reproach is new to me, and I fear I shall not learn to bear it with a good grace from a country which I have ardently loved and faithfully served with the best years of my life. The consciousness that I do not, and cannot deserve it, consoles me in one view, while it mortifies me in another. I am proud of the unqualified conviction of my heart and understanding, that I am incapable of any thing that an honest man should blush to avow; but it gives me pain to find that no purity of motive or integrity of conduct can afford shelter in this world from the vilest and most disgusting imputations. Our country is young, and ought to be generous and charitable, and I believe that the great bulk of our people are so. But I do not need to have my actions *charitably* interpreted. I ask only a *just* construction of them; I care not how rigorous, if it be not malignant. It seemed natural to suppose, that putting former character out of the question, the circumstances under which I last came abroad would at least secure me from the suspicion of selfish views and time-serving policy; and I am, of course, surprised that a man can be found to infer, from my acceptance of the arduous trust in which I am now engaged, 'that I have deserted my principles and my friends, and pledged myself to support the party in power and their measures to every extent?' What principles, in God's name, and what friends have I deserted? The plain matter of fact is thus: A great national crisis occurs, which requires, or is supposed to require, an extraordinary foreign mission. The President, whom I may be said to know only by character, offers this important charge to me. I give up my profession. I surrender all my hopes of future fortune. I forego a second time, and *for ever*, the expectation of placing my numerous and helpless family in a state of independence, and accept this anxious trust, which, instead of promising pecuniary emolument, is likely to bring with it a heavy pecuniary loss, and which, so far from promising to do me honor, puts in hazard the stock of reputation I have before acquired. Now what abandonment of principle is there in all this? I am willing to admit that I may have acted improvidently, as regards myself and my children, and that I may have overrated my capacity, and undertaken a task to which I am not competent. But I am quite sure that I have not deviated from the path of honor in which, with an approving conscience, I have walked from my boyish days. My appointment is known to have been as completely unsolicited as ever appointment was from the beginning of the world. It came to me wholly unsought. It is to the credit of the government that it did so. It came to me unclogged by any terms or conditions. They who talk of a *pledge* on my part, as the consideration of it, know that they insinuate a base and detestable falsehood. No such pledge, no pledge of any kind, was ever proposed to me. I was treated with honor, and delicacy, and confidence ; and I have a firm reliance that I shall continue to be so treated. An attempt to treat me otherwise would drive me in a moment from office, as it would have prevented me from accepting it. As to this *pledge*, the slander is too gross to be believed. I have an intimate persuasion, founded upon a consciousness which I cannot mistake, of integrity without blemish, that no man would undertake to suggest to me so vile and infamous a compact as the price of public station. The acceptance of my appointment may, indeed, *imply* a pledge ; and I am content that it shall be taken to be as large as honor will permit. In its utmost size, whatever that may be, I will faithfully redeem it, and should be ashamed to have it supposed that I could shrink from a duty so pressing and obvious. The foolish, and often hypocritical cant about apostacy and desertion of principles, shall not frighten me from the steady and manly course to which this duty directs me. I have never professed any principles with which my present situation, connected as it unquestionably is with the great interests of my country, is in the slightest degree inconsistent. I find nothing in the objects of it, in the means by which I am instructed to accomplish those objects, or in the measures of the government preparatory to the mission, which I do not entirely approve, and have not uniformly approved.

"As to the friends I have deserted, who are they? I accepted my appointment, as far as I could ascertain, with the entire concurrence of my friends of both parties ; and I rejoice that I have friends of all parties. It was that flattering concurrence which encouraged me to hope that the anxiety inseparable from my undertaking would not be aggravated by unjust and unfeeling prejudices, and that I should have no difficulties to struggle with, but such as I should find here. The affection of many of my friends induced them to express their fears that, as an individual, I should suffer by the mission. But they did not conceal their approbation of my appointment, and did not intimate that any but prudential considerations ought to restrain me from accepting it. I have since been frequently consoled by the recollection of this, the most interesting period of my life."

It will thus appear that Mr. Pinkney embarked in this great national mission, strong in his own integrity and with a bosom glowing with patriotic fervor and zeal. Let us now see what he did or attempted to do, in what spirit and with what ability he conducted his part of the negotiation—and in all that is here said, let it be understood, that so long as his illustrious colleague Mr. Monroe remained, he bore a most distinguished part. They moved in the matter like men above the influence of petty and blinding prejudices, with the broad feelings of American citizens in charge of American rights. With what care he watched the progress of events, and with what solicitude he guarded the national honor, and vindicated the rights of the country, may be seen through the whole period of the negotiation ; but nowhere more conspicuously than in the letter he addressed to President Madison as early as the 31st December, 1807.

"The attitude which our government is now to take,

will fix our destiny for ever ; and my trust is strong and confident that both will be worthy of the high name of our
country.

"In my public letters I have ventured to intimate my
opinions as to the conduct which the crisis demands from
us.   You will excuse me, if in a private letter I speak with
more freedom.

" It will, I sincerely hope, be the solemn conviction of
every man in America (as it is mine) that it has become impossible, without the entire loss of our honor, and the sacrifice
of every thing which it is our duty to protect, to submit in
the smallest degree to that extravagant system of maritime
oppression (proceeding more from jealousy of our rising
greatness than from motives actually avowed) by which Great
Britain every day exemplifies in various modes the favorite
doctrine of her infatuated advisers, that Power and Rightful
Dominion are equivalent terms,

"No man can deprecate war upon light and frivolous
grounds more sincerely than I should do.   But if war arises
out of our resistance to this pernicious career of arrogance
and selfishness, which, while it threatens our best interests
with ruin, is even more insulting than it is injurious, and
more humiliating than it is destructive, can it be doubted
that our cause is a just one, or that we shall be able and
willing to maintain it as a great and gallant nation ought
to do ?

"Our government has shown a laudable solicitude, for
peace with all the world, and has acted wisely in its efforts
to preserve it.   But the time has arrived when it seems to
be certain that we must yield up all that we prize of reputation, of fortune, and of power, to the naval despotism of
this country, or meet it with spirit and resolution ; if not
by war, at least by some act of a strong and decisive character.

" The argument against resistance to British aggression,

founded upon supposed danger from France, if Great Britain should be greatly weakened by that resistance, proves too much, and is otherwise false in fact and reasoning.

"It may be admitted, however, that France is a subject of apprehension to America as well as to Europe ; but are we on that account to suffer with patience every wrong which Great Britain, stimulated by the jealousy of her merchants, or the avarice of her Navy, or the pride of conscious power, may inflict upon us? Such a state of abject slavery to our peers, such a tame surrender of our rights, as the price of British protection against possible and contingent peril, would be a thousand times more degrading than if we were now in the maturity of our years to return openly to the dependence of our colonial infancy upon the guardianship of the parent country. If we once listen to this base and pusillanimous suggestion, we have passed under the yoke and are no longer a nation of freemen ; we shall not only be despised and trampled upon by all the world, but, what is of infinitely more importance, we shall despise ourselves—France will justly become our irreconcilable enemy, and Great Britain will only be encouraged and enabled to stab to the heart the prosperity which she envies, and the power which she begins to dread. By a different course, that which suits with the manly character and the great resources of the American people, we shall show that we rely on ourselves for protection. We shall maintain, with the *gallantry* and firmness which have heretofore characterized us, our station among the powers of the earth. We shall check, while there is yet time, the usurpation of Great Britain, without destroying her salutary strength."

This noble letter breathes a lofty confidence in the integrity of his country's cause. It repudiates indignantly the idea of any compromise of her rights, and points out and severely rebukes the arrogance and presumption of England's claims upon the high seas, and sounds the tocsin of war sooner than submit to a surrender of our rights, by a timid faltering policy, or a base compromise. Mark the date of this letter, at the same time you analyze its tone and temper, and you will see that none saw more clearly or resented more eloquently the odiousness of the decrees in council than Mr. Pinkney, or availed themselves of an earlier opportunity in giving full and free expression to their views and feelings. Speaking to the constitutional head of this government, he spoke with the bold independence of an American citizen in charge of American rights.

In this mission he was unsuccessful. Why? Not because he had failed to exhaust both argument and appeal in his efforts to awaken a sense of justice and true enlightened policy in the bosom of those, whose counsels guided England in that eventful day. Not because he had waxed negligent in making prompt and manly protest against her monstrous aggressions, and tardy and insulting slowness to make amends for the wrongs perpetrated.

True it is, he was under injunction not to jeopard the peace of the countries, by precipitate action or the too free expression of his own excited and wounded pride. Not less true it is that he did restrain, with admirable self-control, his indignation, while compelled to witness aggressions repeated without redress, and diplomatic finesse pushed almost to the verge of open indignity. He did it because it was the will of his government it should be done, not because the peace of the world made it desirable that endurance should be carried to the farthest possible point.

The conduct pursued by our ministers during that critical and most difficult negotiation, beautifully contrasts with that pursued by the English ministry and their deputed agents. The English journalists of that era were compelled, in the hour of calm review and cool investigation, to denounce in tones of indignant rebuke the unmanly and disingenuous policy of a Canning and a Wellesley; and seemed to amuse themselves at our cost, for what they supposed was the weak credulity and want of penetration exhibited by those, who were then in charge of American rights at the court of St. James. A dispassionate examination of the subjoined correspondence will show that they were as correct in the former opinion, as they were egregiously mistaken in the latter. Mr. Pinkney before he embarked on the mission had dissected England's policy with the skill of a master, and exposed her rapacious and grasping ambition and wanton infraction of the law of nations in her aggressions on the freedom of the seas, with resistless eloquence and power of argument. He entered on the mission with open eyes and judgment thoroughly informed. He needed no one to admonish him or put him on his guard. In Mr. Monroe, he found a clear-headed, enlightened, experienced American statesman, in every respect equal to the high trust confided to him. And in all the conferences they had with the British negotiators did he and Mr. Monroe set forth the claims of the United States, and repel the views and pretensions of England. In their frequent interviews with Lords Holland and Auckland, they displayed not less ability than they did zeal and moderation in the assertion of our national honor and rights, and did all that human eloquence could do to secure a full and satisfactory adjustment of all the points in controversy. On 31st Dec., 1806, they concluded a treaty. As that treaty has been the subject of much abuse, I beg leave to insert a few passages from a letter of Mr. Monroe, dated February 28th, 1808, written in its defence.

"The idea (says Mr. Monroe) entertained by the public is, that the rights of the United States were abandoned by the American commissioners in the late negotiation, and that their seamen were left by tacit acquiescence, if not by formal renunciation, to depend for their safety on the mercy of the British cruisers. I have on the contrary always believed and still do believe that the ground on which that interest was placed by the paper of the British commissioners, of Nov. 8th, 1806, and the explanations which accompanied it, was both honorable and advantageous to the United States; that it contained a concession in their favor on the part of Great Britain on the great principle in contestation never before made by a formal and obligatory act of the government, which was highly favorable to their interest; and that it also imposed on her the obligation to conform her practice under it, till a more complete arrangement should be concluded, to the just claims of the United States."

Again. "It is evident that the rights of the United States were expressly to be reserved and not abandoned, as has been most erroneously supposed; that the negotiation on the subject of impressment was to be postponed for a limited time, and for a special object only, and to be revived as soon as that object was accomplished; and in the interim that the practice of impressment was to correspond essentially with the views and interests of the United States." —*State Paper*, vol. 6, page 421.

The whole of this long letter is worthy of a perusal, and less than the whole cannot well exhibit the ground upon which the defence of that treaty is based. This treaty Mr. Jefferson refused to ratify. He did not so much as consult the Senate upon it; but took upon himself the sole responsibility of its rejection. In Hildreth's History of the United States, Vol. V., p. 656, &c., its wisdom, sound policy and propriety the most triumphantly vindicated. "The British negotiators declared that although the ministry could not venture to give up by formal treaty the right of impressment on the high seas, yet that special instructions should be given and enforced for the observance of the greatest caution against subjecting any American born citizen to molestation or injury, and that in case of any such injury, upon representation of it, the promptest redress should be afforded. These assurances were reduced to writing, suggesting at the same time, that while *both parties thus reserved these rights*, this stipulation might *answer temporarily.*   *   *   *   Having obtained every concession on the subject of impressment short of a renunciation by the British government of the claim of right to take British subjects out of American vessels—a claim going back to an indefinite antiquity, strongly supported by the national feeling, and thought at the present crisis of European affairs essential to the national safety—and having thus placed the United States as to this question on ground, short indeed of what justice demanded and perhaps of their rights, but the best, which at present there was the slightest prospect of obtaining ; under these circumstances, imitating the example of Jay and of the commission to France in 1799, Monroe and Pinkney did not deem it consistent either with common prudence or common sense to relinquish the advantage thus secured, and along with it other advantages in prospect, and from a too strict adherence to instructions to leave the country, by breaking up the negotiation, exposed to vast maritime losses, to the continuance and aggravation of present misunderstandings, and to imminent risk of war." This is the verdict passed by faithful and impartial history upon that important transaction. And after the letter of Monroe, and the satisfactory exposition of Hildreth, I feel that I can safely intrust it to the judgment of posterity. True it is, it did leave the question of impressment unsettled. But what became of that question, and how does it stand at the present moment ? It did not surrender the right. It yielded up nothing. It only postponed to future negotiation the adjustment, securing in the meanwhile the most important and desirable modification of its use, in its oppressive bearing upon our interests. Mr. Pinkney and Mr. Monroe were as deeply sensible that the treaty did not secure all that could be desired or reasonably or equitably asked, as Mr. Jefferson or its bitterest assailant. They were called upon to decide between two things, neither of which were to be desired.   They would have spurned, as indignantly as any, a dishonorable adjustment of our difficulties with England.   They felt the injustice of the impressment as practised by her, and would never have consented to a tame surrender of our earnest and decisive protest against that right, as a violation of the law of nations too flagrant to be justified by any supposed exigencies of national defence, that could be pleaded in its extenuation.   They were willing, upon the positive assurance of the British government previously given, that it should be used in essential correspondence with the views of the United States, to leave it among the questions not settled ; not because they were disposed to submit to the practice, but solely, because they thought the permitting it to pass by for the present preferable to war, at a time when we were so little prepared to encounter it.   War came at last, when negotiation failed, and it was hailed with both pride and pleasure by Mr. Pinkney, because the national honor required it, and the patience and forbearance of negotiation had proved inoperative to wring from England the proper redress for wrongs perpetrated.   It was a war that covered our gallant little Navy with deathless glory, and proved to the world that England was no longer mistress of the seas.   A new power was upon that mighty element, capable of maintaining its flag untarnished, whose motto was " Don't give up the ship."

What became of Mr. Jefferson's *sine qua non ?* without which he refused to ratify this treaty.   Was the right of impressment abandoned or surrendered by the treaty that actually followed the war ?   It is as yet among the things not given up.   It is a right, unexercised I grant, and one that will never again be exercised, as far as our flag is concerned.   But the only treaty that reduced it to a mere barren abstract claim of right was the thunder of our little navy on the seas.   Neither Mr. Monroe nor Mr. Pinkney were fully convinced that it would be otherwise settled,

however much they may have hoped and wished that justice
and a sense of right would ultimately prevail in the British
councils ; and, without its settlement, neither of them would
or could have rested satisfied. They did the best they could
in the then state of public affairs, and, in no proper sense
of the word, did they forget what was due to the American
flag, or the brave tars that bore it so gallantly on the seas.
They were not willing to throw away the chances of an
honorable peace by rashness or inconsideration. The postponement for a while of the right of impressment, they
thought, would result in no serious injury to the United
States, after the explicit acknowledgment that, until settled,
it would be used in accordance with our views of interest.
I think, with no impeachment of Mr. Jefferson, that Pinkney and Monroe acted the wiser part.

It is delightful, in recalling, for the vindication of Mr.
Pinkney's character, the odious policy that was pursued by
Great Britain towards the United States prior to the war
of 1812, to reflect that these two great countries are now
bound to each other by the strongest ties of interest and of
amity, which, it is to be hoped, for the sake of the world,
neither of them may be ever tempted to forget or snap
asunder. Speaking the same language, avowedly attached
to the same great principles of political freedom, eminently
commercial in their spirit and destiny, and thereby qualified
to become leaders in the diffusion of light and knowledge
the world over, they may, with exulting pride, forget that
old feuds ever existed, and henceforth live to honor and
respect each other, and work in concert for the welfare of
the nations. We have an interest and a home in the land
of Shakspeare and of Milton. We·love the old cathedrals
and good old church of England. We study the decisions
of her noble and enlightened courts, and claim a copartner-
ship in her splendid literature and stupendous national
glory. And we flatter ourselves that the day has come

when the mother may justly pride herself on the daughter, and feel that we are more than the recipients of her light and lustre. An Englishman may now look upon the land of Washington, and bless God that the name and fame of England are renewed in the name and fame of the United States. The glory of the past of either will not compare with their future, if peace prevail in their mutual councils, and their flags wave over seas covered by their mutual commerce in beauteous harmony. May their towering strength know of no competition but that of friendly rivalry. May their race of glory be henceforth and for ever in parallel lines, whose interests and true national exaltation manifestly lie in one and the same direction.

It becomes now my painful duty in this connection to examine the statements of a work, which was widely circulated at the time it was issued, entitled "The Memoirs of Jefferson." This work was published in 1809. Its authorship was never, that I know of, avowed. It contains very severe and acrimonious animadversions upon the character and conduct of Mr. Pinkney. It charges him with gross duplicity and falsehood. The writer does not mince his words. Destitute of the caution that is usually observed by those who delight in detraction, he is prodigal of his facts in proof, and deals with astounding freedom with dates, those honest tell-tales against such as use them carelessly. I propose to inquire into the nature of the charges made, and the proofs adduced, reaffirming that noble sentiment which this writer had the rashness to indorse, " that if a history wants truth, it wants every thing that can recommend it ;" a sentiment which is more beautifully expressed by Cicero: "Historia. est testis temporum, *lux veritatis, vita memoriæ, magistra vitæ, nuntia vetustatis.*" I shall permit him to speak for himself, judge him by his own words, and then submit his so-called statements to the touchstone of stubborn facts. The author thus writes :

" With this view, Mr. Pinkney was sent to the Court of
St. James, armed, one hand with a falsehood, and the other
with an impudent absurdity."—Vol. II., p. 392.

Again : " On the 10th of October, Mr. Pinkney sent an
answer to Mr. Canning's letter, in which an amount of more
than twenty pages of very large sized octavo, in print, was
occupied in a vain effort to justify the negotiation from the
charge of having failed from his neglecting to make an offer
from government to repeal the embargo ; but in which,
when connected and compared with other parts of the correspondence respecting the negotiation, he appeared manifestly guilty of mistakes or misrepresentations.

" On our first conference (said he to Mr. Canning) *I told
you explicitly,* that *the substance* of what I *suggested* (viz.
that the British orders being repealed, we would suspend
the embargo) *was from my government ;* but the manner
of conducting and illustrating it was all my own. *I even
repeated to you the words of my instructions,* as they were
upon my memory. After this, however doubtful a person
might be as to the assertion of Mr. Pinkney that he had
told Mr. Canning explicitly, that the substance of his suggestion was from his government, he would have a right, at
least, to conclude, that the written authority on which Mr.
Pinkney so confidentially relied, and the words of which he
said he had repeated to Mr. Canning, did at least contain the
words to bear him out. When those very instructions, however, come to be inspected, they are found not to contain one
single word of that import ; but, on the contrary, directions to
the contrary. For his instructions on this head, Mr. Pinkney, it seems, was referred by the Secretary of State (Mr.
Madison) to his (Mr. Madison's) answer to Mr. Erskine, on
the subject of the British orders in council ; and the words
there are as follows : ' The United States are well warranted
in looking for a speedy revocation of a system which is every
day augmenting the mass of injury for which the United

States have the best claims to redress? And then, continues Mr. Madison to Mr. Pinkney himself, '*still it is to be
understood, that while the insult offered in the attack on the
Chesapeake remains unexpiated, you are not to pledge or
commit your government, to consider a recall of the orders in
council as a ground on which a removal of the existing restrictions on the commerce of the United States with Great
Britain may be justly expected.*' Here, then, is a positive
order not to give the British government reason·so much as
to expect that the embargo should be repealed, even though
the orders in council should be rescinded.

"Thus, Mr. Pinkney stands convicted of misrepresentation by the very instructions from which he pretended to have
repeated the words to substantiate the truth of his assertion.
No such words were in it; but words directly the reverse;
so that if he had, as he asserted he did, explicitly told Mr.
Canning that the substance of his suggestions, respecting
the repeal of the embargo, came from his government, he
was guilty of misrepresentation; and if he did make such a
proposal, he was no less guilty of a breach of the orders of
his government, which forbade him to give any such expectation. What makes the matter worse was that Mr. Pinkney
himself, in his letters to Mr. Madison, recognized the policy;
—in one of the month of May, he tells him that he had
taken care to make no proposal. There is still stronger evidence of Mr. Pinkney's conviction, that he was not authorized by his government to offer the repeal of the embargo;
for on the 5th of June he wrote another letter, in which he
informed Mr. Madison that he was to have an interview with
Mr. Canning in a few days, that he would then press the
suggestion of repealing the embargo law. 'But,' adds this
worthy representative of his *honest and honorable cabinet*, 'I
shall, *for obvious reasons*, do this informally, as my own
act.' And further on in the same letter, he says, '*You may

*be assured that I will not commit our government by any
thing I may do or say.'*

" From the whole of this, it is evident that Mr. Pinkney
not only entered into the views of his employers to cajole
the British minister, but even debased himself by palpable
falsehood, to cover them from the effects of that indignation
which their country must necessarily feel, on finding that,
while they affected to negotiate, they only meant to insult
and betray."

Let us now look at the charge and the proof. Is it true,
or is it false ? It is charged that Mr. Pinkney exceeded his
instructions, and endeavored to deceive Mr. Canning by falsely
quoting from them. To substantiate the charge and convict
Mr. Pinkney of a palpable disobedience of the orders of his
government and the perpetration of a gross fraud on Mr.
Canning, this writer affirms that Mr. Pinkney's instructions
were contained in the answer of Mr. Madison to Mr. Erskine,
which made the atonement for the insult offered in the attack on the Chesapeake a *sine qua non*, without which no
expectation of the suspension of the embargo was to be encouraged, éven though the decrees in council should be rescinded. By a reference to the 7th vol. of State Papers,
p. 28, it will be seen, that the letter of Mr. Madison to
Mr. Pinkney, dated April 4th, 1808, contained those instructions. The atonement for the insult offered in the attack on the Chesapeake was made in that letter the *sine
qua non*. Thus far the writer states the truth. The letter
of Mr. Pinkney to Mr. Canning, dated October 10th, 1808,
is adduced in evidence. In it he affirms, that in their first
interview he had notified Mr. Canning of the intention of
our government to suspend the embargo in case the orders
in council were repealed, without any reference to the affair
of the Chesapeake. And that this notification was made in
obedience to the instructions he had received from government. This also is truly stated. These instructions,

this author maintains, do not bear Mr. Pinkney out. They neither sustain him in the assurance given to Mr. Canning, nor the assertion that in giving that assurance he quoted from them correctly. " No such words as Mr. Pinkney pretended to have repeated, were in his letter of instructions, but words directly the reverse." So that "if he had, as he asserted he did, expressly told Mr. Canning that the substance of his suggestions respecting the suspension of the embargo came from his government, he was *guilty* of *misrepresentation ;* and if he did make the proposal, he was not less guilty of a breach of the orders of his government, which forbade him to give any such expectation."

This seems to be a very formidable impeachment. It looks very like the truth. Such a minute and scathing analysis of facts and dates, would seem to indicate a conscious rectitude of purpose and a deep conviction of exactness. Before I proceed farther in the investigation, I beg leave to call attention to another fact contained in this letter of October 10 (concerning which this author is unaccountably silent), because it is material to the issue between us; and that is, that this first interview was held on the 29th of JUNE.

Now I deny that the letter of the 4th of April or the instructions contained in it, which this author quotes with so much seeming exultation, *constituted* the *authority* on *which Mr. Pinkney made* his *overture* in *the interview* of *June 29th ;* and I have the proof to sustain the denial. In a letter, dated April 30th, which may be found in Vol. VII. State Papers, p. 32, Mr. Madison thus wrote to Mr. Pinkney :

" In order to entitle the British government to a discontinuance of the embargo, as it applies to Great Britain, it is evident that all its decrees as well those of January, 1807, as of November, 1807, ought to be rescinded as they apply to the United States, &c. *Should the British govern-*

ment take this course you may authorize an expectation, that the President will within a reasonable time give effect to the authority vested in him on the subject of the embargo laws." This letter was received *anterior* to the interview of the 29th of June, and subsequent to the letter of April the 4th. It was intended to control the overture made by Mr. Pinkney, and it did control it. For in the letter of Mr. Pinkney to Mr. Madison, dated August 4th, he speaks of this very letter of instructions of April 30th, as having been received by him previously to that interview, and used on that occasion. Mr. Pinkney tells Mr. Madison, from whom his instructions were received, and to whom he reported his official conduct, that he made his proposal, which is so summarily condemned by this writer as exceeding his instructions, on the express authority of this letter of the 30th of April. See State Papers, Vol. VII. p. 43.

What now becomes of the assertion that no such words as Mr. Pinkney stated were contained in his instructions, were to be found in them ? And what must be said of an author, who confounds instructions contained in a letter of one date with those of another, and in his eager partisan zeal to find topics of bitter accusation never chances to stumble upon letters, that are in almost immediate juxtaposition, in which the party accused states what he had done, and why he had done it. There was a violation of orders of government in the interview of June 29th, says this author ; and a contemptible attempt at fraud, inasmuch as the instructions of April 4th explicitly required the settlement of the affair of the Chesapeake as the *sine qua non*. There was no violation of the orders of government and no attempt at the perpetration of a fraud, says truthful history, inasmuch as the instructions which Mr. Pinkney expressly declared he followed in that interview are contained in the letter of April the 30th, though not in that of April the 4th, and are rightly quoted.

The proof upon which this author rested his grave allegation, is supposed by him to be strengthened by the fact, that in two letters (one of May, the other of the 5th of June) Mr. Pinkney professes his intention to act in accordance with the instructions of April the 4th. But this, so far from affording proof that Mr. Pinkney exceeded his instructions, proves the very reverse. It shows conclusively that he adhered most rigidly to them, for up to June 5th there is demonstrative evidence that the letter of the 30th of April had not been received. In that very letter of June 5th, which this author had the audacity to quote, Mr. Pinkney acknowledges the receipt of the letter of April 4th. Of course that of April the 30th could not have been received. This letter of April 4th was the only one acted upon up to the 5th of June, and for the best of all reasons, because it was the only one received at that time. The letter of April the 30th, which totally changed the ground and nature of the instructions, was received however before the interview of June the 29th, as Mr. Pinkney declares in his letter of August the 4th.

All these letters were accessible to this anonymous author, and examined by him. It is therefore difficult to conceive of the disingenuousness and want of candor, that pervade his work. When a man so far forgets himself and his own sense of honor and of right, as to hurl accusations of the most offensive kind against the official conduct of another ; and stands convicted, by the very authorities he adduces, of the grossest ignorance or the most glaring misrepresentations, he entitles himself to but little mercy. His ignorance may shield him from the severer condemnation, but it cannot save his book from the infamy assigned to it by his own indorsement of the sentence, " that if a history wants truth it wants every thing that can recommend it." How emphatic are the words of Johnson, " There is such a thing as mistaking the venom of the shaft for the vigor of the bow. It is not hard to be sarcastic in a mask. If we leave such a writer only his merits, where will be his praise?"

Mr. Pinkney was not insensible to the fetters that restrained him in his correspondence with Canning. He was hampered by the exceeding difficulties of his position. Had he been free to address Mr. Canning, as at a subsequent period he did Lord Wellesley, in the strain his own feelings dictated, he would have shown that in sarcasm he was not inferior to that eminent statesman, as he had proved himself to be more than his equal in power of argument and frankness of disposition. If ever honor and a scrupulous conscientiousness adorned the diplomatic conduct of any minister, they did that of the gentleman thus bitterly assailed. I exultingly point to the correspondence hereunto annexed, and am satisfied that it will be found upon examination to be not less conspicuous for high, honorable, manly feeling, than pre-eminent ability. It will bear a favorable comparison with that of any other period of the republic marked by equal hazard, delicacy and difficulty. He uniformly maintained that the embargo was "a measure of wise and peaceful precaution, adopted under the view of reasonably anticipated peril." He was a profound admirer and consistent supporter of the embargo and the non-importation act; and without entering upon the discussion of its merits or demands, I beg leave to introduce to the public for the first time an article of singular force and ability found among the few surviving papers of Mr. Pinkney. It was his habit to throw off hastily his views of such important measures, and then throw them aside. Those who are accustomed to review our past history, will remember that those measures produced at the time a profound sensation in the country. The embargo excited the Eastern States to a most fearful degree, and the non-importation act was not less bitterly opposed. The embargo was the policy of Jefferson's administration, and was laid on the 23d of December, 1807. Its character to respect and its title to support, as the wisest measure that could at that time be adopted, it is not my province to discuss. Suffice it to say, that it was repealed on the 1st of March, 1809, and that a sort of substitute for it was found in the non-intercourse act. Mr. Pinkney thus wrote :

"Will that miserable shadow of a system, called the non-intercourse act, sink even below its own inherent weakness, as we know it will, by the dislike of many and the indifference of all, be such an instrument as our government ought to wield against the most alarming and pernicious of all the pretensions of a jealous and encroaching power—pretensions which, if once allowed to gain the sanction of precedent, can only be beaten down by force ?

" The embargo was a noble and magnificent effort, suited to the extraordinary occasion by which it was suggested, and adequate if persevered in to all its purposes. That great measure being abandoned, no half-way scheme, of the same family, can ever hope to stand in its place, and be effectual.

" The non-intercourse act may furnish incentives to commercial frauds and fuel to faction—it may render government odious by its penalties, and its cause contemptible by its feebleness—it may display anger without spirit, and a more than Christian patience under wrongs which it is forward to proclaim—it may combine a practical submission to injury and insult, with that show and bustle of resentment which produces nearly all the losses and more than the possible disgraces of war without its glory or its graces. It may do all this—but the United States can never stand behind so mean a contrivance and affect to call it resistance, where a *single* power is engaged in systematic attempts to push others from the seas and to cover them with dishonor.

" Nothing seems to me to be more clear, than that such a measure does just enough to demonstrate that we ought to do more. It is at once a Manifesto—and a Capitulation. It struts at the same time that it truckles, and it is so contrived that what it says is the severest censure upon the nothing which it does.

" Every reproach which was falsely cast upon the embargo belongs by indisputable title to this, its crippled and bastard progeny. While France and England, agreeing in nothing else, were in conspiracy to persecute our commerce and violate our neutral rights, the embargo was not only our natural, but our only resource. It promised to be successful when war promised nothing but ruin—and it would have been successful, but that time and prosperity had alloyed our virtue and unfitted us for such a trial. If we had elected war, we must have thrown down the gauntlet in a paroxysm of romantic courage to both England and France ; but it was our business to perceive, and our government did perceive, that the combination of those two gigantic powers in the work of our oppression, made any experiment for reconciling peace with resistance not only prudent but honorable. Any other measure than the embargo would, in such circumstances, have been madness or cowardice. For no others were in our choice but war with both aggressors, or submission to both ; with the certainty too, that that submission would in its progress either lead to war, or to a state of abject degradation."

The letter of President Jefferson, dated August 5th, 1809, expressive of his satisfaction in noting both the matter and manner with which Mr. Pinkney discharged his public duties ; and the unwillingness of Mr. Madison to allow him to return to the United States, at his own urgent request, are his highest vindication.

Success does not always prove the measure of ability and skill employed in negotiation, or the merit of the claims to be adjudicated. England was at that time the proud mistress of the seas. Her sway on that mighty element was

undisputed. She was battling with the powers of France in
a death struggle. She was pushing forward her enterprising
commerce with jealous activity on every sea ; and she looked
with evident suspicion and displeasure on our rising maritime
power. It was with England thus circumstanced in the full
flush of her nautical skill and prowess, "whose drum beat
was echoed" wherever the wail of ocean was heard, that Mr.
Pinkney had to treat ; and the question was one which
touched at once her pride and vaunted supremacy. His
failure does him no discredit as a statesman. He pursued
his work with a steadiness, industry, firmness and ability,
always equal to the occasion, and never allowed himself to
be seduced into chicanery or duplicity by the hopes of ulterior
ends. He was above intrigue, and in the firm belief that
honesty is the only becoming national policy, he stood forth
the plain honest Republican, in the midst of the intrigues
of courts, and the hollow professions of those who represented them.

None knew better than he how to scathe and rebuke oppression and wrong, or could see more thoroughly through
the craftiness, that sometimes disfigures the diplomatic conduct of a Canning and Wellesley. He bore much for his
country's sake, and the love of peace ; for he was emphatically a man of peace. He took no pleasure in sounding the
tocsin of war. But still the letter of December 31st, 1807,
and the whole of his diplomatic correspondence show, that
he loved not peace, when it called for the sacrifice of national
honor and consistency. He no sooner saw that negotiation
must prove fruitless, and that English pride and arrogance
must be humbled before justice could be secured, than he
returned, and aroused his countrymen to war.

There was a beautiful combination of urbanity and firmness, courtesy and independence, a patient spirit of endurance, and keen instinctive repugnance to what was wrong,
in the political character of Mr. Pinkney. So far as I know,

there is not one expression which need cause the most fastidious of his countrymen to blush, or give occasion to the most unrelenting of his opponents to afford even a momentary exultation.

Mr. Pinkney's great abilities, and unparalleled patience of investigation, and keen discrimination of character, and thorough comprehension of all the great questions that at that time agitated and disturbed the world, are not in my opinion to be put in comparison with his love of truth and justice. If intrigue, the ability to prosecute ends in themselves doubtful or manifestly wrong by means not less doubtful and immoral, be constituents in the character of a statesman ; then Mr. Pinkney was no statesman. He scorned to gain an end by tortuous means ; and would have retired instantly, in disgust, from a public service, whose policy he did not believe to be just and upright. His moral perceptions were most delicately attuned, and there pervades his whole foreign correspondence, like a thread of silver hue, a most admirable love of justice and abhorrence of wrong. Let the correspondence speak for itself, and I am silent. Were a witness, above and beyond his correspondence, necessary to enforce this impression of his character upon the heart of his countrymen, we have it. It was a British statesman of distinction who said of him in Parliament, " that he was a man of sound sense and judgment, of an able and astute mind, and of highest reputation ;—that he had conducted himself during his residence in the country in a manner most honorable to himself and likely to benefit both nations—at all times taking the most impartial views of the different interests concerned, his conduct, though firm, had been most conciliatory. Firm to his purpose, and able to elucidate the subjects under discussion, he had never failed in time, punctuality, or mode of procedure in his mission."— *Olive Branch*, p. 356.

This voluntary and noble tribute from a distinguished

stranger, expressed with a nervous comprehensiveness of style and a boldness of panegyric, that cannot but be admired, found an eloquent echo in the following beautiful tribute from the pen of Judge Story. The accomplished American jurist speaks of him as " one who, while abroad, honored his country by an *unparalleled display of diplomatic science;* and on his return illuminated the halls of justice with an eloquence of argument and depth of learned research that have not been exceeded in our day."—*Story* (Vol. I. 276).

A single glance into the Neapolitan mission—Mr. Pinkney's management of affairs on that occasion has been the topic of severe criticism in a high quarter. A writer in the *North American* (Vol. XXI. p. 272), in a quite elaborate review, seems to think that he was caught like a lion in the toils of a wily Neapolitan functionary; and is disposed to condemn him for the exhibition of a weak credulity, that was but too easily snared by the crafty and designing. But what are the facts in the case, and how do they sustain this criticism? I greatly mistake the force of the evidence, if it does not prove, not want of capacity or deficiency of shrewdness in the minister, but want of discernment in the reviewer.

The object of Mr. Pinkney's mission to Naples was, to obtain indemnity for losses sustained by the illegal seizure and confiscation of property belonging to our citizens by the Neapolitan government.

He was instructed to manifest a spirit of conciliation towards the government of Naples.

That Mr. Pinkney acted with great promptitude, secured an early audience, and followed it up with marked decision and firmness, the correspondence conclusively proves. He set forth at once, in a letter of signal ability, published in this memoir, the demands and expectations of our government. The discussion, though temperate and respectful, is perfectly conclusive. It leaves no ground for cavil ; no room for dispute. It must rank, in the estimation of all disinterested and impartial judges, as one of the most lucid and masterly expositions of the subject in controversy that ever emanated from a representative of our glorious Union abroad. His presence in the kingdom, he very well knew, had caused great uneasiness and perplexity. The smallness of the resources of the Neapolitan government, and the extent of our claim, were well calculated to agitate and embarrass the king and his advisers. Mr. Pinkney determined to deepen this impression, and, instead of useless conferences with a minister, who could adjust nothing in dispute, he sent in his letter, setting forth in language not to be misunderstood, and with an array of arguments not to be answered, the justice and equity of our claim.

To this letter Mr. Pinkney received no reply. He "pressed the marquis for an answer, and insisted that if he could not reply to it immediately he would name the time within which it was probable he could do so." Here was no slumbering over duty, no tame submission, no weak irresolution. What was the answer of the Neapolitan minister to the strong and earnest language of Mr. Pinkney? How did he justify the conduct of his government? He said "that an immediate answer was really impossible, and that he could not, without running the risk of misleading Mr. Pinkney, fix any precise time for the giving of such an answer as should be categorical." When asked the reason of this, "he observed that the papers had been scattered about in such a way that, with all the diligence they could use, they had not been able to collect them; that all proper steps had been taken by the king's government for obtaining the papers, &c."

What was the course that propriety, delicacy, and national decorum demanded of our minister under such circumstances? Doubt of the word, impeachment of the motive, or censure of the conduct pursued by his Majesty's government ? Let Mr. Pinkney be heard, and we rest his vindication upon the answer, without fear of the result. "Avoiding extremes of every kind, I have sought to write and speak with politeness, but, at the same time, explicitly and firmly. Without being studiously conciliatory, I have forborne all menaces. I might have contrived to display a more active and zealous importunity than my letters describe ; but it could only have been that teazing importunity which, wanting dignity, and unauthorized by usage, has nothing to recommend its introduction into transactions like this. No proper opportunity has been missed to urge this government to a favorable decision. The reasons suggested for a short postponement of its decision are such as, I suppose, I could not quarrel with without putting myself in the wrong. They are perfectly respectful to the United States, and of real weight in themselves."

What American will impeach the logic or morale of this reasoning ? We had an unsettled claim against a weaker power. That power solicited, in a spirit of seeming fairness, time for collecting the papers in evidence, after having used, as they averred, all proper diligence, to get possession of them. The plea is admitted by our agent. Who will condemn the deed ? and what, though the plea turned out to be deceptive and false, a mere trick of diplomatic finesse, is it admissible to seize hold of a subsequent disclosure, and urge it to the prejudice of the party negotiating ?

If, as the reviewer intimates, Mr. Pinkney was politely bowed out of Naples, and a trick resorted to, to rid the government of the presence of one whom they had good cause to dread, it is to his lasting honor that he scorned the imputation of an unworthy motive to the government of Naples, upon vague suspicion, and dealt with her with a moderation and tender policy worthy of a better cause. His letter of August 24th, was a triumphant vindication of our rights, and his declining to proceed *in extremis*, and lending a favorable ear to what appeared to be reasonable in itself, just, and fair, and could be construed into no want of respect for the United States ; so far from diminishing his reputation as a statesman, and exposing him to censure, is a beautiful illustration of his characteristic fairness and honesty of deportment.

The reviewer wrote under the influence of light thrown upon the transaction by subsequent events. He saw the end from the beginning. The treachery and duplicity of the Court of Naples were, at the time he wrote, things demonstrated. But it is due to Mr. Pinkney to remember, that duplicity proved is quite a different thing from duplicity assumed. Mr. Pinkney was compelled to act upon the alleged reasons of the government of Naples, the distinct and positive assurances of the marquis ; and it would have been rude in the extreme to have called the candor and fair dealing of the Neapolitan government in question upon mere suspicion. In forming our judgment upon the true merits of the case, and deciding upon the wisdom and propriety of the course pursued by Mr. Pinkney, we must place ourselves in his position, and banish from our minds facts that were subsequently revealed.

Mr. Pinkney's ability in discussing great constitutional questions, was often tested in the Supreme Court of the Union and on the floor of Congress ; and he always spoke to command admiration. There was a loftiness of principle, a broad nationality, a dignity and gravity, that indicated a beautiful and abiding appreciation on his part of the vast importance of every constitutional discussion. He never opened his lips in the examination of that august instrument but he seemed to behold his country's honor and true glory involved in the issue. He always merged the advocate in the comprehensive, enlarged, august American statesman. And perhaps on no occasion did he display his profound acquaintance with the great principles of the constitution, or his keen analytic logic, or pure American feeling more conspicuously, than in the discussion on the floor of the Senate, of the great Missouri question.

Mr. Pinkney, it has been shown, was but a short time in Congress. While a member of the lower House he embarked in the discussion of the treaty-making power. Some of the first men in the country figured in that Congress, and participated in that debate. John Randolph, the pride and boast of Virginia, followed in reply. He paid the highest compliment to the eloquence and power of Mr. Pinkney, but wholly discarded his view of the question. The whole force of the opposition was turned against this speech, with what degree of correctness we leave posterity to decide. This was the first time that Randolph and Pinkney encountered each other; and it is gratifying to know, that the conflict was characterized in the beginning with the most cordial expressions of mutual admiration and respect, and ended in the most unlimited homage of the former to the powers of the latter; who, after the delivery of the speech on the Missouri Compromise, it has been said to me, did not hesitate to accord to Mr. Pinkney the rank of the first constitutional lawyer and statesman in the land.

It may be thought that I have consumed too much time, and put myself to needless trouble, in vindicating Mr. Pinkney's title to the name and character of a statesman. But when it is remembered, that so many years have passed since he served the country in that capacity, and that in the only biography written of him there is scarce any mention made of this feature of his character,—when it is remembered that the country was distracted at the time by the most rancorous party dissensions, and that the bitterness of partisan fury was let loose upon him; it will be conceded that his life could not properly be written, or his character drawn, without a calm review of the services rendered, and the accusations hurled against him. The most eloquent of New England's sons and the first of her living lawyers, Rufus Choate, in an eulogy upon recent departed worth, undertook to limit Mr. Pinkney's pre-eminence to the Bar, and to throw a veil over his qualities as a statesman. He either had not looked into this chapter of Mr. Pinkney's life, or else was disposed to overlook its incontestable claims to a nation's gratitude and praise. The time was, when New England thought and spoke differently upon this subject. Her own Story declared, that Mr. Pinkney "honored the country while abroad by an *unparalleled* display of *diplomatic* science, and on his return, illuminated the halls of justice with an eloquence of argument and depth of learned research, that has not been exceeded in our day." The North American Review, speaking the convictions of another of New England's distinguished sons, declared that he was second to none of the great names opposed to him in all the qualities that make up the august character of a statesman. Hundreds who might read and receive as oracular, the burning eloquence of Rufus Choate, if the biography of William Pinkney were wanting in fidelity to his memory, may be induced to pause and consider ere they give too easy credence to the belief that Pinkney's chief excellence was that of a lawyer, when they peruse these pages, and listen, not only to what Story has said, but recall to mind a fact in the history of the past, known at this day to but few, that as early as 1819 he aimed the first decisive blow at the mad spirit of nullification, and brushed away, "as with a mighty besom, the cobweb conceits about State rights and State sovereignty," at a time, too, when their own incomparable Webster was by his side ; and, in 1820, stood forth the defender of the States against the infringement of national usurpation ; thus entitling himself to the lasting gratitude of his country, for so poising the shield of the constitution, as to protect each of these associate powers in its own peculiar and appropriate jurisdiction. I may close this portion of the biography with the expression of surprise, that such distinguished testimony and trumpet-tongued facts should be so soon forgotten, or strangely overlooked in her present eloquent musings of the past.

Vir clarissimus, amantissimus Reipublicæ benefacere amplissimis affectus, summis ornamentis honoris, fortunæ, virtutis ingenii præditus.

The annexed memorial was written by Mr. Pinkney, and pronounced at the time by a distinguished judge to "be a most masterly composition, a complete and unanswerable defence of neutral rights against the belligerent pretensions and encroachments, whose *maxims were worthy of being committed to memory by every statesman in all countries.*"

MEMORIAL ON THE RULE OF THE WAR OF 1756.

To the President of the United States, and the Senate and House of Representatives of the United States of America, in Congress assembled.

THE MEMORIAL OF THE MERCHANTS AND TRADERS OF THE CITY OF BALTIMORE.

Your memorialists beg leave respectfully to submit to your consideration the following statements and reflections, produced by the situation of our public affairs, in a high degree critical and perilous, and peculiarly affecting the commerce of their country.

In the early part of the late war between Great Britain and France, the former undertook to prohibit neutral nations from all trade whatsoever with the colonies of the latter. This exorbitant pretension was not long persisted in. It was soon qualified in favor of a direct trade between the United States and these colonies, and some years afterwards was further relaxed in favor of European neutrals. The United States being thus admitted, by the express acknowledgment of Great Britain, to a direct trade, without limit, between their own ports and the colonies of the opposite belligerents, another trade naturally and necessarily grew out of it, or rather formed one of its principal objects and inducements. The surplus colonial produce, beyond our own consumption, imported here, was to be carried elsewhere for a market ; and it was accordingly carried to Europe, sometimes by the original importer, sometimes by other American merchants, either in the vessels in which the importation was made, or in others. In the course of this traffic, it was understood to be the sense of Great Britain, and was explicitly declared by her courts of prize, that although she had not expressly allowed to the merchants of the United States, by the letter of her relaxations, an immediate trade between the colonies of her enemies and the markets of Europe, a circuitous trade to Europe, in the production of these colonies, was unexceptionable ; and nothing more was necessary to make it so, than that the continuity of the voyage should be broken by an entry, and payment of duties, and the landing of the colonial cargo in the United States. During the greater part of the late war, and the first years of the present, this trade was securely prosecuted by our merchants, in the form which Great Britain had thus thought fit to give it.

The modification of a traffic, in itself entitled to be free, was submitted to, on our part, without repining, because it presented a clear and definite rule of conduct, which, although unauthorized in the light of a restriction, was not greatly inconvenient in its practical operation ; and your memorialists entertained a confident hope, that, while on the one hand, they sought no change of system by which the assumption of Great Britain to impose terms, however mild in their character and effect, upon their lawful commerce, should be repelled ; on the other hand, it would be desired, that the state of things which Great Britain had herself prescribed, and which use and habit had rendered familiar, and intelligible to all, should be disturbed by oppressive innovations ; far less that these innovations should, by a tyrannical retrospection, be made to justify the seizure and confiscation of their property, committed to the high seas, under the protection of the existing rule, and without warning of the intended change.

In this their just hope, your memorialists have been fatally disappointed. Their vessels and effects, to a large amount, have lately been captured by the commissioned cruisers of Great Britain, upon the foundation of new principles, suddenly invented, and applied to this habitual traffic, and suggested, and promulgated, for the first time, by sentences of condemnation ; by which, unavoidable ignorance has been considered as criminal, and an honorable confidence in the justice of a friendly nation, pursued with penalty and forfeiture.

Your memorialists are in no situation to state the precise nature of the rules to which their most important interests have thus been sacrificed : and it is not the least of their complaints against them, that they are undefined, and undefinable, equivocal in their form, and the fit instruments of oppression by reason of their ambiguity.

Your memorialists know that the circumstances which have heretofore been admitted to give legality to their trade, in colonial productions, with their European friends, protect it no longer. But they have not yet been told, and are not soon likely to learn, what other circumstances will be suffered to produce that consequence. It is supposed to have been judicially declared, in general, that a voyage undertaken for the purpose of bringing into the United States the produce of the belligerent colonies, purchased by American citizens, shall, if it appears to be intended that this produce shall ultimately go on to Europe, and an attempt is actually made to re-export and send it thither, be considered, on account of that intention, as a direct voyage to Europe, and therefore illegal, notwithstanding any temporary interruption or termination of it in the United States.

Your memorialists will not here stop to inquire upon what grounds of law or reason the same act is held to be legal when commenced with one intention, and illegal when undertaken with another. But they object, in the strongest terms, against this new criterion of legality, because of its inevitable tendency to injustice; because of its peculiar capacity to embarrass with seizure, and to ruin with confiscation, the whole of our trade with Europe in the surplus of our colonial importations.

The inquiry which the late system indicated was short and simple, and precluded error on all sides; but the new refinement substitutes in its place a vast field of speculation, overshadowed with doubt and uncertainty, and of which the faint and shifting boundaries can never be distinctly known.

Intention, as to the object of our colonial voyages, may be inferred from numerous circumstances, more or less conclusive. To anticipate them all is obviously impracticable; and of course to guard against the inference, in this respect, which British captors and British courts may be disposed to draw, will be impossible. Our property is therefore menaced by a great and formidable danger, which there are no means of eluding; for even if it should chance to escape the condemnation which this pernicious novelty prepares for it, the wound inflicted upon our commerce by arrestations on suspicion, and detentions for adjudication, will be deep and fatal. The efforts of our merchants will be checked and discouraged by more than ordinary inquisitions; our best concerted enterprises broken up, without the hope of retribution, or even reimbursement for actual costs, upon the footing of an intention arbitrarily imputed; and the only alternative which will be presented to our choice will be, either to refrain at once from a traffic which enriches our country while it benefits ourselves, or to see it wasted, and in the end destroyed, by a noxious system of maritime depredation.

Your memorialists are the more alarmed by this departure from a plain and settled rule, in favor of a pliant and mysterious doctrine, so eminently suited to the accomplishment of the worst purposes of commercial jealousy, because the injurious and vexatious qualities of the substituted rule must have been known to those who introduced it, and because, if these qualities did not recommend it to adoption, it is difficult to conceive why it was adopted at all. If it is meant that our trade to Europe shall, notwithstanding this rule, be allowed to continue without being subjected to extraordinary difficulties, operating as actual reductions and mischievous restraints ; if it is meant that a few facts, known and comprehended, shall, as heretofore, form a standard by which the lawfulness of our European voyages may be unequivocally ascertained ; if a wide range has not been designed for the inquiry after intention, and a real effect expected from that inquiry ; if, in a word, the late regulation has not been supposed to be capable of bearing on our trade in a manner new and important, we should hardly have now been called upon to remonstrate against a change. It is not pretended that the rule now enforced against us, is levelled against any practice to which we may be supposed to have lent ourselves, of disguising as our own the property of the enemies of Great Britain. That is not its object ; and if it were, we are enabled to assert, solemnly and confidently, that our conduct has afforded no ground for the injurious suspicion which such an object would imply. The view is professedly to regulate and effect our traffic in articles fairly purchased by us from others; and if the consequences to that traffic were not intended to be serious, and extensive, and permanent, your memorialists search in vain for the motive by which a state, in amity with our own, and moreover connected with it by the ties of com-

mon interest, to which many considerations seem to give peculiar strength, has been induced to indulge in a paroxysm
of capricious aggression upon our rights, by which it dishon-
ors itself without promoting any of those great interests for
which an enlightened nation may fairly be solicitous, and
which only a steady regard for justice can ultimately secure.
When we see a powerful state, in possession of a commerce
of which the world affords no examples, endeavoring ·to in-
terpolate into the laws of nations casuistical niceties and way-
ward distinctions, which forbid a citizen of another independent commercial country, to export from that country
what unquestionably belongs to him, only because he imported it himself, and yet allow him to sell a right of export-
ing it to another ; which prohibit an end because it arises
out of *one* intention, but permit it when it arises out of *two;*
which, dividing an act into stages, search into the mind for
a correspondent division of it in the contemplation of its author, and determine its innocence or criminality accordingly;
which, not denying that the property acquired in an authorized traffic, by neutral nations from belligerents, may become
incorporated into the national stock, and under the shelter of
its neutral character, thus superinduced, and still preserved,
be afterwards transported to every quarter of the globe, reject the only epoch which can distinctly mark that incorpo-
ration, and point out none other in its place ; which, proposing to fix with accuracy and precision the line of demar-
cation, beyond which neutrals are trespassers upon the wide
domain of belligerent rights, involves every thing in darkness
and confusion : there can be but one opinion as to the purpose
which all this is to accomplish.

Your memorialists have endeavored, with all that attention which their natural anxiety was calculated to produce,
to ascertain the various shapes which the doctrine in question
is likely to assume in practice, but they have found it impossible to conjecture in what way, consistently with this doctrine,

the excess of our imports from the belligerent colonies can find its way to foreign markets. The landing of the cargo, and a compliance with all the forms and sanctions, upon which our revenue depends, will not so terminate the voyage from the colonies, as that the articles may be *immediately* re-exported to Europe by the original importer. But if they cannot be exported immediately, what lapse of time will give them a title to be sent abroad, and if not by the original importer, how is he to devolve upon another a power which he has not himself? And if by a sale, he can communicate the power, by what evidence is the transfer to be manifested, so as to furnish an answer to the ready accusation of fraud and evasion? In proportion as this doctrine has developed itself, it has been found necessary to invent plausible qualifications, tending to conceal its real character from observation. It has accordingly been surmised, that, notwithstanding the obstacles which it provides against the re-exportation of a colonial cargo by the importer, such a re-exportation may, perhaps, be lawful. Attempts on his part to sell in the United States, without effect, (which must often happen), may, it is supposed, be sufficient to save him from the peril of the rule. But, admitting it to be certain, instead of being barely *possible*, that these attempts would form any thing like security aganst final condemnation, it is still most material to ask, how they are to afford protection against seizure? By what documents they can be proved to the satisfaction of those to whom interest suggests doubts, and whom impunity encourages to act upon them? The formal transactions of the custom-house once deserted as a criterion, the cargo must be followed, through private transfers, into the warehouses of individual merchants; and when proofs have been prepard, with the utmost regularity, to establish these transfers, or the other facts which may be deemed to be equivalent, they are still liable to be suspected, and will be suspected, as fictitious and colorable, and capture will be the consequence. For the loss and damage which capture brings along with it, British courts of prize grant no adequate indemnity. Redress to *any* extent is difficult ; to a *competent* extent, impossible. And even the costs which an iniquitous seizure compels a neutral merchant to incur, in the defence of his violated rights, before their own tribunals, are seldom decreed, and never paid.

Your memorialists have thus far complained only of the recent abandonment, by Great Britain, of a known rule, by which the oppressive character of an important principle of her maritime code, has heretofore been greatly mitigated. But they now beg leave to enter their solemn protest against the principle itself, as an arbitrary and unfounded pretension, by which the just liberty of neutral commerce is impaired and abridged, and may be wholly destroyed.

The reasons upon which Great Britain assumes to herself a right to interdict to the independent nations of the earth, a commercial intercourse with the colonies of her enemies (out of the relaxation of which pretended right has arisen the distinction in her courts between an American trade from the colonies to the United States, and from the same colonies to Europe) will, we are confidently persuaded, be repelled with firmness and effect by our government.

It is said by the advocates of this high belligerent claim, that neutral nations have no right to carry on with either of the parties at war, any other trade than they have actually enjoyed in time of peace. This position forms the basis upon which Great Britain has, heretofore, rested her supposed title to prevent altogether, or to modify at her discretion, the interposition of neutrals in the colony trade of her adversaries.

But, if we are called upon to admit the truth of this position, it seems reasonable that the converse of it should also be admitted. That war should not be allowed to disturb the customary trade of neutrals in peace ; that the

peace-traffic should, in every view, be held to be the measure
of the war-traffic ; and that, as on the one hand there can
be no enlargement, on the other there shall be no restriction.
What, however, is the fact ?   The first moment of hostilities annihilates the commerce of the nations at peace, in
articles deemed contraband of war ; the property of the bil-
ligerents can no longer be carried in neutral ships ; they are
subject to visitation on the high seas ; to harassing and vexatious search ; to detention for judicial inquiry ; and to the
peril of unjust confiscation : they are shut out from their
usual markets, not only by military enterprises against particular places, carried on with a view to their reduction, but
by a vast system of blockade, affecting and closing up the
entire ports of a whole nation : such have been the recent
effects of an European war upon the trade of this neutral
country ; and the prospect of the future affords no consolation for the past.   The triumphant fleets of one of the con-
tending powers cover the ocean ; the navy of her enemies
has fallen before her ; the communication by sea with France,
and Spain, and Holland, seems to depend upon her will, and
she asserts a right to destroy it at her pleasure : she forbids
us from transporting, in our vessels, as in peace we could,
the property of her enemies ; enforces against us a rigorous
list of contraband ; dams up the great channels of our ordinary trade ; abridges, trammels, and obstructs what she permits us prosecute, and then refers us to our *accustomed
traffic in time of peace,* for the criterion of our commercial
rights, in order to justify the consummation of that ruin
with which our lawful commerce is menaced by her maxims
and her conduct.

This principle, therefore, cannot be a sound one ; it wants
uniformity and consistency; is partial, unequal, and delusive:
it makes every thing bend to the rights of war, while it af-
fects to look back to, and to recognize, the state of things in
peace, as the foundation and the measure of the rights of

neutrals. Professing to respect the established and habitual trade of the nations at peace, it affords no shadow of security for any part of it : professing to be an equitable standard for the ascertainment of neutral rights, it deprives them of all body and substance, and leaves them only a plausible and unreal appearance of magnitude and importance ; it delivers them over, in a word, to the mercy of the states at war, as objects of legitimate hostility; and while it seems to define, does, in fact, extinguish them. Such is the faithful picture of the theory, and practical operation of this doctrine.

But, independent of the considerations thus arising out of the immediate interference of belligerent rights and belligerent conduct with the freedom of neutral trade, by which the fallacy of the appeal to the precise state of our peace-trade, as limiting the nature and extent of our trade in war, is sufficiently manifested, there are other considerations which satisfactorily prove the inadmissibility of this principle.

It is impossible that war among the primary powers of Europe should not, in an endless variety of shapes, materially affect the whole civilized world. Its operation upon the prices of labor and commodities ; upon the value of money; upon exchange ; upon the rates of freight and insurance, is great and important. But it does much more than all this. It imposes upon commerce in the gross, and in its details, a new character ; gives to it a new direction, and places it upon new foundations. It abolishes one class of demands ; creates, or revives others ; and diminishes, or augments the rest. And, while the wants of mankind are infinitely varied by its powerful agency, both in object and degree, the modes and sources of supply, and the means of payment are infinitely varied also.

To prescribe to neutral trade thus irresistibly influenced, and changed, and moulded by this imperious agent, a fixed and unalterable station, would be to say that it shall remain the same, when not to vary is impossible ; and to require, since change is unavoidable, that it shall submit to the ruinous retrenchments and modifications which war produces, and yet refrain from indemnifying itself by the fair advantages which war offers to it as an equivalent, cannot be warranted by any rule of reason or equity, or by any law to which the great community of nations owes respect and obedience.

When we examine the conduct of the maritime powers of Europe, in all the wars in which they have been engaged for upwards of a century, we find that each of them has, occasionally, departed from its scheme of colonial monopoly; relaxed its navigation laws, and otherwise admitted neutrals for a longer or shorter space, as circumstances required, to modes of trade from which they were generally excluded.

This universal practice, this constant and invariable usage, for a long series of years, would seem to have established among the European states a sort of customary law upon the subject of it, from which no single power could be at liberty to depart, in search of a questionable theory at variance with it. Great Britain is known to suspend, in war and on account of war, her famous act of navigation, to which she is supposed to owe her maritime greatness, and which, as the palladium of her power, she holds inviolable in peace; and her colonies are frequently thrown open, and neutrals invited to supply them, when she cannot supply them herself. She makes treaties in the midst of war (she made such a treaty with us), by which neutrals are received into a participation of an extensive traffic, to which before they had no title. And can she be suffered to object, that the same, or analogous acts are unlawful in her enemies; or that, when neutrals avail themselves of similar concessions made by her opponents, they are liable to punishment, as for a criminal intrusion into an irregular and prohibited commerce?

The weight of this consideration has been felt by the advocates of this doctrine, and it has, accordingly, been attempted to evade it by a distinction, which admits the legality of all such relaxations in war, of the general, commercial or colonial systems of the belligerents, as do not arise out of the predominance of the enemy's force, or out of any necessity resulting from it.

It is apparent, however, that such relaxations, whether dictated by the actual ascertained predominance of the enemy's force, or not, do arise out of the state of war, and are almost universally compelled, and produced by it ; that they are intended as reliefs against evils which war has brought along with it, and the opposite belligerent has just as much right to insist, that these evils shall not be removed by neutral aid, or interposition, as if they were produced by the general preponderance of her own power, upon the land or upon the sea, or by the general success of her arms. In the one case, as completely as in the other, the interference of the neutral lightens the pressure of war ; increases the capacity to bear its calamities, or the power to inflict them ; and supplies the means of comfort and of strength. In both cases, the practical effect is the same, and the legal consequences should be the same also.

But whence are we to derive the conclusion of the fact upon which this extraordinary distinction is made to turn ? How are we to determine with precision and certainty, the exact cause which opens to us the ports of a nation at war— to analyze the various circumstances, of which, perhaps, the concession may be the combined effect ; and to assign to each the just portion of influence to which it has a claim ? How easy it is to deceive ourselves on a subject of this kind, Great Britain will herself instruct us, by a recent example. Her courts of prize have insisted that, during the war which ended in the peace of Amiens, France was compelled to open the ports of her colonies, by a necessity created and imposed by the naval prowess of her enemies. And yet these ports were opened in February, 1793, when France and her maritime

adversaries had not measured their strength in a single conflict ; when no naval enterprise had been undertaken by the
latter, far less crowned with success ; when the lists were
not even entered, and when the superiority afterwards acquired, by Great Britain in particular, was yet a problem ;
when the spirit of the French nation and government was
lifted up to an unexampled height, by the enthusiasm of the
day, and by the splendid achievements by which their armies
had recently conquered Savoy, the county of Nice, Worms,
and other places on the Rhine, the Austrian Low Countries,
and Liege.   It would seem to be next to impossible to contend that a concession made by France to neutrals, on the
subject of her colony trade, at such a period of exultation
and triumph, was "compelled by the prevalence of British
arms," that it was "the fruit of British victories," or the result of " British conquest," that it arose out of the predominance of the enemy's force, that it was produced by
" that sort of necessity which springs from the impossibility
of otherwise providing against the urgency of distress inflicted
by the hand of a superior enemy," and that " it was a signal
of defeat and depression."   It would seem to be impossible
to say of a traffic so derived, " that it could obtain or did
obtain, by no other title than the success of the one belligerent against the other, and at the expense of that very belligerent under whose success the neutral sets up his title."
Yet all these things have been said, and solemnly maintained,
and have even been made the foundation of acts, by which
the property of our citizens has been wrested from their hands.
It cannot be believed that the laws of nations have intrusted to
a belligerent the power of harassing the trade, and confiscating
the ships and merchandise of peaceable and friendly nations,
upon grounds so vague, so indefinite, and equivocal.   Of all
law, *certainty* is the best feature ; and no rule can be otherwise
than unjust and despotic, of which the sense and the application are and must be ambiguous.   A *siege* or *blockade* pre-

sents an intelligible standard, by which it may always be known, that no lawful trade can be carried on with the places against which either has been instituted. But the suggestions upon which this new belligerent encroachment, having all the effect of a siege or blockade, is founded, are absolutely incapable of a distinct form, either for the purpose of warning to neutrals or as the basis of a judicial sentence. The neutral merchant finds that, in fact, the colonial ports of the parties to the war are thrown open to him by the powers to which they belong; and he sees no hostile squadrons to shut them against him. Is he to pause, before he ventures to exercise his natural right to trade with those who are willing to trade with him, until he has inquired and determined *why* these ports have been thus made free to receive him? To such a complicated and delicate discussion, no nation has a right to call him. It is enough that an actual blockade can be set on foot to close these ports, and that they may be made the objects of direct efforts, for conquest or occlusion, if the enemy's force is, in truth, so decidedly predominant as is pretended to be. And if it is not predominant to that point, and to that extent, there can be no cause for ascribing to it an effect to which it is physically incompetent, or for allowing it to do that constructively, which it cannot do, and has not done, actually. The pernicious qualities of this doctrine are enhanced and aggravated, as from its nature might be expected, by the fact, that Great Britain gives no notice of the time when, or the circumstances in which she means to apply and enforce it. Her orders of the 6th of November, 1793, by which the seas were swept of our vessels and effects, were, for the first time, announced by the ships of war and privateers by which they were carried into execution. The late decisions of her courts, which are in the true spirit of this doctrine, and are calculated to restore it, in practice, to that high tone of severity which milder decisions had almost concealed from the world, came upon us by surprise; and the captures of which the Dutch complained in the seven years' war, were preceded by no warning. Thus is this principle most rapacious and oppressive in all its bearings. Harsh and mysterious in itself, it has always been and ever must be used to betray neutral merchants into a trade supposed to be lawful, and then to give them up to pillage and to ruin. Compared with this principle, which violence and artifice may equally claim for their own, the exploded doctrine of *constructive blockade*, by which belligerents for a time insulted and plundered the states at peace, is innocent and harmless. That doctrine had something of certainty belonging to it, and made safety at least *possible*. But there can be no security while a malignant and deceitful principle like this hangs over us. It is just what a belligerent chooses to make it—lurking, unseen, and unfelt—or visible, active, and noxious. It may come abroad when least expected; and the moment of confidence may be the moment of destruction. It may sleep for a time, but no man knows when it is to awake, to shed its baleful influence upon the commerce of the world. It clothes itself from season to season, in what are called *relaxations*, but again, without any previous intimation to the deluded citizens of the neutral powers, these relaxations are suddenly laid aside either in the whole or in part, and the work of confiscation commences. Nearly ten months of the late war had elapsed before it announced itself at all, and when it did so, it was in its most formidable shape, and in its fullest power and expansion. In a few weeks it was seen to lose more than half its substance and character, and before the conclusion of the war, was scarcely perceptible. With the opening of the present war it reappeared in its mildest form, which it is again abandoning for another, more consonant to its spirit. Such are its capricious fluctuations, that no commercial undertaking which it can in any way effect, can be considered as otherwise than precarious, whatever may

be the avowed state of the principle at the time of its commencement.

It has been said that, by embarking in the colony trade
of either of the belligerents, neutral nations in some sort interpose in the war, since they assist and serve the belligerent, in whose trade they so embark. It is a sufficient answer to this observation, that the same course of reasoning
would prove that neutrals ought to discontinue all trade
whatsoever with the parties at war. A continuance of their
accustomed peace trade assists and serves the belligerent with
whom it is continued ; and if this effect were sufficient to
make a trade unneutral and illegal, the best established and
most usual traffic would of course become so. But Great
Britain supplies us with another answer to this notion, that
our interference in the trade of the colonies of her enemies
is unlawful, *because they are benefited by it.* It is known
that the same trade is, and long has been, carried on by
British subjects; and your memorialists feel themselves
bound to state that, according to authentic information
lately received, the government of Great Britain does at this
moment grant licenses to neutral vessels, taking in a proportion of their cargoes there, to proceed on trading voyages to
the colonies of Spain, from which she would exclude us, upon
the condition that the return cargoes shall be carried to
Great Britain, to swell the gains of her merchants, and to
give her a monopoly of the commerce of the world. This
great belligerent right then, upon which so much has been
supposed to depend, sinks into an article of barter. It is
used, not as a hostile instrument wielded by a warlike state,
by which her enemies are to be wounded, or their colonies
subdued, but as the selfish means of commercial aggrandize-
ment, to the impoverishment and ruin of her friends; as an
engine by which Great Britain is to be lifted up to a vast
height of prosperity, and the trade of neutrals crippled, and
crushed, and destroyed. Such acts are a most intelligible

commentary upon the principle in question. They show that it is a hollow and fallacious principle, susceptible of the worst abuse, and incapable of a just and honorable application. They show that in the hands of a great maritime state, it is not in its ostensible character of a weapon of hostility that it is prized, but rather as one of the means of establishing an unbounded monopoly, by which every enterprise, calculated to promote national wealth and power, shall be made to begin and end in Great Britain alone. Such acts may well be considered as pronouncing the condemnation of the principle against which we contend, as withdrawing from it the only pretext upon which it is possible to rest it.

Great Britain does not pretend that this principle has any warrant in the opinions of writers on public law. She does not pretend, and cannot pretend, that it derives any countenance from the conduct of other nations. She is confessedly solitary in the use of this invention, by which rapacity is systematized, and a state of neutrality and war are made substantially the same. In this absence of all other authority, her courts have made an appeal to her own early example, for the justification of her own recent practice. Your memorialists join in that appeal, as affording the most conclusive and authoritative reprobation of the practice which it is intended to support by it.

It would be easy to show, by an examination of the different treaties to which Great Britain has been a party from times long past, that this doctrine is a modern usurpation. It would be equally easy to show, that during the greater part of the last century, her statesmen and lawyers uniformly disavowed it, either expressly or tacitly. But it is to a review of *judicial* examples, of all others the most weighty and solemn, that your memorialists propose to confine themselves.

In the war of 1744, in which Great Britain had the power, if she had thought fit to exert it, to exclude the neutral states from the colony trade of France and Spain, her high court of appeals decided that the trade was lawful, and released such vessels as had been found engaged in it.

In the war which soon followed the peace of Aix la Chapelle, Great Britain is supposed to have first acted upon the pretension that such a trade was unlawful, as being shut against neutrals in peace. And it is certain that, during the whole of that war, her courts of prize did condemn all neutral vessels taken in the prosecution of that trade, together with their cargoes, whether French or neutral. These condemnations, however, proceeded upon peculiar grounds. In the seven years' war France did not throw open to neutrals the traffic of her colonies. She established no free ports in the east, or in the west, with which foreign vessels could be permitted to trade, either generally or occasionally *as such*. Her first practice was simply to grant *special licenses* to particular neutral vessels, principally Dutch, and commonly chartered by Frenchmen, to make, under the usual restrictions, particular trading voyages to the colonies. These licenses furnished the British courts with a peculiar reason for condemning vessels sailing under them, viz., "that they became in virtue of them the *adopted or naturalized vessels of France*."

As soon as it was known that this effect was imputed to these licenses they were discontinued, or pretended to be so; but the discontinuance, whether real or supposed, produced no change in the conduct of Great Britain; for neutral vessels, employed in this trade, were captured and condemned as before. The grounds upon which they continued to be so captured and condemned, may best be collected from the reasons subjoined to the printed cases in the prize causes decided by the high court of admiralty (in which Sir Thomas Salisbury at that time presided), and by the lords commisioners of appeals, between 1757 and 1760.

In the case of the America (which was a Dutch ship, bound from St. Domingo to Holland, with the produce of that island belonging to French subjects, by whom the vessel had been chartered), the reason stated in the printed case is, "that the ship must be looked upon as a French ship (coming from St. Domingo), for by the laws of France no foreign ship *can* trade in the French West Indies."

In the case of the Snip, the reason (assigned by Sir George Hays and Mr. Pratt, afterwards Lord Camden) is, "for that the Snip (though once the property of Dutchmen) being employed in carrying provisions to, and goods from a French colony, *thereby became a French ship*, and as such was justly condemned."

It is obvious that the reason, in the case of the *America*, proceeds upon a presumption, that as the trade was, by the standing laws of France, even up to that moment, confined to *French* ships, any ship found employed in it must be a French ship. The reason in the other case does not rest upon this idle presumption, but takes another ground; for it states, that by the reason of the trade in which the vessel was employed, she *became* a French vessel.

It is manifest that this is no other than the first idea of adoption or naturalization, accommodated to the change attempted to be introduced into the state of things by the actual or pretended discontinuance of the special licenses. What then is the amount of the doctrine of the seven years' war, in the utmost extent which it is possible to ascribe to it? It is in substance no more than this, that as France did not, at any period of that war, abandon, or in any degree suspend, the principle of colonial monopoly, or the system arising out of it, a neutral vessel found in the prosecution of the trade, which, according to that principle and that system still continuing in force, could only be a *French* trade and open to *French* vessels, either *became*, or was legally to be *presumed* to be a *French* vessel. It cannot be necessary to

show that this doctrine differs essentially from the principle
of the present day ; but even if it were otherwise, the practice of that war, whatever it might be, was undoubtedly contrary to that of the war of 1744, and as contrasted with it,
will not be considered by those who have at all attended to
the history of these two periods, as entitled to any peculiar
veneration.   The effects of that practice were almost wholly
confined to the Dutch, who had rendered themselves extremely obnoxious to Great Britain, by the selfish and pusillanimous
policy, as it was falsely called, which enabled them during
the seven years' war to profit of the troubles of the rest of
Europe.

In the war of 1744, the neutrality of the Dutch, while
it continued, had in it nothing of complaisance to France ;
they furnished from the commencement of hostilities, on
account of the pragmatic sanction, succors to the confede-
rates ; declared openly, after a time, in favor of the Queen
of Hungary ; and finally determined upon and prepared for
war, by sea and land.   Great Britain, of course, had no inducement in that war to hunt after any hostile principle, by
the operations of which the trade of the Dutch might be harassed, or the advantage of their neutral position, while it
lasted, defeated.   In the war of 1756 she had this inducement in its utmost strength.   Independent of the commercial rivalry existing between the two nations, the Dutch had
excited the undisguised resentment of Great Britain, by declining to furnish against France the succors stipulated by
treaty ; by constantly supplying France with naval and
warlike stores, through the medium of a trade systemat-
ically pursued by the people, and countenanced by the government ; by granting to France, early in 1757, a free passage through Namur and Maestricht, for the provisions, am-
munition, and artillery, belonging to the army destined to act
against the territories of Prussia, in the neighborhood of
the Low Countries ; and by the indifference with which they

saw Nieuport and Ostend surrendered into the hands of France, by the court of Vienna, which Great Britain represented to be contrary to the Barrier treaty and the treaty of Utrecht. Without entering into the sufficiency of these grounds of dissatisfaction, which undoubtedly had a great influence on the conduct of Great Britain towards the Dutch, from 1757 until the peace of 1763, it is manifest that this very dissatisfaction, little short of a disposition to open war, and frequently on the eve of producing it, takes away, in a considerable degree, from the authority of any practice to which it may be supposed to have led, as tending to establish a rule of the public law of Europe. It may not be improper to observe too, that the station occupied by Great Britain in the seven years' war (as proud a one as any country ever did occupy), compared with that of the other European powers, was not exactly calculated to make the measures which her resentments against Holland or her views against France might dictate, peculiarly respectful to the general rights of neutrals. In the north, Russia and Sweden were engaged in the confederacy against Prussia, and were, of course, entitled to no consideration in this respect. The government of Sweden was, besides, weak and impotent. Denmark, it is, true, took no part in the war, but she did not suffer by the practice in question. Besides, all these powers combined would have been as nothing against the naval strength of Great Britain in 1758. As to Spain, she could have no concern in the question, and at length became involved in the war on the side of France. Upon the whole, in the war of 1756, Great Britain had the power to be unjust, and irresistible temptations to abuse it. In that of 1744, her power was, perhaps, equally great, but every thing was favorable to equity and moderation. The example afforded on this subject, therefore, by the first war, has far better titles to respect than that furnished by the last.

In the *American* war the practice and *decisions* on this point, followed those of the war of 1744.

The question first came before the lords of appeal in January, 1782, in the Danish cases of the Tiger, Copenhagen, and others, captured in October, 1783, and condemned at St. Kitts, in December following. The grounds on which the captors relied for condemnation, in the *Tiger*, as set forth at the end of the respondent's printed case, were, "for that the ship, having been trading to Cape Francois, where none but French ships are allowed to carry on any traffic, and having been laden at the same time of the capture, with the produce of the French part of the island of St. Domingo, put on board at Cape Francois, and both ship and cargo taken confessedly coming from hence, must (pursuant to precedents in the like cases in the last war), to all intents and purposes, be deemed a ship and goods belonging to the French, or at least adopted, and naturalized as such."

In the *Copenhagen,* the captor's reasons are thus given : "1st. Because it is allowed that the ship was destined, with her cargo, to the island of *Guadaloupe,* and no other place."

"2dly. Because it is *contrary to the established rule of general law, to admit any neutral ship to go to, and trade at, a port belonging to a colony of the enemy, to which such neutral ship could not have freely traded in time of peace.*"

On the 22d of January, 1782, these causes came on for hearing before the lords of appeal, who decreed *restitution* in all of them : thus in the most solemn and explicit manner disavowing and rejecting the pretended rules of the law of nations, upon which the captors relied ; the first of which was literally borrowed from the doctrine of the war of 1756, and the last of which is that very rule on which Great Britain now relies.

It is true, that in these cases the judgment of the lords

was pronounced upon one shape only of the colony trade of France, as carried on by neutrals ; that is to say, a trade between the colony of France and that of the country of the neutral shipper. But, as no distinction was supposed to exist, in point of principle, between the different modifications of the trade, and as the judgment went upon general grounds applicable to the entire subject, we shall not be thought to overrate its effect and extent, when we represent it as a complete rejection both of the doctrine of the seven years' war, and of that modern principle by which it has been attempted to replace it. But at any rate, the subsequent decrees of the same high tribunal did go that length. Without enumerating the cases of various descriptions, involving the legality of the trade in all its modes, which were favorably adjudged by the lords of appeal after the American peace, it will be sufficient to mention the case of the *Vervagting*, decided by them in 1785 and 1786. This was the case of a Danish ship laden with a cargo of drygoods and provisions, with which she was bound on a voyage from *Marseilles* to *Martinique* and *Cape Francois*, where she was to take in for Europe a return cargo of West India produce. The ship was not proceeded against, but the cargo, which was claimed for merchants of Ostend, was condemned as enemy's property (as in truth it was) by the vice-admiralty of *Antigua*, subject to the payment of freight, *pro rata itineris*, or rather for the whole of the outward voyage. On appeal, as to the cargo, the lords of appeal, on the 8th of March, 1785, reversed the condemnation, and ordered further proof of the property to be produced within three months. On the 28th of March, 1786, no further proof having been exhibited, and the proctor for the claimants daclaring that he should exhibit none, the lords condemned the cargo, and on the same day reversed the decree below, giving freight, *pro rata itineris* (from which the neutral master had appealed), and decreed freight generally, and the costs of the appeal.

It is impossible that a judicial opinion could go more conclusively to the whole question on the colony trade than this ; for it not only disavows the pretended illegality of neutral interpositions in that trade, even directly between France and her colonies (the most exceptionable form, it is said, in which that interposition could present itself), it not only denies that property engaged in such a trade is, on that account, liable to confiscation (inasmuch as, after having reversed the condemnation of the cargo, pronounced below, it proceeds afterwards to condemn it merely *for want of further proof as to the property*), but it holds that the trade is so unquestionably lawful to neutrals, as not even to put in jeopardy the claim to freight for that part of the voyage which had not yet begun, and which the party had not yet put himself in a situation to begin. The force of this, and the other British decisions produced by the American war, will not be avoided, by suggesting that there was any thing peculiarly favorable in the time when, or the manner in which, France opened her colony trade to neutrals on that occasion. Something of that sort, however, has been said. We find the following language in a very learned opinion on this point : " It is certainly true, that in the last war (the American war), many decisions took place which then pronounced, that such a trade between France and her colonies was not considered as an unneutral commerce ; but under what circumstances ? It was understood that France, in opening her colonies during the war, *declared,* that this was not done with a temporary view relative to the war, but on a general permanent purpose of altering her colonial system, and of admitting foreign vessels, universally, and at all times to a participation of that commerce ; taking that to be the fact (however suspicious its commencement might be, during the actual existence of a war), there was no ground to say, that

neutrals were not carrying on a commerce as ordinary as any
other in which they could be engaged ; and therefore in the
case of the *Vervagting*, and in many other succeeding cases,
the lords decreed payment of freight to the neutral ship-
owner.   It is fit to be remembered on this occasion, that the
conduct of France evinced how little dependence can be
placed upon explanations of measures adopted during the
pressure of war ; for, hardly was the ratification of the peace
assigned, when she returned to her ancient system of colonial
monopoly."

We answer to all this, that, to refer the decision of the
lords, in the *Vervagting*, and other succeeding cases, to the
reason here assigned, is to accuse that high tribunal of acting upon a confidence which has no example, in a singularly
incredible declaration (if, indeed, such a declaration was
ever made), after the utter falsehood of it had been, as this
learned opinion does itself inform us, unequivocally and notoriously ascertained.

We have seen that the *Vervagting* was decided by the
lords in 1785 and 1786, at least two years after France had,
as we are told, "returned to her ancient system of colonial
monopoly," and when of course the supposed assertion, of an
intended permanent abandonment of that system, could not
be permitted to produce any legal consequence.

We answer further, that if this alleged declaration was
in fact made (and we must be allowed to say, that we have
found no trace of it out of the opinion above recited), it
never was put into such a formal and authentic shape as to
be the fair subject of judicial notice.

It is not contained in the French *arrêts* of that day,
where only it would be proper to look for it, and we are not
referred to any other document proceeding from the government of France, in which it is said to appear.   There does
not, in a word, seem to have been any thing which an enlightened tribunal could be supposed capable of considering

as a pledge on the part of France, that she had resolved upon or even meditated the extravagant change in her colonial system which she is said, in this opinion, to have been understood to announce to the world. But even if the declaration in question was actually made, and that too with all possible solemnity, still it would be difficult to persuade any thinking man that the sincerity of such a declaration was in any degree confided in, or that any person in any country could regard it in any other light than as a mere artifice, that could give no right which would not equally well exist without it. Upon the whole, it is manifestly impracticable to rest the decisions of the lords of appeal, in and after the American war, upon any dependence placed in this declaration, of which there is no evidence that it ever was made, which it is certain was not authentically or formally made; which, however made, was not, and could not be believed at *any* time, far less in 1785 and 1786, when its falsehood had been unquestionably proved by the public and undisguised conduct of its supposed authors, in direct opposition to it. That *Sir James Marriot*, who sat in the high court of admiralty of Great Britain during the greater part of the late war, did not consider these doctrines as standing upon this ground is evident; for, notwithstanding that in the year 1756 he was the most zealous and perhaps able advocate for the condemnation of the Dutch ships engaged in the colony trade of France, yet, upon the breaking out of the late war, he relied upon the decisions in the American war as authoritatively settling the legality of that trade, and decreed accordingly.

If, as a more plausible answer to these decisions, considered in the light of authorities, than that which we have just examined, it should be said that they ought rather to be viewed as reluctant sacrifices to policy, or even to necessity, under circumstances of particular difficulty and peril, than as an expression of the deliberate opinion of the lords of appeal, or of the government of Great Britain; on the matter of right, it might perhaps be sufficient to reply, that if the armed neutrality coupled with the situation of Great Britain as a party to the war did in any degree compel these decisions, we might also expect to find at the same era some relaxation on the part of that country relative to the doctrine of contraband, upon which the convention of the armed neutrality contained the most direct stipulations which the northern powers were particularly interested to enforce. Yet such was not the fact. But in addition to this, and other considerations of a similar description, it is natural to inquire why it happened that, if the lords of appeal were satisfied that Great Britain possessed the right in question, they recorded and gave to the world a series of decisions against it, founded not upon British *orders of council*, gratuitously relaxing what was still asserted to be the strict right (as in the late war), but upon general principles of public law. However prudence might have required (although there is no reason to believe it did require) an abstinence on the part of Great Britain, from the extreme exercise of the right she had been supposed to claim, still it could not be necessary to give to the mere forbearance of a claim, the stamp and character of a formal admission that the claim itself was illegal and unjust. In the late war, as often as the British government wished to concede and relax, from whatever motive, on the subject of the colony trade of her opponents, an order of council was resorted to, setting forth the nature of the concession or relaxation upon which the courts of prize were afterwards to found their sentences; and, undoubtedly, sentences so passed, cannot, in any fair reasoning, be considered as deciding more than that the order of council is obligatory on the courts, whose sentences they are. But the decrees of the lords of appeal, in and after the American war, are not of this description; since there existed no order of council on the subject of them; and of course they are, and ought to be, of the highest weight and authority against Great Britain, on the questions involved in and adjudged by them.

This solemn reunciation of the principle in question, in the face of the whole world, by her highest tribunal in matters of prize, reiterated in a succession of decrees, down to the year 1786, and afterwards, is powerfully confirmed by the acquiescence of Great Britain, during the first most important and active period of the late war, in the free and unlimited prosecution by neutrals of the whole colony trade of France; she did, indeed, at last prohibit that trade by an instruction unprecedented in the annals of maritime depredation; but the revival of her discarded rule was characterized by such circumstances of iniquity and violence, as rather to heighten, by the effect of contrast, the veneration of mankind for the past justice of her tribunals.

The world has not forgotten the instruction to which we allude, or the enormities by which its true character was developed. Produced in mystery, at a moment when universal confidence in the integrity of her government had brought upon the ocean a prey of vast value and importance; sent abroad to the different naval stations, with such studied secrecy that it would almost seem to have been intended to make an experiment how far law and honor could be outraged by a nation proverbial for respecting both; the heralds, by whom it was first announced, were the commanders of her commissioned cruisers, who at the same instant carried it into effect with every circumstance of aggravation, if of such an act there can be an aggravation. Upon such conduct there was but one sentiment. It was condemned by reason and justice. It was condemned by that law which flows from and is founded upon them; it was condemned, and will for ever continue to be condemned, by the universal voice of the civilized world. Great Britain has made amends, with the good faith which belongs to her councils, for that act of injustice and oppression ; and your memorialists have a strong confidence that the late departure from the usual course of her policy will be followed by a like disposition to atonement and reparation. The relations which subsist between Great Britain and the United States rest upon the basis of recipro- cal interests, and your memorialists see in those interests, as well as in the justice of the British government and the firm- ness of our own, the best reasons to expect a satisfactory answer to their complaints, and a speedy abandonment of that system by which they have been lately harassed and alarmed.

Your memorialists will not trespass upon your time with a recital of the various acts by which our coasts, and even our ports and harbors, have been converted into scenes of violence and depradation ; by which the security of our trade and property has been impaired ; the rights of our territory invaded ; the honor of our country humiliated and insulted ; and our gallant countrymen oppressed and persecuted. They feel it to be unnecessary to ask that the force of the nation should be employed in repelling and chastizing the law- less freebooters who have dared to spread their ravages even beyond the seas which form the principal theatre of their piractical exertions, and to infest our shores with their irre- gular and ferocious hostility.

These are outrages which have pressed themselves in a peculiar manner upon the notice of our government, and cannot have failed to excite its indignation, and a correspond- ent disposition to prevent and redress them.

Such is the view which your memorialists have taken, in this anxious crisis of our public affairs, of subjects which ap- pear to them, in an alarming degree, to affect their country and its commerce, and to involve high questions of national honor and interest, of public law and individual rights, which imperiously demand discussion and adjustment. They do not presume to point out the measures which these great subjects may be supposed to call for. The means of redress for the past and security for the future are respectfully, confidently submitted to your wisdom; but your memorialists cannot forbear to indulge a hope, which they would abandon with deep reluctance, that they may yet be found in amicable explanations with those who have ventured to inflict wrongs upon us, and to advance unjust pretensions to our prejudice.

Baltimore, Jan. 21*st,* 1806.

FOREIGN CORRESPONDENCE.

FROM MR. PINKNEY TO MR. MADISON.

[PRIVATE.]   "LONDON, *October,* 10*th* 1807.

"DEAR SIR :—Mr. Monroe will doubtless sufficiently explain the subject of this letter ; but it seems, notwithstanding, to be proper that I should trouble you with a very brief explanation of it myself.

"This government having determined to send a special envoy to the United States upon the subject of Mr. Monroe's late instructions, and it being probable (although not avowed) that this envoy would have ulterior powers to treat upon all the topics which affect the relations of the two countries, Mr. Monroe expressed a wish to return without delay to the United States, and to leave with me the affairs of our country in quality of Minister Extraordinary and Plenipotentiary. So far as respected the business of the ordinary legation, there was undoubtedly, a difficulty of form, if not of substance, in the way of its coming into my hands in any other than the inadmissible character of a mere *Chargé d'Affaires.* My credentials as Mr. Monroe's successor, expired with the session of the Senate next following their date, and had not been renewed ; and my commission as Minister Extraordinary gave only limited powers for specified objects. It appeared to be my duty, however, in case it should not be unacceptable to the British government to communicate with me in the event of Mr. Monroe's departure, as if I were regularly accredited as the Minister Plenipotentiary of the United States, to consent on my part to such an arrangement, as being more eligible in the present conjuncture than the appointment of a *Chargé d'Affaires*. Mr. Monroe accordingly wrote, with my approbation, a note to Mr. Canning to that effect, to which some personal explanations were added, and received a reply, of which a copy is inclosed, adopting the arrangement proposed.

" You will perceive that, in lending myself to this step, I have ventured to infer the approbation of the President from what certainly does not express it. It would have been much more agreeable to me that a *Chargé d'Affaires* should be left, and that I should remain in my character of Commissioner Extraordinary until the government of the United States should have an opportunity of taking its own course. In that mode I should have been relieved from all embarrassment ; but thinking that the public interest required the course actually adopted, and that it was, moreover, that which was likely to fulfil the expectations of the President, I did not consider myself at liberty to consult my own inclinations.

" The concluding expressions of Mr. Canning's note afford me an opportunity of saying that, in awaiting here the orders of the President, I am ready to return or to remain, as he shall think the interest of our country requires. I beg you to be assured that as I accepted the trust which called me abroad with no selfish motive (although I felt how much I was honored by it), I should regret that any indulgent feeling towards me should in any degree restrain the President from promoting, in the way he thinks best, that which I know is the constant object of his care—the general good. Neither the unfeigned veneration in which I hold his character, nor the grateful recollection which I have not for a moment ceased to cherish of the manner in which he has been so good as to distinguish me, will suffer any abatement, although he should think fit to place some other than myself in the station which he once destined for me. I am quite sure that whatever shall be done, the manner of it will be liberal and kind ; and trusting, as I do most confidently, that I shall carry out of the public service, leave it when I may, the pure name with which I entered it, and the unabated good opinion of the government I have been proud to serve—the rest is of little importance."

In a letter, dated the 21st December, 1807, he says :

"I ought not, perhaps, to have been quite so scrupulous of writing to you on public affairs during the existence of the joint mission ; but you will do me the justice to believe that the scruple was sincerely felt, and yielded to frequently with great reluctance. You will now have reason, perhaps, to complain of me for writing rather too much than too little. I shall, however, continue in general to mark my letters "private," by which their freedom and frequency will be rendered innocent at least, if they shall not be useful.

"You will find that I have been careful to send you by every opportunity, newspapers, pamphlets, &c., since Mr. Monroe's departure ; as indeed I sometimes ventured to do before. May I beg that those from the United States may be sent with more regularity ? I ought to remark, that a pamphlet, favorable to British pretensions, and decrying our own, is no sooner published in America than it finds its way across the Atlantic, gets into general circulation here, and is quoted, praised, and sometimes republished ; whereas those of an opposite description either do not arrive at all, or come too late. Some pamphlets, of a most pernicious kind, having a British character strongly stamped upon them, have lately been imported from the United States, and advertised for republication by English booksellers. I should have been glad to see the antidote accompanying the poison. I am a sincere friend to peace with all the world, while it can be preserved with honor : but the strange productions to which I allude not only dishonor or betray the cause of our country, but tend, if read in Great Britain, to produce a temper unfriendly to accommodation ; and thus, while they inveigh against war, contribute to produce it. The effect of these works is greatly assisted by the wonderful ignorance which has prevailed, and still prevails, among all ranks of people in Great Britain, relative to the reciprocal conduct of France and the United States towards each other. The President's message has, for that reason only, been almost universally misapprehended. Even our best friends have mistaken and complained of it. In the course of my private intercourse (as well with the opposition as with the friends of ministers) I have done all that was consistent with discretion, to give more correct notions on the subject ; but the press only can remove completely the prevailing error, and to that expedient it would be improper that I should have recourse. Some of the most distinguished men in England, however, have been referred to General Armstrong's letter to the French Minister of Marine, and the answer of that Minister, as published in the American newspapers during the last winter, and to our convention with France, and may, perhaps, do what I cannot. Their own newspapers prove in part the practice (even now) under the French decree of November, 1806 ; and it is well known to many persons here (notwithstanding the general ignorance), that France has never acted, and does not at this time act, upon the parts of the decree which might seem intended for external operation, as maritime rules.

"There are rumors of a schism in the cabinet (relative to the Catholics) ; but I am told by a member of the late administration that it will come to nothing."

MR. PINKNEY TO MR. MADISON.

" DEAR SIR :—I inclose a duplicate of my public letter of
the 29th, and my private letter of the 31st, of last month,
to which I am now able to add a copy of the French decree
of the 23d (not, as I had supposed, the 25th) of November. This was sent to me by a Mr. Mitchell, who was proceeding to the United States (as he writes me) in an American vessel (the Ocean), with dispatches for you, from General Armstrong, when the vessel was captured by the Narcis-
sus frigate, and sent into Plymouth, upon the ground that
she took in a part of her cargo in France (*salt* for ballast)
after the day limited in the last British orders in council. I
have thought it proper to interest myself informally in the
case of this vessel, and I have assurance that it shall receive
the promptest attention. I have advised Mr. Mitchell to
wait a few days before he determines upon taking his passage
in another vessel for America, by which he would be likely
to lose time.

" I sent you some days ago a newspaper containing the
French retaliating decree, dated at Milan, the 25th of December. Those which are now forwarded contain the same
decree ; and you will find by the papers of this morning that
it has been followed up by another. This country has ventured
upon an extraordinary struggle with France, by which she
has every thing to lose and nothing to gain. The gross impolicy of the late orders of council (to say nothing of their
insulting tone, and their injustice to neutral states), begins
to develope itself, and will soon be manifest to all. I am
greatly deceived if it will not in a few weeks be matter of
surprise among all descriptions of people here, that a manufacturing and commercial nation like Great Britain, could

have expected any thing but disaster and ruin from such a measure.

" Hopes are entertained in England, that our non-importation act will have been repealed upon the arrival of intelligence of an intended extraordinary mission from this country ! That law passed upon unquestionable grounds of policy and justice ; and, although it has been heretofore properly *suspended*, I do not see how our honor could fail to become a mere shadow, if it should now be abandoned, even for a time. The mission of Mr. Rose would not seem to justify even the *suspension* of it, until the nature and extent of his powers were known ; and after they were known, it could justify nothing. He has no power to arrange on the topic of impressment, the great foundation of the non-importation act ; and his government has not only reasserted its obnoxious pretension on that subject in a public proclamation, but has even gone the length of declaring that it cannot consent to impair it. The unredressed outrages of Love, Whitby, &c., afford no inducement to repeal a law deliberately passed, with the clear approbation of the American people, when all the motives to its passage have received augmented force. But the late orders of council would make the repeal, or even the suspension, of the non-importation act, particularly unfortunate. The time when they were issued—the arrogant claim of maritime dominion, which they suppose and execute—and the contempt which they manifest, in the face of the world, for the rights and the power of our country, make them altogether the most offensive act that can be laid to the charge of any government. The least appearance of a disposition to submit to such an attempt will encourage to further aggressions, until our national spirit will be lost in an habitual sense of humiliation, our character known only to be despised, and our rights considered, like those of the petty states of Europe, the sport and the prey of the strongest. There is an opinion here, that we are likely to become a divided people, when a rupture with Great Britain is in question; but this opinion is founded upon such American publications as those in a Boston paper, signed " Pacificus," and upon some pamphlets and private letters of a similar character, and will, undoubtedly, be gloriously falsified, if there should be occasion, by the patriotism of our people in every quarter of the Union."

MR. PINKNEY TO MR. MADISON.

("Private.")   "London, *April 25th*, 1808.

" Dear Sir :—Mr. Rose has sent me your private letter of the 21st of March; for which I am greatly indebted to you. I know and sincerely regret, the state of your health; and therefore beg you not to make any effort (beyond what may be absolutely necessary for the public service) to write to me. I will take for granted your good will; and, if you will suffer me to do so, will presume upon your esteem. Of course, I shall not be ready to think myself neglected if I hear from you but seldom; and shall not relax in my communications because indisposition, a press of business, or some other reason, prevents you from giving much attention to me or my letters. I will only stipulate for an occasional acknowledgment of them, so that I may know what have been received and what have been miscarried. I need not say that as much more as may be consistent with your convenience, will be in the highest degree acceptable to me. My commissions and credentials, have not yet come to hand. They are perhaps in the Packet, or in the Osage, or in both.

" I feel very sensibly the delicacy and kindness of the assurances which you are so good as to give me, that the purpose of nominating me to the permanent Legation here was never for a moment suspended in the mind of the President.

I am the more gratified by this evidence of the continuing confidence of the President, because I have a firm persuasion that he will never have cause to repent it. I beg you to say for me, to him, that I am truly grateful for this distinction.

"I inclose another copy of the instruction to British cruisers, mentioned and inclosed in my last. Having been confined by indisposition for some days, I cannot yet vouch that it has actually been issued ; but all information concurs to make it sufficiently certain. There is something extremely injudicious in this measure, to say no worse of it. I do not suppose that we ought to consider it (or rather to *appear* to consider it) as offensive to us ; but, undoubtedly, an attempt, in the face of the world, thus to set the people against the government and its laws, is an ungracious act, and rests upon a bad principle. The effect of this wise contrivance in America, can only be, to add to the vigilance of the government in guarding the law, and to render more conspicuous the just pride and the public spirit of our citizens, by an open disdain of all foreign allurements to break it. Such an instruction manifestly reposes upon a foul libel on our patriotism, and is such a sneer upon our honor, national and individual, as should give us virtue, if we had it not before, to resist the temptation which it offers to the worst of our passions.

"P. S.—I have just received my credentials and your letter of the 8th of March, by the Packet, and have sent the customary note to Mr. Canning, requesting an interview for the purpose of presenting them.

"The incident you mention was not the most fortunate that could have happened, but I hope it will produce no bad effect here. I will endeavor to set it to rights without hazarding any thing. The freedom with which I hold it to be my indisputable duty to write to you, renders the delicate caution which the President uses on such occasions, peculiarly proper in my case. But if he should at any time think that the interests of the state require that publicity should be given to any of my dispatches, I do not (because I ought not to) ask to be spared; although certainly the publication of some of them, during my stay in this country, would cause me most serious embarrassment.

"My course will continue to be, to write with candor, frequency and fidelity, and to throw myself upon the kindness and wisdom of those to whom my correspondence belongs. I shall do so without doubt or fear of any kind."

MR. PINKNEY TO MR. MADISON.

"LONDON, *April 27th,* 1808.

" SIR :—I have the honor to inform you, that I have this day had an audience of the King and presented my credentials.

" My reception was particularly kind and gracious; and it is my duty to say, that every evidence, which such an occasion could admit, was afforded, of a desire on the part of the King to continue in friendship with us."

MR. PINKNEY TO THE PRESIDENT OF THE UNITED STATES.

"LONDON, *April 28th,* 1808.

" SIR :—I will trespass on you for a few moments only, for I have very little to say, and that little might have been said, with at least equal propriety, through another.

"I thank you, sir, for the feeling attention which, with your accustomed goodness, you have uniformly shown to the interests of my character, under circumstances which give to that attention even more than its usual value. I thank you, especially, for the recent proof which you have thought fit to afford me of undiminished confidence, in a season when that confidence, at all times flattering, does me peculiar honor.

" Your conduct towards me has been every thing that is delicate and generous and kind, and I should blush for myself, if I did not feel that it had made an impression upon my heart which neither time nor accident can efface. I entreat you to be assured, sir, that it *has* made such an impression ; and that the veneration in which I have always held your virtues and your talents will hereafter be accompanied and enlivened by gratitude and attachment.

" Will you suffer me to avail myself of this opportunity to join to the demonstrations of affectionate regret, which you have received from the different quarters of the Union, the feeble expression of my own, that your country is about to lose the benefit of your services in a station, upon which, although in itself the most exalted to which the virtuous hopes of a citizen can aspire, your patriotism and wisdom have reflected lustre. You will indeed, carry with you from that station all that can give a charm to retirement, the love and veneration of your fellow-citizens, and an approving conscience ; but it is natural that he who can so retire, should be given up with reluctance by the world to the claims of age or even of constitutional principle."

MR. PINKNEY TO MR. MADISON.

("Private.")   "London, *May* 10*th,* 1808.

" Dear Sir :—I received yesterday, after I had finished my public dispatch, a letter from Mr. Otto, who went lately to Holland, and promised while there to give me such intelligence of passing events as might be in his power. I inclose a copy of that letter. It leaves little room to doubt that an obnoxious decree has been recently issued at Bayonne by the

French government, reinforcing its former anti-commercial edicts, and superadding a provision of increased rigor. The decree itself (of which we had an ambiguous and discredited rumor some days ago), has not yet found its way to England.

"I have hardly any thing else worth saying to you. A desire to be friends with us seems now to be almost universal here, and it may I think be safely assumed that it pervades the Cabinet. I believe that the King is so disposed. What will be the practical result of that disposition, with reference to particular measures and pretensions which touch most nearly our honor and prosperity, is far more doubtful. The hostile spirit against France is at its height. Animosity is exasperated by well-founded alarm; and whatever promises annoyance on the one hand, or security on the other, may not easily be yielded to the wish, however strong, to conciliate us. The nation is with the government in that respect; at least such is the appearance.

"There has been sufficient time for sober reflection, to enable the most intemperate advocate for war with America to discover the rashness of his early opinions. The firm attitude taken with such provident foresight by the government of the United States—the combined operation of our embargo, of the other measures of our legislature and executive, of their own orders in council, and the French decrees—the discussions (through the Liverpool papers and others) by which the vital importance of American connection and intercourse (and even of that American trade which their late orders would injudiciously crush) has been demonstrated to all—the still progressive march of the power of France, and the new difficulties and perils which, with a persevering fertility, it produces or threatens—would have created, if it did not exist before, an anxiety to avoid a rupture with us. But if we continue at peace with France (as, if it be possible without dishonor, I trust we shall), they will recede here on certain points with infinite difficulty and reluctance, if they recede at all. They will not go to war if they can help it; but it is to be doubted whether they are prepared to do what may be indispensable to the re-establishment of interrupted friendship. They will be content to leave things as they are, and to trust to the influence of events; and a hope will perhaps be indulged that we cannot persevere in the embargo—that, weary of our system of self-denial, pressed by French aggression, and alarmed by the wide-spread domination and restless ambition of France, we shall at length be induced to acquiesce in the principles and practices of Great Britain (which must necessarily produce a contest with her enemy), or at once to make common cause with her against that enemy. What is to be the system of France, with regard to us, I know not; but it is sufficiently obvious that in the angry struggles of these rival powers, our rights are forgotten by both, and that it requires all the tried wisdom and firmness of our government, and all the virtue of our people, to conduct us in safety and with honor through the tempests that agitate and afflict the world.

" My health has suffered a little since my return to England, and I am disposed to ascribe it to a continued confinement to London, from which I have not been absent a single day for almost two years. I have some thoughts, therefore (but am by no means determined upon it), of going to Cheltenham, for a short time, after the birthday. I shall in that case leave a person in my house to attend to all ordinary business, to forward to me letters, &c.; and shall come to town myself as occasion may require. My son, who has hitherto acted as my secretary, I send home in the Osage to take his station in a counting-house."

MR. PINKNEY TO MR. MADISON.

"LONDON, *June 5th*, 1808.

" SIR :—I have the honor to acknowledge the receipt of your letter of the 4th of April, by Mr. Bethune, together with the printed, and other copies of Papers mentioned in it.

" I am to have an interview with Mr. Canning in a few days (which he will agree to consider extra-official), in the course of which I intend to press, by every argument in my power, the propriety of their abandoning immediately their orders in council, and of proposing by a minister in America (the only becoming course, as you very properly suggest), reparation for the outrage on the Chesapeake. I shall, for obvious reasons, do this informally as my own act.

" Your unanswerable reply to Mr. Erskine's letter of the 23d of February, has left nothing to be urged against the orders in council upon the score of right, and there may be room to hope that the effect, which that reply can hardly have failed to produce upon ministers, as well by its tone as by its reasoning, will, if followed up, become, under actual circumstances, decisive.

" The discussion, which Mr. Rose's preliminary in the affair of the Chesapeake has undergone, gives encouragement to an expectation, that this government will not now be backward to relinquish it, and to renew their overture of satisfaction in a way, more consistent with reason, and more likely to produce a just and honorable result.

" You may be assured that I will not commit our government by any thing I shall do or say, and that if I cannot make things better than they are, I will not make them worse. My view of the course which our honor and interests have required, and still require, is, as you know, in precise conformity with that of the President; but, if it were otherwise, I should make his view, and not my own, the rule of my conduct."

MR. PINKNEY TO MR. MADISON.

"London, *August 4th*, 1808.

" Sir:—The St. Michael arrived at Falmouth, on Thursday the 14th of last month, after a passage of 8 days from L'Orient. Captain Kenyon delivered me on Wednesday, the 20th (upon my arrival from Brighton, where I had been for a short time, on account of my health), your letters of the 30th of April, and your private letter of the 1st of May, together with newspapers, printed copies of the embargo act and its supplements, and of papers laid before Congress at their last session. Mr. Hall brought me a letter from General Armstrong of the 26th of June (of which I send an extract), and Mr. Upson brought me a private letter from him, with the following postscript of the 1st of July. ' An order has been received from Bayonne to condemn eight other of our ships, &c.'

" On Friday the 22d of July I had an interview with Mr. Canning, and renewed my efforts to obtain a revocation of the British orders of January and November, 1807, and of the other orders dependent upon them. I have already informed you in my private letter of the 29th of June that on the morning of its date I had a long conversation with Mr. Canning, which had rendered it somewhat probable that the object mentioned in your letter of the 30th of April (of which I had received a duplicate by the packet) would be accomplished if I should authorize the expectation which that letter suggests; but that some days must elapse before I could speak with any thing like certainty on the subject: and I have mentioned in another private letter (of the 10th of July) that it was understood between Mr. Canning and myself that another interview should take place soon after the prorogation of Parliament. In effect, however, Mr. Canning was not prepared to see me again until the 22d of July, after I had been recalled to London by the arrival of the St. Michael, and had, in consequence, reminded him of our arrangement by a private note.

"In the interview of the 29th of June I soon found it necessary to throw out an intimation, that the power, vested in the President by Congress, to suspend the embargo act and its supplements, would be exercised as regarded Great Britain, if their orders were repealed as regarded the United States.

"To have urged the revocation upon the mere ground of strict right, or of general policy, and there to have left the subject, when I was authorized to place it upon grounds infinitely stronger, would have been, as it appeared to me, to stop short of my duty. Your letters to Mr. Erskine (which Mr. Canning has read and considered) had exhausted the first of these grounds, and endless discussions here, in every variety of form, in and out of Parliament, had exhausted the second. There was, besides, no objection of any force to my availing myself without delay of the powerful inducements which the intimation in question was likely to furnish to Great Britain to abandon her late system ; and it seemed to be certain that, by delaying to present these inducements to Mr. Canning's consideration, I should not only lose much time, but finally give to my conduct a disingenuous air, which, while it would be foreign to the views and sentiments of the President, could hardly fail to make a very unfavorable impression upon the mind of Mr. Canning and his colleagues. I thought, moreover, that, if I should reserve the suggestion for a late state of our discussions, it would be made to wear the appearance of a concession reluctantly extorted, rather than of what it was, the spontaneous result of the characteristic frankness and honorable policy of our government.

" The intimation once made, a complete development of its natural consequences, if properly acted upon, followed of course ; and, taking advantage of the latitude afforded by the informal nature of a mere conversation, I endeavored to make that development as strong an appeal as, consistently with truth and honor, I could (and there was no necessity to do more) to the justice and the prudence of this government. It was not possible, however, that Mr. Canning could require to be assisted by my explanations. It was plain, upon their own principles, that they could not equitably persevere in their orders in council upon the foundation of an imputed acquiescence on our part in French invasions of our neutral rights, when it was become (if it was not *always*) apparent, that this imputation was completely and in all respects an error—when it was manifest that these orders, by letting loose upon our right a more destructive and offensive persecution than it was in the power of France to maintain, interposed between us and France, furnished answers to our remonstrances against her decrees and pretexts for those decrees, and stood in the way of that very resistance to these which Great Britain affected to inculcate as a duty at the moment when she was taking the most effectual steps to embarrass and confound it ; and when it was also manifest that a revocation of those orders would, if not attended or followed by a revocation of the decrees of France, place us at issue with that power, and result in a precise opposition by the United States to such parts of her anti-commercial edicts as it became us to repel.

" In a prudential view any explanations seemed still less to be required. Nothing could be more clear than that if Great Britain revoked her orders, and entitled herself to a suspension of the embargo, her object (if it were any thing short of the establishment and practical support of an exclusive dominion over the seas) must, in some mode or other, be accomplished ; whether France followed her example or not. In the first case the avowed purpose of the British orders would be fulfilled, and commerce would resume its accustomed prosperity and expansion. In the last, the just resistance of the United States (more efficacious than that of the British orders) to French irregularities and aggressions, would be left to its fair operation (of which it was impossible to mistake the consequences), and in the mean time the commercial intercourse between the United States and Great Britain, being revived, would open the way for a return to good understanding, and in the end for an adjustment of all their differences.

" These, and many other reflections of a similiar tendency (which I forbear to repeat), could not have escaped the penetration of Mr. Canning, if they had not been suggested to him in considerable detail. But, whatever might be their influence upon his mind, he certainly did not pronounce any opinion ; and what he said consisted principally of inquiries with a view to a more accurate comprehension of my purpose. He asked if I thought of taking a more formal course than I was now pursuing ; but immediately remarked that he presumed I did not ; for that the course I had adopted was undoubtedly well suited to the occasion. I told him that I was so entirely persuaded that the freedom of conversation was so much better adapted to the nature of our subject and so much more likely to conduct us to a beneficial result than the constraint and formality of written communication, which usually grew into protracted discussion and always produced embarrassment when there was any thing of delicacy in the topics, that I had not intended to present my note.

" The interview (in the progress of which some other points were incidentally touched upon, as mentioned in my private letter of the 29th of June) did not authorize any very confident opinion that Mr. Canning approved of what had *now for the first time* been suggested to him ; and still less could it warrant any anticipation of the final opinion of his government. But the manner in which my communication was received, and the readiness shown by Mr. Canning to proceed in the mode which was peculiarly favorable to my object, connected with the reasonableness of the object itself, induced me to think it rather probable that the issue would be satisfactory.

" The interview of the 22d of July was far from producing any thing of an unpromising complexion. I urged again much of what had been said at the last conference, and suggested such further considerations as had since occurred to me in support of my demand. Mr. Canning was still much more reserved than I had hoped to find him after so much time had been taken for deliberation ; but from all that passed I was more than ever inclined to believe that the orders would be relinquished. He seemed now to be extremely desirous of ascertaining whether I was authorized and disposed, with a view to a final arrangement, to present what I had suggested, as to the suspension of the embargo, in a more precise shape. I told him, after some conversation upon this point, that, although I would prefer that course which was the least formal, yet, if every thing should be first matured, I might be able to combine with a written demand, that their orders would be repealed, such an assurance as I had already mentioned, that the embargo would be suspended, but that I would consider of this with reference to the manner and terms. He then observed that I would perhaps allow him a little time to reflect whether he would put me to the necessity of presenting such a paper, and, upon my assenting to this, he said that he would give me another appointment towards the end of the following week. As I was on the point of leaving him, he asked me if I would endeavor to prepare, before the next interview such a note as we had talked of ; but he had scarcely made this request before he added 'but you will doubtless desire first to know what are our ideas and intentions upon the whole subject.'

"On the 29th of July I met Mr. Canning again ; and was soon apprised that our discussions, if continued, must take a new form.   He began by inquiring if I had received any intelligence of a late affair upon the Lakes which had caused great alarm and anxiety among the British traders, and of which an account had just been put into his hands. He then read very rapidly, from a letter apparently written in Canada, a complaint of an attack upon some British boats in violation of the 3d article of the Treaty of 1794, and observed that this was the more to be regretted, as it followed some recent misunderstanding in the Bay of Passamaquoddy. I told him that I had no intelligence, official or private, of these transactions, which he would perceive took place upon our borders at a great distance from the seat of government, and that of course, I could only express my conviction that the government of the United States would disavow whatever was improper in the conduct of its agents, and would in other respects act as good faith and honor required.   This affair being disposed of, Mr. Canning said that he had thought long and anxiously upon what I had suggested to him at our late conferences—that the subject at first struck him as much more simple and free from difficulty than upon careful examination it was found to be—that in the actual state of the world it behooved both him and me to move in this affair with every possible degree of circumspection (an intimation which he did not explain)—that without some explicit proposal on my part in writing upon which the British government could deliberate and act, nothing could be done ; and, finally, that he must leave me to consult my own discretion whether I would make such a proposal.   I answered that, with such a previous understanding between us as I had counted upon, I should feel no objection to take occasion to say in an official note requiring the revocation of their orders in council, that,

the orders being rescinded as to us, it was the intention of
the President to suspend the embargo as to Great Britain ;
but that I expected to be told, before my note was presented,
what would be the reply to it, and what its consequences in
every direction ; and that I could not conjecture, if it was
really meant to acquiesce in my demand (the exact nature
of it being in point of fact understood by this government
just as well as if it had been made in writing), or if more
time than had already been afforded was required for deliberation, why it was necessary that I should, in the last case
take the step in question at all, or, in the first case, without
being frankly apprised of the effect it would produce.   Mr.
Canning replied that my wish in this particular could not be
acceded to ; that, if I presented a note, they must be left at
perfect liberty to decide upon what it proposed ; that he
could not give me an intimation of the probable consequences
of it ; and in a word, that he would neither invite nor discourage such a proceeding.   He observed, too, that there
were some points belonging to the subject which it was necessary to discuss in writing ; that my suggestion implied that
the embargo was produced by the British orders in council—
that this could not be admitted—and that there were other
questions *necessarily* incident to these two measures with the
examination of which it was proper to begin upon an occasion
like the present.   I remarked in answer that, with an actual
result in view, and with a wish to arrive at that result without delay, nothing could be worse imagined than to entangle
ourselves in a written correspondence, undefined as to its
scope and duration, upon topics on which we were not likely
to agree ; that if I were compelled to frame my note with a
knowledge that it was *only* to provoke argument, instead of
leading at this momentous crisis to a salutary change in the
state of the world, he must be conscious that I too must
argue, and that I could not justify it to my government to
abstain from a complete assertion of all its pretensions and a

full exposure of the true character of those acts of which it complained as illegal and unjust. And where would this end ? To what wholesome consequence could it lead ?

" I ought to mention that I give you in this letter the substance only of the conversations which it states, and that there was nothing in any degree unfriendly in the language or manner of Mr. Canning at either of our conferences. I need not say that I thought it my duty to adopt the same tone and manner."

MR. PINKNEY TO MR. MADISON.

"London, *Sept. 6th*, 1808.

"Sir :—I have an opportunity of writing by Mr. Bethune, who leaves town to-morrow for Falmouth, to embark for the United States in the British packet ; and I cannot omit to take advantage of it, although I have still nothing conclusive to communicate.

" My public letter of the 4th of August will have apprised you of the footing on which my different interviews with Mr. Canning left the subject of the British orders in council ; and my private letter of the 2d of that month will have made you acquainted with my intention to present, in an official note, what I had ineffectually suggested in conference.

" To such a course there could not, even in the first instance, have been any other objection than that it was calculated to lead to discussion rather than to adjustment ; but, whatever might be its tendency, it is certain that I could have no inducement to resort to it until it was indicated by Mr. Canning as indispensable, nor any motive to decline it afterwards.

" At our last interview, and not before, it was unexpectedly found that it was in that mode only that I could obtain a knowledge of the light in which this government thought fit to view the overture I had been directed to make to it ; and I determined, in consequence, to lay before it in writing the intentions of the President, with the same frankness which had characterized my verbal communications.

"I have now the honor to transmit a copy of the note, which, in conformity with that determination, I delivered in person to Mr. Canning, on the 26th of last month, a few days after its date. To this note no answer has yet been returned: but it is to be presumed that it cannot be much longer withheld.

"You will perceive that some time had elapsed, after I had sent off my dispatches by the St. Michael (the 8th of August), before my note was presented. The truth is, that I had employed a part of that time in framing a note of great length, which, when it was nearly completed, I thought it prudent to abandon, in favor of one that held out fewer invitations to unprofitable discussions, which, although I would not shun them if pressed upon me, I did not suppose it proper that I should seek.

"I believed, too, that a little delay on my part would be far from being disadvantageous. There would still be sufficient time for obtaining a final answer to my proposal, in season for the meeting of Congress ; and, as the temper of the government, so far as it had been tried, had not appeared to be favorable to my purpose, I believed that I should act in the spirit of my instructions, and consult the honor of my government, by avoiding, under such circumstances, the appearance of urgency and precipitation.

"Upon the terms, or general plan of my note it is not, I hope, necessary to remark. You will discover that it was prepared under a persuasion that, whatever might be its effect, it was infinitely better to make it as conciliatory as, without a sacrifice of principle or national dignity, was possible.

" The topics to be embraced by it, were such as did not demand, but rather forbade, minute exposition. While it was difficult to urge in their full force without seeming to aim at exciting a disposition unfriendly to the object of my instructions, all the considerations which justified the United States in remonstrating against the British orders, it was yet more difficult, without a degree of harshness scarcely suited to the occasion, and without also the hazard of indiscretion, to display in detail the signal injustice and impolicy of persevering in them, after what I had proposed. This could be done, and had been done, in conversation; but it did not, upon trial, appear to be equally practicable in the more formal and measured proceeding which I was now called upon to adopt.

" I considered, besides, that an overture so advantageous to Great Britain, which the United States were not bound to make to any obligations of equity, although it was wise to make it, did not require, with any view to the character of my country, or even to the success of the overture itself, to be again recommended by an anxious repetition of arguments already fully understood.

" As soon as my note was prepared, I called at the Foreign office to arrange an interview with Mr. Canning, for the purpose of enabling me to accompany the delivery of it with a communication which I deemed important, as well as of affording him an opportunity of making and receiving such explanations as he might desire. The interview took place on the 26th of August.

" It had occurred to me that it would be proper (and could not be injurious) to read to Mr. Canning, from your letter to me of the 18th of July, a brief summary of the instructions under which I was acting. This had not been requested; but it could not be unacceptable; and it was, besides, well calculated to do justice to the liberal sentiments by which my instructions had been dictated, as well as to give weight to my efforts in the execution of them.

"I was led by the reading of these passages (without having originally intended it), into a more extensive explanation than I had before attempted, of the influence which the proposal of my government would have, in truth as well as in the judgment of the world, upon the supposed justice of their new system as it affected the United States. To that explanation, with the particulars of which I will not, and indeed for want of time cannot, at present, trouble you, I added a concise recapitulation of some of the practical considerations which had been so often pressed before ; and there I left the subject.

"Mr. Canning paid great attention to what I said. He spoke, however, of the attack on the Chesapeake and of the President's proclamation, and asked what was to be done with them ? I stated that these two subjects were wholly distinct from the present, but that it was not to be doubted that if the atonement which the United States were authorized to expect, for that admitted outrage upon their sovereignty, were offered in a suitable manner (which I ventured to suggest would be a special mission), it would not be difficult to bring the two governments to a proper understanding on these points—that, as it was fit that the British overture of satisfaction should be renewed in America, and not through me, I could not hope to be the immediate agent in receiving it ; but that I should be happy to contribute informally every assistance in my power to facilitate an adjustment, so much to be desired, upon such terms as it became them to offer and us to accept. Mr. Canning observed, ' that there was a difficulty in *setting about* the adjustment,' and he repeated what he said in our conference of the 29th of June (as mentioned in my private letter on that date), that there would be no objection to restoring the men taken from the Chesapeake ; but he did not say what other reparation they were willing

to propose.   I considered myself at liberty to encourge a disposition, which I thought I perceived in him, to move in that
interesting affair, in such a manner as to promise a satisfactory conclusion of it, and I acted accordingly ; but nothing
passed which could justify me in undertaking to anticipate
the result.

"At the close of the interview I told Mr. Canning that
although I would not be understood to urge an answer to my
note sooner than was consistent with his convenience, I could
not help asking that it might be as prompt as possible.   He
assured me that there should be no unnecessary delay ; and I
took my leave.

"As I have no sufficient grounds, upon which to form an
opinion as to the final course of the British government on
this occasion, I will not fatigue you with mere conjectures.
I have seen Mr. Canning but once (at dinner at his own
house), since the interview of the 26th of August ; and such
an occasion was not suited to official approaches on my part.
A few days, however, will decide what is now perhaps doubtful.   In the mean time the Hope will probably have arrived,
on her return from France ; and I will take care that by her,
and by other opportunities, you shall receive the speediest
information.

"I beg leave to refer to the newspapers herewith sent for
an account of the important events which have lately occurred in Europe."

MR. PINKNEY TO MR. MADISON.

("PRIVATE.)   LONDON, *Sept. 7th,* 1808.

"DEAR SIR :—As Mr. Bethune leaves town in a few hours,
I have only time to write a short private letter in addition
to my public one of yesterday.

"Mr. Atwater delivered your private letter of the 21st
of July, and a duplicate of that of the 15th, and I received

by Mr. Nicolson, on the 24th of last month, your private letters of the 3d and 15th of July.

" I cannot subdue my opinion that the overture on the subject of the orders in council will be either rejected or evaded. What infatuation, if it be so !

" That the embargo pinches here is certain. There is undoubtedly room for alarm on the score of provisions ; and it is confessed that they feel severely the want of our trade. The effect, however, is less than it ought to have been, on account of the numerous evasions of the embargo, and the belief (encouraged in America) that we had not virtue to persist in it. Should it be continued it must be rigorously executed, and our vessels in Europe recalled.

" I send you Marriott's book, entitled " Hints to both Parties." Towards the end you will find a pretty open avowal that even if France should retract her decrees, Great Britain ought to hold on upon the substance of her orders, making them only more *palatable* to us in some of their subordinate provisions. This gentleman is a West India merchant, and a member of Parliament ; and was consulted by ministers when the orders of November were in contemplation.

" It is still believed here that the late events in Spain and Portugal, connected with the British explanations (already forwarded in my private letter of the 17th of August, and now again transmitted) relative to a direct trade between the United States and those countries, will have an irresistible effect on our embargo. They are so misled in this country as to suppose that the embargo has already produced very formidable discontent in America, and I am mistaken if the government has not been inclined to calculate upon that discontent in various ways, and at least *to give it a trial.* But, at any rate, the Spanish and Portuguese trade will, it is imagined, be too great a temptation to be withstood. I know not what we may think of this temptation in America,—but it will be well to reflect that, if we trade under the British orders and go to war with France (as this speculation supposes) while the British orders continue, we not only retreat from the honorable ground we have taken, and admit the right of Great Britain to act at all times upon her new system, to the utter extinction of our commerce, but deliver ourselves up to her mercy in all respects. What would be her course in that respect I know not ; but is there any reason to believe it would be generous or even just ? We should, I incline to think, be in danger of falling into a dependence upon this country fatal to our character, to our institutions, to our navigation, to our strength—and what could we hope to gain ? I profess I am not able to imagine.

" Since the change in Spain and Portugal this nation is not exactly what it was ; and it may be presumed that the government partakes of the universal exaltation. Their dreams of future prosperity are bright and romantic. A *Chateau en Espagne* has become quite common. I have heard it suggested (as a course of *reasoning* not unusual here among merchants and others) that South America, whether dependent or independent, must be thrown commercially into the arms of Great Britain,—that, encouraged to exertion and roused to activity by a new order of things, she will hereafter rival us in all the great agricultural productions of our country—that, under a system friendly to the development of their resources, our southern neighbors will even surpass us as cultivators—that Great Britain will thus become wholly independent of the United States for articles which she has heretofore been obliged to take from them, and in a great degree too, for the consumption of her manufactures—that in other views our importance will be greatly diminished, if not absolutely annihilated, by this new competition—that this result, almost inevitable in any view, is more especially to be counted upon if Great Britain, compelled by the policy of our government, or following the impulse of the jealousy which is imputed to her, should foster (by her capital and her trade), to the full extent of her capacity, the prosperity of the south, in contradistinction to that of the north—that the change in Spain is *otherwise* likely to enable Great Britain to hold towards the United States a higher tone than formerly—that the Spanish deputies here (I doubt this fact), and those who are in the new Spanish interest (this I believe true), begin to talk already of our Louisiana purchase as unfit to be submitted to— that regenerated Spain will certainly question the validity of the cession that preceded our purchase, and reclaim the territory alienated by it—that this and other causes of dissatisfaction (aided by the sentiment of gratitude and the considerations of interest which bind the Spaniards to Great Britain) may be easily fomented into a quarrel with the United States, of which the consequences (Great Britain being a party also) may be most destructive.

"These rhapsodies (which may, however, be worthy of some attention) show how enthusiasm and prejudice can calculate! Spain, assailed by the whole power of France, has already leisure for an American quarrel, and can even spare troops to recover a superfluous territory on the Mississippi! The inveterate habits and pursuits of a whole people, in another hemisphere, are, against the repulsion of still existing causes, to pass to opposite extremes in consequence of a revolution in Europe yet in its earliest infancy, and of which the transatlantic effect (even if in Europe the revolution were established) would be a problem! Great Britain, with a vast increase of debt, is to find her account in casting from her our market for her manufactures, in rejecting our commodities essential to her colonies and convenient to herself, for the purpose of patronizing a country, on the permanency of whose connection she cannot rely, many of whose productions come in competition with those of her own colonies, and in which the passage from the actual state of things to that which is contemplated, must be reluctant and slow, and liable to endless interruptions and relapses ! It is forgotten, too, that this interesting section of the globe during all this tedious and doubtful process, may and must contribute to nourish our growth, while it can scarcely rival us in any thing. It is forgotten that, if it continues to lean upon the parent state, it is not likely, under the pressure of colonial restrictions, to flourish to our prejudice or even to flourish at all, but may serve to strengthen and enrich us ; and that, if it becomes independent, after our example, it will be far more natural that we should benefit and reflect lustre and power upon each other, than that Great Britain should find in the south the means of humbling the other branches of the great family of the west.

"From the newspapers it would seem that France and Austria are on the eve of war. Yet I have been told that it is not so. It is, I believe, certain that France has changed her tone (from haughtiness and menace to conciliation) towards Austria, since the discomfitures in Spain. This is not conclusive proof, however.

"The report that Lucien Bonaparte has requested of a British minister a passport to go to America is, I understand from a very respectable quarter, true.

"The result of our elections will now soon be known. I trust they will be favorable to the measures of our government. I need not say how sincerely and anxiously I wish that, with reference to yourself personally, they may give you all the honor which the suffrages of our people can bestow."

MR. PINKNEY TO MR. MADISON.

("Private.") London, *Sept.* 10*th*, 1808.

"Dear Sir :—I intended to have inclosed in my private letter of the 7th by Mr. Bethune, who left town on the evening of that day for Falmouth, to embark in the British packet, a triplicate of my public letter of the 4th of August, but in my hurry I omitted it. I transmit it now by Mr. Young, our consul at Madrid, who is about to sail from Gravesend for New-York, and I beg to renew my request that the slight variations from the original and duplicate, which you will find in the line marked in the margin with a pencil, may be adopted. The only one of these corrections, however, about which I am in the least anxious, is in the fourth paragraph from the end, which in my rough draft reads thus, "at the close of the *interview*, I observed, that, as the footing upon which this *interview* has, &c." This awkward iteration of the word *interview* (if not actually avoided in the original and duplicate, as perhaps it is) I really wish corrected.

"Mr. Canning's reply to my note not making its appearance, I went this morning to Downing-street to inquire about it; but both Mr. Canning and Mr. Hammond were in the country. I shall not omit to press for the answer (without, however, giving unnecessary offence) until I obtain it, or have the delay explained. It is possible that, when received, it may be found to adopt our proposal, and that they are merely taking time to connect with their compliance a long vindication of their orders. This is one way of accounting for the delay.

"It is also possible that they are actually undecided, and that they wish to procrastinate and keep back their answer until they can understand by the British packet (expected very soon) the workings of the embargo, and of the Spanish views in America; until they can take measure of our elections; until they can ascertain what is to be the course of France towards us; until the state of Europe, so flattering to their hopes, shall improve yet more, or at any rate be past the danger of a relapse, &c., &c. All this is *possible;* but I continue to think that they will reject what I have proposed. Their present *elevation* is exactly calcu-

lated (aided by false estimates of America) to mislead them
to such a conclusion. They are hardly in a temper of mind
to appreciate the motives of the President's conduct. The
chances are that they will ascribe the assurances I have been
authorized to give them, as to the embargo law, to a mere
anxiety to get rid of that law ; and that they will only see
in those assurances a pledge that we are heartily tired of our
actual position, and are ready to abandon it at any rate
They will be apt, in a word, to presume (believing, as I am
sure they do, that we will not venture upon extremities with
them) that, by holding off, they will compel us to retract
our late measures (the most wise and honorable ever adopted
by a government), and to fall at their feet. You must not
be surprised if they should be found to expect even more
than this from the pressure of the embargo. I allude to the
influence which *many* hope it will have upon our elections,
in bringing about a change of *men* as well as of *measures*.
In this I trust they will be signally disappointed.

"If (party spirit out of the question) the conduct of our
government towards the two powers that keep the world in
an uproar with their quarrel, has been *really* disapproved in
the United States, the overture just made to both cannot
fail to subdue it. I anticipate from it a perfect union of
sentiment in favor of any attitude which it may be necessary
to take. It puts us so unequivocally in the right, that,
although we were not, I think, bound to make it, it is impossible not to rejoice that it has been made. In any event
it must be salutary and must do us honor. The overture,
however, would seem to be more advantageous to Great
Britain than France. For if you should take off the embargo
as to France and continue it as to Great Britain, your proceeding would have little substance in it, considered as a
benefit to France, *unless and until you went to war against
Great Britain*. But the converse of this would have a vast

effect in favor of Great Britain, whether you went to war with France or not.

" It does not follow, and certainly is not true, that the overture is for that reason unjust to France ; although I think it the clearest case in the world that Great Britain is (at least) *in pari delicto* with France on the subject of that code of violence which drives neutrals from the seas and justice from the world.

" It is said here, by those who affect to know, that a conciliatory conduct by France toward the United States will not be acceptable to this government ; and certainly Marriott's book affords some reason for suspicion that a repeal of the French decrees would not be followed by that of the British orders. Such infatuation is scarcely credible, yet it would not be much worse than their present backwardness to avail themselves of what has lately been said to them.

" After all, it will be safest (for a time longer) to keep opinion as much as possible in suspense—and I need not repeat my assurances that the moment I receive the information I am expecting, no effort shall be spared to put you in possession of it."

MR. PINKNEY TO MR. MADISON.

("PRIVATE.")   LONDON, *Sept.* 21*st*, 1808.

" DEAR SIR :—The Hope arrived at Cowes from France the 13th.

" Not having heard from Mr. Canning, although he returned to London the 16th, I called again yesterday at Downing-street, and was assured that the answer to my note would be sent to night or early to-morrow morning. Mr. Atwater will of course be able to leave town on Friday, and embark on Saturday with a copy of it.

" I have been told since the arrival of the last British packet (but do not believe it), that there is more probability than I had anticipated, that the late events in Spain and

Portugal (which ought not to be considered as *deciding* on any thing) will have an effect on public opinion in America against the continuance of the embargo, and favorable to all the purposes of Great Britain. If this were true, I should think it was deeply to be lamented. I may misunderstand the subject ; but I cannot persuade myself that any thing that has happened on this side of the Atlantic, ought to induce us in any degree to retreat from our present system.

" If we should resolve to trade with Spain and Portugal (Great Britain and France persisting in their orders and decrees) in any way to which Great Britain would not object, we must suspend the embargo as to those countries only or as to those countries and *Great Britain,* or we must repeal it altogether.

" The temptation to the first of these courses, is, even in a commercial sense, inconsiderable ; the objection to it endless. The object to be gained (if no more was gained than ought to be gained) would be trifling. There could indeed be no gain. An inadequate market redundantly supplied would be more injurious than no market at all ; it would be a lure to destruction, and nothing more. A suspension of the embargo, so limited in its nature as this would be (supposing it to be in fact what it would be in form), would have a most unequal and invidious operation in the different quarters of the Union, of which the various commodities would not in the ports of Portugal and Spain be in equal demand.

" A war with France would be inevitable ; and such a war (so produced), from which we could not hope to derive either honor or advantage, would place us at the mercy of Great Britain, and, on that account, would in the end do more to cripple and humble us than any disaster that could otherwise befall us.

" The actual state of Spain and Portugal is moreover not to be relied upon. My first opinion on that subject remains; but even the most sanguine will admit that there is great

room for doubt.   The Emperor of France is evidently collecting a mighty force for the reduction of Spain ; and Portugal must share its fate.   And even if that force should be
destined (as some suppose) first to contend with Austria, the
speedy subjugation of Spain is not the less certain.   If
France should succeed, Spain and Portugal would again fall
under the British orders of November, as well as under the
operation of the French decrees.   Our cargoes would scarcely
have found their way to the ocean in search of the boasted
market, before they would be once more in a state of prohibition, and we should, in the mean time, have incurred the
scandal of suffering an improvident thirst of gain to seduce
us from our principles into a dilemma presenting no alternative but loss in all the senses of the word.

" But it is not event certain what Great Britain would
herself finally say to such a partial suspension of the embargo.
She would doubtless at *first* approve of it.   But her ultimate
course (especially if war between France and the United
States were not the immediate consequence, or if the measure were eventually less beneficial to herself than might be
supposed at the outset), ought not to be trusted.   That she
should approve at first, is hardly to be questioned, and the
considerations upon which she would do so, are precisely
those which should dissuade us from it.   Some of these are—
the aid it would afford to her allies, as well as to her own
troops co-operating with them, and its consequent tendency
to destroy every thing like system in our conduct—its tendency to embroil us with France, its tendency to induce us,
by overstocking a limited market, to make our commodities
of no value—to dissipate our capital—to ruin our merchants
without benefiting our agriculture—to destroy our infant
manufactures without benefiting our commerce—its tendency
to habituate us to a trammelled trade, and to fit us for acquiescence in maritime despotism.   But there are other
reasons—our trade with Spain and Portugal, while it lasted,

would be a circuitous one with *Great Britain and her colonies*, for their benefit. Our productions would be carried in the first instance to Spain and Portugal, would be bought there for British account, and would find their way to the West Indies or centre here, as British convenience might require, and thus in effect the embargo be removed as to Great Britain, while it continued as to France, and we professed to continue it as to both. And if any profits should arise from this sordid traffic, they would become a fund, to enable us to import into the United States directly or indirectly the manufactures of Great Britain, and thus relieve her in another way, while her orders would prevent us from receiving the commodities of her enemy. It would be far better openly to take off the embargo as to Great Britain, than while affecting to continue it as to that power, to do what must rescue her completely (and that too without advantage to ourselves) from the pressure of it, at the same time that it would promote her views against France in Portugal and Spain.

"As to the withdrawing the embargo as to Great Britain, as well as Spain and Portugal, while the British orders are unrepealed, the objections to that course are just as strong now as they were four months ago. The change in Spain and Portugal (if it were even likely to last) cannot touch the principle of the embargo, as regards Great Britain, who reasserts her orders of November, in the very explanations of the 4th of July, under which we must trade with those countries, if we trade with them at all. If we include Great Britain in the suspension, and exclude France, we do now what we have declined to do before, for the sake of a delusive commerce, which may perish before it can be enjoyed, and cannot in any event be enjoyed with credit, with advantage, or even with safety. We take part at once with Great Britain against France, at a time the least suited that could be imagined to such a determination; at a time when it might be said we were emboldened by French reverses, to do what before we could not resolve upon, or even tempted by a prospect of scanty profit, exaggerated by our cupidity and impatience to forget what was due to consistency, to character, and permanent prosperity. We sanction too the maritime pretensions which insult and injure us; we throw ourselves, bound hand and foot, upon the generosity of a government that has hitherto refused us justice; and all this when the affair of the Chesapeake, and a host of other wrongs, are unredressed, and when Great Britain has just rejected an overture which she must have accepted with eagerness if her views were not such as it became us to suspect and guard against.

"To repeal the embargo altogether would be preferable to either of the other courses, but would notwithstanding be so fatal to us in all respects, that we should long feel the wound it would inflict, unless indeed some other expedient, as strong at least and as efficacious in all it bearings, can (as I fear it cannot) be substituted in its place.

"War would seem to be the unavoidable result of such a step. If our commerce should not flourish in consequence of this measure, nothing would be gained by it but dishonor; and how it could be carried on to any valuable purpose, it would be difficult to show. If our commerce *should* flourish in spite of French and British edicts, and the miserable state of the world; in spite of war with France, if that should happen, it would, I doubt not, be assailed in some other form. The spirit of monopoly has seized the people and government of this country. We shall not under any circumstances be tolerated as rivals in navigation and trade —it is in vain to hope that Great Britain will voluntarily foster the naval means of the United States. All her prejudices—all her calculations are against it. Even as allies we should be subjects of jealousy. It would be endless to enumerate in detail the evils which would cling to us in this

new career of vassalage and meanness, and tedious to pursue
our backward course to the extinction of that very trade to
which we had sacrificed every thing else.

"On the other hand, if we persevere we must gain our
purpose at last. By complying with the little policy of the
moment, we shall be lost. By a great and systematic adherence to principle we shall find the end to our difficulties.
The embargo and the loss of our trade are deeply felt here,
and will be felt with more severity every day. The wheat
harvest is like to be alarmingly short, and the state of the
continent will augment the evil. The discontents among
their manufactures are only quieted for the moment by temporary causes. Cotton is rising, and soon will be scarce.
Unfavorable events on the continent will subdue the temper
unfriendly to wisdom and justice which now prevails here.
But above all, the world will, I trust, be convinced that our
firmness is not to be shaken—our measures have not been
without effect. They have not been *decisive*, because we
have not been thought capable of persevering in self-denial,
if that can be called self-denial which is no more than prudent abstinence from destruction and dishonor.

"I ought to mention that I have been told by a most
respectable American merchant here, that large quantities
of such woollen cloths as are prohibited by our non-importation act, have been and continue to be sent to Canada, with
the view of being smuggled into the United States.

"I beg you to excuse the frequency and length of my
private letters.

"I need not tell you that I am induced to trouble you
with my hasty reflections, because I think you stand in need
of them. I give them merely because I believe that you
are entitled to know the impressions which a public servant
on this side of the water receives from a view of our situation."

MR. PINKNEY TO MR. MADISON.

"LONDON, *September 24th*, 1808.

" SIR :—I am now enabled to transmit to you a copy of Mr. Canning's answer, received only last night, to my note of the 23d of August.

" This answer was accompanied by a letter, of which also a copy is inclosed, recapitulating what Mr. Canning supposes to be 'the substance of what has passed between us at our several interviews, previous to the presentation of my official letter.'

" To the accompanying paper I think it indispensable that I should reply without delay, supporting, with politeness, but with firmness, the statements which I have already had the honor to make to you of the conversations in question, and correcting some errors upon points which Mr. Canning has thought fit to introduce into his letter, but which I had not supposed it necessary to mention in detail in my dispatches.

" I shall not detain Mr. Atwater with a view to this reply ; but will take care to forward a copy of it by an early conveyance. My official note and the answer to it being perfectly intelligible, Mr. Canning's misapprehensions (for such they are) of previous verbal communications, can scarcely be very important in a public view ; but it is, nevertheless, of some consequence that whatever may be the objeet of his statement, I should not make myself a party to its inaccuracies, by even a tacit admission of them.

" I do not perceive that a formal reply to the more official paper, can now be of any advantage ; but I shall probably take occasion to combine with my reply to the one paper some observations upon the other.

" I regret extremely, that the views which I have been instructed to lay before this government have not been met by it as I had at first been led to expect. The overture can-

not fail, however, to place in a strong light the just and liberal sentiments by which our government is animated, and in
other respects to be useful and honorable to our country."

MR. PINKNEY TO MR. MADISON.

"London, *November 25th*, 1808.

" Sir :—I have the honor to send inclosed a copy of a letter, received last night, from Mr. Canning, in answer to my
letter to him of the 10th of last month.

" The tone of this letter renders it impossible to reply to
it with a view to a discussion of what it contains, although
it is not without further inadvertencies as to facts, and many of the observations are open to exception. I intend, however, to combine with an acknowledgment of the receipt of it
two short explanations. The first will relate to the new and
extraordinary conjecture, which it intimates, that my authority was *contingent ;* and the second will remind Mr.
Canning that my letter of the 10th of October does not, as
he imagines, leave unexplained the remark that, " the *provisional* nature of my offer, to make my proposal in writing,
arose out of *circumstances ;* " but, on the contrary, that " the
explanation immediately follows the remark."

MR. PINKNEY TO MR. MADISON.

"London, *December 24th*, 1808.

Sir :—I have had the honor to receive, by the British
packet, your letters of the 9th and 10th of last month.

The assurance contained in the first of these letters, of
the President's approbation of the manner in which my late
instructions were executed, affords me the most lively satis-

faction ; and I beg you to accept my sincere thanks for the kind and flattering terms in which you have been so good as to communicate it."

MR. PINKNEY TO MR. MADISON.

("PRIVATE.) LONDON, *January* 23d, 1809.

"DEAR SIR :—I dined at Mr. Canning's with the *Corps Diplomatique,* on the 18th, the day appointed for the celebration of the Queen's birth-day. Before dinner he came up to me, and, entering into conversation, adverted to a report which he said had reached him, that the American ministers (here and in France) were about to be recalled. I replied that I was not aware that such a step had already been resolved upon. He then took me aside, and observed that, according to his view of the late proceedings of Congress, the resolutions of the House of Representatives in committee of the whole, appeared to be calculated, if passed into a law, to remove the impediments to an arrangement with the United States upon the two subjects of the orders in council and the Chesapeake—that the President's proclamation had in fact formed the great obstacle to the adoption of what we had lately proposed, and that every body knew that it had formed the sole obstacle to adjustment in the other affair—that the renewal of commercial intercourse with America, while that proclamation remained in force, would have been attended with this *embarrassment,* that British merchant vessels, going into our ports, would have found there the commissioned cruisers of the enemy in a capacity to assail them as soon as they should put to sea ; while British armed vessels, having no asylum in those ports, would not have been equally in a situation to afford them protection—that if this was not insisted upon at large in his reply to my official letter of the 23d of August, it was because it was difficult to do so without giving to that paper somewhat of an unfriendly appearance—that as the above mentioned *embarrassment*, produced by the proclamation of the President, and the right which Great Britain supposed she had to complain of the continuance of that proclamation, proceeded, not from the exclusion of British ships of war from American ports, but from the discrimination in that respect between Great Britain and her adversaries; and as the resolutions of the House of Representatives took away that discrimination, although not perhaps in the manner which Great Britain could have wished, they were willing to consider the law to which the resolutions were preparatory, as putting an end to the difficulties which prevented satisfactory adjustments with us. He then said that they were, of course, desirous of being satisfied by us, that the view which they thus took of the resolutions in question was correct; and he intimated a wish that we should say that the intention of the American government was in conformity with that view. He added, that it was another favorable circumstance that the non-importation system was about to be applied to all the belligerents.

" As this occurred rather unexpectedly (although my reception at court, and other circumstances of much more consequence, had seemed to give notice of *some* change), and as I did not think it advisable to say much, even informally, upon topics of such delicacy at so short a warning, I proposed to Mr. Canning that I should call on him in the course of a day or two, for the purpose of a more free conversation upon what he had mentioned, than was then practicable. To this he readily assented; and it was settled that I should see him on the Sunday following (yesterday), at 12 o'clock, at his own house. I thought it prudent, however, to suggest at once, that the resolutions of the House of Representatives struck me as they did Mr. Canning; and (supposing myself to be warranted by your private letter of the 25th of November, in going so far), I added, that although it was evident that if Great Britain and France adhered to their present systems, the resolutions had a necessary tendency to hasten a disagreeable crisis, I was sure that my government, retaining the spirit of moderation which had always characterized it, would be most willing that Great Britain should consider them as calculated to furnish an opportunity for advances to renewed intercourse and honorable explanations.

"The interview yesterday was of some length. An arrangement with me was out of the question. An assurance from me as to the intention of the American government in passing (if indeed it had passed), an Exclusion and Non-intercourse law, applicable to all the powers at war, was equally out of the question. I had no authority to take any official step in the business ; and I should not have taken any without further instructions from you, founded upon the new state of things, even if my former authority had not been at an end. My object, therefore, was merely to encourage suitable approaches on the part of the government by such unofficial representations as I might be justified in making.

"I will not persecute you with a detail of my suggestions to Mr. Canning, intended to place the conduct of our government in its true light, and to second the effect which its firmness and wisdom had manifestly produced. It will be sufficient to state that, while I declined (indeed it was not pressed), giving or allowing Mr. Canning to expect any such assurances as I had understood him to allude to in our last conversation, I said every thing which I thought consistent with discretion, to confirm him in his disposition to seek the re-establishment of good understanding with us, and especially to see in the expected act of Congress, if it should pass, an opening to which the most scrupulous could not object, as well as the strongest motives of prudence for such advances, before it should be too late, on the side of this country, as could scarcely fail to produce the best results.

" It was of some importance to turn their attention here without loss of time, to the manner of any proceeding which might be in contemplation. It seemed that the resolutions of the House of Representatives, if enacted into a law, might render it proper, if not indispensable, that the affair of the Chesapeake should be settled at the same time with the affair of the orders and embargo ; and this was stated by Mr. Canning to be his opinion and his wish. It followed that the whole matter ought to be settled at Washington ; and as this was, moreover, desirable on various other grounds, I suggested that it would be well (in case a special mission did not meet their approbation), that the necessary powers should be sent to Mr. Erskine ; but I offered my intervention for the purpose of guarding them against *deficiencies* in those powers, and of smoothing the way to a successful issue. Mr. Canning gave no opinion on this point.

" Although I forbear to trouble you in detail with what I said to Mr. Canning, it is fit that you should know what was said by him on every point of importance.

" In the course of conversation he proposed several questions for reflection, relative to our late proposal, which, when that proposal was made, were not even glanced at. The principal were the two following :

" 1. In case they should now wish, either through me or *through Mr. Erskine,* to meet us upon the ground of the late overture, in what way was the effectual operation of our embargo as to France, after it should be taken off as to Great Britain, to be secured ? It was evident, he said, that if we should do no more than refuse clearances for the ports of France, &c., or prohibit, under penalties, voyages to such ports, the effect which my letter of the 21st of August, and my published instructions professed to have in view, would not be produced ; for that vessels, although cleared for British ports, might, when once out, go to France instead of coming here. That this would in fact be so (whatever the pen-

alties which the American law might denounce against of-
fenders), could not, he imagined, be doubted ; and he presumed, therefore, as he could see no possible objection to it
(on our part), that the government of the United States
would not, after it had itself declared a commerce with France
illegal, and its citizens who should engage in it delinquents,
complain if the naval force of this country should assist in
preventing such a commerce.

" 2. He asked whether there would be any objection to
asking the repeal of the British orders and of the American
embargo contemporaneous ?   He seemed to consider this as
indispensable.   Nothing could be less admissible, he said,
than that Great Britain, after rescinding her orders, should,
for any time, however short, be left subject to the embargo
in common with France, whose decrees were subsisting, with
a view to an experiment upon France, or with any other view.
The United States could not upon their own principles apply
the embargo to this country one moment after the orders
were removed, or decline after that event to apply it exclusively to France and the powers connected with her.   Great
Britain would dishonor herself by any arrangement which
should have such an effect, &c.

" You will recollect that my instructions (particularly
your letter of the 30th of April), had rather appeared to proceed upon the idea that the British orders were to be repealed
before the embago was removed as to England ; and it is
probable that a perusal of these instructions led to Mr. Canning's inquiry.

" Upon the whole, I thought I might presume that this
government had at last determined to sacrifice to us their
orders in council in the way we had before proposed (although
Mr. Canning once, and only once, talked of *amendment and
modification,* which I immediately discouraged, as well as of
repeal), and to offer the *amende honorable,* in the case of the
Chesapeake, provided Congress should be found to have passed

a law in conformity with the resolutions of the House of Representatives. I ought to say, however, that Mr. Canning did not precisely pledge himself to that effect ; and that the past justifies distrust. The result of the elections in America—the unexpected firmness displayed by Congress and the nation—the disappointments in Spain and elsewhere —a perceptible alteration in public opinion here since the last intelligence from the United States—an apprehension of losing our market, of having us for enemies, &c., have apparently made a deep impression upon ministers ; but nothing can inspire perfect confidence in their intentions but an impossible forgetfulness of the past, or the actual conclusion of an arrangement with us. In a few days I may calculate upon hearing from you. If Congress shall have passed the expected act, the case to which Mr. Canning looks will have been made, and he may be brought to a test from which it will be difficult to escape. Whatever may be my instructions I shall obey them with fidelity and zeal; but I sincerely hope they will not make it my duty to prefer adjustment *here* to adjustment in Washington. I am firmly pursuaded that it will be infinitely better that the business should be transacted immediately with our government ; and, if I shall be at liberty to do so, I shall continue to urge that course.

" You will not fail to perceive that the ground upon which it is now pretended that our proposition of last summer was rejected, is utterly inconsistent with Mr. Canning's note, in which that proposition is distinctly rejected upon other grounds, although in the conclusion of the note, the President's proclamation is introduced *by-the-by*. Besides, what can be more shallow than the pretext of the supposed *embarrassment!*

" I took occasion to mention at the close of our conversation, the recent appointment of Admiral Berkely to the Lisbon station. Mr. Canning said that, with every inclination to consult the feelings of the American government on that subject, it was impossible for the admiralty to resist the claim of that officer to be employed, *after such a lapse of time since his recall from Halifax*, without bringing him to a court-martial. The usage of the navy was in that respect different from that of the army. He might, however, still be brought to a court-martial, and in what he had done, he had acted wholly without authority, &c., &c. I did not propose to enter into any discussion upon the subject, and contented myself with lamenting the appointment as unfortunate.

" The documents laid before Congress and published have had a good effect here. Your letter to Mr. Erskine I have caused to be printed in a pamphlet, with my letter to Mr. Canning of the 23d of August, and his reply. The report of the committee of the House of Representatives is admitted to be a most able paper, and has been published in the Morning Chronicle. The Times newspaper (notwithstanding its former violence against us), agrees that our overture should have been accepted.

" The opposition in Parliament is unanimous on this subject, although divided on others. Many of the friends of government speak well of our overture, and almost every body disapproves of Mr. Canning's note. The tone has changed, too, in the city. In short, I have a strong hope that the eminent wisdom of the late American measures will soon be practically proved to the confusion of their opponents.

" I refer you to the newspapers for news (in the highest degree interesting) and for the debates. See particularly Mr. Canning's speech in the House of Commons, on the 19th, as reported in the Morning Chronicle.

" P. S.—As it was possible that the resolutions of the House of Representatives might not pass into a law, I endeavored to accommodate my conversation of yesterday to that possibility, at the same time that I did not refuse to let Mr. Canning see that I supposed the law would pass.

"I have omitted to mention that we spoke of Mr. Sawyer's letter in our first conversation, and that during the whole of the evening, Mr. Canning seemed desirous of showing, by more than usual kindness and respect, that it had made no unfavorable impression. I incline to think that it has rather done good than harm.

"I have marked this letter *private*, because I understood Mr. Canning as rather speaking confidentially than officially, and I certainly meant so to speak myself; but you will nevertheless make use of it as you think fit : of course it will not in any event be published.

"A third embargo breaker has arrived at Kinsale, in Ireland, on her way to Liverpool. She is called the Sally, and is of Virginia, with more than three hundred hogsheads of tobacco."

MR. PINKNEY TO MR. MADISON.

(" PRIVATE.)   LONDON, *May 3d,* 1809.

"DEAR SIR :—I have had the honor to receive your letter of the 17th of March, and thank you sincerely for your good wishes. Permit me to offer my cordial congratulations upon the manner in which you have been called to the Presidency. Such a majority at such a time is most honorable to our country and to you. My trust is that with the progress of your administration, your friends will grow in strength and numbers, and that the people will see in your future labors new titles to praise and confidence. You have my cordial wishes for your fame and happiness, and for the success of all your views for the public good.

"The publication of my letter of the 21st of September, has not had the effect which malice expected and intended ; and it is not improbable that it has contributed to produce a result directly the reverse of its obvious purpose. Such an incident, however, is injurious to the character of our country, but it will, doubtless, inspire at home such a distrust of the honor of members of Congress, who could condescend to so low and malignant a fraud, as to prevent a repetition of it.

"My letter to the Secretary of State will announce to you the change which has taken place here on the subject of the orders in council. I venture to hope that this measure will open the way to reconcilement between this country and America without any disparagement of our interests or our honor. I have not time (as the messenger leaves town in the morning, and it is now late at night) to trouble you with a detailed statement of my notions on this subject— but I will presume upon your indulgence for a few words upon it.

"The change does undoubtedly produce a great effect in a commercial view, and removes many of the most disgusting features of that system of violence and monopoly against which our efforts have been justly directed. The orders of November were in execution of a sordid scheme of commercial and fiscal advantage, to which America was to be sacrificed. They were not more atrocious than mean. The trade of the world was to be forced through British ports, and to pay British imposts. As a belligerent instrument, the orders were nothing. They were a trick of trade—a huckstering contrivance to enrich Great Britain, and drive other nations from the seas. The new system has a better air. Commerce is no longer to be forced through this country. We may go direct to Russia, and to all other countries, except to France and Holland, and the kingdom of Italy and their colonies. The *duty* system is at an end. We may carry, as heretofore, enemy productions. The provision about certificates of origin is repealed. That about prize ships is repealed also. What remains of the old measure is of a *belligerent* character, and is to be strictly executed as such. No licenses are to be granted even to British merchants to trade to Holland or France.

"There can be no question that this change gives us all the immediate benefits which could have arisen out of the acceptance of our overture of last year. It does not, indeed, give us the same claim to demand from France the recall of her edicts : but, in every other respect, it may be doubted whether it is not more convenient. If that overture had been received, a difficulty would have occurred as to the mode of making it effectual, as mentioned in my private letter of the 23d of January. And if we had agreed, either formally or by mere understanding, to Mr. Canning's suggestion, mentioned in the same letter, the substance of the thing would have approached very nearly to what has since been done. But, at any rate, the manner of the transaction is open to negotiation, and the intimation to that effect which has been made to me, may be an inducement to resume a friendly attitude towards Great Britain, and to put the sincerity of that intimation to the test.

"For the gain actually obtained, we may pay no price. We give no pledge of any sort, and are not bound to take any step whatever. The embargo is already repealed after the end of the approaching session of Congress. The non-intercourse law will expire at the same time. If neither should be continued at the approaching session, negotiation may be tried for obtaining what is yet to be desired, and, that failing, our future measures are in our own power.

"I am not sure that we have not got rid of the most obnoxious portion of the British orders *in the most acceptable way*. To what is left, it is impossible that either the government or the people of this country can be much attached. Having obtained gratuitously the present concessions, we are warranted in hoping that the rest, diminished in value, flattering no prejudices, addressing itself to no peculiar interests, and viewed with indifference by all, will be easily abandoned. In the mean time our peace is preserved, and our industry revived. France can have no cause of quarrel, nor we any inducement to seek a quarrel with her. The United States are no parties to the recent British measure as a measure of pressure and coercion upon France. We may trade in consequence of it, and endeavor to obtain further concessions, without the hazard of war with either party; while what has already been conceded saves our honor and greatly improves our situation. Our overture of last summer, if accepted, must have produced war with France, unless France had retracted her decrees, which was greatly to be doubted. The recent British measure, not being the result of an *arrangement* with America, will not have that tendency. For my own part, I have always believed that a war with France, if it could be avoided, was the idlest thing we could do. We may talk of " unfurling the republican banner against France "—but, when we had unfurled our banner, there would be an end of our exploits. This is precisely such a flourish as might be expected from a heavy intellect wandering from its ordinary track. It is not remembered that if we go to war with France, we shall be shut out from the continent of Europe, without knowing where it would cease to repel us. It is not remembered that in a war with France we might *suffer*, but could not *act*—that we should be an humble ally without hope of honor, and a feeble enemy without a chance of victory. It appears to me that the world would stand amazed if we, a commercial nation, whose interests are incompatible with war, should, *upon the instigation of our passions*, strut into the lists with gigantic France, with a metaphor in our mouths, but with no means of annoyance in our hands, and professing to be the champions of commerce, do just enough to provoke its destruction and make ourselves ridiculous.

" Our friends in this country are all of opinion that we should take in good part the new order in council, and, suf-

fering our restrictive laws to expire, rely upon friendly negotiation and a change of policy in this government, for the
further success of our wishes.   I can assure you with confidence, that they would be greatly disappointed and grieved
if we should be found to take any other course.   Our triumph
is already considered as a signal one by every body.   The
pretexts with which ministers would conceal their motives
for a relinquishment of all which they prized in their system,
are seen through ; and it is universally viewed as a concession
to America.   Our honor is now safe, and by managment we
may probably gain every thing we have in view.   A change
of ministers is not unlikely, and if a change happens, it
will be favorable to us.   Every thing conspires to recommend
moderation.

" I need not, I am sure, make any apology for myself,
even although you should think that less has been obtained
here than ought to have been obtained.   I have endeavored
to do the best with the means put at my disposal, and I have
avoided committing my government.   I am persuaded that
all that was practicable has been accomplished, and I have
a strong confidence that, used and followed up as your wisdom
and that of the legislature will direct, the result will be
good."

MR. PINKNEY TO MR. MADISON.

("Private.)   London, *August 19th,* 1809.

"Dear Sir :—I have had the honor to receive your kind
letter of the 21st of April, and now send the last edition of
War in Disguise as you request.   As we are turning our attention to wool, I have added a tract lately published here on
the merino and Anglo-merino sheep, which may be of use.
I trust that we shall continue to cultivate such manufactures

as suit our circumstances.   Cottons now and woollens *here-after* must flourish among us.

"American newspapers have been received here, showing that the disavowal of Mr. Erskine's arrangement has excited much ferment in the United States.   I cannot subdue my first regret that it was found to be necessary, at the last regular session of Congress, to falter in the course we were pursuing, and to give signs of inability to persevere in a system which was on the point of accomplishing all its purposes. That it *was* found to be necessary, I have no doubt ; but I have great doubts whether, if it had fortunately been otherwise, we should have had any *disavowals*.   It is to be hoped, however, that every thing will yet turn out well.   That *you* will do all that can be done at this perilous moment for the honor and advantage of our country, I am sure.

"I congratulate you heartily on the abundant proofs of public confidence which have marked the commencement of your administration.   I venture to prophesy that they will multiply as you advance, and that your administration will, in its maturity, be identified in the opinions of all men, with the strength and character and prosperity of the state.

"You will see from the English Journals that the British army in Spain has fought gallantly.   They make more of this affair here than perhaps it deserves.

"The French account will not exactly agree with the exulting inferences drawn by the people of England from Sir Arthur Wellesley's dispatch, which indeed leaves a great deal to inference.

"It is clear that the allied army greatly outnumbered the French—that it was advantageously posted—that if the Spaniards (forming the right wing to the amount of upwards of 40,000 men) were not actively engaged, they must have occupied or kept in check an adequate number of the French, *or* have been in a situation to turn the left flank of the

French—that on the first of these suppositions the British (on the left) could not have been attacked (as is here universally supposed) by the *whole* French force—that on the second supposition, it is quite unaccountable that the French were not turned, taken in rear, and utterly exterminated.

"This splendid victory, after all, amounts to no more than a repulse by nearly 70,000 men, enjoying every advantage of position, of between 40 and 50,000. The loss of the British is understood to have been tremendous. What the Spanish loss was is not known, but it was no doubt considerable. Sir Arthur Wellesley admits that the French retired in the most regular order, and it is not pretended that they were pursued or molested in their retreat.

"We have no data to enable us to judge of the probable result of the further projected operations of the British expedition. It will depend of course on the relative strength of its opponents, which cannot be otherwise than great.

"I shall be greatly deceived if France relaxes at this time from her decree against neutral rights. I should rather have expected additional rigor if General Armstrong had not given me reason to hope better things. The maritime arrondissement, now so near its completion, will furnish new inducements to perseverance in the anti-commercial system.

"It appears from the newspapers, that Mr. Adams has been appointed Minister Plenipotentiary to St. Petersburgh. I rejoice at this appointment, for many reasons."

MR. PINKNEY TO MR. MADISON.

("PRIVATE.) LONDON, *Dec.* 10*th*, 1809.

"DEAR SIR:—I see with great pleasure the ground taken by the Secretary of State in his correspondence with Mr. Jackson, connected with the probability that our people are recovering from recent delusion, and will hereafter be disposed to support with *zeal* and *steadiness* the efforts of their government to maintain their honor and character.   Jackson's course is an extraordinary one, and his *manner* is little better.

" The British government has acted for some time upon an opinion, that its partisans in America were too numerous and strong to admit of our persevering in any system of repulsion to British injustice ; and it cannot be denied that appearances countenanced this humiliating and pernicious opinion, which has been entertained by our friends.   My own confidence in the American people was great ; but it was shaken, nevertheless.   I am reassured, however, by present symptoms, and give myself up once more to hope. The prospect of returning virtue is cheering ; and I trust it is not in danger of being obscured and deformed by the recurrence of those detestable scenes which only reduced our patriotism to a problem.

" The *new* ministry (if the late changes entitle it to be so called) is at least as likely as the last to presume upon our divisions.   I have heard it said that it was impossible to form a cabinet more unfriendly to us, more effectually steeped and dyed in all those bad principles which have harassed and insulted us.   I continue to believe that, as it is now constituted, or even with any modifications of which it is susceptible, it cannot last ; and that it will not choose to hazard much in maintaining against the United States the late maritime innovations.

" The people of England are rather better disposed than heretofore to accommodate with us.   They seem to have awaked from the flattering dreams by which their understandings have been so long abused.   Disappointment and disaster have dissipated the brilliant expectations of undefined prosperity which had dazzled them into moral blindness, and had cheated them of their discretion as well as of their sense of justice.   In this state of things America naturally resumes her importance, and her rights become again intelligible. Lost as we were to the view of Englishmen during an overpowering blaze of imaginary glory and commercial grandeur, we are once more visible in the sober light to which facts have tempered and reduced the glare of fiction. The use of this opportunity depends upon ourselves, and doubtless we shall use it as we ought.

"It is, after all, perhaps to be doubted whether any thing but a general peace (which if we may judge from the past, it is not unlikely France will soon propose) can remove all dilemma from our situation. More wisdom and virtue than it would be quite reasonable to expect, must be found in the councils of the two great belligerent parties, before the war in which they are now engaged can become harmless to our rights. Even if England should recall (and I am convinced she could have been, and yet can be, compelled to recall) her foolish orders in council, her maritime pretensions will still be exuberant, and many of her practices most oppressive. From France we have only to look for what hostility to England may suggest. Justice and enlightened policy are out of the question on both sides. Upon France, I fear, we have no means of acting with effect. Her ruler sets our ordinary means at defiance. We cannot alarm him for his colonies, his trade, his manufactures, his revenue. He would not probably be moved by our attempts to do so, even if they were directed exclusively against himself. He is less likely to be so moved while they comprehend his enemy. A war with France, I shall always contend, would not help our case. It would aggravate our embarrassments in all respects. Our interests would be struck to the heart by it. For our honor it could do nothing. The territory of this mighty power is absolutely invulnerable; and there is no mode in which we could make her feel either physical or moral coercion. We might as well declare war against the inhabitants of the moon or of the *Georgium Sidus*. When we had produced the entire exclusion of our trade from the whole of continental Europe, and increased its hazards every where, what else could we hope to achieve by gallantry, or win by stratagem ? Great Britain would go smuggling on as usual; but we could neither fight nor smuggle. We should tire of so absurd a contest long before it would end (who shall say when it should end ?) and we should come out of it, after wondering how we got into it, with our manufactures annihilated by British competition, our commerce crippled by an enemy and smothered by a friend, our spirit debased into listlessness, and our character deeply injured. I beg your pardon for recurring to this topic, upon which I will not fatigue you with another word, lest I should persecute you with many.

" The ministry are certainly endeavoring to gain strength by some changes. It is said that Lord Wellesley is trying to bring Mr. Canning back to the cabinet ; and if so, I see no reason why he should not succeed. One statement is that Mr. Canning is to go to the Admiralty—another, that he is to return to the Foreign Department, that Lord Wellesley is to take the Treasury, and Mr. Percival to relapse into a mere Chancellor of the Exchequer. It is added that Lord Cambden (President of the Council), and Lord Westmoreland (Privy Seal), are to go out.

" If Mr. Canning should not join his old colleagues before the meeting of Parliament, he will probably soon fall into the ranks of opposition, where he will be formidable. There will scarcely be any scruple in receiving him. If he should join his old colleagues, they will not gain much by him. As a debater in the House of Commons, he would be useful to them ; but his reputation is not at this moment in the best possible plight, and his weight and connections are almost nothing. I am not sure that they would not lose by him more than they could gain.

' " If Lord Grenville and Lord Grey should be recalled to

power, Lord Holland would be likely to have the station of Foreign Secretary (Lord Grey preferring, as is said, the Admiralty).

"I believe that I have not mentioned to you that Mr. G. H. Rose was to have been the special envoy to our country, if Mr. Erskine's arrangement had not been disavowed. I am bound to say, that a worse choice could not have been made. Since his return to England, he has, I know, misrepresented and traduced us with an industry that is absolutely astonishing, notwithstanding the cant of friendship and respect with which he overwhelms the few Americans who see him."

MR. PINKNEY TO MR. MADISON.

("PRIVATE.)   LONDON, *August 13th*, 1810.

"DEAR SIR:—I return you my sincere thanks for your letter of the 23d of May. Nothing could have been more acceptable than the approbation which you are so good as to express of my note to Lord Wellesley on Jackson's affairs. I wish I had been more successful in my endeavors to obtain an unexceptionable answer to it. You need not be told that the actual reply was, as to plan and terms, wide of the expectations which I had formed of it. It was, unfortunately, delayed until first views and feelings became weak of themselves. The support which Jackson received in America was admirably calculated to produce other views and feelings, not only by its direct influence on Lord Wellesley and his colleagues, but by the influence which they could not but know it had on the British nation and the Parliament. The extravagant conduct of France had the same pernicious tendency ; and the appearances in Congress, with reference to our future attitude on the subject of the atrocious wrongs inflicted upon us by France and England, could scarcely be without their effect. It is not to be doubted that, with a strong desire in the outset to act a very conciliatory part, the British government was thus gradually prepared to introduce into the proceeding what would not otherwise have found a place in it, and to omit what it ought to have contained. The subject appeared to it every day in a new light, shed upon it from France and the United States ; and a corresponding change naturally enough took place in the scarcely remembered estimates which had at first been made of the proper mode of managing it. The change in Lord Wellesley's notion upon it, between our first interview and the date of his answer, had, without doubt, his full approbation. For, the account of this interview, as given in my private letter to Mr. Smith, of the 4th of January, is so far from exaggerating Lord Wellesley's reception of what I said of him, that it is much below it. It is to be observed that he had hardly read the correspondence, and had evidently thought very little upon it. For which reason, and because he spoke for himself only, and with less care than he would, perhaps, have used if he had considered that he was speaking officially, I am glad that you declined laying my private letter before Congress. The publication of it, which must necessarily have followed, would have produced serious embarrassment.

"Do you not think that, in some respects, Lord Wellesley's answer to my note had not been exactly appreciated in America ? I confess to you that this is my opinion. That the paper is a very bad one is perfectly clear ; but it is not so bad in intention as it is in reality, nor quite so bad in reality as it is commonly supposed to be.

"It is the production of an indolent man, making a great *effort* to reconcile things *almost* incongruous, and just showing his wish without executing it. Lord Wellesley wished to be extremely civil to the American government ; but he was, at the same time, to be very stately—to manage Jackson's situation—and to intimate disapprobation of the suspension of his functions. He was stately, not so much from design as because he cannot be otherwise. In managing Jackson's situation he must have gone beyond his original intention, and certainly beyond any of which I was aware before I received his answer. If the answer had been promptly written, I have no belief that he would have affected to praise Jackson's 'ability, zeal, and integrity,' or that he would have said any thing about his Majesty not having 'marked his conduct with any expression of his displeasure.' He would have been content to forbear to censure him, and *that* I always took for granted he would do.

"For Jackson, personally, Lord Wellesley cares nothing. In his several conferences with me, he never vindicated him, and he certainly did not mean in his letter to undertake his defence. It is impossible that he should not have (*I am indeed sure that he has*) a mean opinion of that most clumsy and ill-conditioned minister. His idea always appeared to be that he was wrong in pressing at all the topic which gave offence ; but that he acted upon good motives, and that his government could not with honor, or without injury to the diplomatic service generally, *disgrace him.* This is explicitly stated in my private letter of the 4th of January to Mr. Smith. There is great difference, undoubtedly, between that idea and the one upon which Lord Wellesley appears finally to have acted. It must be admitted, however, that the praise betowed upon Jackson is very meagre, and that it ascribes to him no qualities in any degree inconsistent with the charge of gross indecency and intolerable petulance preferred against him in my note. He might be honest, zealous, able, and yet be indiscreet, ill-tempered, suspicious, arrogant and ill-mannered. It is to be observed, too, this has no reference whatever to the actual case, and that, when the answer speaks of the offence imputed to Jackson by the American government, it does not say that he gave no such cause of offence, but simply relies on his repeated asseverations that *he did not mean to offend.*

"If the answer had been promptly written, I am persuaded that another feature which now distinguishes it would have been otherwise. It would not have contained any complaint against the course adopted by the American government in putting an end to official communication with Jackson. That Lord Wellesley thought that course objectionable from the first appears in my private letter above-mentioned to Mr. Smith. But he did not urge his objections to it in such a way, at our first interview or afterwards, as to induce me to suppose that he would except to that course in his written answer. He said in the outset that he considered it a *damnum* to the British government, and I know that he was not disposed to acknowledge the regularity of it. There was evidently no necessity, if he did not approve the course, to say any thing about it ; and in our conversations I always *assumed* that it was not only unnecessary but wholly inadmissible to mention it officially for any other purpose than that of approving it.

"After all, however, what he has said upon this point (idle and ill-judged as it is) is the mere statement of the opinion of the British government, that another course would have been more in rule than ours. It amounts to this, then, that we have opinion against opinion and practice ; and that our practice has been acquiesced in.

"As to that part of the answer which speaks of a *chargé d'affaires,* it must now be repented of here, especially by Lord Wellesley, if it was really intended as a threat of future inequality in the diplomatic establishments of the two countries, or even to wear that appearance. Lord Wellesley's letter to me of the 22d ult. abandons that threat, and makes it consequently much worse than nothing. His explanations to me on that head (*not official*) have lately been, that, when he wrote his answer, he thought there was some person in

America to whom Jackson could have immediately delivered his charge, and if he had not been under that impression, he should not probably have spoken in his answer of a *chargé d'affaires,* and should have sent out a minister plenipotentiary in the first instance. I know not what stress ought to be laid upon those private and *ex post facto* suggestions ; but I am entirely convinced that there was no thought of continuing a *chargé d'affaires* at Washington for more than a short time. Neither their pride nor their interests, nor the scantiness of their present diplomatic patronage would permit it. That Lord Wellesley has long been looking out in *his dilatory way* for a suitable character (a man of *rank*) to send as minister plenipotentiary to the United States, I have the best reason to be assured. That the appointment has not yet taken place, is no proof at all that it has not been intended. Those who think they understand Lord Wellesley best, represent him as *disinclined to business*—and it is certain that I have found him upon every occasion given to procrastination beyond all example. The business of the Chesapeake is a striking instance. Nothing could be fairer than his various conversations on that case. He settles it with me verbally over and over again. He promises his written overture in a few days—and I hear no more of the matter. There may be cunning in all this, but it is not such cunning as I should expect from Lord Wellesley.

" In the affair of the blockades, it is evident that the delay arises from the cabinet, alarmed at every thing which touches the subject of blockades, and that abominable scheme of monopoly called the Orders in Council. Yet it is an unquestionable fact that they have suffered, and are suffering severely under the iniquitous restrictions which they and France have imposed upon the world.

" I mean to wait a little longer for Lord Wellesley's reply to my note of the 30th of April. If it is not soon received, I hope I shall not be thought indiscreet if I present a strong remonstrance upon it, and if I take occasion in it to advert to the affair of the Chesapeake, and to expose what has occurred in that affair between Lord Wellesley and me.

" I have a letter from General Armstrong of the 24th of last month. He expects no change in the measures of the French government with regard to the United States. I cannot, however, refrain from hoping that we shall have no war with that government. We have a sufficient cause for war against both France and England—an equal cause against both in point of justice, even if we take into the account the recent violences of the former. But looking to *expediency*, which should never be lost sight of, I am not aware of any considerations that should induce us in actual circumstances to embark in a war with France. I have so often troubled you on this topic, that I will not venture to stir it again."

MR. PINKNEY TO LORD WELLESLEY.

"GREAT CUMBERLAND PLACE, *Nov. 3d*, 1810.

" MY LORD :—In my note of the 25th of August, I had the honor to state to your lordship, that I had received from the minister plenipotentiary of the United States, at Paris, a letter dated the 6th of that month, in which he informed me, that he had received from the French government a written and official notice, that it had revoked the decrees of Berlin and Milan, and that after the first of November, those decrees would cease to have any effect ; and I expressed my confidence, that the revocation of the British orders in council, of January and November, 1807, and April, 1809, and of all other orders dependent upon, analogous to, or in execution of them, would follow of course.

" Your lordship's reply, of the 31st of August, to that note, repeated a declaration of the British minister in America, made, as it appears, to the government of the United States in February, 1808, of 'his Majesty's earnest desire to see the commerce of the world restored to that freedom which is necessary for its prosperity, and his readiness to abandon the system which had been forced upon him, whenever the enemy should retract the principles which had rendered it necessary ;' and added an official assurance, that, ' whenever the repeal of the French decrees should have actually taken effect, and the commerce of neutral nations should have been restored to the condition in which it stood previously to the promulgation of those decrees, his Majesty would feel the highest satisfaction in relinquishing a system which the conduct of the enemy compelled him to adopt.'

" Without departing, in any degree, from my first opinion, that the United States had a right to expect, upon every principle of justice, that the prospective revocation of the French decrees would be immediately followed by at least a like revocation of the orders of England, I must remind your lordship, that the day has now passed when the repeal of the Berlin and Milan edicts, as communicated to your lordship in the note above-mentioned, and published to the whole world by the government of France, in the Moniteur of the 9th of September, was, by the terms of it, to take effect. That it has taken effect, cannot be doubted ; and it can as little be questioned, that, according to the repeated pledges given by the British government on this point (to say nothing of various other powerful considerations), the prompt relinquishment of the system, to which your lordship's reply to my note of the 25th of August alludes, is indispensable.

" I need scarcely mention how important it is to the trade of the United States, that the government of Great Britain should lose no time in disclosing with frankness and precision its intentions on this head. Intelligence of the French repeal has reached America, and commercial expeditions have doubtless been founded upon it. It will have been taken for granted that the British obstructions to those expeditions, having thus lost the support, which, however insufficient in itself, was the only one that could ever be claimed for them, have been withdrawn ; and that the seas are once more restored to the dominion of law and justice.

" I persuade myself that this confidence will be substantially justified by the event, and that to the speedy recall of such orders in council as were subsequent in date to the decrees of France, will be added the annulment of the antecedent order to which my late letter respecting blockades particularly relates. But if, notwithstanding the circumstances which invite to such a course, the British government shall have determined not to remove those obstructions with all practicable promptitude, I trust that my government will be apprised, with as little delay as possible, of a determination so unexpected, and of such vital concern to its rights and interests ; and that the reasons upon which that determination may have been formed, will not be withheld from it."

MR. PINKNEY TO MR. SMITH.

"LONDON, *Nov.* 14*th*, 1810.

" SIR :—I have finally determined not to mention again to Lord Wellesley (as I thought of doing) the subject of a plenipotentiary successor to Mr. Jackson. I think, upon reflection (and shall act accordingly), that I ought, after what has passed, to leave him, without further inquiry or notice on my part, to shape his course upon it ; and that, if an appointment should not be made as soon as the king's health (which would seem to be improving) will permit, I ought at once to send in an official note, announcing my resolution to return to America, and to leave some suitable person as a *chargé d'affaires.*

" My letter of the 23d of July informed you that after
Lord Wellesley's written assurance of the 22d of that month
(which was in conformity, as far as it went, with his assurances in conversation), 'that it was his intention *immediately* to recommend the appointment of an envoy extraordinary and minister plenipotentiary from the king to the
United States,' I did not think myself authorized to take the
step which the instructions contained in your letter of the
23d of May, in certain circumstances, prescribed.

" My opinion was, that whether the prospect which then
existed of bringing to a conclusion the affair of the Chesapeake, were taken into the account or not, it was my obvious
duty to remain at my post, most irksome as it was every day
becoming, until it should incontestably appear that those
assurances were not to be relied upon.

" Before a sufficient time had elapsed to warrant so harsh
a conclusion, I received from Lord Wellesley, on the 28th
of August, a farther *casual* intimation (reported to you in
my letter of the 29th of the same month) that his recommendation of a minister would, as he believed, be made in
the course of that week or the next.

" In the mean time the repeal, by the government of
France, of the Berlin and Milan decrees, had produced a
posture of affairs which, whatever might be Lord Wellesley's
forgetfulness of his own declarations, or the inattention of his
government to what he might advise in consequence of them,
rendered my stay in England for two or three months longer,
indispensable.

" In fine, the effect of that consideration had not ceased
when the illness of the king made it impossible that I
should depart.

" Upon the king's recovery, I shall have every motive for
bringing this matter to an issue, and none for the least hesitation or reserve upon it.   Several months have been allowed

for the performance of an act which might have been completed in as many weeks.

"I shall have done every thing in my power on the subjects connected with the revocation of the French edicts. And the British government will be in a situation to admit of such proceedings on its own part and on mine as the occasion will require.

"From Lord Wellesley's intimation to me on the 28th of August (mentioned above), it is perfectly clear, that he had not then executed the intention so positively announced in his note of the 22d of July. Five or six weeks had passed, and that which he had both said and written he meant to do *immediately*, he was not yet sure that he meant to do within another fortnight. The presumption seems, nevertheless, to be quite unnatural, that Lord Wellesley continued, up to the commencement of the king's malady, to be negligent of a pledge, which he chose to rest not merely on his *official* but his *personal* character—a pledge, of which he knew I could neither question the sufficiency nor doubt the sincerity, and by which, as he also knew, my conduct on an extremely delicate point of duty was wholly determined.

"On the other hand, if Lord Wellesley *has* been mindful of his pledge, and has recommended a minister in compliance with it, how has it happened (how *can* it have happened) that this recommendation has not been followed by an appointment.

"In the midst of all this doubt, which Lord Wellesley might dissipate if he pleased by an explanation apparently necessary for his own sake, there is, as I believe, no uncertainty as to the course which, in the actual state of my instructions (or on the score of general propriety), I ought to pursue; especially as I must infer, from your silence since the arrival of Mr. Morier at Washington (if I had no other reason for that inference), that no such communication was made, either by or through that gentleman to you, as ought in the judgment of the President to have any influence upon my conduct on this occasion."

MR. PINKNEY TO LORD WELLESLEY.

" GREAT CUMBERLAND PLACE, *December* 10*th*, 1810.

" MY LORD:—In compliance with the request contained in your note of the 6th instant, I proceed to recapitulate in this letter (with some variations however) the statements and remarks which I had the honor to make in our conference of the 5th, respecting the revocation of the French decrees, as connected with a change of system here on the subject of neutral rights.

" Your lordship need not be told that I should have been happy to offer, at a much earlier moment, every explanation in my power on matters of such high concern to the rights and commerce of my country, and the future character of its foreign relations, if I had been made to understand that explanation was desired.

" My written communications of August and November were concise, but they were not intended to be insufficient. They furnished evidence which I thought conclusive, and abstained from labored commentary, because I deemed it superfluous. I had taken up an opinion, which I abandoned reluctantly and late, that the British government would be eager to follow the example of France in *recalling*, as it had professed to do in *promulgating*, that extraordinary system of maritime annoyance, which, in 1807, presented to neutral trade, in almost all its directions, the hopeless alternative of inactivity or confiscation ; which considered it as a subject to be regulated, like the trade of the United Kingdoms, by the statutes of the British Parliament ; and undertook to bend and fashion it by every variety of expedient to all the purposes and even the caprices of Great Britain. I had no idea that the remnant of that system, productive of no conceivable advantage to England, and deservedly *odious* for its theory and destructive effects, to others, could survive the public declaration of France that the edicts of Berlin and Milan were revoked. Instructed at length, however, by your lordship's continued silence, and alarmed for the *property of my fellow citizens,* now more than ever exposed by an erroneous confidence, to the ruinous operation of the British orders, I was preparing to support my general representations by detailed remonstrance, when I received the honor of your note of the 4th instant. In the conference which ensued, I troubled your lordship with a verbal communication, of which the following is nearly the substance.

" The doubts which appear to stand in the way of the recall of the British orders in council (under which denomination I include certain orders of blockade of a kindred principle and spirit), must refer to the *manner,* or the *terms,* or the *practical effect* of the alleged repeal of the decrees of France.

" That the *manner* of the proceeding is satisfactory to the British government cannot be questioned ; since it is precisely that in which its own numerous orders for establishing, modifying, or removing blockades and other maritime obstructions, are usually proclaimed to neutral states and merchants.

" The French repeal was officially notified on the 5th of August, to the Minister Plenipotentiary of the United States at Paris, by the French minister for foreign affairs ; as I had the honor to inform your lordship in my letter of the 25th of the same month, which not only gave the import, but (as the inclosed copy will show), adopted the words of General Armstrong's statement to me of the tenor and effect of that notice.

" On the 9th of August the notification to General Armstrong was published in the *Moniteur,* the official journal of the French government, as the act of that government ; and thus became a formal declaration, and a public pledge to all who had an interest in the matter of it.

"It would be a waste of time to particularize the numerous instances of analogous practice in England, by which this course is countenanced ; but a recent example happens to be before me, and may therefore be mentioned. The partial recall or modification of the English blockade of the ports and places of Spain, from Gijon to the French territory (itself known to my government only through a circular notification to me recited afterwards in the London Gazette), was declared to the American and other governments in exactly the same mode.

"I think it demonstrable that the *terms* in which the French revocation was announced, are just as free from well founded objection as the *manner*.

"Your lordship's view of them is entirely unknown to me ; but I am not ignorant that there are those in this country who, professing to have examined them with *care*, and having certainly examined them with *jealousy*, maintain that the revocation on the 1st of November, was made to depend by the obvious meaning of those terms, upon a condition precedent which has not been fulfilled, namely—the revocation by Great Britain of her orders in council, including such blockading orders as France complains of as being illegal.

"If this were even admitted to be so, I am yet to learn upon what grounds of justice the British government could decline to meet, by a similar act on its part, an advance thus made to it by its adversary, in the face of the world, towards a co-operation in the great work of restoring the liberty of the ocean ; so far, at least, as respects the orders in council of 1807 and 1809, and such blockades as resemble them. It is not necessary, however, to take this view of the question ; for the French revocation turns on no condition precedent, is absolute, precise and unequivocal.

"What construction of the document which declares that revocation might be made by determined suspicion and distrust, I have no wish, and am not bound to inquire. Such interpreters would not be satisfied by any form of words, and would be likely to draw the same conclusion from perfect explicitness and studied obscurity. It is enough for me that the fair and natural and necessary import of the paper affords no color for the interpretation I am about to examine.

"The French declaration 'that the decrees of Berlin and Milan *Are Revoked,* and that from the first of November they will cease to have any effect,' is precision itself. But they are followed by these words : 'bien entendu qu'en consequence de cette declaration les Anglois revoqueront leurs arrêts du conseil, et *renonceront* aux nouveaux principes de blocus qu'ils ont voulu etablir, ou bien que les Etats Unis, *conformement à l'acte que vous venez* communique, feront respecter leur droits par les Anglois.'

"If these words state any *condition,* they state *two,* the first depending upon Great Britain, the last upon the United States : and as they are put in the disjunctive, it would be extravagant to hold that the non-performance of one of them is equivalent to the non-performance of both. I shall take for granted, therefore, that the argument against my construction of the Duke of Cadore's letter must be moulded into a new form. It must deal with two conditions instead of one, and considering them equally as conditions precedent to be performed (disjunctively) before the day limited for the operative commencement of the French repeal, must maintain that if *neither* of them should be performed before that day, the decrees were not to be revoked, and, consequently, that as neither of them *has* been so performed, the decrees are still in force.

"If this hypothesis of previous conditions, thus reduced to the only shape it can assume, be proved to be unsound, my construction is at once established ; since it is only upon that hypothesis that any doubt can be raised against the exact and perspicuous assurance that the decrees were actually repealed, and that the repeal would become effectual on the 1st of November. This hypothesis *is* proved to be unsound, by the following consideration.

" It has clearly no foundation in the phraseology of the paper, which does not contain a syllable to put any condition before the repeal. The repeal is represented as a step already taken, to have effect on a day specified. Certain consequences are, indeed, declared to be expected from this proceeding ; but no day is given, either expressly or by implication, within which they are to happen. It is not said, ' bien entendu que les Anglois auront revoqué,' &c., but ' que les Anglois revoqueront,' &c., indefinitely as to time.

" The notion of conditions precedent is, therefore, to say the least of it, perfectly gratuitous. But it is also absurd. It drives us to the conclusion, that a palpable and notorious impossibility was intended to be prescribed as a condition, in a paper which they who think it was meant to deceive, must admit was meant to be plausible.

" It was a palpable and notorious impossibility, that the United States should, before the 1st of November, execute *any condition*, no matter what the nature of it, the performance of which was to follow the ascertained failure of a condition to be executed by Great Britain at *any time* before the same 1st of November. That the act expected from the United States was to be consequent upon the failure of the *other*, is apparent. It is also apparent, that upon any interpretation which would make the act of Great Britain a *condition precedent to the French repeal*, and consequently precedent to the 1st of November (when the repeal was, if ever, to take effect), that condition could not be said to have failed before the whole *period*, from the 5th of August to the 1st of November, had elapsed. But if Great Britain had had the whole time, within which to elect the course which she would pursue, what opportunity would be left to the United States (equally bound, upon this idea of conditions precedent, to act their part within the same period), to become acquainted with that election, and to decide upon and take their own course in consequence ; to say nothing of the transmission of such intelligence of it to Europe as would be indispensable to the efficacy of the conditional revocation.

This general view would be sufficient to discredit the arbitrary construction under consideration. But it will be more completely exposed by an explanation of the nature of the act, which the latter professes to expect from the United States, in case Great Britain should omit to revoke. This act is the *revival* of the non-intercourse law against England, France remaining exempt from it, as well as from the provisions of the subsequent law, commonly called the non-intercourse act. Now, if it is too plain, upon the face of the last mentioned law (to which the letter expressly refers) to escape the most negligent and unskilful observer, that this revival could not, by any industry or chance, be accomplished before the time fixed for the cessation of the French decrees, or even for a considerable time afterwards, it certainly cannot be allowable to assume, that the revival was required by the letter (whatever was the *object* of the writer or his government) to precede the cessation. And if this was not required, it is incontrovertible that the cessation would, by the terms of the letter, take place on the appointed day, whether any of the events disjunctively specified had intervened or not.

" The first step towards a revival of the non-intercourse against England would be the proclamation of the President, that France had so revoked or modified her edicts, as that they ceased to violate the neutral commerce of the United States. But the letter of Monsieur Champagny left the decrees, as it found them, up to the first of November, and, consequently, *up to that day* it could not, for any thing contained in that letter, be said that the rights of American commerce were no longer infringed by them. A prospective proclamation, that they *would* cease to violate those rights, might, perhaps, be issued ; but it could scarcely have any substantial operation, either in favor of France or to the prejudice of England, until the epoch to which it looked had arrived.

"Let it be admitted, however, that all physical and legal obstacles to the issuing, *before the first of November*, of a proclamation, to take effect immediately, were out of the way—how would such a proceeding fulfil, of itself, the expectation that the United States would, before the first of *November*, "cause their rights to be respected by the English," in the mode pointed out in the letter, namely, by the enforcement of the non-intercourse law ? The proclamation would work no direct or immediate consequence against England. Three months from its date must pass away before the non-intercourse law could revive against her ; and when it did so, the revival would not be the effect of the proclamation, but of the continued adherence of England to her obnoxious system. Thus, even if a proclamation, effectual from its date, had been issued by the President on the day when the French declaration of repeal came to the hands of the American minister at Paris, the intercourse between the United States and Great Britain would, on the first of November, have remained in the same condition in which it was found in August. As all this was well understood by the government of France, the conclusion is, that its minister, professing too to have the American law before him, and to expect only what was *conformable with that law*, did not intend to require the revival of the non-intercourse against England as a *condition* to be performed before the first of November.

"It is worthy of remark, as introductory to another view of this subject, that even they who conclude that the repeal of the French decrees has failed are not backward to ascribe to the French declaration a purpose utterly inconsistent with that conclusion. They suppose the purpose to have been to affect the existing relations between America and England, by the only means which the declaration states, the act of non-intercourse. And it is certain that unless England should abandon particular parts of her system, this *was* the result avowedly in view, and meant to be accomplished. But there could be no hope of such a result without a previous effectual relinquishment of the French decrees. A case could not otherwise be made to exist (as the Duke of Cadore was aware) for such an operation of the American law. To put the law before the revocation of the edicts was impossible. With the law in his hand it would have been miraculous ignorance not to know that it was the exact reverse of this which his paper must propose. He would derive this knowledge, not from that particular law only, but from the whole tenor and spirit of American proceedings, ·in that painful and anomalous dilemma, in which Great Britain and France, agreeing in nothing else, had recently combined to place the maritime interests of America. He would collect from those proceedings that, while those conflicting powers continued to rival each other in their aggressions upon neutral rights, the government of the United States would oppose itself impartially to both. The French declaration, then, had either no meaning at all, or it meant to announce to General Armstrong a positive revocation of the French edicts.

"I should only fatigue your lordship by pursuing farther a point so plain and simple. I will, therefore, merely add to what I have already said on this branch of the subject, that the strong and unqualified communication from General Armstrong to me, mentioned in the commencement of this letter, and corroborated by subsequent communications (one of which I now lay before you), may, perhaps, without any great effort of courtesy, be allowed to contain that "authentic intelligence" which your lordship is in search of. He could scarcely have been free from doubt if the occasion was calculated to suggest it, and if he had really doubted, would hardly have spoken to me with the confidence of conviction.

"It only remains to speak of the *practical effect* of the French repeal. And here your lordship must suffer me to remind you that the orders of England in 1807, did not wait for the practical effect of the *Berlin* decree, nor linger till the obscurity, in which the meaning of that decree was supposed to be involved, should be cleared away by time or explanation. They came promptly after the decree itself, while it was not only ambiguous but inoperative, and raised upon an idle prohibition, and a yet more idle declaration, which France had not attempted to enforce, and was notoriously incapable of enforcing a vast scheme of oppression upon the seas, more destructive of all the acknowledged rights of peaceful states than history can parallel. This *retaliation*, as it was called, was so rapid, that it was felt before the injury which was said to have provoked it; and yet, that injury, such as it was, was preceded by the practical assertion, on the part of Great Britain, of new and alarming principles of public law, in the notification of the blockade of May, 1806, and in the judicial decisions of the year before. To uphold the *retaliatory* orders, every thing was *presumed* with a surprising facility. Not only was an impotent, unexecuted, and equivocal menace presumed to be an active scourge of the commerce of neutral nations, but the acquiescence of those nations was presumed against the plainest evidence of facts.

"The alacrity with which all this was done can never be remembered without regret and astonishment; but our regret and astonishment must increase, if, after four years have been given to the *pernicious innovation*, which these presumptions were to introduce and support, something like the same alacrity should not be displayed in seizing an honorable opportunity of discarding it for ever.

"It is not unnatural to imagine that it *will be* discarded with pleasure, *when it is considered*, that having never been effectual as an instrument of hostility, it cannot now lay claim to those *other* recommendations for which it may have heretofore been prized. The orders in council of November have passed through some important changes ; but they have been steady, as long as it was possible, to the *purpose which first impressed on them a character not to be mistaken.*

" In their original plan, they comprehended not only France and such allied or dependent powers as had adopted the edict of Berlin, but such other nations as had merely excluded from their ports the commercial flag of England. This prodigious expansion of the system, was far beyond any intelligible standard of *retaliation;* but it soon appeared that neutrals might be permitted to traffic under certain restrictions, with all these different nations, provided they would submit with a dependence *truly colonial,* to carry on their trade through British ports, and to pay such duties as the British government should think fit to impose, and such charges as British agents and other British subjects might be content to make.

" The United States abstained from this *traffic*, in which they could not embark without dishonor ; and in 1809, the system shrunk to narrower dimensions, and took the appearance of an absolute prohibition of all commercial intercourse with France, Holland, and the kingdom of Italy.

" The prohibition was absolute in appearance, but not in fact. It had lost something of former exuberance, but nothing of former pliancy, and in the event was seen to yield to the demands of *one* trade, while it prevented every other.

"Controlled and relaxed and managed by *licenses*, it did not, after a brief exhibition of impartial sternness, affect to "distress the enemy" by the occlusion of his ports, when the commerce of *England* could advantageously find its way to them. At length, however, this convenience seems to be enjoyed no longer, and the orders in council may apparently be now considered (if indeed they ought not always to have been considered) as affecting England with a loss as heavy as that which they inflict on those whose rights they violate. In such circumstances, if it be too much to expect the *credulity* of 1807, it may yet be hoped, that the evidence of the *practical effect* of the French repeal need not be very strong to be satisfactory. It is however as strong as the nature of such a case will admit, as a few observations will show.

"On such an occasion it is no paradox to say, that the want of evidence is itself evidence : That certain decrees are not in force, is proved by the absence of such facts as would appear if they *were* in force. Every motive which can be conjectured to have led to the repeal of the edicts, invites to the full execution of that repeal, and no motive can be imagined for a different course. These considerations are alone conclusive.

"But farther, it is known that American vessels bound confessedly to England, have, before the 1st of November, been visited by French privateers, and suffered to pass upon the foundation of the prospective repeal of the decree of Berlin, and the proximity of the day when it would become an actual one.

"If there are not even stronger facts to show that the decree of *Milan* is also withdrawn, your lordship can be at no loss for the reason. It cannot be proved that an American vessel is practically held by France. Not to be *denationalized* by British visitation, because your cruisers *visit* only to *capture*, and compel the vessel visited to terminate her voyage not in France, but in England. You will not ask for the issue of an experiment which yourselves intercept, nor complain that you have not received evidence, which is not obtained because you have rendered it impossible. The vessel which formed the subject of my note of the 8th inst., and another more recently seized as a prize, would, if they had been suffered, *as they ought*, to resume their voyages after having been stopped and examined by English cruisers, have furnished on that point unanswerable proof ; and I have reason to know, that precise offers have been made to the British government to put to a practical test the disposition of France in this respect, and that those offers have been refused. Your cruisers, however, have not been able to visit all American vessels bound to France, and it is understood, that such as have arrived have been received with friendship.

" I cannot quit this last question without entering my protest against the pretension of the British government to postpone the justice which it owes to my government and country, for this tardy investigation of consequences. I am not able to comprehend upon what the pretension rests, nor to what limits the investigation can be subjected. If it were even admitted that France was more emphatically bound to repeal her almost nominal decrees than Great Britain to repeal her substantial orders (which will not be admitted), what more can reasonably be required by the latter than has been done by the former ? The decrees are officially declared by the government of France to be repealed. They were ineffectual as a material prejudice to England before the declaration, and must be ineffectual since. There is therefore nothing of substance for this dilatory inquiry, which if once begun may be protracted without end, or at least till the hour for just and *prudent* decision has passed. But, if there were room to apprehend that the repealed decrees might have some operation in case the orders in council were withdrawn, still, as there is no sudden and formidable peril to which Great Britain could be exposed by that operation, there can be no reason for declining to act at once upon the declaration of France, and to leave it to the future to try its sincerity, if that sincerity be suspected.

" I have thus disclosed to your lordship, with that frankness which the times demand, my view of a subject deeply interesting to our respective countries. The part which Great Britain may act on this occasion cannot fail to have important and lasting consequences, and I can only wish that they may be good.

" By giving up her orders in council and the *blockades*, to which my letter of the 21st of September relates, she has nothing to lose in character or strength. By adhering to them, she will not only be *unjust to others* but *unjust to herself*."

MR. PINKNEY TO LORD WELLESLEY.

"Great Cumberland Place, *Jan.* 14, 1811.

" My Lord :—I have received the letter which you did me the honor to address to me on the 29th of last month, and will not fail to transmit a copy of it to my government. In the mean time I take the liberty to trouble you with the following reply, which a severe indisposition has prevented me from preparing sooner.

" The first paragraph seems to make it proper for me to begin by saying, that the topics introduced into my letter of the 10th of December, were intimately connected with its principal subject, and fairly used to illustrate and explain it ; and consequently, that if they had not the good fortune to be acceptable to your lordship, the fault was not mine.

" It was scarcely possible to speak with more moderation than my paper exhibits, of that portion of a long list of invasions of the rights of the United States, which it necessa-

rily reviewed, and of the apparent reluctance of the British
government to forbear those invasions in future. I do not
know that I could more carefully have abstained from whatever might tend to disturb the spirit which your lordship
ascribes to his majesty's government, if, instead of being
utterly barren and unproductive, it had occasionally been
visible in some practical result, in some concession either to
friendship or to justice. It would not have been very surprising, nor very culpable perhaps, if I had wholly forgotten
to address myself to a spirit of conciliation, which had met
the most equitable claims with steady and unceasing repulsion ; which had yielded nothing that could be denied ; and
had answered complaints of injury by multiplying their
causes. With this forgetfulness, however, I am not charge-
able ; for, against all the discouragements suggested by the
past, I have acted still upon a presumption that the disposition to conciliate, so often professed, would finally be
proved by some better evidence than a perseverance in
oppressive novelties, as obviously incompatible with such a
disposition in those who enforce them, as in those whose
patience they continue to exercise.

" Upon the commencement of the second paragraph,
I must observe, that the forbearance which it announces
might have afforded some gratification, if it had been followed by such admissions as my government is entitled to
expect, instead of a further manifestation of that disregard
of its demands, by which it has so long been wearied. It
has never been my practice to seek discussions, of which the
tendency is merely to irritate ; but I beg your lordship to be
assured, that I feel no desire to avoid them, whatever may
be their tendency, when the rights of my country require to
be vindicated against pretensions that deny, and conduct that
infringes them.

" If I comprehend the other parts of your lordship's
letter, they declare in effect, that the British government

will repeal nothing but the *orders in council*, and that it cannot at present repeal even them, because in the first place, the French government has required, in the letter of the Duke of Cadore to General Armstrong, of the 5th of August, not only that Great Britain shall revoke those orders, but that she shall renounce certain principles of blockade (supposed to be explained in the preamble to the Berlin decree) which France alleges to be new ; and, in the second place, because the American government has (as you conclude) demanded the revocation of the British order of blockade of May, 1806, *as a practical instance of that same renunciation*, or, in other words, has made itself a party, not openly indeed, but indirectly and covertly, to the entire requisition of France, as you understand that requisition.

"It is certainly true that the American government has required, as indispensable in the view of its acts of intercourse and non-intercourse, the annulment of the British blockade of May, 1806 ; and further, that it has through me declared its confident expectation that other blockades of a similar character (including that of the island of Zealand) will be discontinued. But by what process of reasoning your lordship has arrived at the conclusion, that the government of the United States intended by this requisition to become the champion of the edict of Berlin, to fashion its principles by those of France while it affected to adhere to its own, and to act upon some partnership in doctrines, which it would fain induce you to acknowledge, but could not prevail upon itself to avow, I am not able to conjecture. The frank and honorable character of the American government justifies me in saying that, if it had meant to demand of Great Britain an abjuration of all such principles as the French government may think fit to disapprove, it would not have put your lordship to the trouble of discovering that meaning by the aid of combinations and inferences discountenanced by the language of its minister, but would have told you so in explicit terms. What I have to request of your lordship, therefore, is, that you will take our views and principles from our own mouths, and that neither the Berlin decree, nor any other act of any foreign state, may be made to speak for us what we have not spoken for ourselves.

" The principles of blockade which the American government professes, and upon the foundation of which it has repeatedly protested against the order of May, 1806, and the other kindred innovations of those extraordinary times, have already been so clearly explained to your lordship, in my letter of the 21st of September, that it is hardly possible to read that letter and misunderstand them. Recommended by the plainest considerations of universal equity, you will find them supported with a strength of argument and a weight of authority, of which they scarcely stand in need, in the papers which will accompany this letter, or were transmitted in that of September. I will not recapitulate what I cannot improve ; but I must avail myself of this opportunity to call your lordship's attention a second time, in a particular manner, to one of the papers to which my letter of September refers. I allude to the copy of an official note of the 12th of April, 1804, from Mr. Merry to Mr. Madison, respecting a pretended blockade of Martinique and Guadaloupe. No comment can add to the value of that manly and perspicuous exposition of the law of blockade, as made by England herself in the maintenance of rules which have been respected and upheld in all seasons and on all occasions, by the government of the United States. I will leave it, therefore, to your lordship's consideration, with only this remark, that, while that paper exists, it will be superfluous to seek in any *French* document for the opinions of the American government on the matter of it.

" The steady fidelity of the government of the United States to its opinions on that interesting subject is known to every body. The same principles which are found in the letter of Mr Madison to Mr. Thornton, of the 27th of October, 1803, already before you, were asserted in 1799, by the American Minister at this court, in his correspondence with Lord Grenville, respecting the blockade of some of the ports of Holland ; were sanctioned in a letter of the 20th of September, 1800, from the Secretary of State of the United States to Mr. King, of which an extract is enclosed ; were insisted upon in repeated instructions to Mr. Monroe and the special mission of 1806 ; have been maintained by the United States against *others* as well as against England, as will appear by the enclosed copy of instructions, dated the 21st of October, 1801, from Mr. Secretary Madison to Mr. Charles Pinckney, then American Minister at Madrid ; and finally, were adhered to by the United States, when belligerent, in the case of the blockade of Tripoli.

"A few words will give a summary of those principles ; and when recalled to your remembrance, I am not without hopes, that the strong grounds of law and right, on which they stand, will be as apparent to your lordship as they are to me.

"It is by no means clear that it may not fairly be contended, on principle and early usage, that a maritime blockade is incomplete with regard to states at peace, unless the place which it would affect is invested by land as well as by sea. The United States, however, have called for the recognition of no such rule. They appear to have contented themselves with urging in substance, that ports not actually blockaded by a present, adequate, stationary force, employed by the power which attacks them, shall not be considered as shut to neutral trade in articles not contraband of war ; that, though it is usual for a belligerent to give notice to neutral nations when he intends to institute a blockade, it is possible that he may not act upon his intention at all, or that he may execute it insufficiently, or that he may discontinue his blockade, of which it is not customary to give any notice ;

that consequently the presence of the blockading force, is the natural criterion by which the neutral is enabled to ascertain the existence of the blockade at any given period, in like manner as the actual investment of a besieged place, is the evidence by which we decide whether the siege, which may be commenced, raised, recommenced and raised again, is continued or not ; that of course a mere notification to a neutral minister shall not be relied upon, as affecting, with knowledge of the actual existence of a blockade, either his government or its citizens ; that a vessel cleared or bound to a blockaded port, shall not be considered as violating in any manner the blockade, unless, on her approach towards such port, she shall have been previously warned not to enter it ; that this view of the law, in itself perfectly correct, is peculiarly important to nations situated at a great distance from the belligerent parties, and therefore incapable of obtaining other than tardy information of the actual state of their ports ; that whole coasts and countries shall not be declared (for they can never be more than *declared*) to be in a state of blockade, and thus the right of blockade converted into the means of extinguishing the trade of neutral nations ; and lastly, that every blockade shall be impartial in its operation, or, in other words, shall not open and shut for the convenience of the party that institutes it, and at the same time repel the commerce of the rest of the world, so as to become the odious instrument of an unjust monopoly, instead of a measure of honorable war.

" These principles are too moderate and just to furnish any motive to the British government for hesitating to revoke its orders in council, and those analogous orders of blockade, which the United States expect to be recalled. It can hardly be doubted that Great Britain will ultimately accede to them in their fullest extent ; but if that be a sanguine calculation (as I trust it is not), it is still incontrovertible, that a disinclination at this moment to acknowledge them, can suggest no national inducement for declining to repeal at once what *every* principle disowns, and what must be repealed at last.

"With regard to the rules of blockades, which the French government expects you to abandon, I do not take upon me to decide whether they are such as your lordship supposes them to be or not. Your view of them may be correct; but it may also be erroneous; and it is wholly immaterial to the case between the United States and Great Britain, whether it be the one or the other.

"As to such *British blockades* as the United States desire you to relinquish, you will not, I am sure, allege that it is any reason for adhering to *them* that *France* expects you to relinquish *others*. If our demands are suited to the measure of our own rights, and of your obligations as they respect those rights, you cannot think of founding a rejection of them upon any imputed exorbitance in the theories of the French government, for which we are not responsible, and with which we have no concern. If, when you have done justice to the United States, your enemy should call upon you to go farther, what shall prevent you from refusing? Your free agency will in no respect have been impaired. Your case will be better, in truth and in the opinion of mankind; and you will be, *therefore*, stronger in maintaining it, provided that, in doing so, you resort only to legitimate means, and do not *once more* forget the rights of others, while you seek to vindicate your own.

"Whether France will be satisfied with what you may do, is not to be known by anticipation, and ought not to be a subject of inquiry. So vague a speculation has nothing to do with your duties to nations at peace, and, if it had, would annihilate them. It cannot serve your interests; for it tends to lessen the number of your friends, without adding to your security against your enemies.

"You are required, therefore, to do right, and to leave

the consequences to the future, when by doing right you have every thing to gain and nothing to lose.

" As to the *orders in council,* which professed to be a reluctant departure from all ordinary rules, and to be justified only as a system of retaliation for a pre-existing measure of France, their foundation (such as it was) is gone the moment that measure is no longer in operation. But the Berlin decree is repealed : and even the *Milan* decree, the successor of your orders in council, is repealed also. Why is it then, that your orders have outlived those edicts, and that ther are still to oppress and harass as before ? Your lordship answers this question explicitly enough, but not satisfactorily. You do not allege that the French decrees are not repealed ; but you imagine that the repeal is not to remain in force, unless the British government shall, in addition to the revocation of its orders in council, abandon its system of blockade. I am not conscious of having stated, as your lordship seems to think, that this is so, and I believe in fact, that it is otherwise. Even if it were admitted, however, the orders in council ought nevertheless to be revoked. Can ' the safety and honor of the British nation,' demand that these orders shall continue to outrage the public law of the world, and sport with the undisputed rights of neutral commerce, after the pretext which was at first invented for them is gone ? But you are menaced with the *revival* of the French system, and consequently may again be furnished with the same *pretext !* Be it so ; yet still, as the system and the pretext are *at present* at an end, so, of course, should be your orders.

" According to your mode of reasoning, the situation of neutral trade is hopeless indeed. Whether the Berlin decree exists or not, it is equally to justify your orders in council. You issued them before it was any thing but a shadow, and by doing so gave to it all the substance it could ever claim. It is at this moment nothing. It is revoked and has passed

away, according to your own admission. You choose, however, to look for its reappearance ; and you make your own
expectation equivalent to the decree itself. Compelled to
concede that there is no anti-neutral French edict in operation upon the ocean, you think it sufficient to say that there
will be such an edict, you know not when ; and in the mean
time you do all you can to verify your own prediction, by
giving to your enemy all the provocation in your power to
resume the decrees which he has abandoned.

" For my part, my Lord, I know not what it is that the
British government requires, with a view to what it calls its
safety and its *honor*, as an inducement to rescind its orders
in council. It does not, I presume, imagine that such a
system will be suffered to ripen into law. It must intend to
relinquish it, sooner or later, as one of those violent experi-
ments for which time can do nothing, and to which submission will be hoped in vain. Yet even after the professed
foundation of this mischievous system is taken away, another
and another is industriously procured for it, so that no man
can tell at what time, or under what circumstances, it is
likely to have an end. When realities cannot be found, possibilities supply their place, and that, which was originally
said to be retaliation for actual injury, becomes at last (if
such a solecism can be endured or imagined) retaliation for
apprehended injuries, which the future may or may not produce, but which it is certain have no existence *now !*

" I do not mean to grant, for I do not think, that the
edict of Berlin did at any time lend even a color of equity
to the British orders in council, with reference to the United
States ; but it might reasonably have been expected that
they, who have so much relied upon it as a justification,
would have suffered it and them to sink together. How this
is forbidden by your *safety* or your *honor* remains to be explained ; and I am not willing to believe that either the one
or the other is inconsistent with the observance of substan-

tial justice, and with the prosperity and rights of peaceful
states.

" Although your lordship has slightly remarked upon certain recent acts of the French government, and has spoken
in general terms of ' the system of violence and injustice now
pursued by France,' as requiring ' some precautions of defence on the part of Great Britain,' I do not perceive that
you deduce any consequence from these observations, in favor
of a perseverance in the orders in council. I am not myself
aware of any edicts of France which, now that the Berlin
and Milan decrees are repealed, affect the rights of neutral
commerce on the seas. And you will yourselves admit that
if any of the acts of the French government, resting on territorial sovereignty, have injured, or shall hereafter injure,
the United States, it is for them, and for them only, to seek
redress. In like manner it is for Great Britain to determine
what precautions of defence those measures of France, which
you denominate unjust and violent, may render it expedient
for her to adopt. The United States have only to insist,
that a sacrifice of their rights shall not be among the number
of those precautions.

" In replying to that passage in your letter, which ad-
verts to the American act of non-intercourse, it is only necessary to mention the proclamation of the President of the
United States, of the 2d of November last, and the act of
congress which my letter of the 21st of September communicated, and to add that it is in the power of the British government to prevent the non-intercourse from being enforced
against Great Britain.

" Upon the concluding paragraph of your letter I will
barely observe, that I am not in possession of any document,
which you are likely to consider as *authentic*, showing that
the French decrees are ' absolutely revoked upon the single
condition of the revocation of the British orders in council,'
but that the information, which I have lately received from

the American Legation at Paris, confirms what I have already stated, and I think proved to your lordship, that those decrees are repealed and have ceased to have any effect. I will now trespass on you no farther than to suggest, that it would have given me sincere pleasure to be enabled to say as much of the British orders in council, and of the blockades from which it is impossible to distinguish them."

MR. PINKNEY TO LORD WELLESLEY.

"GREAT CUMBERLAND PLACE, *February* 17*th*, 1811.

" MY LORD :—Before I reply to your official communication of the 15th instant, you will perhaps allow me, in acknowledging the receipt of the unofficial paper which accompanied it, to trouble you with a few words.

" From the appointment which you have done me the honor to announce to me of a minister plenipotentiary to the United States, as well as from the language of your private letter, I conclude that it is the intention of the British government to seek immediately those adjustments with America, without which, that appointment can produce no beneficial effect. I presume, that, for the restoration of harmony between the two countries, the orders in council will be relinquished without delay ; that the blockade of May 1806 will be annulled ; that the case of the Chesapeake will be arranged in the manner heretofore intended, and, in general, that all such just and reasonable acts will be done as are necessary to make us friends.

" My motives will not, I am sure, be misinterpreted, if, anxious to be enabled so to regulate my conduct in the execution of my instructions as that the best results may be accomplished, I take the liberty to request such explanations on these heads as your lordship may think fit to give me.

"I ought to add, that, as the levee of his royal highness the prince regent has been postponed until Tuesday the 26th instant, I have supposed that my audience of leave is postponed to the same day ; and that I have, on that ground, undertaken to delay my reply to your official communication until I receive an answer to this letter."

MR. SMITH TO MR. PINKNEY

"*March 7th*, 1811.

"SIR :—If, as signified in your letter of the 24th of November, you should persist in the desire of closing your mission at London and of returning to the United States, I have to inform you that the President, from his respect to your wishes, cannot withhold his permission. You will accordingly herewith receive a letter of leave, to be used in such case or in the case pointed out in former instructions.

"It affords me pleasure, and at the same time real happiness, in being authorized to assure you of the high sense entertained by the President, of the distinguished talents and faithful exertions of which you have given so many proofs during a period of public service, frequently not less embarrassing than interesting.

"A blank commission is also inclosed, to be filled, in case of your return to the United States, with the name of some suitable person as secretary of legation."

MR. PINKNEY TO THE MARQUIS DI CIRCELLO.

"NAPLES, *August 24th*, 1816.

"The undersigned, envoy extraordinary of the United States of America, has already had the honor to mention to his excellency the Marquis di Circello, secretary of state and minister for foreign affairs of his majesty the king of the two

Sicilies, the principal objects of his mission ; and he now invites his excellency's attention to a more detailed and formal exposition of one of those objects.

" The undersigned is sure that the appeal, which he is about to make to the well known justice of his Sicilian majesty, in the name and by the orders of his government, will receive a deliberate and candid consideration ; and that, if it shall appear, as he trusts it will, to be recommended by those principles which it is the interest as well as the duty of all governments to observe and maintain, the claim involved in it will be admitted, effectually and promptly.

" The undersigned did but obey the instructions of the President of the United States, when he assured his excellency the Marquis di Circello, at their first interview, that his mission was suggested by such sentiments towards his Sicilian majesty as could not fail to be approved by him. Those sentiments are apparent in the desire which the President has manifested, through the undersigned, that the commercial relations between the territories of his majesty and those of the United States should be cherished by reciprocal arrangements, sought in the spirit of enlightened friendship, and with a sincere view to such equal advantages, as it is for nations to derive from one another.   The representations which the undersigned is commanded to make upon the subject of the present note, will be seen by his majesty in the same light.   They show the firm reliance of the President upon the disposition of the court of Naples impartially to discuss and ascertain, and faithfully to discharge its obligations toward foreign states and their citizens; a reliance which the undersigned partakes with his government ; and under the influence of which, he proceeds to state the nature and grounds of the reclamation in question.

" It cannot but be known to his excellency the Marquis di Circello, that, on the 1st of July, 1809, the minister for foreign affairs of the then government of Naples, addressed to Frederick Degan, Esq., then consul of the United States, an official letter, containing an invitation to all American vessels, having on board the usual certificates of origin and other regular papers, to come direct to Naples with their cargoes ; and that the same minister caused that invitation to be published in every possible mode, in order that it might come to the knowledge of those whom it concerned. It will not be questioned that the promise of security necessarily implied in this measure had every title, in the actual circumstances of Europe, to the confidence of distant and peaceful merchants. The merchants of America, as was to have been expected, *did* confide. Upon the credit and under the protection of that promise, they sent to Naples many valuable vessels and cargoes, navigated and documented with scrupulous regularity, and in no respect obnoxious to molestation ; but scarcely had they reached the destination to which they had been allured, when they were seized, without distinction, as prize, or as otherwise forfeited to the Neapolitan government, upon pretexts the most frivolous and idle. These arbitrary seizures were followed, with a rapacious haste, by summary decree, confiscating in the name and for the use of the same government, the whole of the property which had thus been brought within its grasp ; and these decrees, which wanted even the decent affectation of justice, were immediately carried into execution against all the remonstrances of those whom they oppressed, to enrich the treasury of the state.

" The undersigned persuades himself, that it is not in a note addressed to the Marquis di Circello, that it is necessary to enlarge upon the singularly atrocious character of this procedure, for which no apology can be devised, and for which none that is intelligible has hitherto been attempted. It was, indeed, an undisguised abuse of power of which nothing could well enhance the deformity, but the studied deception that preceded and prepared it ; a deception which, by a sort of treason against society, converted a proffer of hospitality into a snare, and that salutary confidence, without which nations and men must cease to have intercourse, into an engine of plunder.

" The right of the innocent victims of this unequalled act of fraud and rapine, to demand retribution, cannot be doubted. The only question is, from whom are they entitled to demand it ? Those, who at that moment ruled in Naples, and were in fact and in the view of the world, the government of Naples, have passed away before retribution could be obtained, although not before it was required ; and, if the right to retribution regards only the persons of those rulers as private and ordinary wrong-doers, the American merchants, whom they deluded and despoiled in the garb and with the instruments and for the purposes of sovereignty, must despair for ever of redress.

" The undersigned presumes, that such is not the view which the present government will feel itself justified in taking of this interesting subject ; he trusts that it will, on the contrary, perceive that the claim which the injured merchant was authorized to prefer against the government of this country before the recent change, and which, but for that change, must sooner or later have been successful, is now a valid claim against the government of the same country, notwithstanding that change. At least, the undersigned is not at present aware of any considerations which, applied to the facts that characterize this case, can lead to a different conclusion ; and certainly it would be matter for sincere regret, that any consideration should be thought sufficient to make the return of his Sicilian majesty's power fatal to the rights of friendly strangers, to whom no fault can be ascribed.

" The general principle that a civil society may contract obligations through its actual government, whatever that may be, and that it is not absolved from them by reason simply of a change of government or of rulers, is universally received as incontrovertible. It is admitted, not merely by writers on public law, as a speculative truth, but by states and statesmen, as a practical rule ; and, accordingly, history is full of examples to prove, that the undisturbed possessor of sovereign power in any society, whether a rightful possessor or not, with reference to other claimants of that power, may not only be the lawful object of allegiance, but by many of his acts, in his quality of sovereign de facto, may bind the society, and those who come after him as rulers, although their title be adverse to, or even better than his own. The Marquis di Circello does not need to be informed, that the earlier annals of England, in particular, abound in instructions upon this head.

"With regard to just and beneficial contracts, entered into by such a sovereign with the merchants of foreign nations, or (which is the same thing), with regard to the detention and confiscation of their property for public uses, and by his authority, in direct violation of a pledge of safety, upon the faith of which that property arrived within the reach of confiscation, this continuing responsibility stands upon the plainest foundations of natural equity.

" It will not be pretended, that a merchant is called upon to investigate, as he prosecutes his traffic, the title of every sovereign, with whose ports, and under the guarantee of whose plighted word, he trades. He is rarely competent. There are few in any station who are competent to an investigation so full of delicacy, so perplexed with facts and principles of a peculiar character, far removed from the common concerns of life. His predicament would be to the last degree calamitous, if, in an honest search after commercial profit, he might not take governments as he finds them, and consequently rely at all times upon the visible, exclusive acknowledged possession of supreme authority. If he sees all

the usual indications of established rule ; all the distinguish-
ing concomitants of real undisputed power, it cannot be that
he is at his peril to discuss mysterious theories above his capacity or foreign to his pursuits, and moreover, to connect
the results of those speculations with events of which his
knowledge is either imperfect or erroneous. If he sees the
obedience of the people, and the acquiescence of neighboring
princes, it is impossible that it can be his duty to examine,
before he ships his merchandise, whether it be fit that these
should acquiesce, or those obey. If, in short, he finds
nothing to interfere with or qualify the dominion which the
head of the society exercises over it, and the domain which
it occupies, it is the dictate of reason, sanctioned by all experience, that he is bound to look no farther.

"It can be of no importance to him that, notwithstanding all these appearances announcing lawful rule, the mere
right to fill the throne is claimed by, or even resides in,
another than the actual occupant. The latent right (supposing it to exist), disjoined from and controverted by the
fact, is to him nothing while it continues to be latent. It
is only the sovereign in possession that it is in his power
to know. It is with him only that he can enter into engage-
ments. It is through him only that he can deal with the
society. And if it be true, that the sovereign in possession
is incapable, on account of a conflict of title between him and
another, who barely claims, but makes no effort to assert his
claim ; of pledging the public faith of the society and of the
monarch to foreign traders, for commercial and other objects,
we are driven to the monstrous conclusion, that the society
is, in effect and indefinitely, cut off from all communication
with the rest of the world. It has, and can have, no organ
by which it can become accountable to, or make any contract
with foreigners, by which needful supplies may be invited
into its harbors, by which famine may be averted, or redun-
dant productions be made to find a market in the wants of

strangers. It is, in a word, an outcast from the bosom of the great community of nations, at the very moment too, when its existence, in the form which it has assumed, may every where be admitted. And, even if the dormant claim to the throne should, at last, by a fortunate coincidence of circumstances, become triumphant, and unite itself to the possession, this harsh and palsying theory has no assurance to give, either to the society or to those who may incline to deal with it, that its moral capacity is restored, that it is an outcast no longer, and that it may now, through the protecting will of its new sovereign, do what it could not do before. It contains, of course, no adequate and certain provision against even the perpetuity of the dilemma which it creates. If, therefore, a civil society is not competent, by rules in entire possession of the sovereignty, to enter into all such promises to the members of other societies as necessity or convenience may require, and to remain unanswerable for the breach of them, into whatsoever shape the society may ultimately be cast, or into whatsoever hands the government may ultimately fall ; if a sovereign, entirely in possession, is not able, for that reason alone, to incur a just responsibility, in his political or corporate character, to the citizens of other countries, and to transmit that responsibility, even to those who succeed him by displacing him, it will be difficult to show that the moral capacity of a civil society is any thing but a name, or the responsibility of sovereigns any thing but a shadow. And here the undersigned will take the liberty to suggest, that it is scarcely for the interest of sovereigns to inculcate as a maxim, that their lost dominions can only be recovered at the expense of the unoffending citizen of states in amity, or, which is equivalent to it, to make that recovery the practical consummation of intermediate injustice, by utterly extinguishing the hope of indemnity and even the title to demand it.

" The undersigned will now, for the sake of perspicuity

and precision, recall to the recollection of his excellency the
Marquis di Circello, the situation of the government of Murat
at the epoch of the confiscation in question. Whatever
might be the origin or foundation of that government, it
had for some time been *established*. It had obtained such
obedience as in such times was customary, and had manifested itself, not only by active internal exertions of legislative and executive powers, but by important external
transactions with old and indisputably regular governments.
It had been (as long afterwards it continued to be) recognized
by the greatest potentates, as one of the European family
of states, and had interchanged with them ambassadors, and
other public ministers and consuls. And Great Britain, by
an order in council of the 26th of April, 1809, which modified the system of constructive blockade, promulgated by the
orders of November, 1807, had excepted the Neapolitan territories, with other portions of Italy, from the operation of
that system, that neutrals might no longer be prevented
from trading with them.

"Such was the state of things when American vessels
were tempted into Naples, by a reliance upon the passports
of its government, to which perfidy had lent more than ordinary solemnity, upon a declaration as explicit, as it was formal and notorious, that they might come without fear, and
might depart in peace. It was under these circumstances,
that, instead of being permitted to retire with their lawful
gains, both they and their cargoes were seized and appropriated in a manner already related. The undersigned may
consequently assume, that if ever there was a claim to compensation for broken faith, which survived the political power
of those whose iniquity produced it, and devolved in full
force upon their successors, the present claim is of that description.

"As to the demand itself, as it existed against the government of Murat, the Marquis di Circello will undoubtedly

be the first to concede, not only that it is above reproach,
but that it rests upon grounds in which the civilized world
has a deep and lasting interest.   And with regard to the liability of the present government as standing in the place of
the former, it may be taken as a corollary from that concession ; at least until it has been shown, that it is the natural
fate of obligations, so high and sacred, contracted by a government in the full and tranquil enjoyment of power, to perish with the first revolution, either in form or rulers, through
which it may happen to pass ; or (to state the same proposition in different terms), that it is the natural operation of a
political revolution in a state, to strip unfortunate traders,
who have been betrayed and plundered by the former sovereign, of all that *his* rapacity could not reach—the right of
reclamation.

    " The wrong which the government of Murat inflicted
upon American citizens, wanted nothing that might give
to it atrocity, or effect, as a robbery introduced by treachery ;
but however pernicious or execrable, it was still reparable.
It left in the sufferers and their nation a right, which was not
likely to be forgotten or abandoned, of seeking and obtaining
ample redress, not from *Murat* simply (who individually was
lost in the sovereign), but from the government of the country, whose power he abused.   By what course of argument
can it be proved, that this incontestable right, from which
that government could never have escaped, has been destroyed by the reaccession of his Sicilian majesty, after a long in-
terval, to the sovereignty of the same territories ?

    " That such a result cannot in any degree be inferred from
the misconduct of the American claimants, is certain ; for
no misconduct is imputable to them.   They were warranted
in every view of the public law of Europe, in holding commercial communication with Naples in the predicament in
which they found it, and in trusting to the direct and authentic assurances, which the government of the place af-

fected to throw over them as a shield against every danger. Their shipments were strictly within the terms of those assurances ; and nothing was done, by the shippers or their agents, by which the benefit of them might be lost or impaired.

" From what other source can such a result be drawn ? Will it be said that the proceeds of the confiscations were not applied to public purposes during the sovereignty of Murat, or that they produced no public advantages, with reference to which the present government ought to be liable ? The answer to such a suggestion is, that let the fact be as it may, it can have no influence upon the subject. It is enough that the confiscations themselves, and the promise of safety which they violated, were acts of state, proceeding from him who was then, and for several successive years, the sovereign. The derivative liability of the present government reposes, not upon the good, either public or private, which may have been the fruit of such a revolting exhibition of power, emancipated from all the restraints of principle, but upon the general foundation, which the undersigned has already had the honor to expose.

" To follow the proceeds of these spoliations into the public treasury, and thence to all the uses to which they were finally made subservient, can be no part of the duty of the American claimant. It is a task which he has no means of performing, and which, if performed by others, could neither strengthen his case nor enfeeble it. And it may confidently be insisted, not only that he has no concern with the particular application of these proceeds, but that, even if he had, he would be authorized to rely upon the presumption, that they were applied as public money to public ends, or left in the public coffers. It must be remembered, moreover, that whatever may have been the destiny of these unhallowed spoils, they cannot well have failed to be instrumental in meliorating the condition of the country. They afforded extraordinary pecuniary means, which, as far as they extended, must have saved it from an augumentation of its burdens ; or by relieving the ordinary revenue, made that revenue adequate to various improvements, either of use or beauty, which otherwise it could not have accomplished. The territories, therefore, under the sway of Murat, must be supposed to have returned to his Sicilian majesty much less exhausted, more embellished, and more prosperous, than if the property of American citizens had not in the mean time been sacrificed to cupidity and cunning. It must further be remembered, that a part of that property was notoriously devoted to the public service. Some of the vessels seized by the orders of Murat, were, on account of their excellent construction, converted into vessels of war, and as such commissioned by the government ; and the undersigned is informed that they are now in possession of the officers of his Sicilian majesty, and used and claimed as belonging to him.

" The undersigned having thus briefly explained to the Marquis di Circello, the nature of the claim which the government of the United States has commanded him to submit to the reflection of the government of his Sicilian majesty, forbears at present to multiply arguments in support of it. He feels assured that the equitable disposition of his majesty renders superfluous the further illustrations of which it is susceptible."

MISSOURI QUESTION.

It was a splendid spectacle the American Senate Chamber presented, according to contemporaneous authority, the day that William Pinkney arose to participate in this momentous discussion. The reputation of the speaker, just transplanted from the forum to that garden of American legislators, and the magnitude of the question involved, excited the public mind to the highest state of expectation, and brought to the Capitol such a crowd as has rarely if ever been gathered within its walls. Rufus King, an honored son of New-York, a gentleman of enlarged views and commanding abilities, who had borne a conspicuous part in the foreign service of his country as well as her deliberative councils at home, was then a Senator. He was a splendid specimen of a man, and wore his varied honors with wondrous grace.— Otis, Dana, Barbour, Macon and Burril, were his distinguished associates in this first deliberative assembly of the world. Mr. King felt the grandeur and responsibility of the occasion. The country he knew had a deep interest at stake. He knew also that many eyes were upon him, that he was now called upon to give to the country and the world the closing speech of his life, and leave behind him the noblest exposition he could of the constitution. That speech was delivered. Its eloquent warnings filled the land. Many prided themselves upon this effort of the distinguished and venerable champion of the North. A gentleman rose to reply to it, who was not altogether a stranger to the Senate. He came from an arena, on which his powers had been tested by the strongest men of the land ; and if he stood not " quite alone, he had confessedly no superior." Fresh, too, from a diplomatic service, in which he had evinced his usual ability and discretion, he brought with him to that Senate Chamber a world-wide reputation. Already upon this very question, his voice had been heard in a most admirable and powerful speech ; so that, although little more than six weeks a member of the body, we are justified in saying that he was not altogether a stranger. New to the scene ; inexperienced in senatorial life he was, but still not unknown. Deep was the interest awakened in the public mind by this approaching conflict, in which Maryland's favorite son was to measure a lance with the veteran statesman of New-York. It was not a mere personal feeling, not a vainglorious conflict of rivalry, that caused them to assume this antagonistic position. That would have been unworthy of the Senate and the country. It was a high constitutional question that divided them. It was a grave conflict of opinion that made up the struggle. Mr. King had chosen his position—selected his ground—marshalled his arguments—arrayed his facts. He came thoroughly equipped to the battle. The chosen representatives of the views of a portion of the northern wing of the confederacy, he was no mean antagonist. The North had spoken, well and powerfully, through him. Pinkney arose. The occasion was one of imposing sublimity—the scene worthy of the occasion, and the advocate, with whom he was now brought in direct collision, worthy of both.

The talent, the taste, and beauty of the land were there. Crowd upon crowd thronged the galleries. Every nook and corner of the large, capacious hall was filled almost to suffocation. Hundreds went away disappointed, unable to catch a glimpse of the orator or a tone of his powerful and melodious voice. All business was suspended in the Lower House, for the representatives from all parts of the Union participated to the full in the common desire to witness this conflict of mind with mind. The whole country was alive. The public peace and safety had been seriously threatened. Mr. King's dark and dismal picturings had no tendency to allay the popular apprehension or quiet the public agitation. Some hoped—others feared. All partook more or less of the intense anxiety. Pinkney arose. The very novelty of the scene, and the sight of a new antagonist upon a field of such thrilling issues, where all his long cherished principles of constitutional interpretation so thoroughly coincided with the position he occupied, only tended to give greater impetus and wider scope to the workings of his giant intellect. It was in opposition that Mr. Pinkney exhibited to most advantage his wondrous power. Not far from the spot where Webster subsequently encountered Hayne, he stood.. There was unusual fire in his fine blue eye, and exulting hope. Strong in the confidence he reposed in the views he entertained of the constitution, he was not less strong in his reliance " upon the unsophisticated good sense of the American people." Taking up that glorious charter of our liberties, and following Mr. King step by step in argument and illustration, he poured forth the treasures of his mind with a keenness of analysis and a copiousness and concentration of reasoning, that annihilated at once and for ever the position of his opponent. This speech more than sustained the reputation of the orator, and gratified to the full the highest expectations of the audience. It was a surprising combination of eloquence and argument, beauty and strength, amplitude and condensation. Although a close and severe logical discussion, it rivetted attention, and called forth as extraordinary panegyric as was ever vouchsafed to any other parliamentary effort. That speech is a sort of beacon light, by which men may make the most extraordinary developments of oratorical power and ability of argument. One of the most significant proofs of its power was the fact, that Rufus King never answered it. I have been told, upon what I think good authority, that Mr. King himself, with a magnanimity worthy of all praise, took occasion to say that, during the time Mr. Pinkney was speaking, he could not shake off the impression that he must be wrong

A not less significant proof of the rare power of this speech may be found in the fact, that even learned historians at the North, blinded by prejudice, have conspired with stump orators and pamphleteers to misrepresent grossly the views expressed, and the line of argument pursued on that occasion. Hildreth states (vol. 6, 689), that "Pinkney appeared on the other side as leading orator for the extension of slavery." And again, "that Pinkney and Clay, both of whom had begun their political career with earnest efforts for the curtailment and abolition of slavery in their respective States, were now among the most vehement advocates for its extension all over the new West." Let any one read the speech, and if he does not see through the thinly veiled misrepresentation and misconception of this author, he must be blind, indeed. Mr. Pinkney stood up in defence of the constitution. He stood by the States, maintained their original and indestructible equality, and denied that you "could make the Union as to the new States what it is not as to the old." He deprecated the introduction of such extraneous matter as had been unwisely forced into the discussion, and unwove the web so artistically wowen by the Senator from New-York. It was not a discussion on slavery at all. It was a bare, naked, constitutional question, and as such Mr. Pinkney treated it.

It excites a smile to read a little further on in the pages of this recondite historian. "That the idea" that Congress had no power to impose conditions in the admission of new States, "was ridiculous." It may be that the principles of constitutional law, so eloquently enforced by Mr. Pinkney in this speech, and so extensively indorsed, are, after all, mere dreams of the imagination, sickly notions, which, after stalking through the halls of legislation like ghosts, struck northern statesmen dumb, may be dispelled by one wave of the historic wand, never more to mislead or confound the world. It may be that argument unanswered will sink before "assertion without proof"—but really, Mr. Hildreth must excuse us if we prove a little refractory, and refuse to acknowledge any idea ridiculous, which is sustained by such power of argument and force of eloquence. When an historian manifests such carelessness (I had well nigh said, recklessness of assertion), he must bear with us if we demur to his decision of grave points of constitutional law, which he has neither the capacity to decide, nor the authority.

We ask a perusal of the speech, and although it must suffer from the imperfection of the report, we have no fears concerning it. It is a gem of American eloquence, that has lost nothing of its splendor in its passage through the crucible of an unsparing criticism :—

SPEECH ON THE MISSOURI QUESTION.

As I am not a very frequent speaker in this Assembly, and have shown a desire, I trust, rather to listen to the wisdom of others, than to lay claim to superior knowledge by undertaking to advise, even when advice, by being seasonable in point of time, might have some chance of being profitable, you will, perhaps, bear with me if I venture to trouble you once more on that eternal subject which has lingered here, until all its natural interest is exhausted, and every topic connected with it is literally worn to tatters. I shall, I assure you, sir, speak with laudable brevity—not merely on account of the feeble state of my health, and from some reverence for the laws of good taste which forbid me to speak otherwise, but also from a sense of justice to those who honor me with their attention. My single purpose, as I suggested yesterday, is to subject to a friendly, yet close examination, some portions of a speech, imposing certainly on account of the distinguished quarter from whence it came—not *very* imposing (if I may so say, without departing from that respect which I sincerely feel and intend to manifest for eminent abilities and long experience) for any *other* reason.

I believe, Mr. President, that I am about as likely to retract an opinion which I have formed, as any member of this body, who, being a lover of truth, inquires after it with diligence before he imagines that he has found it; but I suspect that we are all of us so constituted as that neither argument nor declamation, levelled against recorded and published decision, can easily discover a practicable avenue through which it may hope to reach either our heads or our hearts. I mention this, lest it may excite surprise, when I take the liberty to add, that the speech of the honorable gentleman from New-York, upon the great subject with which it was principally occupied, has left me as great an infidel as it found me. It is possible, indeed, that if I had had the good fortune to hear that speech at an earlier stage of this debate, when all was fresh and new, although I feel confident that the analysis which it contained of the constitution, illustrated as it was by historical anecdote rather than by reasoning, would have been just as unsatisfactory to me *then* as it is *now*, I might not have been altogether unmoved by those warnings of approaching evil which it seemed to intimate, especially when taken in connection with the observations of the same honorable gentleman on a preceding day, "that delays in disposing of this subject, in the manner he desires, are dangerous, and that we stand on slippery ground." I must be permitted, however (speaking only for myself), to say, that the hour of dismay is passed. I have heard the tones of the larum bell on all sides, until they have become familiar to my ear, and have lost their power to appall, if, indeed, they ever possessed it. Notwithstanding occasional

appearances of rather an unfavorable description, I have long
since persuaded myself that the *Missouri Question*, as it is
called, might be laid to rest, with innocence and safety, by
some conciliatory compromise at least, by which, as is our
duty, we might reconcile the extremes of conflicting views
and feelings, without any sacrifice of constitutional principle;
and in any event, that the Union would easily and triumphantly emerge from those portentous clouds with which this
controversy is supposed to have environed it.

I confess to you, nevertheless, that some of the principles announced by the honorable gentleman from New-York,[*]
with an explicitness that reflected the highest credit on his
candor, did, when they were first presented, startle me not a
little. They were not perhaps entirely new. Perhaps I had
seen them before in some shadowy and doubtful shape,

> "If shape it might be called, that shape had none
> Distinguishable in member, joint, or limb."

But in the honorable gentleman's speech they were shadowy
and doubtful no longer. He exhibited them in forms so
boldly and accurately defined—with contours so distinctly
traced—with features so pronounced and striking, that I was
unconscious for a moment that they might be old acquaintances. I received them as *novi hospites* within these walls,
and gazed upon them with astonishment and alarm. I have
recovered, however, thank God, from this paroxysm of terror,
although not from that of astonishment. I have sought
and found tranquillity and courage in my former consolatory
faith. My reliance is that these principles will obtain no
general currency; for, if they should, it requires no gloomy
imagination to sadden the perspective of the future. My
reliance is upon the unsophisticated good sense and noble
spirit of the American people. I have what I may be allowed to call a proud and patriotic trust, that they will give
countenance to no principles, which, if followed out to their

* Mr. King.

obvious consequences, will not only shake the goodly fabric
of the Union to its foundations, but reduce it to a melancholy ruin. The people of this country, if I do not wholly
mistake their character, are wise as well as virtuous. They
know the value of that federal association which is to them
the single pledge and guarantee of power and peace. Their
warm and pious affections will cling to it as to their only hope
of prosperity and happiness, in defiance of pernicious abstractions, by whomsoever inculcated, or howsoever seductive
and alluring in their aspect.

Sir, it is not an occasion like this, although connected,
as contrary to all reasonable expectation it has been, with
fearful and disorganizing theories, which would make our
estimates, whether fanciful or sound, of natural law, the
measure of civil rights and political sovereignty in the social
state, that can harm the Union. It must, indeed, be a
mighty storm that can push from its moorings this sacred
ark of the common safety. It is not every trifling breeze,
however it may be made to sob and howl in imitation of the
tempest, by the auxiliary breath of the ambitious, the timid,
or the discontented, that can drive this gallant vessel,
freighted with every thing that is dear to an American bosom, upon the rocks, or lay it a sheer hulk upon the ocean.
I may perhaps mistake the flattering suggestions of hope
(the greatest of all flatterers, as we are told), for the conclusions of sober reason. Yet it is a pleasing error, if it be an
error, and no man shall take it from me. I will continue to
cherish the belief, in defiance of the public patronage given
by the honorable gentleman from New-York, with more
than his ordinary zeal and solemnity, to deadly speculations,
which, invoking the name of God to aid their faculties for
mischief, strike at all establishments, that the union of these
States is formed to bear up against far greater shocks than,
through all vicissitudes, it is ever likely to encounter. I
will continue to cherish the belief, that, although like all

other human institutions it may for a season be disturbed, or suffer momentary eclipse by the transit across its disk of some malignant planet, it possesses a recuperative force, a redeeming energy in the hearts of the people, that will soon restore it to its wonted calm, and give it back its accustomed splendor. On such a subject I will discard all hysterical apprehensions—I will deal in no sinister auguries —I will indulge in no hypochondriacal forebodings. I will look forward to the future with gay and cheerful hope ; and will make the prospect smile, in fancy at least, until overwhelming reality shall render it no longer possible.

I have said thus much, Sir, in order that I may be understood as meeting the constitutional question as a mere *question of interpretation,* and as disdaining to press into the service of my argument upon it prophetic fears of any sort, however they may be countenanced by an avowal, formidable by reason of the high reputation of the individual by whom it has been hazarded, of sentiments the most destructive, which, if not borrowed from, are identical with, the worst visions of the political philosophy of France when all the elements of discord and misrule were let loose upon that devoted nation. I mean " the infinite perfectibility of man and his institutions," and the resolution of every thing into a state of nature. I have another motive, which, at the risk of being misconstrued, I will declare without reserve. With my convictions, and with my feelings, I never will consent to hold confederated America as bound together by a silken cord, which any instrument of mischief may sever, to the view of monarchical foreigners, who look with a jealous eye upon that glorious experiment which is now in progress amongst us in favor of republican freedom. Let them make such prophecies as they will, and nourish such feelings as they may, I will not contribute to the fulfilment of the former, nor minister to the gratification of the latter.

Sir, it was but the other day that we were forbidden

(properly forbidden I am sure, for the prohibition came from you) to assume that there existed any intention to impose a prospective restraint on the domestic legislation of Missouri—a restraint to act upon it contemporaneously with its origin as a State, and to continue adhesive to it through all the stages of its political existence. We are now, however, permitted to know that it is determined by a sort of political surgery to amputate one of the limbs of its local sovereignty, and thus mangled and disparaged, and thus only, to receive it into the bosom of the constitution. It is now avowed that, while *Maine* is to be ushered into the Union with every possible demonstration of studious reverence on our part, and on hers with colors flying, and all the other graceful accompaniments of honorable triumph, this ill-conditioned upstart of the West, this obscure foundling of a wilderness that was but yesterday the hunting-ground of the savage, is to find her way into the American family as she can, with an humiliating badge of remediless inferiority patched upon her garments, with the mark of recent, qualified manumission upon her, or rather with a brand upon her forehead to tell the story of her territorial vassalage, and to perpetuate the memory of her evil propensities. It is now avowed that, while the robust district of Maine is to be seated by the side of her truly respectable parent, co-ordinate in authority and honor, and is to be dandled into that power and dignity of which she does not stand in need, but which undoubtedly she deserves, the more infantine and feeble Missouri is to be repelled with harshness, and forbidden to come at all, unless with the iron collar of servitude about her neck, instead of the civic crown of republican freedom upon her brows, and is to be doomed for ever to leading strings, unless she will exchange those leading strings for shackles.

I am told that you have the power to establish this odious and revolting distinction, and I am referred for the proofs of that power to various parts of the constitution, but principally to that part of it which authorizes the admission of new States into the Union. I am myself of opinion that it is in that part only that the advocates for this restriction can, with any hope of success, apply for a license to impose it; and that the efforts which have been made to find it in other portions of that instrument, are too desperate to re quire to be encountered. I shall, however, examine those other portions before I have done, lest it should be supposed by those who have relied upon them, that what I omit to answer I believe to be unanswerable.

The clause of the constitution which relates to the admission of new States is in these words : "The Congress *may* admit new States into this Union," &c., and the advocates for restriction maintain that the use of the word "may" imports discretion to admit or to reject ; and that in this discretion is wrapped up another—that of prescribing the terms and conditions of admission in case you are willing to admit : Cujus est dare ejus est disponere. I will not for the present inquire whether this *involved* discretion to dictate the *terms* of admission belongs to you or not. It is fit that I should first look to *the nature and extent of it*.

I think I may assume that if such a power be any thing but nominal, it is much more than adequate to the present object; that it is a power of vast expansion, to which human sagacity can assign no reasonable limits ; that it is a capacious reservoir of authority, from which you may take, in all time to come, as occasion may serve, the means of oppression as well as of benefaction. I know that it professes at this moment to be the chosen instrument of protecting mercy, and would win upon us by its benignant smiles : but I know too it can frown, and play the tyrant, if it be so disposed. Notwithstanding the softness which it now assumes, and the care with which it conceals its giant proportions beneath the deceitful drapery of sentiment, when it next appears before you it may show itself with a sterner countenance and in more awful dimensions. It is, to speak the truth, Sir, a power of colossal size—if indeed it be not an abuse of language to call it by the gentle name of *a power*. Sir, it is a wilderness of powers, of which fancy in her happiest mood is unable to perceive the far-distant and shadowy boundary. Armed with such a power, with religion in one hand and philanthropy in the other, and followed with a goodly train of public and private virtues, you may achieve more conquests over sovereignties not your own than falls to the common lot of even uncommon ambition. By the aid of such a power, skilfully employed, you may "bridge your way" over the Hellespont that separates State legislation from that of Congress ; and you may do so for pretty much the same purpose with which Xerxes once bridged his way across the Hellespont, that separates Asia from Europe. He did so, in the language of Milton, "the liberties of Greece to yoke." You may do so for the analogous purpose of subjugating and reducing the sovereignties of States, as your taste or convenience may suggest, and fashioning them to your imperial will. There are those in this house who appear to think, and I doubt not sincerely, that the particular restraint now under consideration is wise, and benevolent, and good : wise as respects the Union—good as respects Missouri—benevolent as respects the unhappy victims whom, with a novel kindness, it would incarcerate in the South, and bless by decay and extirpation. Let all such beware, lest in their desire for the effect which they believe the restriction will produce, they are too easily satisfied that they have the right to impose it. The moral beauty of the present purpose, or even its political recommendations (whatever they may be), can do nothing for a power like this, which claims to prescribe conditions *ad libitum*, and to be competent to *this* purpose, because it is competent to *all*. This restriction, if it be not smothered in its birth, will be but a small part of the progeny of that prolific power. It teems with a mighty brood,

of which this may be entitled to the distinction of comeliness
as well as of primogeniture.   The rest may want the boasted
loveliness of their predecessor, and be even uglier than
" Lapland witches."

Perhaps, Sir, you will permit me to remind you that it
is almost always in company with those considerations that
interest the heart in some way or other, that encroachment
steals into the world.   A bad purpose throws no veil over
the licenses of power.   It leaves them to be seen as they are.
It affords them no protection from the inquiring eye of
jealousy.   The danger is when a tremendous discretion like
the present is attempted to be assumed, as on this occasion,
in the names of pity, of religion, of national honor and
national prosperity ; when encroachment tricks itself out in
the robes of piety, or humanity, or addresses itself to pride
of country, with all its kindred passions and motives.   It is
then that the guardians of the constitution are apt to slumber on their watch, or, if awake, to mistake for lawful rule
some pernicious arrogation of power.

I would not discourage *authorized* legislation upon those
kindly, generous, and noble feelings which Providence has
given to us for the best of purposes : but when *power to act*
is under discussion, I will not look to the end in view, lest I
should become indifferent to the lawfulness of the means.
Let us discard from this high constitutional question, all
those extrinsic considerations which have been forced into
its discussion.   Let us endeavor to approach it with a
philosophic impartiality of temper—with a sincere desire to
ascertain the boundaries of our authority, and a determination to keep our wishes in subjection to our allegiance
to the constitution.

Slavery, we are told in many a pamphlet, memorial, and
speech, with which the press has lately groaned, is a foul
blot upon our otherwise immaculate reputation.   Let this
be conceded—yet you are no nearer than before to the con-

clusion that you possess power which may deal with other
subjects as effectually as with this. Slavery, we are further
told, with some pomp of metaphor, is a canker at the root
of all that is excellent in this republican empire, a pestilent
disease that is snatching the youthful bloom from its cheek,
prostrating its honor and withering its strength. Be it so—
yet if you have power to medicine to it in the way proposed,
and in virtue of the diploma which you claim, you have also
power in the distribution of your political alexipharmics to
present the deadliest drugs to every territory that would become a State, and bid it drink or remain a colony for ever.
Slavery, we are also told, is now " rolling onward with a rapid
tide towards the boundless regions of the West," threatening
to doom them to sterility and sorrow, unless some potent
voice can say to it—thus far shalt thou go and no farther.
Slavery engenders pride and indolence in him who commands, and inflicts intellectual and moral degradation on
him who serves. Slavery, in fine, is unchristian and abominable. Sir, I shall not stop to deny that slavery is all this
and more ; but I shall not think myself the less authorized
to deny that it is for you to stay the course of this dark torrent, by opposing to it a mound raised up by the labors of
this portentous discretion on the domain of others—a mound
which you cannot erect but through the instrumentality of a
trespass of no ordinary kind—not the comparatively innocent trespass that beats down a few blades of grass which
the first kind sun or the next refreshing shower may cause
to spring again, but that which levels with the ground the
lordliest trees of the forest, and claims immortality for the
destruction which it inflicts.

I shall not, I am sure, be told that I exaggerate this
power. It has been admitted here, and elsewhere, that I
do not. But I want no such concession. It is manifest,
that as a discretionary power it is every thing or nothing—
that its head is in the clouds, or that it is a mere figment of

enthusiastic speculation—that it has no existence, or that it is an alarming vortex ready to swallow up all such portions of the sovereignty of an infant State, as you may think fit to cast into it as preparatory to the introduction into the Union of the miserable residue. No man can contradict me when I say, that if you have this power, you may squeeze down a new-born sovereign State to the size of a pigmy, and then taking it between finger and thumb, stick it into some niche of the Union, and still continue by way of mockery to call it *a State in the sense of the constitution.* You may waste it to a shadow, and then introduce it into the society of flesh and blood, an object of scorn and derision. You may sweat and reduce it to a thing of skin and bone, and then place the ominous skeleton beside the ruddy and healthful members of the Union, that it may have leisure to mourn the lamentable difference between itself and its companions, to brood over its disastrous promotion, and to seek in justifiable discontent, an opportunity for separation, and insurrection, and rebellion. What may you not do by dexterity and perseverance with this terrific power? You may give to a new State, in the form of terms which it cannot refuse, (as I shall show you hereafter,) a statute book of a thousand volumes—providing not for ordinary cases only, but even for possibilities ; you may lay the yoke, no matter whether light or heavy, upon the necks of the latest posterity; you may send this searching power into every hamlet for centuries to come, by laws enacted in the spirit of prophecy, and regulating all those dear relations of domestic concern, which belong to local legislation, and which even local legislation touches with a delicate and sparing hand. This is the first inroad. But will it be the last? This provision is but a pioneer for others of a more desolating aspect. It is the fatal bridge of which Milton speaks, and when once firmly built, what shall hinder you to pass it when you please, for the purpose of plundering power after power at the expense of

new States, as you will still continue to call them, and rais-
ing up prospective codes, irrevocable and immortal, which
shall leave to those States the empty shadows of domestic
sovereignty, and convert them into petty pageants, in themselves contemptible, but rendered infinitely more so by the
contrast of their humble faculties, with the proud and admitted pretensions of those who, having doomed them to the
inferiority of vassals, have condescended to take them into
their society and under their protection ?

I shall be told, perhaps, that you can have no temptation to do all, or any part of this, and, moreover, that you
can do nothing of yourselves, or, in other words, without the
concurrence of the new State. The last of these suggestions I shall examine by and by. To the first I answer, that
it is not incumbent upon me to prove that this discretion
will be abused. It is enough for me to prove the vastness of
the power as an inducement to make us pause upon it, and
to inquire with attention, whether there is any apartment in
the constitution large enough to give it entertainment. It
is more than enough for me to show that vast as is this power,
it is with reference to mere territories an *irresponsible* power.
Power is irresponsible when it acts upon those who are de-
fenceless against it, who cannot check it, or contribute to check
it, in its exercise, who can resist it only by force. The territory of Missouri has no check upon this power. It has no share
in the government of the Union. In this body it has no representative. In the other House it has, by courtesy, an agent,
who may remonstrate, but cannot vote. That such an irresponsible power is not likely to be abused, who will undertake
to assert ? If it is not, "Experience is a cheat, and fact a liar."
The power which England claimed over the colonies, was such
a power, and it was abused—and hence the revolution. Such
a power is always perilous to those who wield it, as well as
to those on whom it is exerted. Oppression is but another
name for irresponsible power, if history is to be trusted.

The free spirit of our constitution and of our people, is no assurance against the propension of unbridled power to abuse, when it acts upon colonial dependents rather than upon ourselves. Free States, as well as despots, have oppressed those whom they were bound to foster—and it is the nature of man that it should be so. The love of power, and the desire to display it when it can be done with impunity, is inherent in the human heart. Turn it out at the door, and it will in again at the window. Power is displayed in its fullest measure, and with a captivating dignity, by restraints and conditions. The *pruritas leges ferendi* is an universal disease ; and conditions are laws as far as they go. The vanity of human wisdom, and the presumption of human reason, are proverbial. This vanity and this presumption, are often neither reasonable nor wise. Humanity, too, sometimes plays fantastic tricks with power. Time, moreover, is fruitful in temptations to convert discretionary power to all sorts of purposes.

Time, that withers the strength of man, and "strews around him like autumnal leaves, the ruins of his proudest monuments," produces great vicissitudes in modes of thinking and feeling. It brings along with it, in its progress, new circumstances—new combinations and modifications of the old—generating new views, motives, and caprices—new fanaticisms of endless variety—in short, new every thing. We ourselves are always changing—and what to-day we have but a small desire to attempt, to-morrow becomes the object of our passionate aspirations.

There is such a thing as enthusiasm, moral, religious, or political, or a compound of all three ;—and it is wonderful what it will attempt, and from what imperceptible beginnings it sometimes rises into a mighty agent. Rising from some obscure or unknown source, it first shows itself a petty rivulet, which scarcely murmurs over the pebbles that obstruct its way—then it swells into a fierce torrent, bearing

all before it—and then again, like some mountain stream,
which occasional rains have precipitated upon the valley, it
sinks once more into a rivulet, and finally leaves its channel
dry.   Such a thing has happened.   I do not say that it is
now happening.   It would not become me to say so.   But if
it should occur, woe to the unlucky territory that should be
struggling to make its way into the Union at the moment
when the opposing inundation was at its height, and at the
same instant, this wide Mediterranean of discretionary powers, which it seems is ours, should open up all its sluices, and
with a consentaneous rush, mingle with the turbid waters of
the others.

    *   *   *   *   *   *   *   *   *

" New States *may* be admitted by the Congress into this
Union."   It is objected that the word " may" imports power,
not obligation—a right to decide—a discretion to grant or
refuse.

To this it might be answered, that *power* is *duty* on
many occasions.   But let it be conceded that it is discretionary.   What consequence follows ?   A power to refuse,
in a case like this, does not necessarily involve a power to
exact terms.   You must look to the *result*, which is the declared object of the power.   Whether you will arrive at it,
or not, may depend on your will ; but you cannot compromise with the result intended and professed.

What then is the professed result ?   To admit a *State*
into this *Union*.

What is that Union ?   A confederation of States, equal
in sovereignty—capable of every thing which the constitution does not forbid, or authorize Congress to forbid.   It is
an equal Union, between parties equally sovereign.   They
were sovereign, independently of the Union.   The object of
the Union was common protection for the exercise of already
existing sovereignty.   The parties gave up a portion of that
sovereignty to insure the remainder.   As far as they gave it

up, by the common compact, they have ceased to be sovereign. The *Union* provides the means of defending the residue : and it is into that Union that a new State is to come. By acceding to it, the new State is placed on the same footing with the original States. It accedes for the same purpose, *i. e.*, protection for its unsurrendered sovereignty. If it comes in shorn of its beams—crippled and disparaged beyond the original States, it is not into the *original Union* that it comes. For it is a different sort of Union. The first was Union *inter pares :* This is a Union between *disparates*—between giants and a dwarf—between power and feebleness—between full proportioned sovereignties, and a miserable image of power—a thing which that very Union has shrunk and shrivelled from its just size, instead of preserving it in its true dimensions.

It is into "this Union," *i. e.*, the Union of the Federal Constitution, that you are to admit, or refuse to admit. You can admit into no other. You cannot make the Union, as to the new State, what it is not as to the old ; for then it is not *this Union* that you open for the entrance of a new party. If you make it enter into a new and additional compact, is it any longer the same Union ?

We are told that admitting a State into the Union is a compact. Yes—but what sort of a compact ? A compact that it shall be a member of the Union, as the constitution has made it. You cannot new fashion it. You may make a compact to admit, but when admitted, the original compact prevails. The Union is a compact, with a provision of political power and agents for the accomplishment of its objects. Vary that compact as to a new State—give new energy to that political power, so as to make it act with more force upon a new State than upon the old—make the will of those agents more effectually the arbiter of the fate of a new State than of the old, and it may be confidently said that the new State has not entered into *this Union*, but into another Union. How far the Union has been varied is another question. But that it has been varied is clear.

If I am told, that by the bill relative to Missouri, you do not legislate upon a new State—I answer that you do ; and I answer further, that it is immaterial whether you do or not. But it is upon Missouri, as a State, that your terms and conditions are to act. Until Missouri is a State, the terms and conditions are nothing. You legislate in the shape of terms and conditions, prospectively ; and you so legislate upon it, that when it comes into the Union it is to be bound by a contract degrading and diminishing its sovereignty, and is to be stripped of rights which the original parties to the Union did not consent to abandon, and which that Union (so far as depends upon it) takes under its protection and guarantee.

Is the right to hold slaves a right which Massachusetts enjoys ? If it is, Massachusetts is under this Union in a different character from Missouri. The compact of Union for it, is different from the same compact of Union for Missouri. The power of Congress is different—every thing which depends upon the Union is, in that respect, different.

But it is immaterial whether you legislate for Missouri as a State or not. The effect of your legislation is to bring it into the Union with a portion of its sovereignty taken away.

But it is a *State* which you are to admit. What is a State in the sense of the constitution ? It is not a State in the general—but a State as you find it in the constitution. A State, generally, is a body politic or independent political society of men. But the State which you are to admit must be more or less than this political entity. What must it be ? Ask the constitution. It shows what it means by a State by reference to the parties to it. It must be such a State as Massachusetts, Virginia, and the other members of the American confederacy—a State with full sovereignty, except as the constitution restricts it.

It is said that the word *may* ncessarily implies the right of prescribing the terms of admission. Those who maintain this are aware that there are no express words (such as *upon such terms and conditions as Congress shall think fit*), words which it was natural to expect to find in the constitution, if the effect contended for were meant. They put it, therefore, on the word *may*, and on that alone.

Give to that word all the force you please—what does it import? That Congress is not *bound* to admit a new State into this Union. Be it so for argument's sake. Does it follow that when you consent to admit into this Union a new State, you can make it less in sovereign power than the original parties to that Union—that you can make the Union as to it what it is not as to them—that you can fashion it to your liking by compelling it to purchase admission into an Union by sacrificing a portion of that power which it is the sole purpose of the Union to maintain in all the plenitude which the Union itself does not impair? Does it follow, that you can force upon it an additional compact not found in the compact of Union? that you can make it come into the Union less a *State*, in regard to sovereign power, than its fellows in that Union? that you can cripple its legislative competency (beyond the constitution which is the pact of Union, to which you make it a party as if it had been originally a party to it), by what you choose to call a *condition*, but which, whatever it may be called, brings the new government into the Union under new obligations to it, and with disparaged power to be protected by it?

In a word, the whole amount of the argument on the other side, is—that you may refuse to admit a new State, and that therefore, if you admit, you may prescribe the terms.

The answer to that argument is—that even if you can refuse, you can prescribe no terms which are inconsistent with the act you are to do. You can prescribe no condition which, if carried into effect, would make the new State less a sovereign State than, under the Union as it stands, it would be. You can prescribe no terms which will make the compact of Union between it and the original States essentially different from that compact among the original States. You may admit, or refuse to admit : but if you admit, you must admit a State in the sense of the constitution—a State with all such sovereignty as belongs to the original parties : and it must be into *this Union* that you are to admit it, not into a Union of your own dictating, formed out of the existing Union by qualifications and new compacts, altering its character and effect, and making it fall short of its protecting energy in reference to the new State, whilst it acquires an energy of another sort—the energy of restraint and destruction.

I have thus endeavored to show, that even if you have a discretion to refuse to admit—you have no discretion, if you are willing to admit, to insist upon any terms that impair the sovereignty of the admitted State as it would otherwise stand in the Union by the constitution which receives it into its bosom. To admit or not, is for you to decide. Admission once conceded, it follows as a corollary that you must take the new State as an equal companion with its fellows— that you cannot recast or new model the Union *pro hac vice* —but that you must receive it into the *actual Union*, and recognize it as a parcener in the common inheritance, without any other shackles than the rest have, by the constitution, submitted to bear—without any other extinction of power than is the work of the constitution acting indifferently upon all.

I may be told, perhaps, that the restriction, in this case, is the act of Missouri itself—that your law is nothing without its consent, and derives its efficacy from that alone.

I shall have a more suitable occasion to speak on this topic hereafter, when I come to consider the treaty which ceded Louisiana to the United States. But I will say a few words upon it now, of a more general application than it will, in that branch of the argument, be necessary to use.

A territory cannot surrender to Congress by anticipation, the whole, or a part, of the sovereign power which, by the constitution of the Union, will belong to it when it becomes a State and a member of the Union. Its consent is, therefore, nothing. It is in no situation to make this surrender. It is under the government of Congress ; if it can barter away a part of its sovereignty, by anticipation, it can do so as to the whole. For where will you stop ? If it does not cease to be a State, in the sense of the constitution, with only a certain portion of sovereign power, what other smaller portion will have that effect ? If you depart from the standard of the constitution, i. e., the quantity of domestic sovereignty left in the first contracting States, and secured by the original compact of Union, where will you get another standard ? Consent is no standard,—for consent may be gained to a surrender of all.

No State or Territory, in order to become a State, can alienate or surrender any portion of its sovereignty to the Union, or to a sister State, or to a foreign nation. It is under an incapacity to disqualify itself for all the purposes of government left to it in the constitution, by stripping itself of attributes which arise from the natural equality of States, and which the constitution recognizes, not only because it does not deny them, but presumes them to remain as they exist by the law of nature and nations. Inequality in the sovereignty of states is unnatural, and repugnant to all the principles of that law. Hence we find it laid down by the text writers on public law, that "Nature has established a perfect equality of rights between independent nations"— and that "Whatever the quality of a free sovereign nation gives to one, it gives to another." * The constitution of the

* Vattel, Droit des Gens, liv. 2, c. 3. s. 36.

United States proceeds upon the truth of this doctrine. It takes the States as it finds them, FREE AND SOVEREIGN ALIKE BY NATURE. It receives from them portions of their power for the general good, and provides for the exercise of it by organized political bodies. It diminishes the individual sovereignty of each, and transfers, what it subtracts, to the government which it creates : it takes from all alike, and leaves them relatively to each other equal in sovereign power.

The honorable gentleman from New-York has put the constitutional argument altogether upon the clause relative to admission of new States into the Union. He does not pretend that you can find the power to restrain, in any extent, elsewhere. It follows that it is not a particular power to impose this restriction, but a power to impose restrictions *ad libitum*. It is competent to this, because it is competent to every thing. But he denies that there can be any power in man to hold in slavery his fellow-creature, and argues, therefore, that the prohibition is no restraint at all, since it does not interfere with the sovereign powers of Missouri.

   *   *   *   *   *   *   *

One of the most signal errors with which the argument on the other side has abounded, is this of considering the proposed restriction as if levelled at the *introduction or establishment of slavery*. And hence the vehement declamation, which, among other things, has informed us that slavery originated in fraud or violence.

The truth is, that the restriction has no relation, real or pretended, to the right of *making slaves of those who are free*, or of introducing slavery where it does not already exist. It applies to those who are admitted to be already slaves, and who (with their posterity) would continue to be slaves if they should remain where they are at present ; and to a place where slavery already exists by the local law. Their civil condition will not be altered by their removal from Virginia, or Carolina, to Missouri. They will not be more slaves than they now are. Their abode, indeed, will be different, but their bondage the same. Their numbers may possibly be augmented by the diffusion, and I think they will. But this can only happen because their hardships will be mitigated, and their comforts increased. The checks to population, which exist in the older States will be diminished. The restriction, therefore, does not prevent the establishment of slavery, either with reference to persons or place ; but simply inhibits the removal from place to place (the law in each being the same) of a slave, or make his emancipation the consequence of that removal. It acts professedly merely on slavery as it exists, and thus acting restrains its present lawful effects. That slavery, like many other human institutions, originated in fraud or violence, may be conceded : but, however it *originated*, it is established among us, and no man seeks a further establishment of it by new importations of freemen to be converted into slaves. On the contrary, all are anxious to mitigate its evils by all the means within the reach of the appropriate authority, the domestic legislatures of the different States.

It can be nothing to the purpose of this argument, therefore, as the gentlemen themselves have shaped it, to inquire what was the origin of slavery. What is it now, and who are they that endeavor to innovate upon what it now is (the advocates of this restriction who desire change by unconstitutional means, or its opponents who desire to leave the whole matter to local regulation), are the only questions worthy of attention.

Sir, if we too closely look to the rise and progress of long sanctioned establishments and unquestioned rights, we may discover other subjects than that of slavery, with which fraud and violence may claim a fearful connection, and over which it may be our interest to throw the mantle of oblivion. What was the settlement of our ancestors in this country but an invasion of the rights of the barbarians who inhabited it ?

That settlement, with slight exceptions, was effected by the slaughter of those who did no more than defend their native land against the intruders of Europe, or by unequal compacts and purchases, in which feebleness and ignorance had to deal with power and cunning. The savages who once built their huts where this proud Capitol, rising from its recent ashes, exemplifies the sovereignty of the American people, were swept away by the injustice of our fathers, and their domain usurped by force, or obtained by artifices yet more criminal. Our continent was full of those aboriginal inhabitants. Where are they or their descendants ? Either " with years beyond the flood," or driven back by the swelling tide of our population from the borders of the Atlantic to the deserts of the West. You follow still the miserable remnants, and make *contracts* with them that seal their ruin. You purchase their lands, of which they know not the value, in order that you may sell them to advantage, increase your treasure, and enlarge your empire. Yet further—you pursue as they retire ; and they must continue to retire, until the Pacific shall stay their retreat, and compel them to pass away as a dream. Will you recur to those scenes of various iniquity for any other purpose than to regret and lament them ? Will you pry into them, with a view to shake and impair your rights of property and dominion ?

But the broad denial of the sovereign right of Missouri, if it shall become a sovereign State, to recognize slavery by its laws, is rested upon a variety of grounds, all of which I will examine.

It is an extraordinary fact, that they who urge this denial with such ardent zeal, stop short of it in their conduct. There are now slaves in Missouri whom they do not insist upon delivering from their chains. Yet if it is incompetent to sovereign power to continue slavery in Missouri, in respect of slaves who may yet be carried thither, show me the power that can continue it in respect of slaves who are there already.

Missouri is out of the old limits of the Union, and beyond those limits, it is said, we can give no countenance to slavery, if we can countenance or tolerate it any where. It is plain, that there can be no slaves beyond the Mississippi at this moment but in virtue of some power to make or keep them so. What sort of power was it that has made or kept them so ? Sovereign power it could not be, according to the honorable gentlemen from Pennsylvania and New Hampshire : * and if sovereign power is unequal to such a purpose, less than sovereign power is yet more unequal to it. The laws of Spain and France could do nothing—the laws of the territorial government of Missouri could do nothing towards such a result, if it be a result which no laws, in other words, no sovereignty, could accomplish. The treaty of 1803 could do no more, in this view, than the laws of France, or Spain, or the territorial government of Missouri. A treaty is an act of sovereign power, taking the shape of a compact between the parties to it ; and that which sovereign power cannot reach at all, it cannot reach by a treaty. Those who are now held in bondage, therefore, in Missouri, and their issue, are entitled to be free, if there be any truth in the doctrine of the honorable gentlemen ; and if the proposed restriction leaves all such in slavery, it thus discredits the very foundation on which it reposes. To be inconsistent is the fate of false principles—but this inconsistency is the more to be remarked, since it cannot be referred to mere considerations of policy, without admitting that such considerations may be preferred (without a crime) to what is deemed a paramount and indispensable duty.

It is here, too, that I must be permitted to observe, that the honorable gentlemen have taken great pains to show that this restriction is a mere work of supererogation by the principal argument on which they rest the proof of its propriety. Missouri, it is said, can have no power to do what

* Mr. Roberts, Mr. Lowrie, and Mr. Morril.

the restriction would prevent. It would be void, therefore, without the restriction. Why then, I ask, is the restriction insisted upon ? Restraint implies that there is something to be restrained : But the gentlemen justify the restraint by showing that there is nothing upon which it can operate ! They demonstrate the wisdom and necessity of restraint, by demonstrating that with or without restraint, the subject is in the same predicament. This is to combat with a man of straw, and to put fetters upon a shadow.

The gentlemen must, therefore, abandon either their doctrine or their restriction, their argument or their object, for they are directly in conflict, and reciprocally destroy each other. It is evident, that they will not abandon their object, and of course, I must believe, that they hold their argument in as little real estimation as I myself do. The gentlemen can scarcely be sincere believers in their own principle. They have apprehensions, which they endeavor to conceal, that Missouri, as a State, will have power to continue slavery within its limits ; and if they will not be offended, I will venture to compare them, in this particular, with the duelist in Sheridan's comedy of the Rivals, who affecting to have no fear whatever of his adversary, is, nevertheless, careful to admonish Sir Lucius to hold him fast.

Let us take it for granted, however, that they are in earnest in their doctrine, and that it is very necessary to impose what they prove to be an unnecessary restraint : how do they support that doctrine ?

The honorable gentleman on the other side* has told us, as a proof of his great position (that man cannot enslave his fellow man, in which is implied that all laws upholding slavery are absolute nullities), that the nations of antiquity as well as of modern times have concurred in laying down that position as incontrovertible.

* Mr. King.

He refers us in the first place to the Roman law, in which he finds it laid down as a maxim : *Jure naturali omnes homines ab initio liberi nascebantur.* From the manner in which this maxim was pressed upon us, it would not readily have been conjectured that the honorable gentleman who used it had borrowed it from a slave-holding empire, and still less from a book of the Institutes of Justinian, which treats of slavery, and justifies, and regulates it. Had he given us the context, we should have had the modifications of which the abstract doctrine was in the judgment of the Roman law susceptible. We should have had an explanation of the competency of that law, to convert, whether justly or unjustly, freedom into servitude, and to maintain the right of a master to the service and obedience of his slave.

The honorable gentleman might also have gone to Greece for a similar maxim and a similar commentary, speculative and practical.

He next refers us to Magna Charta. I am somewhat familiar with Magna Charta, and I am confident that it contains no such maxim as the honorable gentleman thinks he has discovered in it. The great charter was extorted from John, and his feeble son and successor, by haughty slave-holding barons, who thought only of themselves and the commons of England (then inconsiderable), whom they wished to enlist in their efforts against the crown. There is not in it a single word which condemns civil slavery. Freemen only are the objects of its protecting care, "Nullus *liber* homo," is its phraseology. The serfs, who were chained to the soil—the villeins regardant and in gross, were left as it found them. All England was then full of slaves, whose posterity would by law remain slaves as with us, except only that the issue followed the condition of the father instead of the mother. The rule was "Partus sequitur patrem"—a rule more favorable, undoubtedly, from the very precariousness of its application, to the gradual extinction of slavery, than ours, which has been drawn from the Roman law, and is of sure and unavoidable effect.

Still less has the *Petition of Right,* presented to Charles I., by the Long Parliament, to do with the subject of civil slavery. It looked merely, as Magna Charta had not done before it, to the freedom of England—and sought only to protect them against royal prerogative and the encroaching spirit of the Stewarts.

As to the *Bill of Rights,* enacted by the Convention Parliament of 1688, it is almost a duplicate of the Petition of Right, and arose out of the recollection of that political tyranny from which the nation had just escaped, and the recurrence of which it was intended to prevent. It contains no abstract principles. It deals only with practical checks upon the power of the monarch, and in safeguards for institutions essential to the preservation of the public liberty. That it was not designed to anathematize civil slavery may be taken for granted, since at that epoch and long afterwards the English government inundated its foreign plantations with slaves, and supplied other nations with them as merchandise, under the sanction of solemn treaties negotiated for that purpose. And here I cannot forbear to remark that we owe it to that same government, when it stood towards us in the relation of parent to child, that involuntary servitude exists in our land, and that we are now deliberating whether the prerogative of correcting its evils belongs to the national or the State governments. In the early periods of our colonial history every thing was done by the mother country to encourage the importation of slaves into North America, and the measures which were adopted by the Colonial Assemblies to prohibit it, were uniformly negatived by the crown. It is not therefore our fault, nor the fault of our ancestors, that this calamity has been entailed upon us ; and notwithstanding the ostentation with which the loitering abolition of the slave trade by the British Parliament has been vaunted, the principal consideration which at last reconciled it to that measure was, that by suitable care, the slave population in their West India islands (already fully stocked) might be kept up and even increased without the aid of importation. In a word, it was cold calculations of interest, and not the suggestions of humanity, or a respect for the philanthropic principles of Mr. Wilberforce, which produced their tardy abandonment of that abominable traffic.

Of the Declaration of our Independence, which has also been quoted in support of the perilous doctrines now urged upon us, I need not now speak at large. I have shown on a former occasion how idle it is to rely upon that instrument for such a purpose, and will not fatigue you by mere repetition. The self-evident truths announced in the Declaration of Independence are not truths at all, if taken literally ; and the practical conclusions contained in the same passage of that Declaration prove that they were never designed to be so received.

The Articles of Confederation contain nothing on the subject ; whilst the actual constitution recognizes the legal existence of slavery by various provisions. The power of prohibiting the slave trade is involved in that of regulating commerce, but this is coupled with an express inhibition to the exercise of it for twenty years. How then can that constitution which expressly permits the importation of slaves, authorize the national government to set on foot a crusade against slavery ?

The clause respecting fugitive slaves is affirmative and active in its effects. It is a direct sanction and positive protection of the right of the master to the services of his slave as derived under the local laws of the State. The phraseology in which it is wrapped up still leaves the intention clear, and the words "persons held to service or labor in one State under the laws thereof," have always been interpreted to extend to the case of slaves, in the various acts of Congress which have been passed to give efficacy to the provision, and in the judicial application of those laws. So also in the clause prescribing the ratio of representation—the phrase, "three-fifths of all other persons," is equivalent to *slaves*, or it means nothing. And yet we are told that those who are acting under a constitution which sanctions the existence of slavery in those States which choose to tolerate it, are at liberty to hold that no law can sanction its existence !

It is idle to make the rightfulness of an act the measure of sovereign power. The distinction between sovereign power and the moral right to exercise it, has always been recognized. All political power may be abused, but is it to stop where abuse may begin ? The power of declaring war is a power of vast capacity for mischief, and capable of inflicting the most wide-spread desolation. But it is given to Congress without stint and without measure. Is a citizen, or are the courts of justice to inquire whether that, or any other law, is just, before they obey or execute it ? And are there any degrees of injustice which will withdraw from sovereign power the capacity of making a given law ?

But sovereignty is said to be *deputed* power. Deputed —by whom ? By the people, because the power is theirs. And if it be theirs, does not the restriction take it away ? Examine the constitution of the Union, and it will be seen that the *people* of the States are regarded as well as the *States* themselves. The constitution was made by the people, and ratified by the people.

Is it fit, then, to hold that all the sovereignty of a State is in the government of the State ? So much is there as the people grant : and the people can take it away, or give more, or new model what they have already granted. It is this right which the proposed restriction takes from Missouri. You give them an immortal constitution, depending on your will, not on theirs. The people and their posterity are to be bound for ever by this restriction ; and upon the same prin-

ciple any other restriction may be imposed. Where then is
their power to change the constitution, and to devolve new
sovereignty upon the State government ? You limit their
sovereign capacity to do it ; and when you talk of a State,
you mean the people, as well as the government. The people
are the source of all power—you dry up that source. They
are the reservoir—you take out of it what suits you.

It is said that this government is a government of deputed powers. So is every government—and what power is
not deputed remains. But the people of the *United States*
can give it more if they please, as the people of each State
can do in respect to its own government. And here it is
well to remember, that this is a government of enumerated,
as well as deputed powers ; and to examine the clause as to
the admission of new States, with that principle in view.
Now assume that it is a part of the sovereign power *of the
people of Missouri* to continue slavery, and to devolve that
power upon its government—and then to take it away—and
then to give it again. The government is their creature—
the means of exercising their sovereignty, and they can vary
those means at their pleasure. Independently of the Union,
their power would be unlimited. By coming into the
Union, they part with some of it, and are thus less sovereign.

Let us then see whether they part with this power.

If they have parted with this portion of sovereign power,
it must be under that clause of the national constitution
which gives to Congress "power to admit new States into
this Union." And it is said, that this necessarily implies
the authority of prescribing the conditions, upon which such
new States shall be admitted. This has been put into the
form of a syllogism which is thus stated :

Major. Every universal proposition includes all the
means, manner, and terms of the act to which it relates.

Minor. But this is a universal proposition.

Conclusion. Therefore, the means, manner, and terms, are involved in it.

But this syllogism is fallacious, and any thing else may be proved by it, by assuming one of its members which involves the conclusion.   The *minor* is a mere postulate.

Take it in this way :

Major. None but a universal proposition includes in itself the terms and conditions of the act to be done.

Minor. But this is not such a universal proposition.

Conclusion. Therefore, it does not contain in itself the terms and conditions of the act.

In both cases the minor is a gratuitous postulate.

But I deny that a universal proposition *as to a specific act,* involves the terms and conditions of that act, so as to vary it and substitute another and a different act in its place.   The proposition contained in the clause is *universal* in one sense only.   It is *particular* in another.   It is universal as to the power to admit or refuse.   It is particular as to the being or thing to be admitted, and the compact by which it is to be admitted.   The sophistry consists in extending the universal part of the proposition in such a manner as to make out of it another universal proposition. It consists in confounding the right to produce or to refuse to produce a *certain defined effect,* with a right to produce a *different effect* by refusing otherwise to produce any effect at all.   It makes the *actual right* the instrument of obtaining *another right* with which the actual right is incompatible. It makes, in a word, lawful power the instrument of unlawful usurpation.   The *result* is kept out of sight by this mode of reasoning.   The discretion to decline that result, which is called a universal proposition, is singly obtruded upon us.   But in order to reason correctly, you must keep in view the defined result, as well as the discretion to produce or to decline to produce it.   The result is the particular part of the proposition ; therefore, the discretion to produce or decline it, is the universal part of it. But because the *last* is found to be universal, it is taken for granted that the *first* is also universal. This is a sophism too manifest to impose.

But discarding the machinery of syllogisms as unfit for such a discussion as this, let us look at the clause with a view of interpreting it by the rules of sound logic and common sense.

The power is "to admit new States into this Union;" and it may be safely conceded that here is discretion to admit or refuse. The question is, What must we do if we do any thing ? What must we admit, and into what ? The answer is a *State*—and into *this Union*.

The distinction between federal rights and local rights, is an idle distinction. Because the new State acquires *federal* rights, it is not, therefore, in *this Union*. The Union is a compact ; and is it an equal party to that compact, because it has equal federal rights ?

How is the Union formed ? By equal contributions of power. Make one member sacrifice more than other, and it becomes unequal. The compact is of two parts.

1. The thing obtained—federal rights.

2. The price paid—local sovereignty.

You may disturb the balance of the Union, either by diminishing the thing acquired, or increasing the sacrifice paid.

What were the purposes of coming into the Union among the original States ? The States were originally sovereign without limit, as to foreign and domestic concerns. But being incapable of protecting themselves singly, they entered into the Union to defend themselves against foreign violence. The domestic concerns of the people were not, in general, to be acted on by it. The security of the power of managing them by domestic legislation, is one of the great objects of the Union. The Union is a *means*, not an *end*.

By requiring greater sacrifices of domestic power, the end is sacrificed to the means. Suppose the surrender of all, or nearly all, the domestic powers of legislation were required ; the means would there have swallowed up the end.

The argument that the compact may be enforced, shows that the federal predicament is changed. The power of the Union not only acts on persons or citizens, but on the faculty of the government, and restrains it in a way which the constitution nowhere authorizes. This new obligation takes away a right which is expressly " reserved to the people or the States," since it is nowhere granted to the government of the Union. You cannot do indirectly what you cannot do directly. It is said that *this Union* is competent to make compacts. Who doubts it ? But can you make *this compact ;* I insist that you cannot make it, because it is repugnant to the thing to be done.

The effect of such a compact would be to produce that inequality in the Union, to which the constitution, in all its provisions, is adverse. Every thing in it looks to equality among the members of the Union. Under it, you cannot produce inequality. Nor can you get beforehand of the constitution, and do it by anticipation. Wait until a State is in the Union, and you cannot do it : yet it is only upon the State in the Union that what you do begins to act.

* * * * * * * * *

But it seems, that although the proposed restriction may not be justified by the clause of the constitution which gives power to admit new States into the Union, separately considered, there are other parts of the constitution which combined with that clause will warrant it. And first we are informed that there is a clause in this instrument which declares that Congress *shall* guarantee to every State a republican form of government ; that slavery and such a form of government are incompatible ; and finally, as a conclusion from these premises, that Congress not only have a *right,* but are *bound* to exclude slavery from a new State. Here again, Sir, there is an edifying inconsistency between the argument and the measure which it professes to vindicate. By the argument it is maintained that Missouri cannot have a republican form of government, and at the same time tolerate negro slavery. By the measure it is admitted that Missouri may tolerate slavery, as to persons already in bondage there, and be nevertheless fit to be received into the Union. What sort of constitutional mandate is this which can thus be made to bend, and truckle, and compromise as if it were a simple rule of expediency that might admit of exceptions upon motives of countervailing expediency? There can be no such pliancy in the peremptory provisions of the constitution. They cannot be obeyed by moieties and violated in the same ratio. They must be followed out to their full extent, or treated with that decent neglect which has at least the merit of forbearing to render contumacy obtrusive by an ostentatious display of the very duty which we in part abandon. If the decalogue could be observed in this casuistical manner, we might be grievous sinners, and yet be liable to no reproach. We might persist in all our *habitual* irregularities, and still be spotless. We might, for example, continue to covet our neighbors' goods, provided they were the same neighbors whose goods we had before coveted—and so of all the other commandments.

Will the gentlemen tell us that it is the *quantity of slaves*, not the *quality of slavery*, which takes from a government the republican form? Will they tell us (for they have not yet told us) that there are constitutional grounds (to say nothing of common sense) upon which the slavery which now exists in Missouri may be reconciled with a republican form of government, while any addition to the *number of its slaves* (the quality of slavery remaining the same) from the other States, will be repugnant to that form, and metamorphose it into some non-descript government

disowned by the constitution ?   They cannot have recourse
to the treaty of 1803 for such a distinction, since independently of what I have before observed on that head, the
gentlemen have contended that the treaty has nothing to do
with the matter.   They have cut themselves off from all
chance of a convenient distinction in or out of that treaty,
by insisting that slavery beyond the old United States is rejected by the constitution, and by the law of God as discov-
erable by the aid of either reason or revelation ; and moreover that the treaty does not include the case, and if it did
could not make it better.   They have therefore completely
discredited their own theory by their own practice, and left
us no theory worthy of being seriously controverted.   This
peculiarity in reasoning, of giving out a universal principle
and coupling with it a practical concession that it is wholly
fallacious, has indeed run through the greater part of the
arguments on the other side ; but it is not, as I think, the
more imposing on that account, or the less liable to the criticism which I have here bestowed upon it.

There is a remarkable inaccuracy on this branch of the
subject into which the gentlemen have fallen, and to which
I will give a moment's attention without laying unnecessary
stress upon it.   The government of a new State, as well as
of an old State, must, I agree, be republican in its *form*.
But it has not been very clearly explained what the *laws*
which such a government may enact can have to do with its
form.   The form of the government is material only as it
furnishes a security that those laws will protect and promote
the public happiness, and be made in a republican spirit.
The people being, in such a government, the fountain of
all power, and their servants being periodically responsible
to them for its exercise, the constitution of the Union takes
for granted, (except so far as it imposes limitations,) that
every such exercise will be just and salutary.   The introduction or continuance of civil slavery is manifestly the mere

result of the power of making laws. It does not in any degree enter into the form of the government. It pre-supposes that form already settled, and takes its rise not from the particular frame of the government, but from the general power which every government involves. Make the government what you will in its organization and in the distribution of its authorities, the introduction or continuance of involuntary servitude by the legislative power which it has created can have no influence on its pre-established form, whether monarchical, aristocratical, or republican. The form of government is still one thing, and the law, being a simple exertion of the ordinary faculty of legislation by those to whom that form of government has intrusted it, another. The gentlemen, however, identify an act of legislation sanctioning involuntary servitude with the form of government itself, and then assure us that the last is changed retroactively by the first, and is no longer republican !

But let us proceed to take a rapid glance at the reasons which have been assigned for this notion that involuntary servitude and a republican form of government are perfect antipathies. The gentleman from New-Hampshire* has defined a republican government to be that in which all the *men* participate in its power and privileges : from whence it follows that where there are slaves, it can have no existence. A definition is no proof, however; and even if it be dignified (as I think it was) with the name of a maxim, the matter is not much mended. It is Lord Bacon who says "that nothing is so easily made as a maxim ;" and certainly a definition is manufactured with equal facility. A political maxim is the work of induction, and cannot stand against experience, or stand on any thing but experience. But this maxim, or definition, or whatever else it may be, sets fact at defiance. If you go back to antiquity, you

* Mr. Morril.

will obtain no countenance for this hypothesis ; and if you look at home you will gain still less. I have read that Sparta, and Rome, and Athens, and many others of the ancient family were republics. They were so in form undoubtedly—the last approaching nearer to a perfect democracy than any other government which has yet been known in the world. Judging of them also by their fruits, they were of the highest order of republics. Sparta could scarcely be any other than a republic, when a Spartan matron could say to her son just marching to battle, RE-TURN VICTORIOUS, OR RETURN NO MORE. It was the unconquerable spirit of liberty, nurtured by republican habits and institutions, that illustrated the pass of Thermopylæ. Yet slavery was not only tolerated in Sparta, but was established by one of the fundamental laws of Lycurgus, having for its object the encouragement of that very spirit. Attica was full of slaves—yet the love of liberty was its characteristic. What else was it that foiled the whole power of Persia at Marathon and Salamis ? What other soil than that which the genial Sun of Republican Freedom illuminated and warmed, could have produced such men as Leonidas and Miltiades, Themistocles and Epaminondas ? Of Rome it would be superfluous to speak at large. It is sufficient to name the mighty mistress of the world, before Sylla gave the first stab to her liberties and the great dictator accomplished their final ruin, to be reminded of the practicability of union between civil slavery and an ardent love of liberty cherished by republican establishments.

If we return home for instruction upon this point, we perceive that same union exemplified in many a State, in which "Liberty has a temple in every house, an altar in every heart," while involuntary servitude is seen in every direction. Is it denied that those States possess a republican form of government ? If it is, why does our power of correction sleep ? Why is the constitutional guaranty

suffered to be inactive ?   Why am I permitted to fatigue
you, as the representative of a slaveholding State, with the
discussion of the *nugæ canoræ* (for so I think them)
that have been forced into this debate contrary to all the
remonstrances of taste and prudence ?   Do gentlemen perceive the consequences to which their arguments must lead
if they are of any value ?   Do they reflect that they lead
to emancipation in the old United States—or to an exclusion of Delaware, Maryland, and all the South, and a great
portion of the West, from the Union ?   My honorable
friend from Virginia has no business here, if this disorganizing creed be any thing but the production of a heated
brain.   The State to which I belong, must " perform a lus-
tration"—must purge and purify herself from the feculence
of civil slavery, and emulate the States of the north in
their zeal for throwing down the gloomy idol which we are
said to worship, before her senators can have any title to appear in this high assembly.   It will be in vain to urge that
the old United States are exceptions to the rule—or rather
(as the gentlemen express it), that they have no *disposition*
to apply the rule to them.   There can be no exceptions, by
implication only, to such a rule ; and expressions which justify the exemption of the old States by inference, will justify the like exemption of Missouri, unless they point exclusively to them, as I have shown they do not.   The
guarded manner, too, in which some of the gentlemen have
occasionally expressed themselves on this subject, is somewhat alarming.   They have no *disposition* to meddle with
slavery in the old United States.   Perhaps not—but who
shall answer for their successors ?   Who shall furnish a
pledge that the principle once engrafted into the constitution, will not grow, and spread, and fructify, and overshadow
the whole land ?   It is the natural office of such a principle
to wrestle with slavery, wheresoever it finds it.   New
States, colonized by the apostles of this principle, will

enable it to set on foot a fanatical crusade against all who
still continue to tolerate it, although no practicable means
are pointed out by which they can get rid of it consistently
with their own safety. At any rate, a present forbearing
disposition, in a few or in many, is not a security upon
which much reliance can be placed upon a subject as to
which so many selfish interests and ardent feelings are connected with the cold calculations of policy. Admitting,
however, that the old United States are in no danger from
this principle—why is it so ?   There can be no other answer (which these zealous enemies of slavery can use) than
that the constitution recognizes slavery as existing or
capable of existing in those States. The constitution, then,
admits that slavery and a republican form of government
are not incongruous. It associates and binds them up together, and repudiates this wild imagination which the gentlemen have pressed upon us with such an air of triumph.
But the constitution does more, as I have heretofore proved.
It concedes that slavery may exist in a new State, as well as
in an old one—since the language in which it recognizes
slavery comprehends new States as well as actual.   I trust
then that I shall be forgiven if I suggest, that no eccentri-
city in argument can be more trying to human patience,
than a formal assertion that a constitution, to which slave-
holding States were the most numerous parties, in which
slaves are treated as property as well as persons, and provision is made for the security of that property, and even for
an augmentation of it, by a temporary importation from
Africa, a clause commanding Congress to guarantee a republican form of government to those very States, as well as to
others, authorizes you to determine that slavery and a republican form of government cannot coexist.

But if a republican form of government is that in which
all the men have a share in the public power, the slave-
holding States will not alone retire from the Union. The

constitutions of some of the other States do not sanction universal suffrage, or universal eligibility. They require citizenship, and age, and a certain amount of property, to give a title to vote or to be voted for ; and they who have not those qualifications are just as much disfranchised, with regard to the government and its power, as if they were slaves. They have civil rights indeed (and so have slaves in a less degree) ; but they have no share in the government. Their province is to obey the laws, not to assist in making them. All such States must therefore be forisfamiliated with Virginia and the rest, or change their system : for the constitution being absolutely silent on those subjects, will afford them no protection. The Union might thus be reduced from an Union to an unit. Who does not see that such conclusions flow from false notions—that the true theory of a republican government is mistaken—and that in such a government, rights political and civil, may be qualified by the fundamental law, upon such inducements as the freemen of the country deem sufficient ? That civil rights may be qualified as well as political, is proved by a thousand examples. Minors, resident aliens, who are in a course of naturalization—the other sex, whether maids or wives, or widows, furnish sufficient practical proofs of this.

Again; if we are to entertain these hopeful abstractions, and to resolve all establishments into their imaginary elements in order to recast them upon some Utopian plan, and if it be true that all the *men* in a republican government must help to wield its power, and be equal in rights, I beg leave to ask the honorable gentleman from New Hampshire— and why not all the *women ?* They too are God's creatures, and not only very fair but very rational creatures ; and our great ancestor, if we are to give credit to Milton, accounted them the " wisest, virtuousest, discreetest, best ;" although to say the truth he had but one specimen from which to draw his conclusion, and possibly if he had had more, would not have drawn it at all. They have, moreover, acknowledged civil rights in abundance, and upon abstract principles more than their masculine rulers allow them in fact. Some monarchies, too, do not exclude them from the throne. We have all read of Elizabeth of England, of Catharine of Russia, of Semiramis, and Zenobia, and a long list of royal and imperial dames, about as good as an equal list of royal and imperial lords. Why is it that their exclusion from the power of a popular government is not destructive of its republican character ? I do not address this question to the honorable gentleman's gallantry, but to his abstraction, and his theories, and his notions of the infinite perfectibility of human institutions, borrowed from Godwin and the turbulent philosophers of France. For my own part, Sir, if I may have leave to say so much in the presence of this mixed uncommon audience, I confess I am no friend to female government, unless indeed it be that which reposes on gentleness, and modesty, and virtue, and feminine grace and delicacy ; and how powerful a government that is, we have all of us, as I suspect, at some time or other experienced ! But if the ultra republican doctrines which have now been broached should ever gain ground among us, I should not be surprised if some romantic reformer, treading in the footsteps of Mrs. Wolstoncraft, should propose to repeal our republican law salique, and claim for our wives and daughters a full participation in political power, and to add to it that domestic power, which in some families, as I have heard, is as absolute and unrepublican as any power can be.

I have thus far allowed the honorable gentlemen to avail themselves of their assumption that the constitutional command to guarantee to the States a republican form of government, gives power to coerce those states in the adjustment of the details of their constitutions upon theoretical speculations. But surely it is passing strange that any man, who thinks at all, can view this salutary command as the grant of a power so monstrous ; or look at it in any other light than as a protecting mandate to Congress to interpose with the force and authority of the Union against that violence and usurpation, by which a member of it might otherwise be oppressed by profligate and powerful individuals, or ambitious and unprincipled factions.

In a word, the resort to this portion of the constitution for an argument in favor of the proposed restriction, is one of those extravagancies (I hope I shall not offend by this expression) which may excite our admiration, but cannot call for a very rigorous refutation. I have dealt with it accordingly, and have now done with it.

We are next invited to study that clause of the constitution which relates to the migration or importation, before the year 1808, of such persons as any of the States then existing should think proper to admit. It runs thus : "The migration or importation of such persons as any of the States now existing shall think proper to admit, shall not be prohibited by the Congress prior to the year one thousand eight hundred and eight, but a tax or duty may be imposed on such importation not exceeding ten dollars for each person."

It is said that this clause empowers Congress, after the year 1808, to prohibit the passage of slaves from State to State, and the word "migration" is relied upon for that purpose.

I will not say that the proof of the existence of a power by a clause which, as far as it goes, denies it, is always inadmissible ; but I will say that it is always feeble. On this occasion, it is singularly so. The power, in an affirmative shape, cannot be found in the constitution; or if it can, it is equivocal and unsatisfactory. How do the gentlemen supply this deficiency ? by the aid of a negative provision in an article of the constitution in which many restrictions are inserted *ex abundanti cautela*, from which it is plainly im-

possible to infer that the power to which they apply would
otherwise have existed.   Thus : " No bill of attainder or *ex
post facto* law shall be passed."   Take away the restriction,
could Congress pass a bill of attainder, the trial by jury in
criminal cases being expressly secured by the constitution ?
The inference, therefore, from the prohibition in question,
whatever may be its meaning, to the power which it is supposed to restrain, but which you cannot lay your finger upon
with any pretensions to certainty, must be a very doubtful
one.   But the import of the prohibition is also doubtful, as
the gentlemen themselves admit.   So that a doubtful power
is to be made certain by a yet more doubtful negative upon
power—or rather a doubtful negative, where there is no evidence of the corresponding affirmative, is to make out the
affirmative and to justify us in acting upon it, in a matter
of such high moment, that *questionable* power should not
dare to approach it.   If the negative were perfectly clear in
its import, the conclusion which has been drawn from it
would be rash, because it might have proceeded, as some of
the negatives in whose company it is found evidently did
proceed, from great anxiety to prevent such assumptions of
authority as are now attempted.   But when it is conceded,
that the supposed import of this negative (as to the term
migration) is ambiguous, and that it may have been used in
a very different sense from that which is imputed to it, the
conclusion acquires a character of boldness, which, however
some may admire, the wise and reflecting will not fail to
condemn.

In the construction of this clause, the first remark that
occurs is, that the word MIGRATION is associated with the
word IMPORTATION.   I do not insist that *noscitur a sociis* is
as good a rule in matters of interpretation as in common
life ; but it is, nevertheless, of considerable weight when the
associated words are not qualified by any phrases that disturb
the effect of their fellowship ; and unless it announces (as

in this case it does not), by specific phrases combined with the associated term, a different intention. Moreover, the ordinary unrestricted import of the word *migration* is what I have here supposed. A removal from district to district, within the same jurisdiction, is never denominated a *migration* of persons. I will concede to the honorable gentlemen, if they will accept the concession, that ants may be said to migrate when they go from one ant-hill to another at no great distance from it. But even then they could not be said to migrate, if each ant-hill was their home in virtue of some federal compact with insects like themselves. But, however this may be, it should seem to be certain that human beings do not *migrate*, in the sense of a constitution, simply because they transplant themselves, from one place, to which that constitution extends, to another which it equally covers.

If this word *migration* applied to freemen, and not to slaves, it would be clear that removal from State to State would not be comprehended within it. Why then, if you choose to apply it to slaves, does it take another meaning as to the place from whence they are to come ?

Sir, if we once depart from the usual acceptation of this term, fortified as it is by its union with another in which there is nothing in this respect equivocal, will gentlemen please to intimate the point at which we are to stop ? *Migration* means, as they contend, a removal from State to State, within the pale of the common government. Why not a removal also from county to county within a particular State—from plantation to plantation—from farm to farm—from hovel to hovel ? Why not any exertion of the power of locomotion ? I protest I do not see, if this arbitrary limitation of the natural sense of the term *migration* be warrantable, that a person to whom it applies may not be compelled to remain immovable all the days of his life (which could not well be many) in the very spot, literally speaking, in which it was his good or his bad fortune to be born.

Whatever may be the latitude in which the word "persons" is capable of being received, it is not denied that the word "importation" indicates a bringing in from a jurisdiction foreign to the United States. The two *termini* of the *importation*, here spoken of, are a foreign country and the American Union—the first the *terminus a quo*, the second the *terminus ad quem*. The word *migration* stands in simple connection with it, and of course is left to the full influence of that connection. The natural conclusion is, that the same *termini* belong to each, or in other words, that if the *importation* must be abroad, so also must be the *migration*—no other termini being assigned to the one which are not manifestly characteristic of the other. This conclusion is so obvious, that to repel it, the word *migration* requires, as an appendage, explanatory phraseology, giving to it a different beginning from that of *importation*. To justify the conclusion that it was intended to mean a removal from State to State, each within the sphere of the constitution in which it is used, the addition of the words *from one to another State in this Union*, were indispensable. By the omission of these words, the word "migration" is compelled to take every sense of which it is fairly susceptible from its immediate neighbor "importation." In this view it means a *coming*, as "importation" means a *bringing*, from a foreign jurisdiction into the United States. That it is susceptible of this meaning, nobody doubts. I go further. It can have no other meaning in the place in which it is found. It is found in the constitution of this Union—which, when it speaks of *migration* as of a general concern, must be supposed to have in view a migration into the domain which itself embraces as a general government.

Migration, then, even if it comprehends slaves, does not mean the removal of them from State to State, but means the coming of slaves from places beyond their limits and their power. And if this be so, the gentlemen gain nothing for their argument by showing that slaves were the objects of this term.

An honorable gentleman from Rhode Island,* whose speech was distinguished for its ability, and for an admirable force of reasoning, as well as by the moderation and mildness of its spirit, informed us, with less discretion than in general he exhibited, that the word "migration" was introduced into this clause at the instance of some of the Southern States, who wished by its instrumentality to guard against a prohibition by Congress of the passage into those States of slaves from other States. He has given us no authority for this supposition, and it is, therefore, a gratuitous one. How improbable it is, a moment's reflection will convince him. The African slave-trade being open during the whole of the time to which the entire clause in question referred, such a purpose could scarely be entertained ; but if it had been entertained, and there was believed to be a necessity for securing it, by a restriction upon the power of Congress to interfere with it, is it possible that they who deemed it important would have contented themselves with a vague restraint, which was calculated to operate in almost any other manner than that which they desired ? If fear and jealousy, such as the honorable gentleman has described, had dictated this provision, a better term than that of "migration," simple and unqualified, and joined too with the word "importation," would have been found to tranquillize those fears and satisfy that jealousy. Fear and jealousy are watchful, and are rarely seen to accept a security short of their object, and less rarely to shape that security, of their own accord, in such a way as to make it no security at all. They always seek an explicit guaranty ; and that this is not such a gua-

* Mr. Burrill.

ranty this debate has proved, if it has proved nothing else.

Sir, I shall not be understood by what I have said to admit that the word *migration* refers to *slaves*. I have contended only that if it does refer to slaves, it is in this clause synonymous with *importation;* and that it cannot mean the mere passage of slaves, with or without their masters, from one State in the Union to another.

But I now deny that it refers to slaves at all. I am not for any man's opinions or his histories upon this subject. I am not accustomed *jurare in verba magistri*. I shall take the clause as I find it, and do my best to interpret it.

❊   ❊   ❊   ❊   ❊   ❊

[After going through with that part of his argument relating to this clause of the constitution, which I have not been able to restore from the imperfect notes in my possession, Mr. Pinkney concluded his speech by expressing a hope that (what he deemed) the perilous principles urged by those in favor of the restriction upon the new State would be disavowed or explained, or that at all events the application of them to the subject under discussion would not be pressed, but that it might be disposed of in a manner satisfactory to all by a prospective prohibition of slavery in the territory to the north and west of Missouri.]

SPEECH IN THE HOUSE OF REPRESENTATIVES ON THE TREATY-MAKING POWER.

In the debate upon the bill to carry into effect the British convention of 1815, Mr. Pinkney said: He intended yesterday, if the state of his health had permitted, to have trespassed on the House with a short sketch of the grounds upon which he disapproved of the bill. What I could not do then, (said he,) I am about to endeavor now, under the pressure, nevertheless, of continuing indisposition, as well as under the influence of a natural reluctance thus to manifest an apparently ambitious and improvident hurry to lay aside the character of a listener to the wisdom of others, by which I could not fail to profit, for that of an expounder of my own humble notions, which are not likely to be profitable to any body. It is, indeed, but too probable that I should best have consulted both delicacy and discretion, if I had forborne this precipitate attempt to launch my little bark upon what an honorable member has aptly termed " the torrent of debate " which this bill has produced. I am conscious that it may with singular propriety be said of me, that I am *noves hospes* here ; that I have scarcely begun to acquire a domicil among those whom I am undertaking to address ; and that recently transplanted hither from courts of judicature, I ought for a season to look upon myself as a sort of exotic, which time has not sufficiently familiarized with the soil to which it has been removed, to enable it to put forth either fruit or flower. However all this may be, it is now too late to be silent. I proceed, therefore, to entreat your indulgent attention to the few words with which I have to trouble you upon the subject under deliberation.

That subject has already been treated with an admirable force and perspicuity on all sides of the House. The strong power of argument has drawn aside, as it ought to do, the veil which is supposed to belong to it, and which some of us seem unwilling to disturb ; and the stronger power of genius, from a higher region than that of argument, has thrown upon it all the light with which it is the prerogative of genius to invest and illustrate every thing. It is fit that it should be so ; for the subject is worthy by its dignity and importance to employ in the discussion of it all the powers of the mind, and all the eloquence by which I have already felt that this assembly is distinguished. The subject is the fundamental law. We owe it to the people to labor with sincerity and diligence, to ascertain the true construction of that law, which is but a record of their will. We owe it to the obligations of the oath which has recently been imprinted upon our consciences, as well as to the people, to be obedient to that will when we have succeeded in ascertaining it. I shall give you my opinion upon this matter, with the utmost deference for the judgment of others ; but at the same time with that honest and unreserved freedom which becomes this place, and is suited to my habits.

Before we can be in a situation to decide whether this bill ought to pass, we must know precisely what it is ; what it is not is obvious. It is not a bill which is auxiliary to the treaty. It does not deal with details which the treaty does not bear in its own bosom. It contains no subsidiary enactments, no dependent provisions, flowing as corollaries from the treaty. It is not to raise money, or to make appropriations, or to do any thing else beyond or out of the treaty. It acts simply as the echo of the treaty.

Ingeminat voces, auditaque verba reportat. It may properly be called the twin brother of the treaty; its duplicate, its reflected image, for it re-enacts with a timid fidelity, somewhat inconsistent with the boldness of its pretensions, all that the treaty stipulates, and having performed that work of supererogation, stops. It once attempted something more, indeed ; but that surplus has been expunged from it as a desperate intruder, as something which might violate, by a misinterpretation of the treaty, that very public faith which we are now prepared to say the treaty has never plighted in any the smallest degree. In a word, the bill is a *fac-simile* of the treaty in all its clauses.

I am warranted in concluding, then, that if it be any thing but an empty form of words, it is a *confirmation* or *ratification* of the treaty; or, to speak with a more guarded accuracy, is an act to which only (if passed into law) the treaty can owe its being. If it does not spring from the *pruritas leges ferendi,* by which this body can never be afflicted, I am warranted in saying, that it springs from an hypothesis (which may afflict us with a worse disease) that no treaty of commerce can be made by any power in the state but Congress. It stands upon that postulate, or it is a mere bubble, which might be suffered to float through the forms of legislation, and then to burst without consequence or notice.

That this postulate is utterly irreconcilable with the claims and port with which this convention comes before you, it is impossible to deny. Look at it! Has it the air or shape of a mere pledge that the President will recommend to Congress the passage of such laws as will produce the effect at which it aims? Does it profess to be preliminary, or provisional, or inchoate, or to rely upon your instrumentality in the consummation of it, or to take any notice of you, however distant, as actual or eventual parties to it? No, it pretends upon the face of it, and in the solemnities with which it has been accompanied and followed, to be a pact with a foreign state, complete and self-efficient, from the obligation of which this government cannot now escape, and to the perfection of which no more is necessary than has already been done. It contains the clause which is found in the treaty of 1794, and substantially in every other treaty made by the United States under the present constitution, so as to become a formula, that, when ratified by the President of the United States, by and with the advice and consent of the Senate, and by his Britannic majesty, and the respective ratifications mutually exchanged, it shall be binding and obligatory on the said states and his majesty.

It has been ratified in conformity with that clause. Its ratifications have been exchanged in the established and stipulated mode. It has been proclaimed, as other treaties have been proclaimed, by the executive government, as an integral portion of the law of the land, and our citizens at home and abroad, have been admonished to keep and observe it accordingly. It has been sent to the other contracting party with the last stamp of the national faith upon it, after the manner of former treaties with the same power, and will have been received and acted upon by that party as a concluded contract, long before your loitering legislation can overtake it. I protest, Sir, I am somewhat at a loss to understand what this convention has been since its ratifications were exchanged, and what it is now, if our bill be sound in its principle. Has it not been, and is it not an unintelligible, unbaptized and unbaptizable thing, without attributes of any kind, bearing the semblance of an executed compact, but in reality a hollow fiction ; a thing which no man is led to consider even as the germ of a treaty, entitled to be cherished in the vineyard of the constitution ; a thing which, professing to have done every thing that public honor demands, has done nothing but practise delusion ? You may ransack every diplomatic nomenclature and run through every vocabulary, whether of diplomacy or law, and you shall not find a word by which you may distinguish, if our bill be correct in its hypothesis, this " deed without a name." A plain man who is not used to manage his phrases, may, therefore, presume to say that if this convention with England be not a valid treaty, which does not stand in need of your assistance, it is an usurpation on the part of those who have undertaken to make it ; that if it be not an act within the treaty-making capacity, confided to the President and Senate, it is an encroachment on the legislative rights of Congress.

I am one of those who view the bill upon the table, as declaring that it is not within that capacity, as looking down upon the convention as the still-born progeny of arrogated power, as offering to it the paternity of Congress, and affecting by that paternity to give to it life and strength ; and as I think that the convention does not stand in need of any such filiation, to make it either strong or legitimate, that it is already all that it can become, and that useless legislation upon such a subject is vicious legislation, I shall vote against the bill. The correctness of these opinions is what I propose to establish.

I lay it down as an incontrovertible truth, that the constitution has assumed (and, indeed, how could it do otherwise ?) that the government of the United States might and would have occasion, like the other governments of the civilized world, to enter into treaties with foreign powers, upon the various subjects involved in their mutual relations ; and further, that it might be, and was proper to designate the department of the government in which the capacity to make such treaties should be lodged. It has said, accordingly, that the President, with the concurrence of the Senate, shall possess this portion of the national sovereignty. It has, furthermore, given to the same magistrate, with the same concurrence, the exclusive creation and control of the whole machinery of diplomacy. He only, with the approbation of the Senate, can appoint a negotiator, or take any step towards negotiation. The constitution does not, in any part of it, even intimate that any other department shall possess either a constant or an occasional right to interpose in the preparation of any treaty, or in the final perfection of it. The President and Senate are explicitly pointed out as the sole actors in that sort of transaction. The prescribed concurrence of the *Senate,* and that too by a majority greater than the ordinary legislative majority, plainly excludes the necessity of congressional concurrence. If the consent of Congress to any treaty had been intended, the constitution would not have been guilty of the absurdity of first putting a treaty for ratification to the President and Senate exclusively, and again to the same President and Senate as portions of the legislature. It would have submitted the whole matter at once to Congress, and the more especially, as the ratification of a treaty by the Senate, as a branch of the legislature, may be by a smaller number than a ratification of it by the same body, as a branch of the executive government. If the ratification of any treaty by the President, with the advice and consent of the Senate, must be followed by a legislative ratification, it is a mere nonentity. It is good for all purposes, or for none. And if it be nothing in effect, it is a mockery by which nobody would be bound. The President and Senate would not themselves be bound by it—and the ratification would at last depend, not upon the will of the President and two-thirds of the Senate, but upon the will of a bare majority of the two branches of the legislature, subject to the qualified legislative control of the President.

Upon the power of the President and Senate, therefore, there can be no doubt. The only question is as to the extent of it, or in other words, as to the subject upon which it may be exerted. The *effect* of the power, when exerted within its lawful sphere, is beyond the reach of controversy. The constitution has declared, that whatsoever amounts to a treaty, made under the authority of the United States, shall immediately be supreme law. It has contradistinguished a *treaty* as law from *an act of Congress* as law. It has erected treaties, so contradistinguished, into a binding judicial rule. It has given them to our courts of justice, in defining their jurisdiction, as a portion of the *lex terræ*, which they are to interpret and enforce. In a word, it has communicated to them, if ratified by the department which it has specially provided for the making of them, the rank of law, or it has spoken without meaning. And if it has not elevated them to that rank, it is idle to attempt to raise them to it by ordinary legislation.

Upon the extent of the power, or the subjects upon which it may act, there is as little room for controversy. The power is to make *treaties*. The word treaties is *nomen generalissimum*, and will comprehend *commercial* treaties, unless there be a limit upon it by which they are excluded. It is the *appellative*, which will take in the whole species, if there be nothing to narrow its scope. There is no such limit. There is not a syllable in the context of the clause to restrict the natural import of its phraseology. The power is left to the force of the generic term, and is, therefore, as wide as a treaty-making power can be. It embraces all the varieties of treaties which it could be supposed this government could find it necessary or proper to make, or it embraces none. It covers the whole treaty-making ground which this government could be expected to occupy, or not an inch of it.

It is a just presumption, that it was designed to be co-extensive with all the exigencies of our affairs. Usage sanctions that presumption—expediency does the same. The omission of any exception to the power, the omission of the designation of a mode by which a treaty, not intended to be included within it, might otherwise be made, confirms it. That a commercial treaty was, above all others, in the contemplation of the constitution, is manifest. The immemorial practice of Europe, and particularly of the nation from which we emigrated, the consonance of enlightened theory to that practice, prove it. It may be said, indeed, that at the epoch of the birth of our constitution, the necessity for a power to make commercial treaties was scarcely visible, for that our trade was then in its infancy. It was so ; but it was the infancy of another Hercules, promising, not indeed a victory over the lion of Nemæa, or the boar of Erymanthus, but the peaceful conquest of every sea which could be subjected to the dominion of commercial enterprise. It was then as apparent as it is now, that the destinies of this great nation were irrevocably commercial ; that the ocean would be whitened by our sails, and the *ultima Thule* of the world compelled to witness the more than Phœnician spirit and intelligence of our merchants. With this glorious anticipation dawning upon them—with this resplendent Aurora gilding the prospect of the future ; nay, with the risen orb of trade illuminating the vast horizon of American greatness, it cannot be supposed that the framers of the constitution did not look to the time when we should be called upon to make commercial conventions. It needs not the aid of the imagination to reject this disparaging and monstrous supposition. Dulness itself, throwing aside the lethargy of its character, and rising for a passing moment to the rapture of enthusiasm, will disclaim it with indignation.

It is said, however, that the constitution has given to Congress the power to regulate commerce with foreign nations ; and that, since it would be inconsistent with that power, that the President, with the consent of the Senate, should do the same thing, it follows, that this power of Congress is an exception out of the treaty-making power. Never were premises, as it appears to my understanding, less suited to the conclusion. The power of Congress to regulate our foreign trade, is a power of municipal legislation, and was designed to operate as far, as, upon such a subject, municipal legislation can reach. Without such a power, the government would be wholly inadequate to the ends for which it was instituted. A power to regulate commerce by treaty alone, would touch only a portion of the subject. A wider and more general power was therefore indispensable, and it was properly devolved on Congress, as the legislature of the Union.

On the other hand, a power of mere municipal legislation, acting upon views exclusively our own, having no reference to a reciprocation of advantages by arrangements with a foreign state, would also fall short of the ends of government in a country of which the commercial relations are complex and extensive, and liable to be embarrassed by conflicts between its own interests and those of other nations. That the power of Congress is simply legislative in the strictest sense, and calculated for ordinary domestic regulation only, is plain from the language in which it is communicated. There is nothing in that language which indicates regulation, by compact or compromise, nothing which points to the co-operation of a foreign power, nothing which designates a treaty-making faculty. It is not connected with any of the necessary accompaniments of that faculty ; it is not furnished with any of those means, without which it is impossible to make the smallest progress towards a treaty.

It is self-evident, that a capacity to regulate commerce by treaty, was intended by the constitution to be lodged somewhere. It is just as evident, that the legislative capacity of Congress does not amount to it ; and cannot be exerted to produce a treaty. It can produce only a statute, with which a foreign state cannot be made to concur, and which will not yield to any modifications which a foreign state may desire to impress upon it for suitable equivalents. There is no way in which Congress, as such, can mould its laws into treaties, if it respects the constitution. It may legislate and counter-legislate ; but it must for ever be beyond its capacity to combine in a law, emanating from its separate domestic authority, its own views with those of other governments, and to produce a harmonious reconciliation of those jarring purposes and discordant elements which it is the business of negotiation to adjust.

I reason thus, then, upon this part of the subject. It is clear that the power of Congress, as to foreign commerce, is only what it professes to be in the constitution, a legislative power, to be exerted municipally without consultation or agreement with those with whom we have an intercourse of trade ; it is undeniable that the constitution meant to provide for the exercise of another power relatively to commerce, which should exert itself in concert with the analo-

gous power in other countries, and should bring about its
results, not by statute enacted by itself, but by an international compact called a treaty ; that it is manifest, that
this other power is vested by the constitution in the President and Senate, the only department of the government
which it authorizes to make any treaty, and which it enables
to make all treaties ; that if it be so vested, its regular exercise must result in that which, as far as it reaches, is law
in itself, and consequently repeals such municipal regula-
tions as stand in its way, since it is expressly declared by
the constitution that treaties regularly made shall have, as
they ought to have, the force of law.　In all this, I perceive
nothing to perplex or alarm us.　It exhibits a well digested
and uniform plan of government, worthy of the excellent
men by whom it was formed.　The ordinary power to regulate commerce by statutory enactments, could only be devolved upon Congress, possessing all the other legislative
powers of the government.　The extraordinary power to regulate it by treaty, could not be devolved upon Congress,
because from its composition, and the absence of all those
authorities and functions which are essential to the activity
and effect of a treaty-making power, it was not calculated
to be the depository of it.　It was wise and consistent to
place the extraordinary power to regulate commerce by
treaty, where the residue of the treaty-making power was
placed, where only the means of negotiation could be found,
and the skilful and beneficial use of them could reasonably
be expected.

That Congress legislates upon commerce, *subject to the
treaty-making power*, is a position perfectly intelligible ; but
the understanding is in some degree confounded by the other
proposition, that the legislative power of Congress is an exception out of the treaty-making power.　It introduces into
the constitution a strange anomaly—a commercial state, with
a written constitution, and no power in it to regulate its

trade, in conjunction with other states, in the universal mode
of convention.   It will be in vain to urge, that this anomaly
is merely imaginary ; for that the President and Senate may
make a treaty of commerce for the consideration of Congress.   The answer is, that the treaties which the President
and Senate are entitled to make, are such, as when made,
become a law ; that it is no part of their functions simply
to initiate treaties, but conclusively to make them ; and
that where they have no power to make them, there is no
provision in the constitution, how or by whom they shall be
made.

That there is nothing new in the idea of a separation of
the legislative and conventional powers upon commercial
subjects, and of the necessary control of the former by the
latter, is known to all who are acquainted with the constitution of England.   The parliament of that country enacts
the statutes by which its trade is regulated municipally.
The crown modifies them by a treaty.   It has been imagined, indeed, that parliament is in the practice of confirming such treaties ; but the fact is undoubtedly otherwise.
Commercial treaties are laid before parliament, because the
king's ministers are responsible for their advice in the making of them, and because the vast range and complication of
the English laws of trade and revenue, render legislation
unavoidable, not for the ratification, but the execution of
their commercial treaties.

It is suggested, again, that the treaty-making power
(unless we are tenants in common of it with the President
and Senate, to the extent at least of our legislative rights)
is a pestilent monster, pregnant with all sorts of disasters !
It teems with " Gorgons, and Hydras, and Chimeras dire ! "
At any rate, I may take for granted that the case before us
does not justify this array of metaphor and fable ; since we
are all agreed that the convention with England is not only
harmless but salutary.   To put this particular case, how-

ever, out of the argument, what have we to do with considerations like these ? are we here to form, or to submit to, the constitution as it has been given to us for a rule by those who are our masters ? Can we take upon ourselves the office of political casuists, and because we think that a power ought to be less than it is, compel it to shrink to our standard ? Are we to bow with reverence before the national will as the constitution displays it, or to fashion it to our own, to quarrel with that charter, without which we ourselves are nothing ; or to take it as a guide which we cannot desert with innocence and safety ? But why is the treaty-making power, lodged, as I contend it is, in the President and Senate, likely to disaster us, as we are required to apprehend it will ? Sufficient checks have not, as it seems, been provided, either by the constitution or the nature of things, to prevent the abuse of it. It is in the House of Representatives alone, that the amulet, which bids defiance to the approaches of political disease, or cures it when it has commenced, can in all vicissitudes be found. I hold that the checks are sufficient, without the charm of our legislative agency, for all those occasions which wisdom is bound to foresee and to guard against ; and that as to the rest (the eccentricities and portents which no ordinary checks can deal with) the occasions must provide for themselves.

It is natural, here, to ask of gentlemen, what security they would have ? They cannot " take a bond of Fate ;" and they have every pledge which is short of it. Have they not, as respects the President, all the security upon which they rely from day to day for the discreet and upright discharge of the whole of his other duties, many and various as they are ? What security have they that he will not appoint to office the refuse of the world ; that he will not pollute the sanctuary of justice by calling vagabonds to its holy ministry, instead of adorning it with men like those who now give to the bench more dignity than they receive from it : that he will not enter into a treaty of amnesty with every conspirator against law and order, and pardon culprits from mere enmity to virtue ?. The security for all this, and infinitely more, is found in the constitution and in the or- der of nature ; and we are all satisfied with it. One should think that the same security, which thus far time has not discredited, might be sufficient to tranquillize us upon the score of the power which we are now considering.

We talk of ourselves as if we only were the representa- tives of the people. But the first magistrate of this country is also the representative of the people, the creature of their sovereignty, the administrator of their power, their steward and servant, as you are—he comes from the people, is lifted by them into place and authority, and after a short season returns to them for censure or applause. There is no ana- logy between such a magistrate and the hereditary monarchs of Europe. He is not born to the inheritance of office ; he cannot even be elected until he has reached an age at which he must pass for what he is ; until his habits have been formed, his integrity tried, his capacity ascertained, his cha- racter discussed and probed for a series of years, by a press, which knows none of the restraints of European policy. He acts, as you do, in the full view of his constituents, and un- der the consciousness that on account of the singleness of his station, all eyes are upon him. He knows, too, as well as you can know, the temper and intelligence of those for whom he acts, and to whom he is amenable. He cannot hope that they will be blind to the vices of his administra- tion on subjects of high concernment and vital interest ; and in proportion as he acts upon his own responsibility, unre- lieved and undiluted by the infusion of ours, is the danger of ill-advised conduct likely to be present to his mind.

Of all the powers which have been intrusted to him, there is none to which the temptations to abuse belong so little as to the treaty-making power in all its branches ; none which can boast such mighty safeguards in the feelings, and views, and passions which even a misanthrope could attribute to the foremost citizen of this republic. He can have no motive to palsy by a commercial or any other treaty the prosperity of his country. Setting apart the restraints of honour and patriotism, which are the characteristic of public men in a nation habitually free, could he do so without subjecting himself as a member of the community (to say nothing of his immediate connections) to the evils of his own work ? A commercial treaty, too, is always a conspicuous measure. It speaks for itself. It cannot take the garb of hypocrisy, and shelter itself from the scrutiny of a vigilant and well instructed population. If it be bad, it will be condemned, and if dishonestly made, be execrated. The pride of country, moreover, which animates even the lowest of mankind, is here a peculiar pledge for the provident and wholesome exercise of power. There is not a consideration by which a cord in the human breast can be made to vibrate that is not in this case the ally of duty. Every hope, either lofty or humble, that springs forward to the future ; even the vanity which looks not beyond the moment ; the dread of shame and the love of glory ; the instinct of ambition ; the domestic affections ; the cold ponderings of prudence ; and the ardent instigations of sentiment and passion, are all on the side of duty. It is in the exercise of this power that responsibility to public opinion, which even despotism feels and truckles to, is of gigantic force. If it were possible, as I am sure it is not, that an American citizen, raised, upon the credit of a long life of virtue, to a station so full of honor, could feel a disposition to mingle the little interests of a perverted ambition with the great concerns of his country, as embraced by a commercial treaty, and to sacrifice her happiness and power by the stipulations of that treaty, to flatter or aggrandize a foreign state, he would still be saved from the perdition of such a course, not only by constitutional checks, but by the irresistible efficacy of responsibility to public opinion, in a nation whose public opinion wears no mask, and will not be silenced. He would remember that his political career is but the thing of an hour, and that when it has passed he must descend to the private station from which he rose, the object either of love and veneration, or of scorn and horror. If we cast a glance at England, we shall not fail to see the influence of public opinion upon an hereditary king, an hereditary nobility, and a House of Commons elected in a great degree by rotten boroughs, and overflowing with place-men. And if this influence is potent there against all the efforts of independent power and wide spread corruption, it must in this country be omnipotent.

But the treaty-making power of the President is further checked by the necessity of the concurrence of two-thirds of the Senate, consisting of men selected by the legislatures of the States, themselves elected by the people. They too must have passed through the probation of time before they can be chosen, and must bring with them every title to con-fidence. The duration of their office is that of a few years ; their numbers are considerable ; their constitutional respon-sibility as great as it can be ; and their moral responsibility beyond all calculation.

The power of impeachment has been mentioned as a check upon the President in the exercise of the treaty-mak-ing capacity. I rely upon it less than upon others, of, as I think, a better class ; but as the constitution places some re-liance upon it, so do I. It has been said, that impeachment has been tried and found wanting. Two impeachments have failed, as I have understood, (that of a judge was one)—but they may have failed for reasons consistent with the general efficacy of such a proceeding. I know nothing of their merits, but I am justified in supposing that the evidence was defective, or that the parties were innocent as they were pronounced to be :—Of this, however, I feel assured, that if it should ever happen that the President is found to deserve the punishment which impeachment seeks to inflict, (even for making a treaty to which the judges have become parties,) and this body should accuse him in a constitutional way, he will not easily escape. But, be that as it may, I ask if it is nothing that you have power to arraign him as a culprit ? Is it nothing that you can bring him to the bar, expose his misconduct to the world, and bring down the indignation of the public upon him and those who dare to acquit him ?

If there be any power explicitly granted by the constitution to Congress, it is that of declaring war ; and if there be any exercise of human legislation more solemn and important than another, it is a declaration of war. For expansion it is the largest, for effect the most awful of all the enactments to which Congress is competent ; and it always is, or ought to be, preceded by grave and anxious deliberation. This power, too, is connected with, or virtually involves, others of high import and efficacy; among which may be ranked the power of granting letters of marque and reprisal, of regulating captures, of prohibiting intercourse with, or the acceptance of protections or licenses from the enemy. Yet farther; a power to declare war implies, with peculiar emphasis, a negative upon all power, in any other branch of the government, inconsistent with the full and continuing effect of it. A power to make peace in any other branch of the government, is utterly inconsistent with that full and continuing effect. It may even prevent it from having any effect at all ; since peace may follow almost immediately (although it rarely does so follow) the commencement of a war. If, therefore, it be undeniable that the President, with the advice and consent of the Senate, has power to make a treaty of peace, available *ipso jure*, it is undeniable that he has power to repeal, by the mere operation of such a treaty, the highest acts of congressional legislation. And it will not be questioned that this repealing power is, from the eminent nature of the war-declaring power, less fit to be made out by inference than the power of modifying by treaty the laws which regulate our foreign trade. Now the President, with the advice and consent of the Senate, has an incontestable and uncontested right to make a treaty of peace, of absolute inherent efficacy, and that too in virtue of the very same general provision in the constitution which the refinements of political speculation, rather than any known rules of construction, have led some of us to suppose excludes a treaty of commerce.

By what process of reasoning will you be able to extract from the wide field of that general provision the obnoxious case of a commercial treaty, without forcing along with it the case of a treaty of peace, and along with that again the case of every possible treaty? Will you rest your distinction upon the favorite idea that a treaty cannot repeal laws competently enacted, or, as it is sometimes expressed, cannot trench upon the legislative rights of Congress? Such a distinction not only seems to be reproached by all the theories, numerous as they are, to which this bill has given birth, but is against notorious fact and recent experience. We have lately witnessed the operation in this respect of a treaty of peace, and could not fail to draw from it this lesson; that no sooner does the President exert, with the consent of the Senate, his power to make such a treaty, than your war-denouncing law, your act for letters of marque, your prohibitory statutes as to intercourse and licenses, and all the other concomitant and dependent statutes, so far as they affect the national relations with a foreign enemy, pass away as a dream, and in a moment are 'with years beyond the flood.' Your auxiliary agency was not required in the production of this effect; and I have not heard that you even tendered it. You saw your laws departing as it were from the statute books, expelled from the strong hold of supremacy by the single

force of a treaty of peace ; and you did not attempt to stay
them ; you did not bid them linger until you should bid them
go ; you neither put your shoulders to the wheel of expulsion
nor made an effort to retard it.   In a word, you did nothing.
You suffered them to flee as a shadow, and you know that
they were reduced to shadow, not by the necromancy of
usurpation, but by the energy of constitutional power.   Yet,
you had every reason for interference then which you can
have now.   The power to make a treaty of peace stands upon
the same constitutional footing with the power to make a
commercial treaty.   It is given by the same words.   It is
exerted in the same manner.   It produces the same conflict
with municipal legislation.   The ingenuity of man cannot
urge a consideration, whether upon the letter or the spirit of
the constitution, against the existence of a power in the President and Senate to make a valid commercial treaty, which
will not, if it be correct and sound, drive us to the negation
of the power exercised by the President and Senate, with
universal approbation, to make a valid treaty of peace.

Nay, the whole treaty-making power will be blotted from
the constitution, and a new one, alien to its theory and practice, be made to supplant it, if sanction and scope be given
to the principles of this bill.   This bill may indeed be considered as the first of many assaults, not now intended perhaps, but not therefore the less likely to happen, by which
the treaty-making power, as created and lodged by the constitution, will be pushed from its place, and compelled to
abide with the power of ordinary legislation.   The example
of this bill is beyond its ostensible limits.   The pernicious
principle, of which it is at once the child and the apostle,
must work onward and to the right and the left until it has
exhausted itself ; and it never can exhaust itself until it has
gathered into the vortex of the legislative powers of Congress the whole treaty-making capacity of the government.
For if, notwithstanding the directness and precision with

which the constitution has marked out the department of the government by which it wills that treaties shall be made, and has declared that treaties so made shall have the force and dignity of law, the House of Representatives can insist upon some participation in that high faculty, upon the simple suggestion that they are sharers in legislative power upon the subjects embraced by any given treaty, what remains to be done, for the transfer to Congress of the entire treaty-making faculty, as it appears in the constitution, but to show that Congress have legislative power direct or indirect upon every matter which a treaty can touch ? And what are the matters within the practicable range of a treaty, which your laws cannot either mould, or qualify, or influence ? Imagination has been tasked for example, by which this question might be answered. It is admitted that they must be few, and we have been told, as I think, of no more than one. It is the case of *contraband of war*. This case has, it seems, the double recommendation of being what is called an international case, and a case beyond the utmost grasp of congressional legislation. I remark upon it, that it is no more an international case than any matter of collision incident to the trade of two nations with each other. I remark farther, that a treaty upon the point of contraband of war may interfere, as well as any other treaty, with an act of Congress. A law encouraging, by a bounty or otherwise, the exportation of certain commodities, would be counteracted by an insertion into the list of contraband of war, in a treaty with England or France, any one of those commodities. The treaty would look one way, the law another. And various modes might readily be suggested in which Congress might so legislate as to lay the foundation of repugnancy between its laws and the treaties of the President and Senate with reference to contraband. I deceive myself greatly if a subject can be named upon which a like repugnancy might not occur. But even if it should be practicable to furnish, after laborious inquiry and meditation, a meagre and scanty inventory of some half dozen topics, to which domestic legislation cannot be made to extend, will it be pretended that such was the insignificant and narrow domain designed by the constitution for the treaty-making power ? It would appear that there is with some gentlemen a willingness to distinguish between the legislative power expressly granted to Congress and that which is merely implied, and to admit that a treaty may control the results of the latter. I reply to those gentlemen that one legislative power is exactly equivalent to another, and that, moreover, the whole legislative power of Congress may justly be said to be expressly granted by the constitution, although the constitution does not enumerate every variety of its exercise, or indicate all the ramifications into which it may diverge to suit the exigencies of the times. I reply, besides, that even with the qualification of this vague distinction, whatever may be its value or effect, the principle of the bill leaves no adequate sphere for the treaty-making power. I reply, finally, that the acknowledged operation of a treaty of peace in repealing laws of singular strength and unbending character, enacted in virtue of powers communicated *in terminis* to Congress, gives the distinction to the winds.

And now that I have again adverted to the example of a treaty of peace, let me call upon you to reflect on the answer which that example affords to all the warnings we have received in this debate against the mighty danger of intrusting to the only department of the government, which the constitution supposes can make a treaty, the incidental prerogative of a repealing legislation. It is inconsistent, we are desired to believe, with the genius of the constitution, and must be fatal to all that is dear to freemen, that an Executive magistrate and a Senate, who are not immediately elected by the people, should possess this authority. We hear from one quarter that if it be so, the public liberty is

already in the grave ; and from another, that the public interest and honor are upon the verge of it.   But do you not
perceive that this picture of calamity and shame is the mere
figment of excited fancy, disavowed by the constitution as
hysterical, and erroneous in the case of a treaty of peace ?
Do you not see that if there be any thing in this high colored peril, it is a treaty of peace that must realize it ?
Can we in this view compare with the power to make such a
treaty, that of making a treaty of commerce ?   Are we
unable to conjecture, while we are thus brooding over anticipated evils which can never happen, that the lofty character
of our country (which is but another name for strength and
power) may be made to droop by a mere treaty of peace ;
that the national pride may be humbled ; the just hopes of
the people blasted ; their courage tamed and broken ; their
prosperity struck to the heart ; their foreign rivals encouraged into arrogance and tutored into encroachment, by a
mere treaty of peace ?   I confidently trust that, as this
never has been so, it will never be so ; but surely it is just
as possible as that a treaty of commerce should ever be made
to shackle the freedom of this nation, or check its march to
the greatness and glory that await it.   I know not, indeed,
how it can seriously be thought that our liberties are in
hazard from the small witchery of a treaty of commerce,
and yet in none from the potent enchantments by which a
treaty of peace may strive to enthral them.   I am at a loss to
conceive by what form of words, by what hitherto unheard-
of stipulations, a *commercial* treaty is to barter away the
freedom of United America, or of any the smallest portion
of it.   I cannot figure to myself the possibility that such a
project can ever find its way into the head or heart of any
man, or set of men, whom this nation may select as the
depositories of its power ; but I am quite sure that an attempt to insert such a project in a commercial treaty, or in
any other treaty, or in any other mode, could work no other

effect than the destruction of those who should venture to
be parties to it, no matter whether a President, Senate, or a
whole Congress. Many extreme cases have been put for illustration in this debate ; and this is one of them ; and I take
the occasion which it offers to mention, that to argue from
extreme cases is seldom logical, and upon a question of interpretation, never so. We can only bring back the means of
delusion, if we wander into the regions of fiction, and explore the wilds of bare possibility in search of rules for real
life and actual ordinary cases. By arguing from the possible
abuse of power against the use or existence of it, you may
and must come to the conclusion, that there ought not be,
and is not, any government in this country, or in the world.
Disorganization and anarchy are the sole consequences that
can be deduced from such reasoning. Who is it that may not
abuse the power that has been confided to him ? May not
we, as well as the other branches·of the government ? And
if we may, does not the argument from extreme cases
prove that we ought to have no power, and that we
have no power ? And does it not, therefore, after having served for an instant the purposes of this bill, turn
short upon and condemn its whole theory, which attributes to us, not merely the power which is our own, but
inordinate power, to be gained only by wresting it from
others ? Our constitutional and moral security against the
abuses of the power of the executive government have already been explained. I will only add, that a great and manifest abuse of the delegated authority to make treaties would
create no obligation any where. If ever it should occur, as I
confidently believe it nèver will, the evil must find its cor-
rective in the wisdom and firmness, not of this body only,
but of the whole body of the people co-operating with it.
It is, after all, in the people, upon whose Atlantean shoulders our whole republican system reposes, that you must expect that recuperative power, that redeeming and regenerat-

ing spirit, by which the constitution is to be purified and redintegrated when extravagant abuse has cankered it.

In addition to the example of a treaty of peace which I have just been considering, let me put another, of which none of us can question the reality. The President may exercise the power of pardoning, save only in the case of impeachments. The power of pardoning is not communicated by words more precise or comprehensive than the power to make treaties. But to what does it amount? Is not every pardon, *pro hac vice*, a repeal of the penal law against which it gives protection? Does it not ride over the law, resist its command, and extinguish its effect? Does it not even control the combined force of judicature and legislation? Yet, have we ever heard that your legislative rights were an exception out of the prerogative of mercy? Who has ever pretended that this faculty cannot, if regularly exerted, wrestle with the strongest of your statutes? I may be told, that the pardoning power necessarily imports a control over the penal code, if it be exercised in the form of a pardon. I answer, the power to make treaties equally imports a power to put out of the way such parts of the civil code as interfere with its operation, if that power be exerted in the form of a treaty. There is no difference in their essence. You legislate, in both cases, subject to the power. And this instance furnishes another answer, as I have already intimated, to the predictions of abuse, with which, on this occasion, it has been endeavored to appal us. The pardoning power is in the President alone. He is not even checked by the necessity of Senatorial concurrence. He may by his single *fiat* extract the sting from your proudest enactments —and save from their vengeance a convicted offender.

Sir, you have my general notions upon the bill before you. They have no claim to novelty. I imbibed them from some of the heroes and sages who survived the storm of that contest to which America was summoned in her cradle. I imbibed them from the father of his country. My understanding approved them, with the full concurrence of my heart, when I was much younger than I am now ; and I feel no disposition to discard them, now that age and feebleness are about to overtake me. I could say more—much more—upon this high question ; but I want health and strength. It is, perhaps, fortunate for the House that I do ; as it prevents me from fatiguing them as much as I fatigue myself.

I have searched in vain for the authorship of the " Political Sketches," or even a sight of the book. There is a vague impression on my mind, that it was the production of one of our northern stars. But whoever the author may be, or what may have become of the work, the following remarks will reward perusal. It is a most masterly dissertation on style ; singularly rich, discriminating and profound. Elevated above the asperity of captious criticism by a nice and accurate perception of true beauty and force, it is a jewel of its kind. For imagination in its highest form and noblest development Mr. Pinkney possessed the most unbounded admiration, and gave to the country and the world the most perfect and exquisite illustration of it. But for it, in its uncurbed irregularity and mystical dreamings, he expressed, as he felt, the most unmixed disgust and contempt.

It must not be supposed that Mr. Pinkney, in the close of this article, designed to intimate that Dr. Johnson wrote with *difficulty*, for no one knew better than he the actual rapidity with which he wrote ; but only to reaffirm what Johnson said of himself, " that whenever he said a good thing he seemed to labor." Dr. Johnson, speaking of Addison, used to say that he was the *Raphael* of essay writers.

REMARKS ON "POLITICAL SKETCHES.'

BY WILLIAM PINKNEY.

WHEN I first perused this valuable performance, I condemned it without hesitation, as a work wherein the imagination had been permitted to flutter at large, unaccompanied by the judgment. I thought the great subject of the author's consideration lightly and gracefully handled ; and the remarks he has bestowed on Montesquieu, at the end of his section on Virtue, more properly applicable to himself. He appeared to me far more solicitous to please his reader by a labored floridity of style, and a succession of gay images, than to enlighten the understanding, by accuracy of thought and justness of conception.

But upon a more attentive perusal of his work, I am thoroughly convinced of its merits. As far as I am able to decide, it discovers a clear discriminating head—a solidity of reflection—an acquaintance with history, men, and the principles of government, and an animated fancy. It is not however without faults. Want of originality is apparent in the two sections of Virtue and Religion. Again ; the author's meaning is often so concealed by a redundancy of uncommon and figurative expressions, that it is accessible to none, but those geniuses whom Johnson speaks of, who "grasp a system by intuition," except through the medium of unremitted application. Perspicuity is frequently sacrificed to that anxiety which is natural to a young writer, of strewing over his subject with the flowers of rhetoric, and embellishing reflection with the graces of expression. The tinsel of Lexiphanic language in many places involves his argument in almost inextricable mystery, and pains whom it was intended to please, by making them toil for instruction, when an easy, natural communication was practicable. To be learnedly incomprehensible was certainly not the author's intention. He wrote to be *admired*, but he wrote also to be *understood*. The cool approbation which is given to solidity of thought, could not content him. He sought by splendid imagery to gain that tribute of approbation from the heart, which is given to the warm glow of rhetoric. But nothing more completely removes an argument from the reach of general comprehension, than what is commonly, though falsely called, an elegance of diction. Paradoxically as it may sound, its very lustre is the parent of darkness. By fascinating the imagination it monopolizes the attention, and the plain simplicity of truth, surrounded by the dazzling glitter of a highly colored style escapes the eye of observation. In works of mere entertainment, the impropriety of this species of writing in some measure ceases ; but surely to support a train of reasoning in such a manner as to oblige a majority of readers to apply almost every moment to a dictionary, upon a question, too, where the nicety of discrimination is necessary at every turn, to destroy apparent analogies—where the understanding (independent of the obstacles thrown in its way by perplexing figures and unusual words) can with difficulty pursue the chain of reflection ; and where, in the combined consideration of human nature, facts, and principles, the conclusions must be embarrassed rather than illustrated, if not perspicuously treated—is at least impolitic in him who seeks to lead the mind to information and conviction.

In the world of taste, the plain simple language of Addison has been preferred to that of the Rambler. The periods of the last impress us with the painful idea of labor ; and give us a disagreeable conception of a tedious process by which every sentence was tortured into form. I would apply the same remark to the Political Sketches.

When the ardor of our author's fancy shall have cooled by time—when his notions of a writer's true reputation shall have become juster—when he shall have learned to prefer that style which explains his subject, instead of plunging it into obscurity ; and when he shall be convinced that to bury the matter of his discussion beneath a profusion of gaudy trappings, is only the *affectation* of elegance, he will in all probability be among the first ornaments of the literary world, and do honor to his country and himself.

———

I come now to consider the character of Mr. Pinkney as a man ; to sum up with an impartial and truthful pen those moral and intellectual qualities that united to make him an ornament of society.

His personal appearance possessed a goodly degree of dignity and grace. Tall and finely formed, with a head exquisitely shaped, forehead high, broad, massive and slightly retreating, eyes of the softest blue, rather heavy in repose, but capable of the intensest and most varied expression when roused in the excitement of debate, a mouth of uncommon sweetness and flexibility, soft brown hair, scarcely tinged with gray when death laid him low, and a characteristic neatness and elegance of address—he was a man remarkable to look upon. It is almost amusing to glance at the caricature of him published many years ago in the " North American," and one can only smile in wonder at the strange want of resemblance it exhibits.

Affable in the immediate circle of his friends, he was rather inaccessible to strangers. He was never very talkative ; and yet when disengaged and not too much abstracted by press of business, he was the life and light of society.

On such occasions his wit sparkled and flashed, giving to

his conversation a nameless and indescribable charm, not unlike intellectual fascination. His very taciturnity gave to his colloquial powers, when he chose to exercise them, a more remarkable and striking effect. He was a great admirer of ladies, and always paid a marked tribute of respect to that refinement and elegance of taste and intuitive perception, which constitute at once the beauty and marvel of the female character. No one knew better than he how to draw out its peculiar powers, and elicit to advantage its finer and softer sensibilities. During his frequent visits to Annapolis, he loved to while away an hour of the evening in an old mansion, which was the home of elegance and the chief centre of attraction, the residence of the late Mrs. L———, a lady of whom it were impossible to speak without seeming exaggeration, whose loveliness of character was only equalled by her vigor of intellect and suavity of manners—who in life was the honored companion of the young and the old ; and at whose funeral the legislature of Maryland considered it a sad privilege to walk as mourners. For this lady, and the circle of beauty and intelligence that was ever congregated around her, Mr. Pinkney entertained the most unbounded admiration ; and on more than one occasion of public interest, in the discussion of the forum, did he exhibit his sense of her presence by a display of eloquence which he knew she could both appreciate and understand. He never presumed to talk nonsense to ladies, or lowered himself, as some great men are wont to do, to the supposed measure of their ability, for he was one of those who believed them to be in all respects, by character, education, and intellect, worthy of the companionship of those who are so much dependant upon them for sympathy and support. He had without doubt formed his opinion of the mind and heart of woman from the noblest specimen ; and knew by early experience that there was nothing too abstruse or sublime for the one to grasp, or too magnanimous, exalted, or ennobling for the other to embrace. Believing them to be capable of the highest intellectual enjoyment, and eminently skilled in intellectual taste, he conversed with them as equals ; and his conversation was on that account peculiarly attractive and instructive. He often expressed the opinion, that no great man ever lived, who had not a highly intellectual and clear-headed mother. Of one of the ladies of his acquaintance now living (with whom he corresponded when abroad), he was accustomed to say, that her letters gave him more real pleasure and delight, than those received from any other source. The letters which passed between them were for a long time in the possession of my own family ; and were a truly brilliant passage of arms, in which grace and beauty triumphed on either side. They were, however, lost, to the regret of the author of this memoir.

He was singularly free from the spirit of detraction. Tender of the feelings and motives of others, he seldom, if ever, permitted any thing of the sort to pass by without rebuke. In the company of the young, especially, who are too liable to be betrayed into sarcastic and ill-natured comment upon the conduct of others, he was ever ready to pour oil on the troubled waters, and vindicate the aspersed, or at all events silence and confound the asperser.

He possessed very high veneration for consistent and humble piety. Well versed in the best old Church of England theology, and accustomed to hold frequent and delighted converse with Hooker, Taylor, *et id omne genus,* he was peculiarly clear in his views of its true character. On one occasion, illustrative of this high veneration for all that was pure and holy, and this aversion to disparaging comment, when seated at a festive board in the city of Annapolis, a young member of the bar chanced to mention the insanity of a lady of distinction, and as a proof conclusive of the fact, stated that she was running into all the lanes and alleys of Baltimore, and ferreting out objects of charity from among their filthy and wretched inmates. Mr. Pinkney turned and said, with one of his sweetest smiles, and in a tone of most melting pathos, "what a beautiful combination of moral virtues to constitute mental derangement, piety towards God, and benevolence towards man." The only criticism, said a lady to me, who often went with him to public worship, I ever remember to have heard him make was, "praise that sermon if you dare."

He was a stanch friend; although in the selection of a friend, he followed the rule so beautifully and forcibly laid down by Shakspeare:

> " The friends thou hast and their adoption tried,
> Grapple them to thy soul with hooks of steel,
> But do not dull thy palm with entertainment
> Of each new hatched unfledged comrade."

HAMLET.

His sensibilities were singularly warm for a man of reserve. His heart beat responsive to the touch of kindness. His zeal in the service of those he loved knew no bounds. His eloquence and legal learning were not unfrequently poured forth in pleading their cause and defending their rights and honor; and the offering was made altogether without the hope or the acceptance of reward. A gentleman, not now living, who lost a suit in chancery which involved his all, as he supposed, because of some incidental expression of Mr. Pinkney, went to him; and he told me that he entered immediately with all his heart and soul into the investigation, and never rested until he had reversed the decision of the court below, and established him in the full possession of his lost estate, and would never hear of the least compensation. It was a friend's claim upon his sympathy in a cause he knew to be just, and the only remuneration he could or would receive, separate and above the pleasure of the deed, was gratitude for the service rendered. The audience were in tears, no eye was dry, while a friend's voice was uplifted in the defence of a friend's rights. There are witnesses to the truth of this simple fact, now alive, whose testimony could be invoked were it necessary. This was by no means an uncommon occurrence. One of the most powerful and touching speeches he ever delivered before a jury was in defence of a near relative of a lady with whom he boarded ; and long will the echoes of that memorable effort live in the memory of those who heard it. Upper Marlborough was the place, a jury of Prince George's County the arbiters, and the tears of a lone widow restored to the embrace of one she loved, the only reward of the eloquent advocate. This kindness of disposition and warmth of friendship were exhibited in behalf of the poor and uninfluential more readily, than those whom it might appear to be politic to defend.

One of the strongest proofs of the warmth and generosity of his feelings is furnished in the fact, that he never forfeited a friendship he once learned to honor and trust. With Jefferson, Madison and Monroe, he continued on terms of the closest intimacy and confidence. The following extract, from a letter written just before his final return to the country and but a short time before his death, will show in what light the last continued to regard him ; and there were few men living, who had a better opportunity of knowing and understanding Mr. Pinkney's character :—

"I pray you be assured that I view your forbearing to name me for the court of England exactly as you do, and that I rejoice you took that course. It would certainly have been hazardous, and moreover, I had no wish to go to England, or to remain any longer abroad. The office of Attorney-General would not have suited me, as I have some time since taken measures for resuming my residence in Baltimore, where I hope to retrieve the losses, which my missions could not fail to inflict upon me in a pecuniary sense ; but they have been incurred in the public service, and if *Providence spares* and *assists me* will not long be felt. Your friendly wishes are really invaluable. I do not want office, but I highly prize your esteem.

"Notwithstanding my anxiety to get home, I shall quit this station with some regret. They have been very kind to me here. My place will doubtless be supplied by a man much more able and distinguished, and at the same time of equal discretion."

This letter was written from St. Petersburg, where Mr. Pinkney was highly esteemed.

Although not indiscriminate in his friendships, where his heart was given, it was the heart in its fulness, warm, gushing, simple and confiding as a child's. To both the friends and the scenes of his early youth, he turned with undiminished interest and pleasure in the close of his brilliant career.

He was an affectionate husband and father ; and evinced the greatest anxiety to promote the welfare of his children in every way possible. He had noble views on the subject of education. I have it in my power to present those views to the public, for the first time, in a letter written by him to my father. It contains the very breathings of his soul, and possesses an additional value, viz., that it was intended solely for the eye of a brother's sympathy, from whom he concealed nothing, and was never designed for publication. It is just what he thought on a subject of the most absorbing interest.

MR. PINKNEY TO HIS BROTHER NINIAN.

"LONDON, 1st *June*, 1800.

"DEAR NINIAN,—Your last letter has given me great hopes of William. If I should be disappointed in regard to him, I shall feel it severely, and I shall certainly form my judgment of him impartially when I return. We are sometimes disposed to think too favorably of our own, and to

permit our understandings to be blinded by our affections.
I am not of that temper. He will find me able to determine accurately of his progress, without being biassed by a
parent's fondness, to imagine excellence where it does not
exist. I have perfect confidence, however, that he will not
need this sort of bias. On your care of him (for which I
cannot be too grateful), I have implicit reliance that you
will give him sound principles, both by your instruction and
example ; that you will incite him to early habits of honorable thinking and manly feeling ; that you will teach him
that the whole complexion of his future life depends upon
his boyish years ; that you will inspire him with that just
ambition, which, having excellence for its object, is the best
security for its attainment ; that you will impress upon his
mind the indispensable necessity of regular application and
systematic industry as the only sure aids of talent where it
exists, and the only effectual substitute for it where it is
wanting ; and in a word, that you will form him to knowledge and virtue, with skill and attention equal, if not superior, to my own, I have no doubt. There are, indeed,
some things in the education of a boy which men are apt to
neglect, but which, I trust, you will think too important to
be slighted. I mean certain principles, moral and religious,
which we allow ourselves to refer to the future, in the hope
that they will grow up of themselves or be acquired as the
mind advances to maturity. A *mother* teaches them in infancy, and stamps them upon the heart, not by formal lec-
tures, but by reiterated admonition or reproof, as occasions
present themselves. Among those principles the detestable
nature of a falsehood deserves to be strongly inculcated.
This is a subject upon which half mankind are casuists ; but
I would not have my son among this class of moralists—with
the great and essential truths of religion, the outline of the
Christian creed, and the prominent duties involved in it, a
boy cannot be too soon possessed. I would have my son in

early life instructed, to avoid the fashionable infidelity of the times. I would have him reared in the bosom of a faith, by which no man was ever made worse, and all may hope to be made better : a sound and rational piety (the surest warrant of happiness in *this world* as well as in the next) is rarely to be expected, unless it be the result of instruction commenced when the mind is susceptible of deep impressions, and continued till they are firmly fixed. The fanatic is usually a recent convert to mystical doctrines he does not understand ; and the sceptic in religion too often owes the doubts that torment him to the unpardonable negligence of those to whose care his childhood was confided.

" I know it is unnecessary to write thus to you ; but you will place what I have said to the account of my anxiety for this boy's welfare, and excuse it.

" I have nothing to add to this scrawl, worth the writing. The French have opened the campaign on the Rhine with brilliant success ; and in Italy, the early prosperity of the Austrians seems likely to end in defeat and ruin. A friend to the peace of the world knows not to which side he should give his wishes. The ambitious views of the Emperor of Germany &c., &c., are little better than those of republican France.

" Each party is tolerably honest in adversity, and becomes the reverse in the hour of triumph. Americans should learn to be the partisans of neither. I beg you to be assured that I think of you always with true affection.

" P.S.—1*st July*, 1800.—I have kept this letter for the purpose of sending it by ＊ ＊ ＊ who has remained here longer than was expected.

" You will see by the public papers that my conjecture as to the result of the campaign in Italy was correct, although at that time the general opinion was rather the other way. The overthrow of the Austrians is signal and decisive. Nothing could be more absolute and complete. The Emperor will now be driven to make peace, and Bonaparte offers it to him in the hour of success and triumph, and doubtless with sincerity. This country must follow the example of Austria."

The campaign on the Rhine has hitherto been manifestly subservient to that of Italy, but it seems already to assume a more active character, and if peace does not speedily interpose the Austrians under *Kray* will experience a fate similar to those under *Melas*. Such a constellation of military talent has seldom (if ever) been seen as may now be found in the French armies and at the head of French affairs. It is to this circumstance that have been principally owing the splendid events in Italy and the masterly though less active operations in Germany. That Kray and Melas have been *outgeneralled* is universally admitted. The precise co-operation between the two French armies, although so far apart, towards the accomplishment of one object, is a proof, if any was wanting, of the superior intelligence of those by whom their movements were planned and conducted.

" We hear nothing of our commissioners at Paris. It is believed that they are going on well ; but with what speed (although I hear from Murray now and then) we are ignorant.

" You are likely I perceive to have a contest for President and Vice-President. So far removed as I am, I ought to abstain from all interference on the subject ; but I must express an opinion that Mr. Adams's administration has been, in the main, wise and proper. So far as I have been able to judge of the leading measures of his administration they have been politic and just in substance. That some of them should create clamor was to be expected—and this must be looked for let who will be President.

" Mr. Adams has done nothing to deserve to be discarded. He came into power at a very delicate crisis, and the delicacy of that crisis was much increased by the circumstance of his having General Washington for his immediate and only predecessor in office. Slight errors should be overlooked in a man who means well, and who has acted essentially right in situations peculiarly arduous and embarrassing."

This letter abounds in wise and judicious sentiments. It is a faithful transcript of his paternal feelings, and will secure for him the thanks of all, who are themselves concerned for the proper training of their children.

Mr. Pinkney was too severe a student to mingle much in general society. His practice was too extensive to admit of much recreation. Duty triumphed over the yearnings of a social disposition; and pleasure with him was always made secondary to duty. But still at home, in the privacy of his own hearthstone, or abroad, in the centre of society, he was the finished gentleman, and contributed all in his power to the pleasure and entertainment of those around him. Never, as many can testify, did the charm of his eloquence or the salient vigor of his intellect appear more fascinating, than in the presence of a friendship he loved and trusted.

He was a man of elegant hospitality, and always welcomed to his board those who chose to share in its conviviality. He knew not the love of money, and nothing gave him truer delight than to shower it down in blessings on the pathway of others.

His favorite literary works are not known. But that he delighted especially in Shakespeare, Milton, Addison and Johnson, is well known. The former he never tired in reading, and thoroughly comprehended. Perfectly at home in all the polite literature of the mother country, and extensively and critically read in the poets, he was admirably qualified to appreciate that splendid monument of wise and judicious criticism, " The Lives of the Poets," and detect its faults. The copy now in my possession affords abundant proof of both the pleasure and care with which he read.

The Bible he was accustomed to regard not only as the word of God, but as the very first of literary works ; incomparably above and beyond them all, of ancient or modern times. He studied it closely, and his mind teemed with its beauties. Hooker was also an especial favorite, particularly his magnificent first book. He loved the Church of England, and esteemed its theologians perfect masters of style and matter.

He was fond of his pencil, and often sketched for the amusement and gratification of his children—and singular to state, his sketches were executed with the skill of a master, and only wanted the aid of experience to entitle them to the highest rank in artistic excellence. He was passionately fond of nature, and loved to revel in its beauties. In the very trees and flowers he found a sort of companionship. On one occasion, illustrative of this ardent attachment for external nature, he observed that a favorite tree, one of the monarchs of the forest, had been cut down, and it stirred his soul to the highest degree of eloquent rebuke. He inveighed against the deed, and in his own expressive language affirmed "that the growth of centuries was ever venerable."

His recreation was walking and hunting. Of the latter he was particularly fond. There was an excitement about it congenial to his ardent temperament. He was a capital shot, and was capable of great endurance. He was a man of heart in every thing he undertook. His soul was in his business and his pleasures, his study and his pastime. He did nothing languidly. Enthusiastic and aspiring, he strove to excel in every thing he attempted.

He was a man of the nicest sense of honor. Truth was the grace he was most ambitious to exhibit in all his intercourse with his fellow men. A gentleman now residing in New-York, whose letter is before me, relates the following conversation that passed between Mr. Emmet and himself. I cannot, said this celebrated and eloquent lawyer, pay Mr. Pinkney a greater compliment than by telling you that in all his arguments before the Supreme Court he was never known to cite a single authority that was not on record precisely as he cited it, and so fully was the court satisfied with this fact, that they never thought it necessary to test the accuracy of the citation. It gives me the more pleasure to refer to this, because it proves what Mr. Emmet thought of his illustrious rival, and how he spoke of him in the freedom of conversation. Mr. Pinkney was not a man of professions, and yet to use his own language in a letter to a friend, "he had a good memory and a grateful heart." The reciprocation of kindness was the cordial of his life. Domestic in his tastes and habits, nothing afforded him more lively satisfaction, when the calls of business permitted, than to gather around him his children and the old friends whom he never changed for new ones, and the young men of promise in whose advancement he took an intense interest, and live over again the days of his boyhood and indulge in a real sunshine of heart cheerfulness. Even when he could not afford from press of business to contribute his full share to the pleasure of his friends, he would pass to and fro from his study to his parlor in the course of the evening and endeavor to make the best atonement in his power for the stern necessity of his absence. Such was the discipline of his mind, he could resume the thread of his most abstruse argument in an instant, and go on consolidating the chain, as though he had suffered no interruption. There was in one word a sort of pensive cheerfulness about him that captivated the heart, and a warm sympathy where the friends of his bosom were concerned, which none who ever shared it can forget.

It is said that Mr. Pinkney was inordinately ambitious; and I am not disposed to deny that his ambition may have exceeded the limits that are wisely and in mercy prescribed to the aspirations of men. But there was nothing low or sordid in his thirst after distinction. If he were ambitious, it was not to appear to be what he was not, but to be what he felt he should become. He was ambitious to be truly learned and truly great. He selected the profession of the law, and always continued to pursue it with delight, because it was not possible to acquire in it a spurious and undeserved reputation. If he sought to occupy the rank of the first of orators, or the greatest of lawyers, it was by giving expression to such sentiments as could alone proceed from the lips of that rarest and most brilliant creation of God, and exhibiting those unquestionable fruits of ripe and profound legal learning, that could alone proceed from the other. He knew that the path of solid distinction was only open to the patient and laborious student, and in striving to make the most rapid and advanced progress in it, he was contented to toil on, amid drudging labor to the end, in his endeavor and determination to win the unfading laurel. He never resorted to low and vulgar artifice to gain a fraudulent reputation. He built upon no other man's foundation the superstructure of his vast renown. He rose on no other man's ruin. In fair and open contest, by dint of persevering and indefatigable and intense exertion, he fought for victory ; and it may be truly said of him that he wore not a garland he did not fairly win. Self-culture in the exercise of a self-discipline, rarely if ever equalled, was the true secret of his success. Conscious of the possession of rare intellectual endowments, and grateful for the gift, he labored to make the most of them by constant and unremitting diligence. Thus far he was ambitious. Eager to excel, but only by endeavoring to deserve the pre-eminence he sought. Too eager to excel it may have been for his own happiness and good ; but still neither moved by envy nor poisoned by jealousy, in his efforts to excel. He recognized in his competitors the first men of the old and the new world, and he met them like a man, in the spirit of a man, who felt the terrible strokes of their stalwart arms, and acknowledged their inimitable power and dialectic skill, and who spurned the resort to underhand trick as self-degradation. Feeling the grandeur of the exciting race, he laid aside every thing that could impede his progress. Pleasure, self-ease, society, were all not only resolutely but cheerfully relinquished, to secure the palm for which he struggled. Superficial he was not ; self-sufficient he was not. Never satisfied to remain where he was, his motto was ever onward. His constant aim was to be what he wished men to think him ; and what he knew, by a prudent husbandry of his resources, he could readily make himself to be. There was a sublimity in this deathless desire to improve to the highest possible degree the faculties of a noble intellect, which commands our admiration. There was a moral power in that severe discipline of the mind, for its own improvement, which was never relaxed for a moment, that made its influence felt by the very first minds of the profession. It sought no ephemeral end by illegitimate means. Distinction alone was not the boon it craved. Applause was not alone the incense it coveted. Distinction as the reward of real attainment ; professional applause as the fruit of gigantic professional labor,—this it was which moved the soul of Pinkney, and fired his noble spirit. Solid reputation, based upon real merit, was what he desired. So exceedingly jealous was he of the moral beauty of this element in the reputation he sought, that his friends were apprised of his intention to abandon the field of professional duty, the very moment he was conscious of any diminution of zeal in study or inherent failure of his mental faculties. With less labor he might have lived upon the reputation he had acquired, and occasionally poured forth the higher specimens of his power ; but that would not have filled the measure, or realized the idea he had formed of the ambition worthy of his profession. Ambition I know is a dangerous thing. It sometimes degenerates into a mean and pitiful vice. But such was not the ambition of William Pinkney. There is nothing even in his most private correspondence, or the most unreserved communings of his friendship, that savored of illiberality or

meanness.   There was, it is true, a reserve in his professional bearing, that was distasteful to many, and misinterpreted
by more.   Mr. Kennedy has done him justice in this respect.
He appeared in the forum in the midst of his competitors
like a knight ever equipped for battle, and he walked the
field with knit brow and cautious step, ready for a tilt wherever he met a foeman worthy of his steel.   On such occasions
there was at times too much the semblance of hauteur
imparted to his air and mien.   But still he was not wanting
in courtesy.   He always engaged his adversary in fair fight
and with honorable weapons.   It will be remembered that
Judge Story said of him (page 252, vol. i.), "that he was
fair in not urging points on which he did not rely with confidence, and acute in seizing the proper point of attack, and
driving the enemy from it by storm."   This is the deliberate and honest asseveration of one who knew him well.   It
was a grapple of mind with mind, learning with learning,
eloquence with eloquence.

His ambition did not blind him to the real merit of others, neither did it excite envy in his bosom.   He admired the
talents of a Hamilton, Madison, Dexter, Dallas, Jones, Emmet, Story, Marshall, Webster, Clay and others ; and to the
worth of most, if not all of them, there are interspersed
either in his letters or his speeches, most explicit and noble
tributes of praise.   They were, most of them, his competitors, and he disputed with them, inch by inch, the palm of
ascendency ; and he disputed to the last with the keen
eye and practised skill of the most consummate gladiator.
But although he was accustomed to press his advantages with
vast dexterity, he was not blind to their exalted mental and
moral worth.   I very much question whether any man ever
paid more frequent and spontaneous tribute to the genius or
acquirements of his competitors than he.   One thing is certain ; his private correspondence is defiled by as little acrimony or bitterness of criticism upon his contemporaries, or

disgusting egotism, as any. In his more familiar converse he spoke freely of measures and of works ; sparingly of men and of motives. He was perhaps as little personal in his many earnest struggles of the forum and the Senate chamber, as the least offensive and most guarded of his competitors.

To the younger members of the bar he was, at all times, the kind, considerate and sympathizing friend, the delighted and interested eulogizer of their endeavors to ascend the rugged hill of fame, " to drink the nectar and breathe the ambrosial perfume." He loved to encourage them in their first struggles to be great, and sought to stimulate their ambition, and elevate their professional self-respect by judicious praise and well directed criticism.

I do not question that Mr. Pinkney had his faults and weaknesses like other men. But, with Story, I aver they were trivial, when compared with his virtues—"lighter than the linnet's wing." To use the language of Virginia's noble orator, Randolph of Roanoke: " He had indeed his faults, his foibles ; I should rather say sins. Who is without them ? Let such, such only, cast the first stone. And these foibles, if you will, which every body could see, because every body is clear-sighted with regard to the faults and foibles of others, he I have no doubt would have been the first to acknowledge on a proper representation of them." These are noble words, uttered in the same breath that told the world that the last act of intercourse between them was an act the recollection of which he would not be without for all the offices that all the men in the United States have filled or ever shall fill. What that act was, was only known to him who witnessed it ; but where the recollection is so sweet and fragrant, the knowledge is a thing of naught. I am not conscious that I have colored too highly a single trait ; and full well I know, I have not so combined or developed them as they were combined and developed in the daily walk.

Justum et tenacem propositi virum.

MARSHALL, STORY, WEBSTER, CLAY, CALHOUN, PINKNEY.

Marshall, Story, Pinkney, and Webster, four of the greatest names in American jurisprudence. All now gone to their rest. The first two may be said without a figure to linger still in the highest forum of this nation, and give forth law to the country and the world. The forms of Marshall and of Story (alike calm and dignified, and yet all unlike in the living lineaments of manly beauty), the befitting sanctuaries of minds free from prejudice, and well nigh intuitive in judgment, have not yet faded from the memory of the living. The form of the third is not yet a stranger to the hall, that has oft resounded with his trumpet tones. Marshall and Story dictated law to the nation. They expounded the constitution of the freest and noblest Republic known to the page of history. The world has learned to venerate their judgments. They were *lumina justitiæ in foro justitiæ.* All men loved to do them reverence. No man can wish, for the judicatures of the land, a more exalted destiny or a fuller measure of glory, than the permission to wear their mantle and emulate their greatness, by imbibing their lofty principles. Pinkney took, in his hands, the same inimitable constitution. Fresh from the society of its most revered authors, and animated by its stupendous principles, he unfolded it to the view of the American people, and assisted in the establishment of those great principles of construction, which are at once the ornament and the strength of that more than Egyptian pyramid, reared by the hands of a Marshall and a Story, to the lasting honor of American jurisprudence. Webster lived to prove that the highest intellectual endowments and the profoundest legal learning perished not with them. He wore the mantle of his three great predecessors (for a time his cotemporaries on earth), with not less grace than dignity. He enjoyed the enviable title of defender and expounder of the constitution. It is not transcending truth to say of him, that that precious instrument has been made more illustrious by the surpassing brilliancy and depth of his giant intellect, and that ages yet to come will hold it in still higher reverence as they view it in the gorgeous light of his masterly commentary. There was a rare combination in the character of Pinkney and Webster ; solid as the granite, profound as the ocean, brilliant as the diamond, they were, it seems to me, the purest specimens of all that was great in oratory and masterful in reasoning. And now that the shades of Marshall and Story live but in name, and the echoes of Pinkney's eloquence and profound legal learning are heard amid the hills of his own beautiful Potomac, and Webster, too, is dead, and Marshfield is desolate ; we may say, with proud exultation, in Webster's own words, " the past, at least, is secure," and Columbia shall be remembered as the abode of eloquence and the home of genius. In naming Mr. Pinkney and Mr. Webster together, and weaving a like brilliant and imperishable garland for each, it must not be supposed that I mean to intimate that they were wholly alike in the quality and character of their minds. They resembled each other in that feature which made them so unlike any other of their illustrious compeers. They were alike in the wonderful combination of depth and brilliancy. But in most other respects they differed from each other as widely as they did from the more distinguished of their competitors. Clay was far reaching, endowed with extraordinary sagacity, full of sterling common sense, bold as a lion, the most perfect mas-

ter of the power to move and mould the masses, emphatically and *par excellence* the orator of the people. He was
the first statesman of the world. Almost intuitive in judgment, he was equal to any emergency, and could steer the
noble ship of state through the most difficult and appalling
crisis. His courage always rose with the occasion, and his
admirable decision of character gave a sort of charm to
the policy he pursued, and was the chief element of his success. His tall and majestic figure beautifully harmonized
with his frankness of disposition ; while his voice, which was
the very melody of eloquence, capable of the most marvellous modulation, pre-eminently fitted him for a leader in
the fervor and excitement ot debate. The great pacificator
of the country, he more than once calmed the spirit of the
storm, as it rose in its fury, and threatened to pour desolation in its whirlwind path ; so that without the charge of
extravagance, we may apply to him those beautiful words of
the poet :

> " Tumida æquora placat
> Collectasque fugat nubes, solemque reducit."

He led on in the Missouri compromise, and Pinkney followed. He led on in the last, not less glorious, compromise,
and Webster followed. The glory of the invention and
guiding policy was in either case Clay's ; the noblest defence
was Pinkney's and Webster's. The chivalrous and heroic
Clay will be remembered as long as the Union lasts, and the
marvel of his eloquence, identified with the floating stars,
will recall the splendors of the elder Pitt, and make immortal the principles of freedom it so brilliantly illustrated.
His name is still the watchword which is recognized by
every sentinel on guard, as the countersign ; and his memory
is still, as it ever will be, a tower of strength.

The genius of Calhoun (which delighted to revel in the
midst of its own splendid theories, remarkably rich and

fruitful), united to his singularly strong and vigorous intellect, will command the admiration of the world, so long as originality and force are properly appreciated. But Clay, with all his incomparable excellence as a popular orator and statesman, was defective in profound logical power ; and Calhoun, with all his unquestioned intellectuality, was defective in judgment and splendor of eloquence. Their eminence was restricted to the two great departments of oratory and statesmanship.

Mr. Pinkney and Mr. Webster were left to illustrate that rare combination, which secured for them like pre-eminence as lawyers, orators, and statesmen. For close, severe, connected, logical reasoning, they were unsurpassed. Perfect masters of the science of the law ; inimitable expounders of the constitution, they were as profound as brilliant, as deep as eloquent. They were tried in the severest school and in the presence of the most critical and competent judges. The very first court of the nation, in the very zenith of its fame, was not ashamed to sit at the feet of either, and learn the true principles of constitutional interpretation. They were, indeed, amici curiæ. But still they were very unlike each other, notwithstanding this wonderful resemblance. Pinkney was rapid. He poured forth torrents of forensic eloquence and vehement argumentation in a swollen stream, that seemed to be absolutely exhaustless. Engaged in the most diversified and extensive practice, he never failed to infuse the magic of his eloquence and transparency of his reasoning into his numberless arguments. Mr. Webster could be eloquent ; at times most eloquent ; and on such occasions the effect was irresistible. He was calm, collected, deliberate in the main ; and yet his great soul was sometimes roused, and his lion spirit stirred, and then there was the lightning flash in his eye, and the thunder tone on his tongue. At such times, there was an awful sublimity in his thoughts, and a bold, massive structure in his style, that were admirably adapted to the occasion. He bore down, like a roused lion, upon his antagonist, and desperate and well-timed were the blows of his stalwart arm. He was master of every passion, and his countenance glowed with the most varying expression. I was privileged to witness one of those noblest bursts of oratorical power in the celebrated Gerard Will case. Never shall I forget the withering scorn, the biting sarcasm, the deep affecting pathos and fearful sublimity, that alternately thrilled and delighted the wrapt assembly.

Mr. Pinkney was not less self-collected. But fired by the brilliancy of his genius, and transported by the sublimity of his thoughts, his warm southern temperament was more quickly and keenly roused, and he always rose in grandeur before the court, and was not confessedly excelled by any. He saw his conclusion with an eagle eye, hurried on with giant strides to reach it, and failed not of his mark. He forced you along " pari passu" in breathless wonder, in a very whirl, not of declamation, but of overpowering and matchless argumentation. And yet, in the highest excitement of his fervor and rushing impetuosity, he was ever perfect master of himself.

Webster required some powerful stimulus to draw out his giant faculties. Pinkney never was without such stimulus. It was as natural for him to be eloquent as to speak. Pinkney's, was the outgushing of thought and expression from an overflowing fountain ; Webster's, the welling up of thought and expression, not less rich, but less copious and free in its flow. They were more Demosthenic than Ciceronian in their style of eloquence, and yet modelled upon neither. *Vigor* and *perspicuity* were the chief characteristics. Admirable scholars, they were singularly happy in the choice and arrangement of their words ; not less admirable logicians, they were equally happy in the classification and disposition of their ideas. Webster never had occasion to recall a word or re-arrange a sentence ; but then he was, even in his most excited mood, what would be termed a slow speaker. Pinkney was not less skilful in the structure of his sentences and the choice of his words. He was never known to be at fault for either. This was the more wonderful, because, in the greatest rapidity of utterance, there was never a pause for either language or ideas. Neither of them was ever excelled in the ability to explore all the depths of a subject ; and though differing widely in their peculiar powers of imagination, neither of them was ever excelled in the beauty and magnificence of coloring they could impart to the deductions and processes of reasoning. Mr. Webster sometimes drew a vast crowd to the courts of justice, and at times riveted the attention of the audience. Mr. Pinkney never spoke without drawing a crowd, and wielding a tremendous influence over the promiscuous assemblage ; and this he did with such consummate skill, that he never weakened his argument or made it nerveless. Men are as fond of eloquence now as they were then ; and yet, taking the whole professional life together, it may be truly affirmed that no man ever drew together such crowds with like power to keep them spell-bound, without the weakening of a single link in the chain of severe logical discussion. It was, indeed, a rare and wonderful gift.

It is to be deeply regretted that these two great men, so much alike in towering strength, transparency of reasoning, copiousness and concentration of thought and wealth of imagination, were never brought into direct antagonism. They were engaged in the great Bank cause ; and there, according to Story's estimate, Pinkney was the bright peculiar star. But to the best of my knowledge, they were never engaged as opposite counsel in any cause. It is a well known fact, that Mr. Pinkney's highest powers were always more signally displayed in such antagonism. It was then, that his ingenuity in the conduct of a cause, his quickness of perception, his accuracy of law knowledge, his powers of scathing analysis, his almost intuitive perception of the weak points, and ardent spirit (that, like Napoleon's, would scarce admit the possibility of defeat) shone out in all their strength.

When it is said that Webster stated, that he had met Pinkney, Emmet and Wirt, but never feared either of them as much as he did Jeremiah Mason, it should not be forgotten that he had never encountered Pinkney. He had argued by his side ; never in opposition to him. It would have been a glorious contest, and I regret that their mutual friends were not permitted to witness it, knowing that it would have been conducted in a way to reflect honor upon both.

If, as I have shown, they were alike in combination of talent (however much they differed in their idiosyncrasies of intellect), they were not unlike in the destiny that befel them. Neither of them was ever vanquished. They never suffered a Waterloo defeat, although they passed the bridge of Lodi, and scaled the passage of the Alps.

Mr. Pinkney could never be followed by a reporter. He soon gave up the task in despair, in the fascinating spell of the orator. And from the constant multiplicity of his efforts, another consequent necessity for extraordinary exertion, unassisted by reporters, it was impossible for him to revise and prepare for publication any of his speeches. Thoughts struck out in the excitement of debate, and beauties of expression and flashes of eloquence emitted by the mind, when roused by the fervor of discussion, can never be recalled ; and consequently, if the reporter from any cause prove unequal to the task, the speech is lost. It was Mr. Pinkney's misfortune to live and die, without meeting the man, who could write down those splendid passages, or even preserve unbroken the chain of his argument ; and it is the misfortune of the lovers of true eloquence, that such was the melancholy fact. Mr. Webster in this respect has the advantage over all others.   He has left a monument behind him worthy of his vast fame.

Not too rapid to be followed, in the present improved state of stenography, his speeches were happily preserved ; and that without any great labor on his part.   In his speech on Foote's resolution, he had the advantage of a report from the pen of the senior editor of the Intelligencer, who is second to none of his cotemporaries in the best qualities of a statesman.   It is not, therefore, possible to conceive of a richer mine of all that is grand in eloquence, stupendous in genius, and conclusive in argument, than the speeches of Daniel Webster afford, caught up as they fell from his lips, with the glow fresh upon them, and reviewed by himself in the sunset of his splendid career, when not a faculty was dimmed, nor a ray obscured.

No man can accord to the lamented Webster a pre-eminence I do not accord to him.   No man can take a prouder pleasure in contemplating the rising columns of his fame, which, " piercing the skies, is gilded by the first and latest rays of the sun" in his circuit of glory.

I have thus ventured to give to the public my estimate of the character of these two remarkable men, Webster and Pinkney.   I waved the expression of my opinion until the facts that illustrated the latter were spread out before it. That estimate must pass for what it is worth.   For a rare combination of all the elements of true greatness, they were, in my opinion, proudly pre-eminent.   For massive grandeur of intellect and granite strength, solidity of judgment and sublime eloquence, they were principes inter pares.   Pinkney was Webster's equal in depth and brilliancy ; more varied in his gifts and uniformly great in the use of them.   His oratory was more splendid and overpowering if viewed in the aggregate ; fully its equal, viewed in any other light. They were, however, kindred orbs, stars of the first magnitude.   In all that is worthy of lasting renown, in devotion

to the Union, power of argument, conservative statesmanship and majesty of eloquence, their names will be handed
down to coming generations—the first of lawyers, orators
and statesmen. Equalled, it may be, by some, in one or
other of those departments ; they were unequalled in the
exquisite union of pre-eminent excellence in all. I award
to them like honor and distinction, satisfied that our country will never want a title to the name of eloquence and
force of intellect, so long as either name shall survive to be
remembered.

CONCLUSION.

HAVING caught up the true echoes of Mr. Pinkney's fame, I may be permitted in conclusion to address a few words to the young men of the United States ; and enforce the sublime moral, which they so impressively inculcate. I had a higher object in undertaking this work than the mere desire of paying a merited tribute to the subject of this memoir. For although the part enacted by Mr. Pinkney in the past history of the country, and his brilliant achievements in Parliamentary and forensic eloquence are worthy of perpetuation ; although his name and character are a portion of our common heritage of glory, and therefore justly entitle him to be held in grateful remembrance—it strikes me that the powerful influence, which such an example ought to exert upon the enterprising youth of the present day, constitutes the most important and attractive aim of the biography. Example is ever more potent for good than precept. The present receives its wisest lessons and most exciting stimulus from the past, and the future will, for the most part, take its hue from the past and the present combined. Youth has always been nerved to patriotism and excited to eloquence by the great and the virtuous, whose footprints are left on the paths they tread. It will be so, so long as the human soul retains its love of virtue and admiration of distinguished talent. The tombs of the departed great, the mausoleums of the illustrious dead, are the best schools for the mental and moral training of those who follow them. Oblivion may have its sweets, and forgetfulness its charms

and usefulness, but not where the fragrance of noble principles is scenting the air, and the fruits of gigantic exertion
are clustering on the boughs. He, who strives to deserve
well of his country and of mankind, and consecrates his rich
and varied powers to the service of his fellows, is a beacon
light, set up by Divine Providence for the encouragement
and imitation of succeeding ages. It is not possible to
multiply too much the exemplars, who have illustrated the
page of history and made it glorious. Each additional star
swells the brilliancy of the constellation, and the eye never
tires in gazing upon its beauty, for to each there is its own
peculiar fascination. There is no antagonism in those cu-
mulating rays. It is one harmonious blended light, that
gathers intensity and strength from the burning splendors of
the whole.

Our young countrymen have an awful trust committed
to their charge, a magnificent present, and a future such as
never before dawned upon the world. The blessings they
enjoy are not the birth and growth of a single day. They
see the gorgeous blossom of the flower that was but yesterday in the bud ; the mighty development of the seed that
was but just now in the germ. The United States of
America are a new star in the political firmament—a
federative government not known to any other confederation
of the old or the new world—without a parallel in the history of the past. A distinguished writer of England, in a
disquisition concerning the power and stability of federative
governments, of singular force and discrimination, asserts
that ours "is a new creation in politics ; that our union has
avoided the glaring errors of former confederacies—that our
forefathers studied the models of antiquity in the true spirit
of political wisdom. With a view to balance the powers of
the central and state governments, and to prevent the former
from overstepping its proper limits, a power has been there
conceded to the judiciary, which has in no other instance

been vested in that department." These United States then, the invention and discovery of the patriots of '87, men of the lion heart and patriot will, the cool sagacity to discern what was best and the enlargement of soul to adopt what they discerned, is the country of your hopes and allegiance. Its principles, institutions, resources, power and future destiny, have been long the topic of eloquent discussion. It is history known by heart to each one of you. In territory, for extent, richness and variety of soil; in beauty of scenery, and mineral resources, and every other quality that could fit it to be the fairest heritage that ever fell to the lot of any people, whose bosoms beat high with love of liberty, social, civil, and religious—it is unsurpassed. Mountain and vale, woodland and prairie, bay, river, and lake, constitute it the consecrated land of liberty. Possessed of every variety of climate, from the ice-bound shores of the Atlantic to the warm and genial breezes of the tropics, it is adapted to the growth of every luxury that the palate can crave, and suited to the wants and tastes of the millions who have sought upon it a shelter and a home. Dotted over by the footsteps of the arts and sciences with beauty and comfort; covered with railroads, which promise in a few brief years to form a complete iron web for the diffusion of commerce and the propagation of light and liberty from the centre to the circumference of its wide-spread domain; blessed with institutions, free, nicely balanced, beautifully and wondrously harmonized, where the freedom of each is as large as the security of the whole will permit, and the power of the whole is so tempered and guarded that it cannot well become the oppression of the few—such is the land of your birth.

Those who intelligently read the past and then contemplate the present, must feel more than ever convinced that our growth is full as marvellous as our birth. The ægis of the constitution now covers an immense area. The very sentinels, who cry out the watchword of freedom on the shores of the Atlantic, may hear the echo that sends it back from the mild Pacific wave. These separate and independent sovereignties have multiplied ; and each in turn has taken its place beneath the floating stars without so much as a jar in the glorious constellation. The weak and the strong have been gathered into the same clustering group without so much as the loss of a single beam, save where that beam was voluntarily surrendered to be absorbed into the splendors of the whole.

And yet our growth has been singularly guarded against those dangers that follow the widening of the bands of empire, by the discoveries of science which have brought the most distant States of the Union into close proximity. The pulsations of the great national heart may be heard and felt at almost every beat to the farthest verge of the body politic.

We are a nation among men, a power on the earth. Our influence for good or evil can be circumscribed by no limits. Liberty in union is the true genius of our institutions, and who shall fetter or restrain them ? Our power is in the justice of our political principles. It is a moral power, the greatest and most masterful of all powers. Adherence to what is constitutional law at home, and a due observance of what is clear international law abroad, are the very elements of our greatness. Our power is not a thing of force. Muttering cannon and frowning battlements do not aptly represent it. These appendages of power we possess, it is true, and the thunders of Lake Erie and the bloody plains of New Orleans proclaim to all the surrounding nations, that while we love peace and cultivate it, we know how to meet force by force and uphold the dignity of the flag. But still our power is pre-eminently and characteristically the power of moral suasion, high example and noble unselfish principle. We have had a brilliant past. We have a glorious present. We shall have a future. But what a future ? Shall it be

a future of joy and hope to ages yet unborn, or blacker than
midnight when it settles all gloomily on the fretted bosom
of the sea ?

The ship of State has passed through sea and fire. More
than once has she been driven furiously among the breakers,
until her very beams seemed to bend and crack in the shock,
and the pilot hung doubtingly at the helm.

> " Ponto nox incubat atra
> Intonuere poli et crebris micat ignibus æther."

More than once has she been conducted in safety through
the howlings of the tempest to mild waters and a friendly
harbor, where the storm spent its fury in impotency.   Bright
skies are once more above her—a clear pathway before her—
calmly, quietly, and beneath the beauteous banner of peace,
she circumnavigates the world.   The true glory of a country
does not consist in a fruitful soil, overflowing treasury, well
equipped and well disciplined armies, fortified cities, frowning batteries, or a splendid naval force, ships manned by
brave tars and governed by gallant officers.   It does not
consist in wide extent of territory or a crowded population.
These things are valuable in themselves, images of power
and where rightly used and honestly obtained images of
greatness.   But they do not constitute true national glory.
The day was when we had them not—a day of darkness,
peril, fierce and desperate conflict.   And yet the measure of
our glory was never fuller.   Our name was for praise on the
lips of all.

The true glory of a nation consists in moral elevation, high-
toned principle, love of justice, adherence to right, schools
and colleges, the purity of her statesmen, the intelligence
and patriotism of her yeomanry, and above all incomparably,
the vital godliness of each.

It is for the young men of the Union, thus circumstanced,
I write.   I write to them because they are young men,
young in hopes, young in energy, young in the fervor and

freshness of an enterprising enthusiastic public spirit. Youth is generally represented as a sort of holiday of sunshine, a pleasure-taking, gay, joyous, buoyant season; when the prisoner just escaped from the painful restraints of his alma mater may give himself up to those waking dreams, which Prior seems disposed in a very mockery of refinement to dignify with the name of hopes. I would not take one ray of real sunshine from its path. I would not dim one rush candle that flickers by its way. I would not put into its sparkling chalice one drop of bitterness, to mar the buoyancy and elasticity of this sweet spring-time of existence. Youth when virtuously spent, is an oasis in this bleak, drear wilderness. It is the dew-drop on the trembling leaf, the petal of the flower not yet blown, the acorn of the oak not yet developed. It is pre-eminently the season of hope, the hour of visions bright and golden fancies, when the mind may weave the garland of its future fame and regale itself amid scented bowers and golden fruit. But youth is something more, something vastly higher, nobler, more august. It is the period for the moulding of the immortal mind and heart; and gives the coloring and character to the days to come.

It is for the young men of the Union I write. It is for them I have endeavored to draw this character and disclose the life of one of our distinguished sons—satisfied that every exemplar of noble energy and aspiring character, set before them, must tend to stimulate their efforts and awaken emulation in their bosoms.

In his loyalty to the Union—in his deep and patient examination of its stupendous principles—in his awful reverence for the constitution—in his broad and expansive patriotism that scorned all sectional boundaries, and aspired to be coextensive with the limits of the land of his fondest love —in his high toned, and energetic endeavor to assist in the establishment of the true principle of its interpretation—in all those respects we fancy we may behold in Mr. Pinkney an example worthy of their imitation in this day of ultraisms on either side of the line that separates between North and South. Like him, see to it that nothing is wanting on your part to uphold the constitution of this Union and cause it to be reverenced and obeyed. Look upon it as the strong bond of society—cherish it in your inmost soul. Let your fealty to it be above suspicion and reproach. In all your expositions of it, learn with him, while you do all in your power to enlighten its duly commissioned expounders, to bow with deference to their decisions, satisfied that the constitution, *constitutionally interpreted,* is the law of safety, honor, prosperity, and peace to all. Should you enter the halls of legislation or rise to address courts of justice, be ever ready to resist by argument and eloquence the slightest encroachment of State sovereignty on the national jurisdiction, and vindicate the States from national usurpation. Like him never approach the discussion of any constitutional question without an overawing sense of the responsibility of the deed, and feel as though your country is standing before you to be elevated or depressed, as the constitution triumphs or is impaired.

In your youthful preparations for the onerous duties that must devolve upon you as the future guardians of your country's honor and interests, should difficulties rise up to impede your progress or dampen your energies—should poverty bow down your souls in the dust, and patronage be wanting to give you confidence and inspire you with hope —should the sad defects of early education conspire to abate your ardor in the exciting race of honorable distinction, I would point you to the youthful Pinkney, who was compelled to grapple with fiercer difficulties, and alone, without money or patronage, the smile of friends, or the favors of the rich, push forward his onward and upward career ; and bid you take courage and never yield to despondency and gloom. If

endowed with genius (the real power to scale the loftiest eminence of professional renown), remember that genius alone
will not suffice to crown you with complete success. Like
Pinkney, you must study to be great. Close, diligent, searching mental discipline must be the very aliment of your
life. Your motto, like his, must be "plus ultra." Knowledge, coextensive with the widest range of the profession of
the law and the science of government, must be not only
sought by you but obtained, and that, too, by labor continued without intermission. You must realize what is so beautifully recorded of Publius Scipio, "illum et in otio de ne-
gotiis cogitare et in solitudine secum loqui soletum ; ut neque cessaret unquam et interdum colloquio non egeret.
Hæque duæ res quæ langorem afferunt cæteris illum accue-
bant otium et solitudo." Never forget the lessons which
those echoes teach so conclusively, and always bear in mind,
that no matter how prodigal Providence may have been in
her gifts to you, all must at last depend upon yourselves.
Work you must, and that, too, in the close as in the beginning of your professional life ; or you may never hope to scale
the summit and reflect lasting renown and distinction on the
land of your birth. In this strenuous desire and exertion to
do your best, to add something daily to the stores of your
mental resources, you must, like him, give your days and
nights to study ; so that when you arise to address juries, or
courts, or legislators, you may reasonably expect to instruct
and delight them, having mastered your subject and threaded
all its intricacies.

The benefit and importance of such an example cannot be
better stated than in the language of Mr. Wirt. "No man
dared to grapple with him without the most perfect preparation and the full possession of all his strength. He kept
the bar on the alert and every horse with his traces tight. It
will be useful to remember him, and in every case imagine
him the adversary with whom we have to cope." Years have

passed since these words were penned, but the power of such
an example is imperishable. So far from losing, it acquires
strength by age, and comes to us clothed with all the dignity
and veneration of a relic of times gone by. This ceaseless mental struggle (that never so much as winked its eye, but always
marched steadily to the point and made preparation a delight) is less the habit of our day than it was ; and, therefore, there is peculiar propriety in calling up this marked and
striking feature in Pinkney's character for renewed imitation
and study.

Above all, like him, keep your professional integrity as
an advocate unimpeached and unimpeachable. Never rest
your defence upon weak points—spurn all captious cavillings
—and when you grapple with your adversary, meet him like
a man and storm the very bulwarks of his argument.

Be it your ambition, like him, to be truly great, *because
truly learned and upright*. Aim to be what you would have
the world suppose you to be. Let your confidence be the result of diligent preparation, and then, although like him,
you may never rise without embarrassment, you will find
yourselves more and more assured. Your pathway of argument and eloquence will be clear before you.

I hand you this simple record of a man who has been
said, somewhat reproachfully, to live in the mere echoes of
his fame. You have heard those echoes coming up from the
courts before which he plead—the public service he so much
adorned by his wise, moderate and patriotic principles—the
Congress of the Union, where he always stood forth the
champion of the people's rights, and where his eloquence
and his logic were the breathings of a conservative statesmanship—and the private walks of life, which he illustrated
by a moderation, temperance, and kindliness of heart, that
might be said, without a figure, to have been that chorus of
the virtues which Cicero so much lauds. You can now
judge whether these echoes be not convincing proofs of the

more than gothic splendors of the original. Pinkney's fame may live for the most part in the echoes of the past. But still they are the echoes of the great, the learned, and the wise, who have left behind them the most undoubting testimony to the wonders of his mind—echoes not of the envious or fawning parasite, but the honest and upright, men of mental enlargement and well cultivated taste, giants of the age in which they lived. The speeches that survive him are all fragmentary. They lost so much in the effort to report them, that you can scarce discern the resemblance. Such was the discipline of his mind and his skill in extemporaneous discussion, that when fully prepared (and he never spoke when he was not), he poured forth his arguments in a stream of the purest English, fresh and gushing from the " well undefiled."

Is it hoping too much ; is it asking too much of the young men of the United States, who are now treading in his footsteps and the footsteps of the other giants of his day, that, thrilled by such glowing reminiscences of genius, patriotism and labor, they would redeem the promise of the future and hand on the record to succeeding ages, bright with new names, that shall live after them ?

In a country like ours, where each citizen has his full share in the affairs of the body politic,—and no one can tell what positions of power and influence he may have to fill,—and where in the most retired sphere he may choose to occupy " procul a republica," he can hope to serve the country most effectually—it is his bounden duty to prepare himself by a careful training of both mind and heart for any and every possible public emergency. He belongs to the republic, for the republic is but an aggregate of personal individuality. He cannot lead a solitary, selfish existence without the guilt of moral treason against her pride and power.

Diligence and application are tremendous levers and the fulcrum on which they rest is the might and majesty of your individual will. *Possunt, quia posse videntur,* was a

favorite maxim in the olden time.   Who can calculate what
moderate abilities will accomplish, when stirred into action
and kept vigorously at work by plodding industry and steady
perseverance ?   Application works wonders.   Bacon has said
that " crafty men contemn studies, simple men admire them,
wise men use them."   " Read to weigh and consider," continues
that master mind.   " Some books are to be tasted, others to
be swallowed, and some few are to be chewed and digested."
With some such maxims in your view, and the firm determination to make the most of your powers, you must live
benefacere Reipublicæ and reflect upon it fadeless lustre and
renown.

Shun superficiality in every thing you undertake.   The
habit will soon become a palsy upon your mental faculties.
Take a step at a time, and no step without a full comprehension of its use and aim.   " Festina lente."   Be satisfied to
move a step at a time, and rest assured that your progress
will be rendered thereby the more rapid and certain.

The republic expects each one to do his duty, and we
would therefore urge upon you the importance and necessity
of diligent preparation to do it well and faithfully.

Your fathers, " Patres conscripti," were wise men all, of
the most approved patriotism, calm philosophic wisdom,
patient study, and intense application.   Washington, Adams,
Hamilton, Marshall led them on in their bright career, a
career carved out for them on the blood-washed fields of the
Revolution.   They left their impress on the history of the
world—and that history must be torn to tatters before their
memory can begin to fade, and then so long as the shreds
remain, the disjecta membra will hand down their names to
confound tyrants on their thrones and rebuke the myrmidons
of despotism.   Wise men will be needed, wise councils, wise
measures, for the future guardians of our ship of State.
Patriotism and intelligence, in combination with moral virtue

and a pure Christian faith—these are the gothic and corinthian pillars of the noble edifice.

Your country looks to you. Shall she look in vain ? To uphold her ancient renown and fulfil her exalted destiny, she craves your warmest sympathies and most substantial aid. Will you refuse her the just demand ? None but true hearts, enlightened minds, heroic wills can serve her as she needs.

You are young and vigorous. There is nothing that you may not do which she has either the right to expect or the authority to exact. She neither exacts nor expects of you impossibilities. Girded in by an example ever powerful to thrill and stimulate you—surrounded by the monuments of a prudence, moderation, and patriotism, that have pervaded the land in all the beauty and impressiveness of an august reality, she would have you only re-enact the magnificence and glory of the past. Worthy sons of worthy sires is all she desires you to be. She would have you imitate virtues that have already found an impersonation on the earth, and emulate a patriotism that knew of no measure short of the highest national exaltation.

Aim to be real characters. There is power in reality. This was Mr. Pinkney's crowning characteristic.

The age in which we live is an age of activity, rather than patient, laborious, plodding industry and attention to study. Even among professional men there is far less of the "labor limæ" than existed in the generation just passed. There is not the same ambition to excel, the same emulation in the path of honorable distinction. The dust actually accumulates on the pages of splendid libraries that were thoroughly conned by the fathers of the present generation, who possessed no more time for literary and learned pursuits than those who have inherited their names and fortunes, but not their thirst for knowledge or distinction.

The great Roman Satirist thus wrote in the decline of his country's literary and political glory.

> "Indocti primum, quamquam plena omnia gypso
> Chrysippi invenias. Nam perfectissimus horum est,
> Si quis Aristotelem similem vel Potticon emit
> Et jubet archetypos pluteum servare Cleanthes."

He rebuked those who aped learning without undergoing the fatigues and toil of study, and flattered themselves, that by filling their studios with the busts of deceased logicians and statues of renowned philosophers, they would merit and win for themselves honorable and lasting distinction. May we not, without charge of presumption, warn you against this folly, and by the hard-earned laurels of your ancestors, and ours, inculcate the all-important truth, that nothing truly great can be accomplished without intense application. It will not do to have the images of Lord Bacon, Shakspeare, Hooker, Taylor, Coke, Mansfield, Steward, Sir Matthew Hale, Johnson, looking down upon us with calm beauty and inspiring earnestness. It will not suffice to gaze upon the statues of Aristotle, Cicero, Quintillian, Thucydides, Herodotus, as though the cold marble would warm us into life and transfuse into our bosoms their own bright thoughts and deeds. It will not do to stand in the shadow of the fathers of the republic and feast our eyes upon their calm philosophic features. We must study their immortal works to emulate their greatness. However eagerly we may pursue the discoveries made in science and government since their day, we must remember that these are fixed stars which can never lose their brilliancy or their use. Their works are solid gold, hammered out, which must constitute the warp and woof of every character which like theirs would aspire to like immortality.

The mention of Cleanthes recalls to mind an historic fact of pregnant interest to the young. It proves what the heart of oak, and iron will can accomplish. He was a Stoic philosopher, surnamed Hercules, because of his excessive labors

to amass knowledge. He was so poor that he was accustomed
to get his living by drawing water for the gardens at night,
that he might apply himself to the study of philosophy by
day.   It was even said of him that he wrote the doctrines of
his master upon ox bones and broken tiles for want of money
to purchase befitting materials.   And we know that some
other immortal works have been since written on scraps of
paper picked up accidentally in the streets.   The home of
genius is not in the palaces of luxury or the gardens of delight, but the workshops of patient and secluded labor.
Great names are enrolled, not upon the fleeting, unsubstantial
cloud, which receives its roseate hue from the hand of an excited fancy or a rich and discursive imagination, but on the
marble dug from the quarry and polished by industry and
perseverance.

   We know that we are oftentimes charged with egotistic
folly as a nation, because we regard ourselves as the world's
trustees.   But we plead not guilty to the impeachment.   We
hold that this western continent is destined for the enact-
ment of a grand drama in the world's history.   We see the
hand of Providence in her birth and growth.   We have no
prophet's vision to read the future ; but we can sit down in
the light of the past and read enough to thrill and fill us
with awe and pleasure.   Our fathers copied after no model.
It was all their own brilliant creation ; God's blessing on
their honest patriotism, love of justice, moderation and fear
of wrong.   Liberty and equality constitutionally guarded,
were the magic words they emblazoned upon their high
floating standard.   They kindled a flame that still cheers the
world, amid the darkness of misrule and the clouds of political superstition and antiquated error.

   In handing over this precious legacy to you, are you surprised that our anxiety and our fears are awakened, as well
as our patriotic exultation and pride.   Your fathers will soon
lie down to die, and the floating stars will wave before their

dying eye in all the beauty of unity and harmony of their
blended rays. Her martial airs will float triumphantly on
every breeze, and mingle, as they fall upon their ear, in death,
with those other sounds that will soothe and compose them
to their final rest. They will soon cease to be actors in this
busy scene. Their last prayer offered up for the country's
weal, their last deed of loyalty performed, they will pass from
off this stage of action and leave you the responsibility and
privilege of being alone in your glory. Their solicitude is for
you and yours, not for themselves. Their task is well-nigh
concluded ; their responsibility well-nigh accomplished.
The past is theirs. The present and the future belong to
you. "The past is secure." It gives neither anxiety nor
concern. The stars and stripes cover it with glory. But
the present and the future are laden with hopes and fears.
Will you make it the heritage of good or the prognosticator
of evil?

You have the hopes of the world in your care and keeping. You are each one of you sentinels on the watch-tower
of liberty. The countersign from your lips is echoed from
the Atlantic to the Pacific wave, and the world honors and
respects it. It finds a welcome response in thousands, who
dare not whisper even to their trembling hearts the solace
and the comfort it affords. Be it your highest earthly ambition to live as men should live who are put in charge of such
a dread trust. Let your policy be just and upright. Cultivate peace, and let the repose of nations be undisturbed by
you. Suffer the country to grow. Intermeddle not with
her inner life, for it constitutes at once her truest power and
highest renown. God, in His wise overruling Providence,
will develope her as rapidly as her safety and honor will permit. Let the American name, under your guardianship, be, as
it ever has been, the watchword of honesty and truth. Her
flag, let it wave the symbol of equal-handed justice and enlarged civil and religious liberty, the pledge of protection to

the rights of all and the stern, unbending, unyielding exactor of our own.

Promote purity of morals and elevation of principle. Frown upon vice. Revive, as far as you can, the self-sacrificing habits that characterized the infancy of the republic. Do all in your power to bring back again the period of '76 ; and let the heroic deeds and virtues of that golden age be your constant study and imitation.

And above all, learn to estimate, as you ought, the power of individual influence, the force and might of individual example. " Rivulets are made up of drops—mountains of grains of sand." The onward rushing stream of political power, which on this continent, and in these United States, occasionally swells with more than the majesty and impetuosity of the Mississippi, when a flood is upon her, is only the swollen aggregate of private views and principles. Each gives an impetus to the whole. There is no danger so subtle, crafty, and insidious in its first approaches, and after workings for evil, as the secret conviction that it matters not what this or that private citizen does or thinks—the persuasion that the man is absorbed and swallowed up in the multitude. It is the most bitter drop of political poison ever distilled into the cup of a freeman—it is the first weaving of the chain of the despot on his stalwart arm. He has read history to but little practical profit, who does not know that every thought and deed of each and every freeman is incorporated by the mysterious law which pervades all human society into the grand aggregate ; and that the citadel is never so safe as when each watchman, feeling her to be in danger, is wide awake and at his post.

That my young countrymen may live to realize their most sanguine hopes, and reflect new lustre on the land of their birth; that they may be happy and useful in their retirement, if they should prefer the quiet shade—and respected and revered for their public and private virtues, should they be called to serve their country in the legislative halls, at the council board, or in the courts of justice ; that they may cultivate their minds and hearts, and refresh themselves at the well-springs of eloquence and of learning; and, above all, that they may be strong in wisdom, and show themselves as men, keeping the statutes of the Lord, and walking in His ways, and thus diffuse all around them the fragrance of a holy and virtuous life, is my most earnest prayer. They must expect difficulties, look for trials, and encounter many rude shocks as they traverse the sea of life. The very castles they build in what may be called the mock grandeur of their youth, "when life is like a summer dream," will be soon demolished, and the solid superstructure of a sure and enduring renown will cost them many days of anxious toil in its erection. But still, if true to themselves, the country and the world, they will not fail to be honored and revered as public benefactors. " There is an intimate connection between private virtue and public greatness. The most honorable and liberal, the most benevolent and religious man is in the first instance, and will eventually appear to have been, the best friend to his country and the noblest benefactor to mankind."

I have a deep and unfeigned veneration for the memory of lofty talent and high-toned manly principle, consecrated through long years of public service, by single-minded earnestness and self-sacrificing labor; and if I mistake not, there is that in the bosom of my fellow-men which beats responsive to my own. He who erects a monument to departed worth, and by his art and skill causes the marble or the brass to speak trumpet-tongued to the present of the past, is a benefactor of his race. Every monument thus erected to lend beauty to the streets of the crowded city, is a pillar of national security, which strengthens while it adorns the great temple of freedom. It speaks in a language free from passion, and with the awful impressiveness of the tomb, which consecrates all that is virtuous and ennobling among men. A monument of marble or of brass, it was not possible for me to raise. It is not often the privilege of descent to engrave on the cold marble the image of a loved ancestry. True it is, the world is occasionally cheered by the sight of the filial deed ; and even now the American can look with pride upon the enterprising artist, who calmly and patiently continues at his work, and will not abandon it until his countrymen shall hail the consummation of the deed. Justice Story will live, not only in his own imperishable works, but in the life-revealing pen and chisel of his son.

Mine is an humble task. To the memory of William Pinkney after a long lapse of years, during which his form has neither moved among men, nor his tongue electrified them, and when the prejudices of rivalry may be supposed to have given place to nobler sentiments, I have erected this modest and unpretending monument. Inscribed upon it is his character as I have studied and understand it. In the fourfold aspect of orator, lawyer, statesman, and man, you may read it there. I have asserted nothing without proof. I have weighed well the facts stated. I have uniformly permitted other lips to speak forth his praise. In my own estimate of his mental and moral character, I have studied to be impartial, and although it would be disgusting presumption to affirm that I have not unconsciously yielded somewhat to the power of those feelings of partiality which almost always give a coloring to our views, I can truly say, that I believe that the work contains intrinsic internal evidence of its truthfulness and fidelity. Will any cynic chide me for the work ? He may rebuke the rashness of the undertaking, and I bow to the sad, though just impeachment. But the desire to rescue from oblivion the memory of departed worth is immortal, and none may dare rebuke it. That desire, united to the deep interest I take in the young men of the land, is my only

apology for what I know and feel, as deeply as the most unsparing critic of my work, to be its rashness.

Quid erit tutius quam eam exercere artem quâ semper
armatus, presidium amicis, opem alienis, salutem periclitanti-
bus, invidis vero et inimicis metum et terrorem, ultro feras,
ipse securus et velut quâdam perpetuâ potentiâ ac potestate
munitus ?

THE END.